Mesoamerican Rituals
and the Solar Cycle

Indigenous Cultures of Latin America: Past and Present

Gabrielle Vail

Series Editor

Vol. 1

The Indigenous Cultures of Latin America: Past and Present series
is part of the Peter Lang Regional Studies list.
Every volume is peer reviewed and meets
the highest quality standards for content and production.

PETER LANG
New York • Bern • Berlin
Brussels • Vienna • Oxford • Warsaw

Mesoamerican Rituals and the Solar Cycle

New Perspectives on the *Veintena* Festivals

Edited by
Élodie Dupey García
and Elena Mazzetto

PETER LANG
New York • Bern • Berlin
Brussels • Vienna • Oxford • Warsaw

Library of Congress Cataloging-in-Publication Data

Names: Dupey García, Élodie, editor. | Mazzetto, Elena, editor.
Title: Mesoamerican rituals and the solar cycle: new perspectives on the
veintena festivals/edited by Élodie Dupey García and Elena Mazzetto.
Description: New York: Peter Lang, 2021.
Series: Indigenous cultures of Latin America: past and present; vol. 1
ISSN 2689-8217 (print) | ISSN 2689-8225 (online)
Includes bibliographical references and index.
Identifiers: LCCN 2019055966 | ISBN 978-1-4331-7540-4 (hardback: alk. paper)
ISBN 978-1-4331-7544-2 (paperback: alk. paper)
ISBN 978-1-4331-7541-1 (ebook pdf) | ISBN 978-1-4331-7542-8 (epub)
ISBN 978-1-4331-7543-5 (mobi)
Subjects: LCSH: Aztecs—Rites and ceremonies. | Aztec calendar.
Classification: LCC F1219.3.R38 M49 2021 | DDC 529/.32978452—dc23
LC record available at https://lccn.loc.gov/2019055966
DOI 10.3726/b16286

Bibliographic information published by **Die Deutsche Nationalbibliothek.**
Die Deutsche Nationalbibliothek lists this publication in the "Deutsche
Nationalbibliografie"; detailed bibliographic data are available
on the Internet at http://dnb.d-nb.de/.

Cover image: Toci-Tlazolteotl gives birth to Cinteotl, the Maize God.
Source: *Codex Borbonicus*, pl. 13 (detail),
courtesy of Bibliothèque de l'Assemblée nationale, Paris.

The publisher has the non-exclusive right to use the image of the *Codex Borbonicus* in all
languages, forms, media, editions and printings as part of the scientific volume *Mesoamerican
Rituals and the Solar Cycle: New Perspectives on the Veintena Festivals*.
Bibliothèque de l'Assemblée nationale retains ownership and copyright of the image and all
other rights not specified.

To Michel Graulich, in gratitude for passing on
his passion for Mesoamerican myths and rituals.

Table of Contents

Illustrations

Tables

Acknowledgments

We would like to express our gratitude to the institutions and individuals who have supported this book project and have assisted us during the process. Foremost we thank the Universidad Nacional Autónoma de México, where we are conducting our research on ancient Nahua culture and religion, principally the Instituto de Investigaciones Históricas that hosted the international conference "Las fiestas de las veintenas. Nuevas aportaciones en homenaje a Michel Graulich" in 2016, which was the first step in the long journey of making this volume. A very special acknowledgment goes to Gabrielle Vail, who invited us to submit this book to be the inaugural volume of Peter Lang's series "Indigenous Cultures of Latin America: Past and Present": thank you for the help in establishing the fruitful contact with the publisher, the guidance during the development of the book proposal, and the detailed review of specific parts of this work. We also owe a debt of gratitude to the colleagues and students who have provided their support at different stages, foremost the contributors of the present volume who have encouraged us and have placed their trust in us, as well as Cecelia F. Klein, Leonardo López Luján, and John Pohl, who have penned the endorsements. Likewise, we are grateful to Cynthia Vail, Debra Nagao, Chet Van Duzer, Michael Parker, Wendy Aguilar, Stan Declercq, Omar Tapia, Ilse Flores, and Jesús López del Río, who have taken care of the translation and correction of the written contents; to Elbis Domínguez, Nicolas Latsanopoulos, and Rodolfo Ávila, for creating the drawings that illustrate several chapters; and to Mara Vargas and Alicia Cervantes, for helping us to access some essential information. We also thank the anonymous reviewer selected by Peter Lang, whose careful reading of our manuscript and detailed remarks have contributed significantly to the final form of this work. Very important, too, was the support received from the Biblioteca Medicea Laurenziana in Florence, the Bibliothèque de l'Assemblée nationale in Paris, the Museo de América in Madrid, and the Proyecto Templo Mayor in Mexico City, which have allowed us to reproduce images of Mesoamerican codices and artifacts that are fundamental to the academic quality of this book. Finally, we sincerely acknowledge Emma Clarke, Erika Hendrix, and the editorial team at Peter Lang for their interest in our project, as well as their professionalism and all their hard work in preparing this publication.

Introduction

ELENA MAZZETTO AND ÉLODIE DUPEY GARCÍA

This book explores a seminal topic concerning the Mesoamerican past: the festivals that took place during the eighteen periods of twenty days, or *veintenas*, into which the solar year was divided. In the final stage of Pre-Columbian history—commonly known as the Late Postclassic (AD 1200–1521)—some Mesoamerican societies celebrated these festivals through complex rituals, which included sacrifices, offerings, singing and dancing, ceremonial itineraries and feigned battles. In each festival, the rites involved the priests and the gods themselves, embodied in diverse beings, artifacts, and natural elements. Specific sectors of society—the king, nobles, warriors, merchants, midwives, slaves, and so forth—also participated in these festivals, while the populations of major cities or more modest settlements usually attended public ceremonies. As a consequence, this ritual cycle appears to be a significant thread in Mesoamerican religious life; at the same time, it informs us about social relations in Pre-Columbian societies. Both religious and social aspects of the solar cycle festivals are addressed in the twelve contributions in this book, which aims to improve our understanding of this ceremonial sequence: its actors and rites, its structure and categories, its correspondence to myths, as well as its continuities and meaning in colonial and contemporary times.

TIME COMPUTATION SYSTEMS IN MESOAMERICA

Since the earliest stages of civilization, Mesoamerican cultures have created complex calendar systems that measured and organized time. These time computation systems were of fundamental significance in the Pre-Columbian era. Not only sophisticated tools for recording the passage of time, they were schemata that structured ancient thought and understanding of the world. In fact, these calendar systems influenced the conduct of all members of society and determined their future. They were also frameworks for explaining events that affected the natural environment, in particular the alternation of day and night, as well as seasonal cycles.

Mesoamerican civilizations primarily used two systems of time computation. One of them was a divinatory 260-day count, called the *tonalpohualli* in Nahuatl, a term that literally means "day-count" or "count of the fates."[1] This divinatory calendar was formed by the association of twenty calendrical signs[2] and thirteen successive numerals—1-Crocodile/Earth Monster, 2-Wind, 3-House, etc.—whose combination led to the division of the cycle in periods of 13 days. Each day and each 13-day series were placed under the ascendency of a divinity, who imbued them with positive or negative influences that had an impact on all human activities, whether in everyday life or in ritual contexts. Information about the fortune of these temporal periods was recorded in "books of fate," manuscripts where the count was depicted in various forms. Such manuscripts were used by calendar specialists in order to predict omens, which were taken into account, for example, when sowing and harvesting, as well as to choose the name of a newborn, to determine the start of war or a trade expedition, or to find the date for a wedding or a ruler's accession to the throne.[3]

The second system of time computation, the subject of this book, was a solar calendar of 365 days, called the *xiuhpohualli*, "year-count," in Nahuatl, and *haab'*, *cuiya*, and *iza*, "year," respectively in Maya (Yucatec), Mixtec, and Zapotec. It was generally formed by eighteen periods of twenty days, plus a period of five days that was seen as unlucky: this was a time when ordinary activities, such as lighting a fire to cook, were forbidden, and the destiny of individuals born during these days was prophesied as being extremely inauspicious, which was reflected in the name they were given.[4] At the time of contact, the Spaniards began calling the 20-day interval *veintena*, the Spanish translation of the Nahuatl word *cempohualli*, "twenty." In the account known as "Anales de Cuauhtitlan" (2011, 27) and in the *Primeros Memoriales* (1997, 55) the calendar divided into periods of twenty days is named *cecempohuall-apohualiztli* or *cecempoallapualli* "count twenty by twenty" in Nahuatl, an expression used by scholars such as Patrick Johansson (2005), Andrea Rodríguez Figueroa and Leopoldo Valiñas Coalla (2010, 2014), Marc Thouvenot (2015, 2019), and Ana Díaz (2011). In colonial times, the solar count was also known as the "calendar of the fixed festivals" (*calendario de las fiestas fijas*) (Sahagún 1979, bk 2: fol. 3r), because, in the eyes of the Spaniards, the religious events celebrated throughout this cycle of time always occurred on the same dates during the year, while the ceremonies corresponding to the divinatory calendar were movable, for they followed the 260-day count.[5]

In the Late Postclassic, these two systems of time measurement were considered extremely ancient, and their invention was often attributed to the gods or the forefathers of humankind; in some contexts, the two counts were even conceived of as divinities. In Central Mexico, for example, according to the "Historia de los mexicanos por sus pinturas" (2002, 27–29), the days, the "months,"[6] and the solar calendar were created by the gods Quetzalcoatl and Huitzilopochtli, before they made the primordial waters and the earth's surface. Similarly, the "Anales de Cuauhtitlan" (2011, 27), together with the *Florentine Codex* compiled by the Franciscan friar Bernardino de Sahagún (1950–82, bk 4: 4), recount that the creation of the divinatory count of 260 days and the organization of the solar cycle in 20-day periods were established by the ancestral couple Cipactonal and Oxomoco. The Maya, in turn, thought that the great temporal cycles belonged to ancient times even predating the creation of the world (Velásquez García 2017, 8), and they conceived of them as divinities, in other words as beings endowed with consciousness, reason, knowledge, and will.

HISTORICAL SOURCES ON THE SOLAR CYCLE FESTIVALS

Although the 365-day calendar was in use since the early stages of Mesoamerican history, almost all aspects of the celebration of festivals during the solar cycle prior to the Postclassic period remain unknown, given the absence of ancient iconographic testimonies and written records clearly focused on these religious practices. In contrast, the festival sequence held during the *veintenas* in Late Postclassic societies was chronicled by the sixteenth-century Spaniards as soon as they initiated the conquest and colonization of Mexico (1519). Their writings, though, do not offer a full and consistent account of the festival cycle for all Mesoamerica. On the one hand, we have thorough information regarding the cultures they investigated in detail, in particular the Nahua from Central Mexico and, to a lesser extent, the Maya of Yucatan; and on the other hand, we know that other ethnic groups, such as the Mixtecs, Zapotecs, Totonacs, Otomi, Matlatzinca, and Purepecha, used a 365-day calendar, but the data concerning their specific celebration of festivals are fragmentary. For these societies, we sometimes have lists of the *veintena* names in native languages—for instance, in Mixtec (Caso 1956, 1967), Otomi (Carrasco 1987 [1950]; Lastra 2006; Wright 2009), Matlatzinca (Caso 1946), Zapotec (Alcina Franch 1993; Oudijk 2018), Maya Quiché and Cakchiquel (Caso 1967; Edmonson 1988)—that were collected in colonial times; in other cases, we rely upon reconstructions provided by ethnologists on the basis of present-day practices (Stresser-Péan 2005; Torres Cisneros 2001, 2011).

The record is considerably different for the cultures of Late Postclassic Central Mexico and Yucatan. Some Pre-Columbian manuscripts—specifically the Borgia, Dresden, and Madrid codices—include iconographic representations of rites that have been interpreted by some scholars as images of solar cycle ceremonies (Bill 1997; Brotherston 2003; Jansen and Pérez 2017; Milbrath 1989, 2007, 2013a, 2013b; Vail 2002, 2005; Vail and Hernández 2013). Furthermore, the powerful Nahua societies of the Valley of Mexico and the Puebla-Tlaxcala region were extensively studied by the Spanish conquistadors and missionaries throughout the sixteenth century. The missionaries, in particular, engaged deeply with indigenous people in gathering and recording information, and they also wrote their chronicles with the invaluable help of native contributors. In this way, the friars obtained rich descriptions of Late Postclassic Nahua festivals (see Table 0.1), as part of their research focused on indigenous rituals in order to destroy the original religion and supplant it with Christianity. Among the notable works carried out by Franciscan and Dominican friars in Central Mexico during the second half of the sixteenth century are the *Primeros Memoriales* and *Historia general de las cosas de la Nueva España*—the unique extant copy of which is known as the *Florentine Codex*—of Bernardino de Sahagún, as well as the chronicles by Diego Durán, Toribio de Benavente Motolinía, and Diego Muñoz Camargo. The *Relación de las cosas de Yucatán* attributed to Diego de Landa is the foremost source on religious life and especially the *haab'* festivals among the Postclassic Maya.

Moreover, the Spaniards and especially the friars encouraged the creation of painted manuscripts that address the pre-Hispanic past. With regard to the solar cycle festivals, the most interesting images are contained in Sahagún's *Primeros Memoriales* and in the *Codex Borbonicus*, a traditional screenfold manuscript created in the Valley of Mexico and whose probable colonial dating is still disputed. These and other post-Conquest codices were painted by indigenous artists and they often include glosses recording data provided by native interlocutors, which supplement the information in the chronicles. It should be stressed, however, that while the iconographic contents of these manuscripts refer to pre-Hispanic practices and beliefs, their structure and style do not always correspond to ancient Mesoamerican canons; instead, they frequently follow European standards. This has led scholars to debate whether these colonial images were copied from ancient codices or, at least, originated in the indigenous milieu (Baird 1993, 116–17), or if these representations were created under the patronage of the missionaries, seeking alignments between the Nahua and European calendar systems (Kubler and Gibson 1951, 52). Henry B. Nicholson (2002, 96–99) and Eloise Quiñones Keber (in Sahagún 1997, 28) have proposed that the most complex images of the *veintenas* in the colonial documentation were probably copies of Pre-Columbian manuscripts used by the ancient priests to plan the ceremonies and the required offerings.

Table 0.1. Common names of the *veintenas* and gods celebrated among the Mexica according to the sources of the sixteenth century

RAINY SEASON

13/2–4/3	Atlcahualo, "Water Ceases" Aquatic gods, Xipe Totec
5–24/3	Tlacaxipehualiztli, "Flaying of Men" Huitzilopochtli, Xipe Totec
25/3–13/4	Tozoztontli, "Little Vigil" Earth, aquatic and maize gods
14/4–3/5	Huey Tozoztli, "Great Vigil" Aquatic and maize gods, Quetzalcoatl
4–23/5	Toxcatl, "Dryness" Tezcatlipoca, Huitzilopochtli, Tlacahuepan Cuexcotzin
24/5–12/6	Etzalcualiztli, "Eating of *etzalli* (a dish of maize and bean)" Tlaloc, Chalchiuhtlicue, Quetzalcoatl, Xolotl
13/6–2/7	Tecuilhuitontli, "Little Feast of the Lords" Huixtocihuatl (Salt Goddess), Xochipilli-Macuilxochitl
3–22/7	Huey Tecuilhuitl, "Great Feast of the Lords" Xilonen, Cihuacoatl, Quetzalcoatl, Xochipilli-Macuilxochitl
23/7–11/8	Tlaxochimaco, "Offering of Flowers" All the gods, Huitzilopochtli
12–31/8	Xocotl Huetzi, "The Fruit Falls" Otontecuhtli-Huehueteotl, gods of the merchants

DRY SEASON

1–20/9	Ochpaniztli, "Sweeping" Toci-Teteo Innan, Chicomecoatl, Atlatonan, telluric goddesses
21/9–10/10	Teotleco, "The Gods Arrive" All the gods, Huitzilopochtli, Xiuhtecuhtli, Tlamatzincatl, gods of the merchants
11–30/10	Tepeilhuitl, "Feast of the Mountains" Gods of the mountains
31/10–19/11	Quecholli, "Roseate Spoonbill" Mixcoatl, Coatlicue, Centzon Totochtin (pulque gods)
20/11–9/12	Panquetzaliztli, "Banner Are Raised" Huitzilopochtli, Tezcatlipoca, Tlacahuepan Cuexcotzin, gods of the merchants and feather workers
10–29/12	Atemoztli, "Water Descends" Aquatic gods
30/12–18/1	Tititl (debated meaning) Ilamatecuhtli, Mictlantecuhtli

Continued

Table 0.1. Continued

DRY SEASON	
19/1–7/2	Izcalli, "Growth," "Resuscitation"
	Xiuhtecuhtli, pulque and aquatic goddesses
8–12/2	Nemontemi, "Empty/Vain Days"

On the whole, the quantity of historical sources that deal with the solar cycle festivals in Postclassic Central Mexico is exceptional, yet, at the same time, it emphasizes the disparity of information available on this religious phenomenon throughout Mesoamerica. Additionally, Central Mexican sources are diverse, which invites comparison of data from different authors, media, and contexts. In this regard, we should stress that the *veintena* analyses for societies in the Valley of Mexico have also benefited from archaeological data obtained through the last 40 years of excavations in the former ceremonial center of Mexico-Tenochtitlan, especially the Templo Mayor.[7] Last but not least, some of the colonial texts on the pre-Hispanic cultures of Central Mexico were written in Nahuatl. This significantly enhances the quality of the data because scholars can access the indigenous categories through their original names and their descriptions in a native language. A noteworthy example may be found in the identification of the two main classes of victims of human sacrifices practiced by the Nahua, and of one of the more intriguing and complex categories in their religion, that of *ixiptla*.

For its significance at the heart of this book, the category of **ixiptlatl* requires a brief elucidation.[8] In Nahua culture, the two principal categories of victims for human sacrifice were enemy warriors captured on the battlefield and bathed— that is, purified—slaves who became living embodiments of the divinities. The latter were known as *teoixiptla*, a term that has been translated as "image", "representative", "substitute", or "impersonator" of the gods. In fact, the *ixiptla* actually embodied the gods for specific periods of time: they dressed and spoke like the divinities, and they were sacrificed in festivals to mark cycles in the life and death of divine entities. However, the appellation *ixiptla* was not only a prerogative of the victims. It also applied to any individual or material regarded as the embodiment of a divine entity and that was adorned with the divinity's symbols. The priests who wore the divine garments at specific moments of the calendar cycle were thus conceived as *ixiptla*, as were the stone or wood effigies and the edible maize and amaranth figures in the form of the supernatural beings.[9] Interestingly, archaeological research at the Templo Mayor of Tenochtitlan has uncovered remains of animals associated with gods' insignia (López Luján and Chávez Balderas 2010; López Luján et al. 2012), suggesting the existence of animal *ixiptla*, although this category is not mentioned in historical sources.

150 YEARS OF RESEARCH ON THE *VEINTENAS*

The crucial role of the solar cycle in Pre-Columbian religions has made the *veintena* festivals a significant subject of debate among historians, historians of religions, and anthropologists since the late nineteenth century, beginning in the 1880s, but the disparity of historical records pertaining to the different Mesoamerican cultures is mirrored in the academic literature: scholars have principally focused on the celebration of the *veintenas* among the Nahua societies of Central Mexico.

In the mid-nineteenth century, José Fernando Ramírez (1903[1867], 2001) began to show interest in the time computation systems of Mesoamerica, which he came to explore through his study of the sixteenth-century sources, whereas, almost 20 years later, Alfredo Chavero (1884) offered the first precise description of the *veintenas* also based on the historical accounts. In the same period, the first works that provide an interpretation of the Nahua festivals appeared, including those of Albert Réville (1885) and James Frazer (1911 [1890]). Both scholars were influenced by an evolutionist ideology that was the theoretical framework of the natural and social sciences during the nineteenth century, leading to the classification of human cultures into successive levels of development. In the case of the *veintenas*, however, Réville's and Frazer's research principally looks for correspondence between sacrificial rituals, on the one hand, and on the other the sequence of plant growth and the agricultural cycle, specifically the phases of sowing and harvesting. According to them, the efficacy of the Nahua rites lies in their ability to imitate nature: these scholars perceived gestures that refer to natural phenomena—for example, rainfall—in the ritual activities, which they interpret as a means to propitiate the continuity of the natural cycle. As a result, the natural environment was expected to replicate the ritual actions performed in the festivals with positive effects, such as the arrival of the rainy season and the harvest of abundant crops.

The creation of the German Mexicanist School—heralded by the cultural relationship between Germany and Mexico forged by Alexander von Humboldt— strongly influenced the study of ancient Mesoamerican religions during the first half of the twentieth century, first in Germany and later in the rest of the world (Tapia 2017, 53). The German contribution included the work of renowned scholars such as Eduard Seler, Konrad T. Preuss, and Hermann Beyer.[10] Their theoretical position was founded on the assumptions of the Nature-Mythology School, derived from the field of literature and folklore studies of the European Romantic period. Mythology was conceived of as a "religion of nature," that is a religion based on the personification of the forces of nature. Therefore, these scholars believed the divinized forces of nature played a key role in rituals. Seler and Preuss, in particular, analyzed the solar cycle festivals as religious events in which the natural elements were embodied by ritual protagonists, who manifested their creative or destructive potential through the passing seasons. Equally important was the role that German Mesoamericanists assigned to the celestial bodies (the Sun, the Moon, Venus, and the stars) and the perpetual struggle between the forces of light and darkness—a topic to which later researchers also contributed (e.g. Graulich 1987; Milbrath 2013a, 2013b).

Beginning at the end of the nineteenth century, Seler—and after him Beyer—contributed to the discussion of the *veintenas*, particularly the debate revolving around the adjustment—or not—of the calendar (365 days) to the actual duration of the solar year (approximately 365.2422 days). Previously, Alfredo Chavero (1884, 1: 680) had raised this question and proposed that the religious festivals of the Aztecs were left to shift in relation to the natural phenomena during their migration, but when they first came in contact with the heirs of the Toltec civilization, they adopted their system of adjustment. In 1891, Seler rejected the possibility of an adjustment (Seler 1904a; see also Seler and Seler-Sachs 1902), but he changed his mind twelve years later and proposed that an intercalation of ten days to the 365-day count occurred every 42 years (Seler 1903). Two decades later, Beyer (1965b [1925]) presented examples coming from the *Codex Vaticanus A* that led him to posit that the ancient Nahua did not make any intercalations of days to adjust their 365-day calendar to the length of the solar year. As we will see, this key topic for the understanding of the solar cycle festivals has continued to be debated throughout the twentieth century and until today.

Returning to the contributions of the German Mexicanist School, Seler also commented on the antiquity of the solar calendar and the cycle of festivals related to it, as well as their manifestations in a broad area of Mesoamerica that encompassed various indigenous cultures (Seler and Seler-Sachs 1902, 507–54). Thus, his work emphasized the need for studies that would examine time periods and regions beyond the Late Postclassic in Central Mexico.[11] Finally, Seler (1899, 1963 [1904–06]) and Preuss (1929) undertook a mythical approach to the solar cycle festivals that turned out to be particularly fruitful. It was based on the search for the specific myths mirrored and re-enacted in the rites, as well as on the mimetic relation between these religious expressions. The results of this comparison of myths and rites—enriched, in the case of Preuss, by the use of ethnographic data obtained during his visits to the Gran Nayar, among the Cora, Huichols, and Mexicaneros—were essential for the initial elucidation of a number of rituals and provided a promising path for the scholars who followed.

The study of the Nahua solar cycle festivals developed more broadly between the 1950s and the 1980s, when multiple aspects of these religious activities, as well as the question of the adjustment or, to the contrary, the shifting of the *veintenas* were discussed by leading Americanist scholars such as Ángel María Garibay (1958), Alfonso Caso (1967), Alfredo López Austin (1967, 1970), Víctor Castillo Farreras (1971), Thelma Sullivan (1976), Charles Dibble (1980), and Yólotl

González Torres (1985). Karl Nowotny, Paul Kirchhoff and, later, Pedro Carrasco should be credited with the first attempts to systematically study the structure of the 365-day calendar and the contents of the Nahua festivals.[12] Indeed, Nowotny (1968) stressed that the *veintenas* sequence needs to be studied as a complex made up of distinct units, whose interpretation can be achieved by analyzing the connections among such units. This idea led him to identify major rituals that repeated throughout the cycle and to propose a classification of the different types of sacrifice. In the same vein, Kirchhoff (1971) identified six of the eighteen festivals as "single fiestas" and twelve as "double fiestas." For Kirchhoff, the latter were "double" because they evinced a continuity in the ritual activities and they celebrated the same gods. Following him, Carrasco (1979) proposed an organization of the eighteen *veintenas* into four blocks whose themes coincided. His proposal also associated the rites and elements of the festivals with astronomical phenomena, in particular the equinoxes and the solstices, as well as with economic and political activities (*cf.* Tapia 2017).

We also owe a remarkable debt to the study of the *veintenas* to Johanna Broda, whose works on a series of topics began to appear in the 1970s and have continued until now. In her early studies, Broda (1970, 1971, 1983) made a profound contribution by analyzing the ritual elements and meanings in the Nahua ceremonies. In particular, she explored how they related to agricultural fertility, as well as to the seasons and the sun's movements during the year, while also comparing the ancient rituals with the religious practices of present-day indigenous communities. Some years later she delved into the social, political, and economic dynamics involved in the organization and execution of the festivals, which led her to propose that the structure of society—that is, the different social sectors and their respective political roles—were reflected in the *veintena* ceremonies (Broda 1976, 1978, 1979). Her subsequent contributions were to the field of archaeoastronomy and the study of the ritual landscape of the Valley of Mexico, especially of the mountains involved in the *veintena* festivals (Broda 1991a, 1991b, 1997, 2001, 2019).

Another outstanding contribution occurred in the late 1980s, when Michel Graulich published his PhD dissertation, *Mythes et rituels du Mexique ancien préhispanique*, which remains today the only comprehensive and detailed study of the entire Nahua ceremonial cycle (Graulich 1987; see also Graulich 1981, 1997, 1999). Graulich came to investigate the solar year festivals through his interest in human sacrifice and mythology. Indeed, he perceived a natural link between the eighteen *veintenas* and the mythical corpus, noticing that myths and rites shared themes and protagonists. In this sense, Graulich's work followed in the footsteps of Seler, as well as the methodologies of preeminent figures such as Georges Dumézil and Claude Lévi-Strauss, for whom mythology and rituals reflect each other.

One of Graulich's crucial contributions to the study of the *veintenas* involved his theory regarding the structure of the sequence of festivals and the lack of an adjustment between the 365-day count and the actual length of the year. Graulich (1986, 1987, 1999) postulated that the decision not to insert days to adjust for the respective length of the calendar and the solar cycle was a conscious strategy adopted by the Mesoamericans in order to maintain the perfect coincidence between the divinatory count and the solar calendar—an idea previously formulated by Chavero (1884), Seler (1904a), Beyer (1965b), and Caso (1967), among others, but never fully developed prior to Graulich's work. Thus, Graulich argued that the Nahua *veintena* festivals were never celebrated on the same dates and that, year after year, they shifted in relation to the periods of time—particularly the seasons—that structured the tropical year.

The construction of this model led him to attempt to put each festival back into its original position. To do so, he analyzed the Nahuatl names of some of the *veintenas* that had ties to specific periods of the year, for example Atlcahualo, "Arrest of Water," Atemoztli, "Descent of Water," and Toxcatl, "Dryness." He concluded that, in 1519, when the Spaniards landed in Mexico, there was a gap of 209 days between the date on which the festivals were originally celebrated—which was in line with the seasons and the corresponding agricultural activities—and the date on which they were actually celebrated (see Table 0.2). Graulich estimated that, due to the lack of intercalations, the last time the festivals were in their correct positions was around AD 680–683, a period in which several significant religious and calendrical reforms occurred in Mesoamerica. Interestingly, Victoria Bricker used a method similar to Graulich's and studied the names of some *veintenas* in Mayan languages that were also originally related to climate and agriculture, but at Conquest showed that the calendar "gradually slipped out of phase with the seasons" (Bricker 1982, 101).

Table 0.2. Chronology and parallelism of the festivals according to the interpretation of Michel Graulich

RAINY SEASON		DRY SEASON	
3–22/4	Ochpaniztli	30/9–19/10	Tlacaxipehualiztli
23/4–12/5	Teotleco	20/10–8/11	Tozoztontli
13/5–1/6	Tepeilhuitl	9–28/11	Huey Tozoztli
2/6–21/6	Quecholli	29/11–18/12	Toxcatl
22/6–11/7	Panquetzaliztli	19/12–7/1	Etzalcualiztli
12–31/7	Atemoztli	8–27/1	Tecuilhuitontli
1–20/8	Tititl	28/1–16/2	Huey Tecuilhuitl
21/8–9/9	Izcalli	17/2–8/3	Tlaxochimaco
10–29/9	Atlcahualo	9–28/3	Xocotl Huetzi
		29/3–2/4	Nemontemi

Graulich's extensive analysis of the solar cycle festivals and his efforts to rediscover their original positions also led him to note an interesting phenomenon: the parallelism of the Nahua festivals. In particular, he suggested that Ochpaniztli, the first festival of the year that originally inaugurated the arrival of the rainy season,[13] and Tlacaxipehualiztli, positioned half a year later, formerly at the beginning of the dry season, were *veintenas* that respectively opened two series of nine festivals whose rites display relations of similarity, opposition, and complementarity (see Table 0.1). For example, the festivals that inaugurated each series, Ochpaniztli and Tlacaxipehualiztli, shared features such as the flaying of sacrificial victims, but in the first case they were women, while in the second they were men. The parallelism of the Nahua festivals turned out to be an important factor for understanding apparently obscure rites, which, in fact, echo rites that occurred in the other half of the year (Graulich 1986, 1999).

During and following Graulich's investigations, the Nahua solar year festivals have captured the attention of Mesoamericanists, although no new comprehensive analysis of the whole cycle of fiestas was undertaken after his. Instead, scholars have focused on particular topics, with monographs on specific festivals or rites that sometimes delve into their relationship with mythology (Arnold 1999; Baudez 2010; Botta 2004, 2009; Brown 1984, 1988; Brylak 2011; Carrasco 1991, 2002; Clendinnen 1991; Danilović 2016; Dehouve 2008, 2009, 2011; Díaz Barriga Cuevas 2013; DiCesare 2009; Durand-Forest 2002; Dupey García 2013; González González 2010, 2011; Heyden 1991; Kruell 2011; Limón Olvera 2001a, 2001b; López Luján 2005; López Austin and López Luján 2004; Margáin Araujo 1945; Mazzetto, forthcoming; Olivier 2002, 2003, 2015; Olmedo Vera 2008; Ragot 2011; Reyes Guerrero 2015; Schwaller 2019; Veliz Ruiz Esparza 2018; Vié-Wohrer 1999, 2008). In direct connection with this matter, we should also mention the thorough analysis of Mesoamerican mythology by Alfredo López Austin (1998b [1990]) in *Los mitos del tlacuache* and his concise, though insightful, reflections on its complex relationship with rituals, even if he did not specifically address the *veintenas*. Indeed, without negating the close links between myths and rites, López Austin has gone beyond the idea of the rituals as mere re-enactments of myths, stressing their autonomous operation, as well as structures and functions.

Since 1980, scholarly works have also continued to focus on the complete cycle of the *veintena* cycle, but through the prism of specific subjects, for instance, the references to rituals in the hymns to the gods (Saurin 1999), the iconographic and stylistic analysis of images of the *veintena* festivals (Baird 1993; Batalla Rosado 1993, 1994, 2011; Brotherston 2003; Brown 1984; Couch 1985; Espinosa Pineda 2010; Granicka 2015; Jansen and Pérez 2017; Milbrath 1989, 2007, 2013a, 2013b; Nicholson 2002), the theatrical dimensions of the rites (Brylak 2015; Proenza 1993), the ritual food consumed during these religious events (Brylak 2013; Mazzetto 2013, 2014d, 2015, 2017, 2019b; Morán 2016; Velasco Lozano

2001), as well as the sacred spaces and ceremonial paths used in the rituals (Aveni 1991; Broda 1991a, 1991b, 1997, 2001; Mazzetto 2014a, 2014b, 2014c, 2016, 2019a; Mazzetto and Rovira-Morgado 2014; Proenza 2011; Rodríguez Figueroa 2010, 2014).

Likewise, the question of whether the Nahua did or did not make an adjustment between the 365-day count and the actual length of the solar year has continued to be a hotly debated topic since Graulich formulated his theory (Broda 1983; Díaz Cíntora 1994; Flores Gutiérrez 1995; Iwaniszewski 2019; Kruell 2019; Prem 2008, 89–99; Sprajc 2000; Tena 1987), because central Mexican historical sources do not provide conclusive evidence. Also, the key topic of pre-Conquest reforms to the Nahua calendar has been discussed by Edward Calnek (2007), while the structure of the solar cycle and the political and religious motivations of Motecuhzoma Xocoyotzin's calendrical change regarding the New Fire celebration were analyzed by Graulich (1993, 1994, 1995), Ross Hassig (2001), and John Schwaller (2019). In the Maya area, the absence of an adjustment between the calendar and the duration of the year has been supported by Victoria and Harvey Bricker, who find that the halfway point of the *haab'*—0 Yax—was measured against the summer solstice to determine the movement of the former against the latter over time (H. Bricker and V. Bricker 2011; also Bricker 1982; V. Bricker and H. Bricker 1988). If their interpretation is correct, this would indicate that corrections were not made to keep the rituals aligned with seasonal events, at least among the Postclassic Maya.

With regard to the identification, reconstruction, and interpretation of rituals celebrated in the *haab'* festivals of the Maya, studies have been authored by Karl Taube (1988), Cassandra Bill (1997), Cassandra Bill and colleagues (2000), Gabrielle Vail (2002, 2005), Harvey Bricker and Victoria Bricker (2011), and Gabrielle Vail and Christine Hernandez (2013). In particular—following in the footsteps of Cyrus Thomas (1882), Ernst Förstermann (1906), and Eric Thompson (1934)—scholars have commented on the Wayeb'/yearbearer pages in the Dresden and Madrid codices. Likewise, several works on the Zapotec solar cycle, or *yza*, were produced over the years, some of which examined its correlation with the Western calendar (Alcina Franch 1993; Caso 1965; Justeson and Tavárez 2007; Lind 2015; Tavárez 2011); a complex question that has also been addressed by Hanns Prem (2008) for the Nahua calendar through a comparison of an impressive number of historical sources. Additionally, building on Caso's (1946) and Carrasco's (1987 [1950]) early attempts to reconstruct the Matlatzinca and Otomi festivals respectively, through a study of the names of the *veintenas* and their possible connections with Nahua rituals and divinities, Yolanda Lastra (2006) more recently conducted the same type of work. Similar comparative approaches examining the structure and names of the *veintena* festivals across Mesoamerica have also been undertaken by Munro Edmonson (1988). Broadening the horizons towards the north,

Gustavo Torres Cisneros (2008) looked for connections between the solar calendar used by the Nahua and the ritual calendar of the Hopi and Pueblo communities of the Southwest of the United States, grounded on the importance of maize agriculture in these native American societies, as well as the division of time based on opposite and complementary poles.

In summary, we observe some common threads in the study of the solar year festivals. First, attention has been given almost exclusively to Nahua festivals; few approaches consider the phenomenon through the prism of other Mesoamerican traditions. Furthermore, scholarly investigation has principally targeted a limited list of specific rituals, with particular attention focused on those apparently related to agricultural practices, in conjunction with the complete absence, after Graulich's contribution, of any attempt to analyze the structure and meaning of the overall ceremonial cycle. Lastly, several authors have discussed the existence of a method—and its characteristics—used by the ancient Mesoamericans to adjust the 365-day calendar to the true length of the solar year, in particular combining archaeoastronomical studies with data from Maya epigraphy and colonial sources.

THEMATIC CONTENTS, METHODOLOGY, AND STRUCTURE OF THIS BOOK

Based on prior research trajectories, we have chosen to focus the present book on an analysis of the meanings of solar cycle rituals for the societies that created and performed them, an analysis that attempts to cover the entire *veintena* sequence and as much of the territory and history of Mesoamerica as possible.[14] Indeed, although the primary emphasis is on Late Postclassic Central Mexico—due to the nature and contents of historical sources on Pre-Columbian societies—an important characteristic of this collective contribution is that it examines the *veintenas* within a broader framework of native religious practices. This is reflected in the comparisons the authors make among cultures distant in space and time, from the Maya area to the Central Highlands and, further north, the Sierra Madre Occidental, and spanning Classic traditions to the present.

Specifically, the orientation we have adopted involves revisiting long-term discussions on the solar cycle festivals, as well as exploring these religious practices in original ways, not only through the investigation of understudied rituals, but also by offering new interpretations for rites that have been extensively analyzed, through comparisons with other ancient and recent cultures, or in light of current anthropological theories. In parallel to these approaches to specific rituals, another path followed by the volume's contributors is to consider the entire *veintena* sequence through the prism of specific topics, for instance, a particular god, a mythical event, a category of priests, or dance practice. Such efforts provide multiple, often complementary, interpretations of the same rituals or festivals, which taken as a whole enrich our knowledge of the *veintenas*. Finally, the present book delves not only into the rites—their contents and structures, their definition and categorization—but also into the identity of the social actors who were directly or indirectly involved in the ritual activities, for instance, the rulers, warriors, prostitutes, practitioners of various professions, and priests, who are of course essential figures for understanding this religious cycle, but who have never been thoroughly investigated.

As a consequence of these orientations, we have organized the chapters of the book around three principal themes. First, we offer a re-examination of the fundamental connection between rites and myths through the analysis of new examples that shed light on this relationship; second, we provide detailed and original explanations for particular ritual practices and actors in Maya and Nahua societies; and third, we present an innovative reflection on some native categories and colonial interpretations concerning the *veintenas*. Despite the division of the book into three sections, the coherence of the volume is ensured by a shared methodology that promotes a dialogue among diverse corpuses of sources, from pre-Hispanic manuscripts, ceramics, and sculptures, to colonial illustrated treatises, chronicles, maps, trial testimonies, and ethnographic field surveys.

The first part of the book, entitled "Rites and Myths in Pre-Columbian Mesoamerica," traces the path forged by the first Mesoamericanists and builds on Graulich's model in order to re-examine the relationship between mythology and ritual and enrich this essential discussion in various ways. Demonstrating the potential of a comparative approach, Oswaldo Chinchilla Mazariegos (Chapter One) shows that a mythical corpus from the Classic Maya Lowlands revolving around the Maize God echoes the fiesta celebrated by the Nahua during the *veintena* of Toxcatl. He thus augments the mythical dimension of this festival previously uncovered by Guilhem Olivier (2003). Also inspired by Graulich's work, Guilhem Olivier's contribution (Chapter Two) shows an interest in the ritual re-enactment of the myths that relate the birth of the gods, while it also demonstrates that unknown myths can be discovered and reconstructed through the study of rituals. Examining the god Quetzalcoatl in the *veintena* cycle, Élodie Dupey García (Chapter Three) discusses the structural relationship between mythology and rituals, questioning an absolute correspondence between the festival sequence and the chronology of mythical episodes. The repetition of mythical motifs throughout the *veintenas* suggests that the same myth could be evoked in several ritual contexts, while all parts of a mythical story were not necessarily evoked together in a festival. Moving away from the classical paradigms, Johannes Neurath (Chapter Four) weaves connections between pre-Hispanic Nahua and modern Huichol myths and rites, at the same time carrying out a critical historiographic revision of the studies on rituals in ancient Mesoamerica, which are too often seen as reflections of the mythology. Instead, he proposes that the concept of antagonistic identification can add another layer of depth to the discussion of Pre-Columbian festivals.

The second section of the book, "Ritual Actors and Activities in the *Veintena* Festivals," begins with a contribution on the *veintenas* among the Postclassic Maya of Yucatan (Chapter Five), in which Gabrielle Vail compares colonial data and the iconography of Pre-Columbian codices to discuss a selection of rituals that reveals the centrality of renovation and renewal ceremonies in this religious cycle. The chapters that follow in the second part of the volume specifically focus on the Nahua of Central Mexico. The emphasis on this civilization in the historical sources has provided considerable and detailed evidence that allows for a reconstruction of the content and sequence of certain rituals, some understudied to date, while others have been more extensively analyzed over time, but are of a complexity that suggests additional layers of meaning. This is the case of the skin flaying ritual, which is the subject of Elena Mazzetto's contribution (Chapter Six) that revisits and questions well-established analyses of the *veintena* ceremonies as mimetic reproductions of natural phenomena and agricultural activities, specially the relationship between the post-mortem rite of flaying and the act of husking corn ears. The manufacture of amaranth images of the gods is addressed by John Schwaller (Chapter Seven) in a contribution that seeks to disambiguate the uses and meanings of this material employed to embody the divine. Finally, Sylvie Peperstraete (Chapter Eight) explores a category of priest—the *huixtotin*—and their spheres of action, which allows her to illustrate the complexity and dynamism that characterized the Meso-american gods' and priests' identities and functions. Her study likewise corroborates the parallelism and continuity among certain festivals, thus confirming the importance of a comprehensive analysis of the *veintena* cycle.

The third part of the volume, "Pre-Columbian Categories, Colonial Interpretations," opens with a contribution by Mirjana Danilović (Chapter Nine) on dance performances and their interaction with sacrifice. The author reviews historical texts to identify the Nahua category of dance, concluding that our own categories—in which actions such as dancing, singing, fighting, and forming a procession are clearly distinct—fail to explain certain pre-Hispanic practices that join dance and sacrifice. Posing an essential question for this volume, Andrea Rodríguez Figueroa, Mario Cortina Borja, and Leopoldo Valiñas Coalla (Chapter Ten) focus on defining the Nahua category of ritual and its differences with respect to the Western concept, through a meticulous linguistic analysis of sixteenth-century texts in Nahuatl and Spanish that describe solar cycle festivals. In so doing, they also demonstrate that the Spanish chroniclers often altered data on the *veintenas* provided by native people in order to reinterpret this ritual cycle in light of the structure and ideas of the Christian liturgy. A related proposal is developed by Sergio Botta (Chapter Eleven), who shows that Franciscan discourses on the *veintenas* evolved over time in response to historical contexts, thus illustrating how this Mendicant Order interacts with otherness—in this case, the Nahua religion—to serve its own agenda. This thorough historiographic investigation marks a turning point with regard to previous studies of colonial texts on the *veintenas*, which have tended to simplistically consider them an impartial source of information on the pre-Hispanic past. Finally, Rossend Rovira-Morgado (Chapter Twelve) analyzes some plausible survivals of two Pre-Columbian *veintenas* in certain Christian festivals as part of the political and social history of colonial Mexico City, at the same time that he considers the role of specific social actors in these celebrations.

In addition to bringing together recent findings from academic research on the *veintenas*, this volume also engages its readers in central and current debates on Mesoamerican religions. In particular, Chinchilla Mazariegos and Vail participate in the discussion on the antiquity and the profound unity of the beliefs underlying the *veintena* rites, and also discuss their dissemination through space and time in various forms, thus corroborating the observations first made by Seler, as well as the existence of the "hard nucleus" theorized by López Austin (1980, 1998b [1990], 2001).[15] Several authors are also concerned with the structure of Mesoamerican religions, in particular the kinship relationships of the divinities, their coexistence, rivalry, and complementarity, as well as their possible equivalence or substitution among different societies or within the same culture (Chapters One, Two, Three, Six). Other contributors address the relationship and interaction of people and gods, and more broadly of humankind with the supernatural, formulating new ideas concerning the Nahua concepts of *nahualli* and *ixiptla*, as well as the tendency for fusion and fission of the Mesoamerican gods (Chapters Two, Six, Eight).[16] Finally, the epilogue by Danièle Dehouve appraises the collective input of the twelve chapters of the book for the understanding of the solar cycle festivals, as well as for the advancement of Mesoamerican studies. In fact, this final contribution to *Mesoamerican Rituals and the Solar Cycle* outlines perspectives for future research, which shows that, after 150 years of study, this classic topic is still very much alive and will certainly continue to be so, for the puzzle that the *veintenas* pose to the community of scholars through their plurality of meanings and the endless wealth of knowledge they offer on the Pre-Columbian past.

ACKNOWLEDGMENTS

The authors are profoundly grateful to Gabrielle Vail, Debra Nagao, Charlotte Steinhardt, and the anonymous reader selected by Peter Lang, for their constructive criticism and stimulating commentaries which have contributed to improving the writing and contents of this introduction.

NOTES

1. Maya epigraphers have named this calendar the *tzolk'in*, meaning "count of days," but we do not know what the pre-Hispanic Maya called it. With reference to the *tonalpohualli*, the term "fate" is understood as the fortune associated with a calendrical sign and, in general, by everything that was decided for the persons since the moment of their birth (Wimmer 2006, entry "*tonalli*").

2. In Nahua culture, the 20 signs are Crocodile/Earth Monster, Wind, House, Lizard, Serpent, Death, Deer, Rabbit, Water, Dog, Monkey, Grass, Reed, Jaguar, Eagle, Vulture, Movement, Flint, Rain, and Flower. Some of these are shared with other Mesoamerican cultures, although there are also variations.

3. After the conquest, the mantic or divinatory nature of this count and its structure, which was judged "idolatrous" because it had no equivalent in the Western world, unleashed the hostility of the Franciscans in charge of the natives' evangelization (with a few exceptions). The friars were consistent in their efforts to eradicate its use and the knowledge surrounding the 260-day count, through attempts to denigrate its importance and to reduce its function to that of an instrument of astrological divination. On the Nahua *tonalpohualli*, see Boone (2006, 2007), Caso (1967), Díaz Álvarez (2011, 2013, 2016), Mikulska (2016), Seler (1901–02, 1902–03, 1963 [1904–06]), and Siarkiewicz (1995); on the Maya *tzolk'in*, see Thompson (1971) and more recent discussions in Bricker and Bricker (2011), and Vail and Aveni (2004). On the divinatory 260-day count among the Zapotecs, known as *biyee*, see Oudijk (2020).

4. These periods of five days were known as Nemontemi in Nahuatl and Wayeb' in Maya (Yucatec).

5. The Maya also used a third system of time computation, known as the "Long Count," which originated in the Mixe-Zoque area. It was an absolute dating system that counted the time that had elapsed since a starting date of August 11, 3114 BC.

6. The Spaniards also equated the 20-day periods of the solar calendar to the concept of "month," recorded as *metztli*, literally, "moon," in some texts written in Nahuatl under Spanish rule.

7. We are referring, in particular, to the "Proyecto Templo Mayor" (begun in 1978) and the "Programa de Arqueología Urbana" (started in 1994). Some of the archaeological materials excavated in the framework of these projects, for example the Huey Cuauhxicalco, the Huey Tzompantli, the ballcourt, and Ehecatl's Temple are particularly interesting, for these buildings were important ritual stages during the *veintena* festivals (López Luján and Chávez Balderas 2019). Also, the discovery of an oak (*Quercus*) in 2011, seems to be directly related to the Xocotl Huetzi rituals (Nebot García 2013).

8. We place an asterisk in front of *ixiptlatl* because it is a hypothetical reconstruction. Indeed, this noun only existed in a possessed form and, therefore, it is always found with a prefix, as in *i-ixiptla*, "his/her/its embodiment" (which often appears as *ixiptla* in written accounts, eliding the two initial *i* letters) , or *te-ixiptla*, "someone's embodiment." In the rest of this introduction we will use the fixed form *ixiptla* (in singular and plural and without a prefix), which is profusely employed in academic publications.

9. The etymology of the word *ixiptlatl*, and specifically the identification and meaning of the initial *ix-* or *i-* that could belong to the word *ixtli*, "face, eye, surface", or be the mark of the possession in Nahuatl, has sparked a debate among the specialists that has had important repercussions for the understanding of this category. Information and discussions on this topic can be found in Bassett (2015), Dehouve (2016, 2020), Hvidtfeldt (1958), Karttunen (1993), López Austin (1980, 1998a [1973], 1998b [1990]), and Wimmer (2006, entry.*ixiptlahtli*), among others.

10. The publications of these authors that specially interest us here—that is, that directly focus on the *veintenas* cycle or discuss topics related to the 365-day calendar and the seasons—are the following: Seler 1899, 1903, 1904a, 1904b, 1963 [1904–06]; Preuss 1905, 1929, 1998; Beyer 1965a [1908], 1965b [1925].

11. The use of similar calendrical systems by Mesoamerican peoples was also vigorously espoused by Alfonso Caso (1967), who was convinced of the cultural unity of Mesoamerica.

12. Previously, Cottie Arthur Burland (1967) offered a relatively undeveloped interpretation of the structure of the *veintenas* sequence, in which he proposed that it was organized in four blocks dedicated to the cycle of maize, the rain and mountain gods, the demiurges, and the fire gods.

13. Graulich's effort to restore each *veintena* to its original position led him to propose that the *veintena* that opened the year was not Atlcahualo, as observed by the sixteenth-century authors, but Ochpaniztli.

14. The debate surrounding the existence, or not, of an adjustment of the Mesoamerican 365-day calendar to the actual length of the solar year is not directly addressed in the book, although several chapters contribute to the discussion of this topic.

15. The "hard nucleus" has been defined by López Austin as the elements of a cultural worldview (*cosmovisión*) that show a strong resistance to historical changes. As such, the hard nucleus gives a particular worldview its structure and specificity, at the same time that it contributes to the assimilation of new elements over time.

16. The theory of the fusion and fission of the Mesoamerican gods theorized by López Austin (1983, 76; see also Thompson 1934, 1970) refers to the cases in which a group of gods is also conceived of as a singular, single divinity; and the opposite cases in which a divinity is manifested in various deities, each having some of its attributes.

REFERENCES

Alcina Franch, José. 1993. *Calendario y religión entre los zapotecos*. Mexico City: Universidad Nacional Autónoma de México-Instituto de Investigaciones Históricas.

Anales de Cuauhtitlan. 2011. Edited by Rafael Tena. Mexico City: Consejo Nacional para la Cultura y las Artes.

Arnold, Philip. 1999. *Eating Landscape: Aztec and European Occupation of Tlalocan*. Niwot: University Press of Colorado.

Aveni, Anthony F. 1991. "Mapping the Ritual Landscape: Debt Payment to Tlaloc During the Month of *Atlcahualo*." In *Aztec Ceremonial Landscapes*, edited by Davíd Carrasco, 58–73. Boulder: University Press of Colorado.

Baird, Ellen. 1993. *The Drawings of Sahagún's Primeros Memoriales: Structure and Style*. Norman: University of Oklahoma Press.

Bassett, Molly H. 2015. *The Fate of Earthly Things: Aztec Gods and God-Bodies*. Austin: University of Texas Press.

Batalla Rosado, Juan José. 1993. "La perspectiva planigráfica precolombina y el *Códice Borbónico*: página 31, escena central." *Revista Española de Antropología Americana* 23: 113–34.

———. 1994. "Datación del Códice Borbónico a partir del análisis iconográfico de la representación de la sangre." *Revista Española de Antropología Americana* 24: 47–74.

———. 2011. "El *Códice Borbónico*. Reflexiones sobre la problemática relativa a su confección y contenido." In *La Quête du serpent à plumes. Arts et religions de l'Amérique précolombienne*, edited by

Sylvie Peperstraete, Nathalie Ragot, and Guilhem Olivier, 197–211. Turnhout: Brepols Publishers, Bibliothèque de l'École Pratique des Hautes Études-Sciences religieuses.

Baudez, Claude-François. 2010. "Sacrificio de sí, sacrificio del 'otro'." In *El sacrificio humano en la tradición mesoamericana*, edited by Leonardo López Luján and Guilhem Olivier, 431–51. Mexico City: Instituto Nacional de Antropología e Historia, Universidad Nacional Autónoma de México.

Beyer, Hermann. 1965a [1908]. "El sur en el pensamiento del México antiguo." *El México Antiguo* 10 (Hermann Beyer, *Mito y simbología del México antiguo*. Translated by Carmen Cook de Leonard): 34–38.

——. 1965b [1925]. "Prueba de que los mexicanos no intercalaban días durante el ciclo de 52 años." *El México Antiguo* 10 (Hermann Beyer, *Mito y simbología del México antiguo*. Translated by Carmen Cook de Leonard): 300–02.

Bill, Cassandra. 1997. "The Roles and Relationships of God M and Other Black Gods in the Codices, with Specific Reference to Pages 50–56 of the Madrid Codex." In *Papers on the Madrid Codex*, edited by Victoria R. Bricker and Gabrielle Vail, 111–45. New Orleans: Tulane University.

Bill, Cassandra, Christine Hernández, and Victoria Bricker. 2000. "The Relationship Between Early Colonial Maya New Years' Ceremonies and Some Almanacs in the Madrid Codex." *Ancient Mesoamerica* 11, no. 1: 149–68.

Boone, Elizabeth H. 2006. "Marriage Almanacs in the Mexican Divinatory Codices." *Anales del Instituto de Investigaciones Estéticas* 89: 71–92.

——. 2007. *Cycles of Time and Meaning in the Mexican Books of Fate*. Austin: University of Texas Press.

Botta, Sergio. 2004. "Los dioses preciosos. Un acercamiento histórico-religioso a las divinidades aztecas de la lluvia." *Estudios de Cultura Náhuatl* 35: 89–120.

——. 2009. "De la tierra al territorio. Límites interpretativos del naturismo y aspectos políticos del culto a Tláloc." *Estudios de Cultura Náhuatl* 40: 175–99.

Bricker, Harvey M., and Victoria R. Bricker. 2011. *Astronomy in the Maya Codices*. Philadelphia: American Philosophical Society.

Bricker, Victoria R. 1982. "The Origin of the Maya Solar Calendar." *Current Anthropology* 23, no. 1: 101–03.

Bricker, Victoria R., and Harvey M. Bricker. 1988. "The Seasonal Table in the Dresden Codex and Related Almanacs." *Archaeoastronomy* 12, *JHA* 19: S1–S62.

Broda, Johanna (de Casas). 1970. "Tlacaxipehualiztli: A Reconstruction of an Aztec Calendar Festival from 16th Century Sources." *Revista Española de Antropología Americana* 5: 197–274.

——. 1971. "Las fiestas aztecas de los dioses de la lluvia: una reconstrucción según las fuentes del siglo XVI." *Revista Española de Antropología Americana* 6: 245–327.

——. 1976. "Los estamentos en el ceremonial mexica." In *Estratificación social en la Mesoamérica prehispánica*, edited by Pedro Carrasco, Johanna Broda et al., 37–65. Mexico City: Centro de Investigaciones y Estudios Superiores en Antropología Social, Instituto Nacional de Antropología e Historia.

——. 1978. "Relaciones políticas ritualizadas: el ritual como expresión de una ideología." In *Economía política e ideología en el México prehispánico*, edited by Pedro Carrasco and Johanna Broda, 219–55. Mexico City: Centro de Investigaciones y Estudios Superiores en Antropología Social, Instituto Nacional de Antropología e Historia.

——. 1979. "Estratificación social y ritual mexica: un ensayo de antropología social de los mexica." *Indiana* 5: 45–82.

————. 1983. "Ciclos agrícolas en el culto: un problema de correlación del calendario mexica." In *Calendars in Mesoamerica and Peru. Native American Computations of Time, Proceedings of the 44th International Congress of Americanists, Manchester 1982*, edited by Anthony F. Aveni and Gordon Brotherston, 145–64. Oxford: British Archaeological Reports.

————. 1991a. "Cosmovisión y observación de la naturaleza: el ejemplo del culto a los cerros en Mesoamérica." In *Arqueoastronomía y etnoastronomía en Mesoamérica*, edited by Johanna Broda, Stanislaw Iwaniszewski, and Lucrecia Maupomé, 461–500. Mexico City: Universidad Nacional Autónoma de México-Instituto de Investigaciones Históricas.

————. 1991b. "The Sacred Landscape of Aztec Calendar Festivals: Myth, Nature, and Society." In *Aztec Ceremonial Landscapes*, edited by Davíd Carrasco, 74–120. Boulder: University Press of Colorado.

————, ed. 1997. *Graniceros: Cosmovisión y meteorología indígenas de Mesoamérica*. Mexico City: El Colegio Mexiquense, Universidad Nacional Autónoma de México.

————. 2001. "Ritos mexicas en los cerros de la Cuenca: Los sacrificios de niños." In *La montaña en el paisaje ritual*, edited by Johanna Broda, Stanislaw Iwaniszewski, and Ismael Arturo Montero García, 173–98. Mexico City: Universidad Autónoma de Puebla, Universidad Nacional Autónoma de México, Consejo Nacional para la Cultura y las Artes, Instituto Nacional de Antropología e Historia.

————. 2019. "La fiesta de Atlcahualo y el paisaje ritual de la Cuenca de México." *Trace* 75: 9–45.

Brotherston, Gordon. 2003. "The Year in the Mexican Codices. The Nature and Structure of the Eighteen Feasts." *Estudios de Cultura Náhuatl* 34: 67–98.

Brown, Betty Ann. 1984. "Ochpaniztli in Historical Perspective." In *Sacrifice in Mesoamerica*, edited by Elizabeth H. Boone, 195–209. Washington, DC: Dumbarton Oaks

————. 1988. "All Around the Xocotl Pole: Reexamination of an Aztec Sacrificial Ceremony." In *Smoke and Mist: Mesoamerican Studies in Memory of Thelma D. Sullivan*, edited by Kathryn Josserand and Karen Dakin, 173–89. Oxford: British Archaeological Reports.

Brylak, Agnieszka. 2011. "Rivalidad y ritual. Agon en la religion nahua." In *De dioses y hombres. Creencias y rituales mesoamericanos y sus supervivencias*, edited by Katarzyna Mikulska Dąbrowska and José Contel, 121–45. Warsaw, Toulouse: University of Warsaw, Université de Toulouse.

————. 2013. "La cocina ritual azteca en el *Códice Florentino*. Algunos tipos de comida." In *Códices del centro de México. Análisis comparativos y estudios individuales*, edited by Miguel Ángel Ruz Barrio and Juan José Batalla Rosado, 331–58. Warsaw: University of Warsaw.

————. 2015. "Los espectáculos de los nahuas prehispánicos: entre antropología y teatro." PhD diss., University of Warsaw.

Calnek, Edward E. 2007. "Kirchhoff's Correlations and the Third Part of the Codex Borbonicus." In *Skywatching in the Ancient World. New Perspectives in Cultura Astronomy*, edited by Clive Ruggles and Gary Urton, 83–94. Boulder: University Press of Colorado.

Carrasco, Davíd. 1991. "The Sacrifice of Tezcatlipoca: To Change Place." In *To Change Place: Aztec Ceremonial Landscapes*, edited by Davíd Carrasco, 31–57. Boulder: University Press of Colorado.

————. 2002. "The Sacrifice of Women in the *Florentine Codex*. The Hearts of Plants and Players in War Games." In *Representing Aztec Ritual: Performance, Text, and Image in the Work of Sahagún*, edited by Eloise Quiñones Keber, 197–225. Boulder: University Press of Colorado.

Carrasco, Pedro. 1979. "Las fiestas de los meses mexicanos." In *Mesoamérica. Homenaje al doctor Paul Kirchhoff*, edited by Dahlgren Barbro, 52–60. Mexico City: Instituto Nacional de Antropología e Historia.

————. 1987 [1950]. *Los otomíes. Cultura e historia prehispánica de los pueblos mesoamericanos de habla otomiana*. Toluca: Gobierno del Estado de México.

Caso, Alfonso. 1946. "El calendario matlatzinca." *Revista mexicana de estudios antropológicos* 8, no. 1–2–3: 95–109.

———. 1956. "El calendario mixteco." *Historia mexicana* 5, no. 4: 481–97.

———. 1965. "Zapotec Writing and Calendar." In *Handbook of Middle American Indians*. Vols. 2–3, *Archaeology of Southern Mesoamerica*, edited by Gordon R. Willey, series editor Robert Wauchope, 931–47. Austin: University of Texas Press.

———. 1967. *Los calendarios prehispánicos*. Mexico City: Universidad Nacional Autónoma de México-Instituto de Investigaciones Históricas.

Castillo Ferreras, Víctor. 1971. "El bisiesto náhuatl." *Estudios de Cultura Náhuatl* 9: 75–104.

Chavero, Alfredo. 1884. "Tomo I. Historia antigua y de la conquista." In *México a través de los siglos. Historia general y completa del desenvolvimiento social, político, religioso, militar, artístico, científico y literario de México desde la antigüedad más remota hasta la época actual*, edited by Vicente Riva Palacio. Mexico City, Barcelona: Ballesca and Comp. Editores, Espasa y Comp. Editores.

Clendinnen, Inga. 1991. *Aztecs: An Interpretation*. Cambridge: Cambridge University Press.

Couch, Christopher N. C. 1985. *The Festival Cycle of the Aztec Codex Borbonicus*. Oxford: British Archaeological Reports.

Danilović, Mirjana. 2016. "El concepto de danza entre los mexicas." PhD diss., Universidad Nacional Autónoma de México.

Dehouve, Danièle. 2008. "El venado, el maíz y el sacrificado." *Diario de campo. Cuadernos de Etnología* 4: 1–39.

———. 2009. "El lenguaje ritual de los mexicas. Hacia un metodo de análisis." In *Image and Ritual in the Aztec World*, edited by Sylvie Peperstraete, 19–33. Oxford: British Archaeological Reports.

———. 2011. *L'imaginaire des nombres chez les anciens Mexicains*. Rennes: Presses Universitaires de Rennes.

———. 2016. "El papel de la vestimenta en los rituales mexicas de 'personificación'." *Nuevo Mundo Mundos Nuevos*. https://journals.openedition.org/nuevomundo/69305?lang=en

———. 2020. "The Notion of Substitution in Aztec Kingship." In *Anthropomorphic Imagery in the Mesoamerican Highlands. Gods, Ancestors, and Human Beings*, edited by Brigitte Faugère and Christopher S. Beekman, 355–85. Louisville: University Press of Colorado.

Díaz Álvarez, Ana. 2011. "Las formas del tiempo: tradiciones cosmográficas en los calendarios indígenas del Centro de México." PhD diss., Universidad Nacional Autónoma de México.

———. 2013. "*Tlapohualli*, la cuenta de las cosas. Reflexiones en torno a la reconstrucción de los calendarios nahuas." *Estudios de Cultura Náhuatl* 46: 159–97.

———. 2016. *El maíz se sienta a platicar. Códices y formas de conocimiento nahua, más allá del mundo de los libros*. Mexico City: Bonilla Artigas Editores.

Díaz Barriga Cuevas, Alejandro. 2013. "Ritos de paso de la niñez nahua en la fiesta de Izcalli." *Estudios de Cultura Náhuatl* 46:199–221.

Díaz Cíntora, Salvador. 1994. *Meses y cielos: Reflexiones sobre el origen del calendario de los nahuas*. Mexico City: Universidad Nacional Autónoma de México.

DiCesare, Catherine. 2009. *Sweeping the Way. Divine Transformation in the Aztec Festival of Ochpaniztli*. Boulder: University Press of Colorado.

Dibble, Charles. 1980. "The Xalaquia Ceremony." *Estudios de Cultura Náhuatl* 14: 197–202.

Dupey García, Élodie. 2013. "De pieles hediondas y perfumes florales. La reactualización del mito de creación de las flores en las fiestas de las veintenas de los antiguos nahuas." *Estudios de Cultura Náhuatl* 45: 7–36.

Durand-Forest, Jaqueline. 2002. "Los oficios de la religión mexica." *Estudios de Cultura Náhuatl* 33: 15–24.

Edmonson, Munro S. 1988. *The Book of the Year: Middle American Calendrical Systems*. Salt Lake City: University of Utah Press.

Espinosa Pineda, Gabriel. 2010. "Las viñetas de las 18 fiestas del año en los *Primeros memoriales*." In *Tepeapulco: región en perspectivas*, edited by Manuel Alberto Morales Damián, 69–116. Pachuca, Mexico City: Universidad Autónoma del Estado de Hidalgo, Plaza y Valdés.

Flores Gutiérrez, Daniel. 1995. "El problema del inicio del año y el origen del calendario meso-americano: un punto de vista astronómico." In *Coloquio Cantos de Mesoamérica: metodologías científicas en la búsqueda del conocimiento prehispánico*, edited by Daniel Flores Gutiérrez, 117–32. Mexico City: Universidad Nacional Autónoma de México-Instituto de Astronomía-Facultad de Ciencias.

Förstemann, Ernst. 1880. *Die Maya Handschrift der Königlichen öffentlichen Bibliothek zu Dresden*. Mit 74 Tafeln in Chromo-Lightdruck. Verlag der A. Leipzig: Naumannschen Lichtdruckeret.

Förstemann, Ernst. 1906. *Commentary on the Maya Manuscript in the Royal Public Library of Dresden*. Papers of the Peabody Museum of American Archaeology and Ethnology, vol. 4, n. 2. Cambridge: Harvard University.

Frazer, James George. 1911 [1890]. *The Golden Bough: A Study in Magic and Religion*. Vol. 1, *The Magic Art and the Evolution of Kings*. 3rd ed. London: MacMillan.

Garibay K., Ángel María. 1958. *Veinte himnos sacros de los nahuas*. Mexico City: Universidad Nacional Autónoma de México-Instituto de Historia.

González González, Carlos. 2010. "El sacrificio humano como generador de prestigio social. Los mexicas y el llamado sacrificio gladiatorio." In *El sacrificio humano en la tradición religiosa meso-americana*, edited by Leonardo López Luján and Guilhem Olivier, 419–30. Mexico City: Instituto Nacional de Antropología e Historia, Universidad Nacional Autónoma de México.

———. 2011. *Xipe Tótec. Guerra y regeneración del maíz en la religión mexica*. Mexico City: Instituto Nacional de Antropología e Historia, Fondo de Cultura Económica.

González Torres, Yólotl. 1985. *El sacrificio humano entre los mexicas*. Mexico City: Fondo de Cultura Económica.

Granicka, Katarzyna. 2015. "En torno al origen de las imágenes de la sección de las veintenas en los 'Primeros Memoriales' de fray Bernardino de Sahagún." *Revista Española de Antropología Americana* 45: 211–27.

Graulich, Michel. 1981. "The Metaphor of the Day in Ancient Mexican Myth and Ritual." *Current Anthropology* 22: 45–50.

———. 1986. "El problema del bisiesto mexicano y las *xochipaina* de *Tititl* y de *Huey Tecuilhuitl*." *Revista Española de Antropología Americana* 16: 19–33.

———. 1987. *Mythes et rituels du Mexique ancien préhispanique*. Brussels: Académie Royale de Belgique.

———. 1993. "Aspects religieux du règne de Montezuma II." *Annuaire de l'École Pratique des Hautes Études, Section des Sciences Religieuses* 100: 31–37.

———. 1994. "Aspects religieux du règne de Montezuma II (suite)." *Annuaire de l'École Pratique des Hautes Études, Section des Sciences Religieuses* 101: 29–35.

———. 1995. "Les réformes politiques et religieuses de Motecuhzoma II Xocoyotzin." In *Hommage à Jacques Soustelle*, edited by Jacqueline de Durand-Forest, 211–24. Paris: L'Harmattan.

———. 1997. *Myths of Ancient Mexico*. Norman: University of Oklahoma Press.

———. 1999. *Ritos aztecas. Las fiestas de las veintenas*. Mexico City: Instituto Nacional Indigenista.

Hassig, Ross. 2001. *Time, History, and Belief in Aztec and Colonial Mexico*. Austin: University of Texas Press.

Heyden, Doris. 1991. "Dryness Before the Rains: Toxcatl and Tezcatlipoca." In *To Change Place: Aztec Ceremonial Landscapes*, edited by Davíd Carrasco, 188–202. Boulder: University Press of Colorado.

"Historia de los mexicanos por sus pinturas." 2002. In *Mitos e historias de los antiguos nahuas*, edited by Rafael Tena. Mexico City: Consejo Nacional para la Cultura y las Artes.

Hvidtfeldt, Arild. 1958. *Teotl and *Ixiptlatli: Some Central Conceptions in Ancient Mexican Religion*. Copenhagen: Muksgaard.

Iwaniszewski, Stanislaw. 2019. "Michel Graulich y el problema del desfase estacional del año vago mexica." *Trace* 75: 128–84.

Jansen, Maarten, and Gabina Aurora Pérez Jiménez. 2017. *Time and the Ancestors: Aztec and Mixtec Ritual Art*. Leiden: Brill.

Johansson, Patrick. 2005. "*Cempoallapohualli*. La cronología de las veintenas en el calendario solar náhuatl." *Estudios de Cultura Náhuatl* 36: 149–84.

Justeson, John S., and David Tavárez. 2007. "The Correlation of the Colonial Northern Zapotec Calendar with European Chronology." In *Skywatching in the Ancient World*, edited by Clive Ruggles and Gary Urton, 17–81. Boulder: University Press of Colorado.

Kirchhoff, Paul. 1971. "Las 18 fiestas anuales en Mesoamérica: 6 fiestas sencillas y 6 fiestas dobles." In *Verhandlungen des XXXVIII Internationalen Amerikanisten-Kongresses, Stuttgart-München, 12 bis. 18 August 1968*. Vol. 3, 207–21. Munich: Klaus Renner Verlag.

Kruell, Gabriel. 2011. "Panquetzaliztli: El nacimiento de Huitzilopochtli y la caída de Tezcatlipoca." *Estudios Mesoamericanos* 10: 81–93.

———. 2019. "Revisión histórica del 'bisiesto náhuatl': en memoria de Michel Graulich." *Trace* 75: 155–87.

Kubler, Georges, and Charles Gibson. 1951. *The Tovar Calendar: An Illustrated Mexican Manuscript ca. 1585*. Memoirs of the Connecticut Academy of Arts and Sciences 11. New Haven: Yale University Press.

Lastra, Yolanda. 2006. *Los otomíes: su lengua y su historia*. Mexico City: Universidad Nacional Autónoma de México-Instituto de Investigaciones Antropológicas.

Limón Olvera, Silvia. 2001a. *El fuego sagrado: ritualidad y simbolismo entre los nahuas según las fuentes documentales*. Mexico City: Instituto Nacional de Antropología e Historia, Universidad Nacional Autónoma de México.

———. 2001b. "El dios del fuego y la regeneración del mundo." *Estudios de Cultura Náhuatl* 32: 51–68.

Lind, Michael. 2015. *Ancient Zapotec Religion: An Ethnohistorical and Archeological Perspective*. Boulder: University Press of Colorado.

López Austin, Alfredo. 1967. *Juegos rituales aztecas. Versión, introducción y notas de Alfredo López Austin*. Mexico: Universidad Nacional Autónoma de México-Instituto de Investigaciones Históricas.

———. 1970. "Religión y magia en el ciclo de las fiestas aztecas." In *Religión, mitología y magia*, 3–29. Mexico City: Museo Nacional de Antropología.

———. 1980. *Cuerpo humano e ideología. Las concepciones de los antiguos nahuas*. 2 vols. Mexico City: Universidad Nacional Autónoma de México-Instituto de Investigaciones Antropológicas.

———. 1983. "Nota sobre la fusión y fisión de los dioses en el panteón mexica." *Anales de Antropología* 20, no. 2: 75–87.

———. 1998a [1973]. *Hombre-Dios. Religión y política en el mundo náhuatl*. 3rd ed. Mexico City: Universidad Nacional Autónoma de México-Instituto de Investigaciones Históricas.

————. 1998b [1990]. *Los mitos del tlacuache. Caminos de la mitología mesoamericana*. 4th ed. Mexico City: Universidad Nacional Autónoma de México-Instituto de Investigaciones Antropológicas.

————. 2001. "El núcleo duro, la cosmovisión y la tradición mesoamericana." In *Cosmovisión, ritual e identidad de los pueblos indígenas de México*, edited by Johanna Broda and Félix Báez-Jorge, 47–65. Mexico City: Fondo de Cultura Económica.

López Austin, Alfredo, and Leonardo López Luján. 2004. "El Templo Mayor de Tenochtitlan, el Tonacatépetl y el mito del robo del maíz." In *Acercarse y mirar. Homenaje a Beatriz de la Fuente*, edited by María Teresa Uriarte and Leticia Staines Cicero, 403–55. Mexico City: Universidad Nacional Autónoma de México-Instituto de Investigaciones Estéticas.

López Luján, Leonardo. 2005. *The Offerings of the Templo Mayor of Tenochtitlan*. Albuquerque: University of New Mexico Press.

López Luján, Leonardo, and Ximena Chávez. 2010. "Al pie del Templo Mayor: excavaciones en busca de los soberanos mexicas." In *Moctezuma II. Tiempo y destino de un gobernante*, edited by Leonardo López Luján and Colin McEwan, 294–303. Mexico City: Instituto Nacional de Antropología e Historia.

————, ed. 2019. *Al pie del Templo Mayor de Tenochtitlan. Estudios en honor de Eduardo Matos Moctezuma*. 2 vols. Mexico City: El Colegio Nacional.

López Luján, Leonardo, Ximena Chávez Balderas, Belem Zúñiga-Arellano, Alejandra Aguirre Molina, and Norma Valentín Maldonado. 2012. "Un portal al inframundo: ofrendas de animales al pie del Templo Mayor de Tenochtitlan." *Estudios de Cultura Náhuatl* 44: 9–40.

Margáin Araujo, Carlos. 1945. "La fiesta azteca de la cosecha Ochpanistli." *Anales del Instituto Nacional de Antropología e Historia* 1: 157–74.

Mazzetto, Elena. 2013. "La comida ritual en las fiestas de las veintenas mexicas. Un acercamiento a su tipología y simbolismo." *Amérique Latine Histoire & Mémoire, Les Cahiers ALHIM* 25. https://journals.openedition.org/alhim/4461.

————. 2014a. *Lieux de culte et parcours cérémoniels dans les fêtes des vingtaines à Mexico-Tenochtitlan*. Oxford: British Archaeological Reports.

————. 2014b. "Las *ayauhcalli* en el ciclo de las veintenas del año solar. Funciones y ubicación de las casas de niebla y sus relaciones con la liturgia del maíz." *Estudios de Cultura Náhuatl* 48: 135–75.

————. 2014c. "Tlacochcalco, el 'lugar de la casa de los dardos' y la materialización del Inframundo. Homologías funcionales de un espacio sagrado mexica." *Studi e Materiali di Storia delle Religioni* 80: 226–44.

————. 2014d. "Le metafore alimentari e vegetali del guerriero defunto nella cultura azteca." *Studi Tanatologici* 7: 135–56.

————. 2015. "El simbolismo de la *yotextli* en las fiestas del año solar mexica." *Itinerarios* 21: 147–70.

————. 2016. "La veintena de Ochpaniztli. Una posible metáfora del crecimiento del maíz en los espacios del Templo Mayor de México-Tenochtitlan." In *El maíz nativo en México. Una aproximación desde los estudios rurales*, edited by Ignacio López Moreno and Ivonne Vizcarra Bordi, 65–92. Mexico City: Universidad Autónoma Metropolitana.

————. 2017. "¿Miel o sangre? Nuevas problemáticas acerca de la elaboración de las efigies de *tzoalli* de las divinidades nahuas." *Estudios de Cultura Náhuatl* 53: 73–118.

————. 2019a. "Mitos y recorridos divinos en la veintena de Panquetzaliztli." *Trace* 75: 46–85.

————. 2019b. "Vapores, lumbres y serpientes. Apuntes sobre algunas técnicas de cocción ritual y sus significados entre los antiguos nahuas." *Itinerarios* 29: 63–95.

————. Forthcoming. "Cuando la tierra ríe. Apuntes sobre el humor ritual entre los nahuas prehispánicos." *Revista Española de Antropología Americana*.

Mazzetto, Elena, and Rossend Rovira-Morgado. 2014. "Sobre la orilla del agua: En torno a la dignidad de *atenpanecatl* y de ciertos espacios de culto a la diosa Toci en México-Tenochtitlan." *Cuicuilco* 21, no. 59: 93–120.

Mikulska Dąbrowska, Katarzyna. 2016. *Tejiendo destinos: un acercamiento al sistema de comunicación gráfica de los códices adivinatorios.* Warsaw, Zinacantepec: University of Warsaw, El Colegio Mexiquense.

Milbrath, Susan. 1989. "A Seasonal Calendar with Venus Periods in *Codex Borgia 29–46*." In *Imagination of Matter: Religion and Ecology in Mesoamerican Traditions*, edited by Davíd Carrasco, 103–27. Oxford: British Archaeological Reports.

———. 2007. "Astronomical Cycles in the Imagery of Codex Borgia 29–46." In *Skywatching in the Ancient World. New Perspectives in Cultural Astronomy*, edited by Clive Ruggles and Gary Urton, 157–208. Boulder: University Press of Colorado.

———. 2013a. *Heaven and Earth in Ancient Mexico. Astronomy and Seasonal Cycles in the Codex Borgia.* Austin: University of Texas Press.

———. 2013b. "Seasonal Imagery in Ancient Mexican Almanacs of the Dresden Codex and Codex Borgia." In *Das Bild der Jahreszeiten im wandel der kulturen un zeiten*, edited by Thierry Greub, 117–42. Munich: Wilhelm Fink Verlag.

Morán, Elizabeth. 2016. *Sacred Consumption: Food and Ritual in Aztec Art and Culture.* Austin: University of Texas Press.

Nebot García, Edgar. 2013. "El Xochitlicacan y el Quauitl-xicalli del recinto sagrado de México Tenochtitlan: el árbol como símbolo de poder en el México antiguo." *Dimensión Antropológica* 59: 7–50. http://www.dimensionantropologica.inah.gob.mx/?p=11371

Nicholson, Henry B. 2002. "Representing the *Veintena* Ceremonies in the *Primeros Memoriales*." In *Representing Aztec Ritual: Performance, Text, and Image in the Work of Sahagún*, edited by Eloise Quiñones Keber, 63–106. Boulder: University Press of Colorado.

Nowotny, Karl A. 1968. "Die aztekischen Festkreise." *Zeitschrift für Ethnologie* 93: 84–106.

Olivier, Guilhem, 2002. "The Hidden King and the Broken Flutes: The Mythical and Royal Dimension of Tezcatlipoca's Feast of Toxcatl." In *Representing Ritual: Performance, Text, and Image in the Work of Sahagún*, edited by Eloise Quiñones Keber, 107–42. Boulder: University Press of Colorado.

———. 2003. *Mockeries and Metamorphoses of an Aztec God: Tezcatlipoca, "Lord of the Smoking Mirror."* Translated by Michel Besson. Niwot: University Press of Colorado.

———. 2015. *Cacería, sacrificio y poder en Mesoamérica. Tras las huellas de Mixcóatl, "Serpiente de Nube."* Mexico City: Fondo de Cultura Económica, Universidad Nacional Autónoma de México, Centro de Estudios Mexicanos y Centroamericanos.

Olmedo Vera, Bertina. 2008. "Fiesta pequeña de los señores." In *Análisis etnohistórico de códices y documentos coloniales*, edited by Celia Isla Jiménez, María Teresa Sánchez Valdés, and Lourdes Suárez Diez, 15–29. Mexico City: Instituto Nacional de Antropología e Historia.

Oudijk, Michel R. 2018. "La reconstrucción del calendario zapoteco." https://www.academia.edu/36451010/La_reconstrucci%C3%B3n_del_calendario_zapoteco.

———. 2020. "Nuevas fuentes para la interpretación del *Códice Vaticano B*." In *Comentario al Códice Vaticano B (3773)*, edited by Katarzyna Mikulska Dąbrowska, 229–71. Mexico City: Universidad Nacional Autónoma de México, University of Warsaw, Vatican Apostolic Library.

Prem, Hanns. 2008. *Manual de la antigua cronología mexicana.* Mexico City: Centro de Investigaciones y Estudios Superiores en Antropología Social, Porrúa.

Preuss, Konrad Theodor. 1905. "Der Einfluß der Natur auf die Religion in Mexiko und den Vereinigten Staaten." *Zeitschrift der Gesellschaft für Erdkunde Berlin* 5–6: 361–80, 433–60.

————. 1929. "Das Frühlingsfest im Alten Mexiko und bei den Mandan Indianern der Vereinigten Staaten von Nordamerika." In *Donum Natalicum Schrijnen. Verzameling van opstellen door oud-leerlingen en bevriende vakgenooten opgedragen aan Mgr. Prof. Dr. Jos. Schrijnen bij Gelegenheid van zijn zestigsten verjaardag 3 Mei 1929*, 825–37. Chartres: Imprimerie Durand.

————. 1998. *Fiesta, literatura y magia en el Nayarit. Ensayos sobre coras, huicholes y mexicaneros de Konrad Theodor Preuss*. Edited by Jesús Jáuregui and Johannes Neurath. Mexico City: Instituto Nacional Indigenista, Centro de Estudios Mexicanos y Centroamericanos.

Proenza, Martha T. 1993. *La fiesta prehispánica: un espectáculo teatral. Comparación de las descripciones de cuatro fiestas hechas por Sahagún y Durán*. Mexico City: Instituto Nacional de Bellas Artes.

————. 2011. *Teatralidad y poder en el México antiguo: la fiesta Toxcatl celebrada por los mexicas*. Mexico City: Instituto Nacional de Bellas Artes, Consejo Nacional para la Cultura y las Artes.

Ragot, Nathalie. 2011. "Ad Memoriam: cérémonies post-funéraires et hommages aux défunts chez les Aztèques." In *La quête du Serpent à Plumes. Arts et religions de l'Amérique précolombienne. Hommage à Michel Graulich*, edited by Nathalie Ragot, Sylvie Peperstraete, and Guilhem Olivier, 157–73. Turnhout: Brepols Publishers, Bibliothèque de l'École Pratique des Hautes Études-Sciences Religieuses.

Ramírez, José Fernando. 1903 [1867]. "Códices mexicanos de Fr. Bernardino de Sahagún", *Anales del Museo Nacional de México* 1: 1–34.

Ramírez, José Fernando. 2001. *Obras históricas: época prehispánica*. Mexico City: Universidad Nacional Autónoma de México.

Réville, Albert. 1885. *Les religions du Mexique, de l'Amérique centrale et du Pérou*. Paris: Librairie Fischbacher.

Reyes Guerrero, María Eugenia. 2015. "Transgresiones y sanciones durante los actos rituales en las fiestas de las veintenas de Etzalcualiztli y Huey Tecuilhuitl." MA thesis, Universidad Nacional Autónoma de México.

Rodríguez Figueroa, Andrea Berenice. 2010. "Paisaje e imaginario colectivo del altiplano central mesoamericano: el paisaje ritual en *atl cahualo* o *cuahuitl ehua* según las fuentes sahaguntinas." MA thesis, Universidad Nacional Autónoma de México.

————. 2014. "El paisaje festivo en el *cecempohuallapohualli* de la cuenca de México del siglo XVI, según las fuentes sahaguntinas." PhD diss., Universidad Nacional Autónoma de México.

Sahagún, Bernardino de. 1950–82. *Florentine Codex: General History of the Things of New Spain, Fray Bernardino de Sahagún*. Translated with notes and illustrations by Arthur J. O. Anderson, and Charles E. Dibble. 13 vols. Santa Fe: The School of American Research, University of Utah Press.

————. 1979. *Códice Florentino. El manuscrito 218–220 de la colección palatina de la Biblioteca Medicea Laurenziana*. 3 vols. Florence, Mexico City: Giunti Barbéra, Archivo General de la Nación.

————. 1997. *Primeros Memoriales*. Edited and translated by Thelma Sullivan. Completed and revised, with additions, by Henry B. Nicholson, Arthur J. O. Anderson, Charles E. Dibble, Eloise Quiñones Keber, and Wayne Ruwet. Norman: University of Oklahoma Press.

Saurin, Patrick. 1999. *Teocuicatl. Chants sacrés des anciens mexicains*. Paris: Publications Scientifiques du Muséum.

Schwaller, John F. 2019. *The Fifteenth Month. Aztec History in the Rituals of Panquetzaliztli*. Norman: University of Oklahoma Press.

Seler, Eduard. 1899. "Die Achtzehn Jahresfeste der Mexikaner (Erste Hälfte)." *Veröffentlichungen aus dem Kgl. Museum für Völkerkunde* 6: 67–209.

————. 1901–02. *Codex Fejérváry Mayer. An Old Mexican Picture Manuscript in the Liverpool Free Public museums (12014/M) [...]*. Berlin, London: Hazell, Watson, & Viney, ld.

————. 1902–03. *Codex Vaticanus 3773. An Old Mexican Pictorial Manuscript in the Vatican Library [...]*. 2 vols. Berlin, London: Hazell, Watson, & Viney, ld.

————. 1903. "Die Korrecturen der Jahreslänge und der Länge der Venusperiode in den mexikanischen Bilderschriften." *Zeitschrift für Ethnologie* 35: 27–49.

————. 1904a. "The Mexican Chronology with Special Reference to the Zapotec Calendar." In *Mexican and Central American Antiquities, Calendar Systems, and History*, edited by Charles P. Bowditch, 11–55. Smithsonian Institution Bulletin 28. Washington, DC: Smithsonian Institution.

————. 1904b. "Wall Paintings of Mitla: A Mexican Picture Writing in Fresco." In *Mexican and Central American Antiquities, Calendar Systems, and History*, edited by Charles P. Bowditch, 243–324. Smithsonian Institution Bulletin 28. Washington, DC: Smithsonian Institution.

————. 1963 [1904–06]. *Comentarios al Códice Borgia*. Vols. I and II, In *Códice Borgia y comentarios de Eduard Seler*. 3 vols. Mexico City: Fondo de Cultura Económica.

Seler, Eduard, and Caecilie Seler-Sachs. 1902. *Gesammelte abhandlungen zur amerikanischen sprachund alterthumskunde*. Vol. 1. Berlin: A. Asher.

Siarkiewicz, Elżbieta. 1995. *El tiempo en el tonalamatl*. Warsaw: University of Warsaw.

Sprajc, Ivan. 2000. "Problema de ajuste del año calendárico mesoamericano al año trópico." *Anales de Antropología* 34, no. 1: 133–60.

Stresser-Péan, Guy. 2005. *Le Soleil-Dieu et le Christ. La christianisation des Indiens du Mexique, vue de la Sierra de Puebla*. Paris: L'Harmattan.

Sullivan, Thelma D. 1976. "The Mask of Itztlacoliuhqui." In *Actas del XLI Congreso Internacional de Americanistas, Mexico 1974*, 252–62. Mexico City: Instituto Nacional de Antropología e Historia.

Tapia, Omar. 2017. "Las fiestas de las veintenas. Análisis historiográfico de la historia mesoamericana." BA thesis, Universidad Nacional Autónoma de México.

Taube, Karl A. 1988. "The Ancient Yucatec New Year Festival: The Liminal Period in Maya Ritual and Cosmology." PhD diss., Yale University.

Tavárez, David. 2011. *The Invisible War. Indigenous Devotions, Discipline, and Dissent in Colonial Mexico*. Redwood City: Stanford University Press.

Tena, Rafael. 1987. *El calendario mexica y la cronografía*. Mexico City: Instituto Nacional de Antropología e Historia.

Thomas, Cyrus. 1882. *A Study of the Manuscript Troano*. U.S. Department of the Interior Contributions to North American Ethnology 5. Washington, DC: Government Printing Office.

Thompson, J. Eric S. 1934. *Sky Bearers, Colors, and Directions in Maya and Mexican Religion*. Contributions to American Archaeology 10. Washington, DC: Carnegie Institution.

————. 1970. *Maya History and Religion*. Norman: University of Oklahoma Press.

————. 1971. *Maya Hieroglyphic Writing: An Introduction*. Norman: University of Oklahoma Press.

Thouvenot, Marc. 2015. "*Ilhuitl* (día, parte diurna, veintena) y sus divisiones." *Estudios de Cultura Náhuatl* 49: 93–160.

————. 2019. "El mundo del *ilhuitl*. Sus ritmos y duraciones." *Trace* 75: 86–127.

Torres Cisneros, Gustavo. 2001. "Les visages de Soleil el Lune (*Xëëw po'o yë' ajkxy ywiinjëjp*): configurations calendaires, mythiques et rituels du temps chez del Mixes de l'Oaxaca, Mexique." PhD diss., École Pratique des Hautes Études.

————. 2008. "El calendario ceremonial hopi comparado con el calendario azteca." In *Por los caminos del maíz. Mito y ritual en la periferia septentrional de Mesoamérica*, edited by Johannes Neurath, 387–457. Mexico City: Fondo de Cultura Económica, Consejo Nacional para la Cultura y las Artes.

————. 2011. "Los meses dobles en el calendario mixe y sus implicaciones para el estudio de las fiestas en Mesoamérica." In *La quête du Serpent à Plumes. Arts et religions de l'Amérique précolombienne. Hommage à Michel Graulich*, edited by Nathalie Ragot, Sylvie Peperstraete, and Guilhem Olivier, 175–94. Turnhout: Brepols Publishers, Bibliothèque de l'École Pratique des Hautes Études-Sciences Religieuses.

Vail, Gabrielle. 2002. *Haab' Rituals in the Maya Codices and the Structure of Maya Almanacs*. Washington, DC: Center for Maya Research.

————. 2005. "Renewal Ceremonies in the Madrid Codex." In *Painted Books and Indigenous Knowledge in Mesoamerica: Manuscript Studies in Honor of Mary Elizabeth Smith*, edited by Elizabeth H. Boone, 179–209. New Orleans: Tulane University.

Vail, Gabrielle, and Anthony Aveni, ed. 2004. *The Madrid Codex: New Approaches to Understanding an Ancient Maya Manuscript*. Boulder: University Press of Colorado.

Vail, Gabrielle, and Christine Hernández. 2013. *Re-Creating Primordial Time: Foundation Rituals and Mythology in the Postclassic Maya Codices*. Boulder: University Press of Colorado.

Velasco Lozano, Ana María. 2001. "Los cuerpos divinos: la utilización del amaranto en el ritual mexica." In *Animales y plantas en la cosmovisión mesoamericana*, edited by Yolotl González Torres, 39–63. Mexico City: Consejo Nacional para la Cultura y las Artes, Instituto Nacional de Antropología e Historia.

Velásquez, Erik. 2017. "Códice de Dresde. Parte 1." Facsimil edition. *Arqueología mexicana*, edición especial 69.

Veliz Ruiz Esparza, Luis Alejandro. 2018. "Complejo sonoro y representaciones rituales en un texto sahaguntino: el caso de la veintena de Etzalcualiztli." PhD diss., Universidad Nacional Autónoma de México.

Vié-Wohrer, Anne-Marie. 1999. *Xipe Totec notre seigneur l'écorché: étude glyphique d'un dieu aztèque*. 2 vols. Mexico City: Centro de Estudios Mexicanos y Centroamericanos.

————. 2008. "Hypothèses sur l'origine et la diffusion du complexe rituel du *tlacaxipehualiztli*." *Journal de la Société des Américanistes* 94, no. 2. https://journals.openedition.org/jsa/10602.

Wimmer, Alexis. 2006. *Dictionnaire de la langue nahuatl classique*. http://sites.estvideo.net/malinal/.

Wright Carr, David Charles. 2009. "El calendario mesoamericano en las lenguas otomí y náhuatl." *Tlalocan* 16: 217–53.

PART I

Rites and Myths in Pre-Columbian Mesoamerica

CHAPTER ONE

Tezcatlipoca and the Maya Gods of Abundance

The Feast of Toxcatl and the Question of Homologies in Mesoamerican Religion

OSWALDO CHINCHILLA MAZARIEGOS

In this feast, they killed a young man of very polished appearance, whom they had raised for a year in luxuries. They said that he was the image of Tezcatlipoca. After killing the young man who was raised for a year, they promptly put another in his place ... They chose them among all the captives, the most pleasant men, and the *calpixques* guarded them. They put great diligence in [ensuring] that they were the ablest and better disposed that there could be, and without any corporal defect.

(Sahagún 1989, 1: 115–16)[1]

Yn aquin pepenaloia, in teixiptla, atle yiaioca.

He who was chosen as impersonator was without defects.

(Sahagún 1950–82, bk 2: 66)

In their account of the feast of Toxcatl, Bernardino de Sahagún's informants devoted several paragraphs to describe the young man who impersonated Tezcatlipoca, only to be sacrificed at the end of the feast. They heaped praise on him, "who had no flaw, who had no defects, who had no blemish, who had no mark, who had no wart, small tumor" (*atle itlacauhca, atle yiaioca, atle ytlaciuhca, atle ytlaciuizço, atle ytech ca etzotzocatl*) (translation to English modified from Sahagún 1950–82, bk 2: 68). The physical perfection of Tezcatlipoca's impersonator is one of the reasons that lead me to compare him with the Maya Maize God, and to compare the ritual events that transpired during the Toxcatl celebrations with the Maize God's death and rebirth, known from artistic representations in Classic Maya ceramics.

The correspondences that emerge from these comparisons suggest that the Nahua feast evoked mythical events that were also recognizable in the earlier and variant versions that were depicted in Classic Maya vessels.

These comparisons stretch across many centuries, and refer to the religious beliefs of peoples who spoke different languages and lived in different environments, separated from each other by vast distances. Nevertheless, they were participants in the broad cultural milieu that modern scholars identify with Mesoamerican civilization. The Classic Maya, the sixteenth-century Nahua, and other indigenous peoples of Mesoamerica share a core system of religious beliefs that become manifest in ways that show surprising affinities, notwithstanding the discontinuities imposed by language and ethnicity, geography, and time (López Austin 1993, 15–23; 2001, 2003; Monaghan 2000; Van der Loo 1987).

Several authors have debated the homologies between Tezcatlipoca and the Maya god K'awiil. In this chapter, I review those arguments and involve a third party, the Maya Maize God. I will not offer a complete analysis of each deity, an endeavor that would escape the scope of this chapter and would duplicate the work of earlier scholars.[2] Nor will I attempt a detailed explanation of Tezcatlipoca and the feast of Toxcatl, whose multiple facets have received much specialized attention.[3] Instead, I will focus on the intersections that appear to bring these gods together in ways that most likely did not result from independent invention or convergence. The discussion is based mainly on Sahagún's accounts of the feast in the *Florentine Codex* (Sahagún 1950–82, bk 2: 66–77). A variant account from Durán (1984, 2: 37–45) also referred to the Tezcatlipoca impersonator and his sacrifice, but without highlighting his youthfulness and physical beauty. De la Serna's (2003, 98–99) early seventeenth-century description largely paralleled Sahagún's, although he added intriguing details that are discussed below.

At the outset, I address the theoretical and methodological problems involved in my comparison of Classic Maya and sixteenth-century Nahua deities. Next, I discuss the parallels between the Maya Maize God and K'awiil, and compare the Maize God's myths with the rituals dedicated to Tezcatlipoca during Toxcatl. Rather than equating them with each other, I note the commonalities that link them as members of a broad category of young gods in Mesoamerican religion.

DESCENT AND TRANSLATION OF MESOAMERICAN GODS

In his pioneering book *The Maya Scribe and his World* and subsequent works, Michael Coe pointed out connections between Tezcatlipoca and the Lowland Maya god K'awiil, also known as God K (Coe 1973, 16). Coe's proposition was consonant with his conviction—stated in the same work—that Mesoamerican peoples shared a common religion (Coe 1973, 8). He followed the path that authors such as Paul Schellhas, Eduard Seler, and Eric Thompson had taken before him, searching for commonalities among the Maya and Nahua gods (Schellhas 1904; Seler 1904; Thompson 1934, 1939). But this path is fraught with difficulties. While most scholars acknowledge close correspondences in the religious beliefs of Mesoamerican peoples, attempts to trace specific links among gods and goddesses across geographic, temporal, ethnic, and linguistic provinces face multiple concerns related to possible disjunctions of form and meaning. The homologies are never complete, and even if noticeable, it is rarely possible to trace the historical processes that brought them about.

The problem goes beyond the specific parallels between K'awiil and Tezcatlipoca, and applies to other Mesoamerican deities that appear in separate, sometimes distant communities. Homologies may result from two distinct but not mutually exclusive processes: "descent" and "translation." Descent refers to derivation from an ancestor. This process involves the common, ancient origins of religious concepts and deities, and their divergent evolution in separate communities, resulting in related manifestations that are not translations of each other. Alfredo López Austin stressed the unity of Mesoamerican religion, derived from ancient common roots that go back to the early agricultural villages of the Archaic period (López Austin 1993, 15–20; 2001). A common background, extended in those early communities—not necessarily pinpointed to a specific community or region—explains the fundamental unity of Mesoamerican religion, which López Austin (1993, 19) conceived as an organized whole, not "a mere aggregate of parts assembled from all the corners of Mesoamerica."

Reconstructing the descent of Mesoamerican gods and religious beliefs is a difficult task, complicated by the vagaries of preservations and the uneven distribution of extant pictorial and textual records. Miguel Covarrubias made an early effort to trace the descent of rain gods from Central Mexico, the Gulf Coast, Oaxaca, and the Maya area back to prototypes in Olmec art (Covarrubias 1946). More recently, Karl Taube amended some of the misidentified examples in Covarrubias's chart and made a similar effort to trace the descent of Mesoamerican maize gods (Taube 1996; 2004, 29–34). While concentrating on the deities' representations, Taube (1996, 54) pointed out that the continuities also involved their qualities and associations. Indeed, we should assume that successive generations learned not only the gods' iconographic conventions from their forebears, but also the complex of mythical beliefs and religious rituals that were germane to their cult. The transmission was not seamless, and there were important episodes of transformation, adaptation, and disjunction that should be kept in mind. Nevertheless, those processes should not obscure the importance of descent processes that ultimately linked together the religious beliefs and rituals of Mesoamerican peoples.

Covarrubias's and Taube's charts suggest that Mesoamerican gods diverged progressively from common sources, forming independent descent lines that had few points of contact with each other after the initial splits. Generally missing from these charts are the horizontal links that resulted in translations of deities and religious beliefs across regions, among peoples who spoke different languages, and were ruled by different lords who were often at odds with each other. In a recent contribution, Guilhem Olivier and Roberto Martínez discussed the translation of foreign gods in Postclassic Mesoamerica (Olivier and Martínez 2015). In English, the verb "translate" has multiple meanings, referring to movements from one place or condition to another, changes in appearance, or the expression of words in different languages (Merriam-Webster 2019). This range of meanings applies well to processes that include the acquisition of deities from other regions and communities and their assimilation with previously existing ones. Mediated through economic and political interaction—from trade and diplomacy to warfare and imperial expansion—and sometimes responding to migratory movements, translations resulted from intense and sustained interaction between different communities and regions through time. Foreign gods, their iconographic representations, and their associated rituals were transferred from one region to another, either directly—through contact among individuals from both communities— or indirectly, through the mediation of individuals from other communities or through the transportation of books, effigies, or other materials that may have carried the information.[4] But López Austin (1993, 19) warned that those exchanges rarely resulted in the introduction of completely new gods and beliefs. From his perspective, the gods that appear to be imported from elsewhere at certain sites or regions are best understood as reinterpretations of deities that were already present, although they may appear under new names or new shapes.

While citing examples from the Old World and early colonial instances in which the Christian saints and Jesus Christ himself were assimilated with Mesoamerican gods, Olivier and Martínez (2015, 365) showed that this was not a colonial innovation but, rather, a long-established Mesoamerican tradition. Focusing on Postclassic cases, Olivier and Martínez recognized "a structure of shared thought in conceptions of deities," and suggested that it might relate to a remote and mythologized "Toltec" past. Not coincidentally, Taube included a Postclassic convergence between the highland Mexican and Maya rain gods in his revised version of Covarrubias's chart. Thus, scholars are willing to acknowledge translations, but they tend to situate them mostly in the Postclassic period. I suspect that the translation of Mesoamerican gods involved much longer processes of interaction and exchange, and multiple contacts that spanned many centuries, reaching far beyond the Postclassic.

Pre-Hispanic examples of translation include the Nahua deities Xiuhtecuhtli and Tlahuizcalpantecuhtli in the Venus pages of the *Dresden Codex* (Taube and Bade 1991; Whittaker 1986). The scribes rendered the names of both gods using syllabic spellings in the Maya script. Xiuhtecuhtli's portrait displays the god's usual attributes in central Mexican art (perhaps reflecting a recent translation). Tlahuiz-calpantecuhtli took an animal shape that departed markedly from representations of the Nahua Venus god, suggesting more complex processes of translation, prob-ably spanning a longer time range. An earlier case is attested in the Late Classic inscription from Copan Temple 26. David Stuart noted that the text was written with parallel blocks that contained equivalent phrasings, one in the Maya logosyl-labic script, and the other using a fancifully devised script that employed Teotihua-can motifs to "translate" the Maya words (Stuart 2000, 497). One pairing in this "bilingual" inscription contains the name of the ruler Waxaklajuun Ubaah K'awiil, in which the "Teotihuacan" equivalent of the Maya god K'awiil is a serpent-footed Storm God with a smoking mirror in the forehead (Figure 1.1). This may suggest that the Copan Maya conceived of an aspect of the Storm God as the Teotihuacan counterpart of K'awiil, but the inscription's uniqueness, coupled with problems in its decipherment leave much room for uncertainty. These translations may or may not convey central Mexican beliefs credibly, but at the very least, they reflect an awareness that the local gods had counterparts in highland Mexico.

Early colonial texts are sometimes explicit. Notably, a passage in the *Popol Vuh* explained that the K'iche' god Tohil was the same as a foreign god, named Yolcuat and Quitzalcuat (*Popol Vuh* 1996, 162). Modern scholars have questioned whether this translation reflected an accurate understanding of the Nahua gods. Dennis Tedlock asserted that the K'iche' equivalent of Quetzalcoatl was not Tohil, but Q'ukumatz, while Tohil found a better counterpart in Tezcatlipoca (see *Popol Vuh* 1996, 305–06). Olivier and Martínez (2015) favored homologies between Tohil,

Figure 1.1. An apparent translation of K'awiil (right) into a Teotihuacan-style god (left) in Late Classic Copan. Detail of Temple 26 Inscription, Copan. Source: Drawing by Oswaldo Chinchilla Mazariegos.

Mixcoatl, and Curicaueri, the tutelary god of the P'urhepecha. Writing from a detached perspective, informed by multiple sources from many regions of Mesoamerica, modern observers tend to search for the closest possible fits among the gods of different communities. Even conceding the loss of vast amounts of information and the uneven contents of the extant records, it is unlikely that the authors of the *Popol Vuh* were equally informed. The question is not whether the K'iche' writers had clear notions of the complexity of the gods of the Nahua or P'urhepecha, but rather, which of the multiple attributes and manifestations of a complex god like Quetzalcoatl did they regard as akin to those of their own patron god.

The homologies are never neat. We can only expect perfect fits in cases where the beliefs and the associated iconography were transmitted directly from one place and people to another within a relatively short period of time. In the absence of detailed written sources or archaeological materials that would confirm such processes, we can rarely prove that this was the case. Correspondences are significant, not because they signify the wholesale adoption of gods from one community by another, but because they reveal the diverse manners in which Mesoamerican religious concepts were manifested while retaining core features, despite the bewildering variations that we perceive in iconographic forms and ritual practices. Classic and Postclassic Mesoamerican peoples inherited core religious concepts that originated in remote antiquity, reinterpreted them and blended them with related concepts and images acquired from other communities, which, nevertheless, were not entirely novel to them. Mesoamerican religious specialists did not just incorporate motifs and concepts that originated elsewhere, but recombined them in ways that were coherent and significant in particular social and historical circumstances.

TEZCATLIPOCA AND THE FEAST OF TOXCATL

Modern interpreters are often bewildered by the complexity of Tezcatlipoca. The god's numerous names and manifold aspects defy simple characterization (Heyden 1989; Nicholson 1971; Olivier 2003, 31). Among other attributions, he was regarded as a warrior and a sorcerer, associated with the night and the wind, the earth and the moon. He was related to many gods, including the lunar god Tecciztecatl-Meztli, Tepeyollotl, the jaguar heart of the mountains, and Itztlacoliuhqui-Ixquimilli, the faceless god of frost and maize.[5] He was a main actor in creative myths about the rise and fall of former suns, the formation of the earth, the fall of Tollan, and the legendary rise of the Mexica.[6]

For present purposes, I will emphasize Tezcatlipoca's youthfulness, his relationship with wealth and abundance, and his active sexuality. While these attributes of the deity cannot be artificially separated from others, they are especially relevant to analyze his links with the Maya gods. Tezcatlipoca held sway over all kinds of wealth and abundance, "and they said that he alone gave prosperity and riches, and he alone took them away at his whim" (*Y decían que él solo daba las prosperidades y riquezas, y que él solo las quitaba cuando se le antojaba*) (Sahagún 1989, 1: 38). He presided over the day 1-Death, and those who were born on that day were destined to be prosperous and wealthy, if they were devout and did penance. If not, the god took away their riches at will, turning masters into slaves at the slightest offense (Sahagún 1989, 1: 245–46). Olivier and Michel Graulich noted that this aspect was especially apparent in his manifestation as Omacatl, the god of feasting, who had to be pleased by those who organized banquets and celebrations. If they failed to appease him, the god would appear in dreams and spoil the food and drink, bringing sickness to the guests and dishonoring the hapless hosts (Sahagún 1989, 1: 51–52, also Graulich 2002a; Olivier 2003, 80–82).

During the feast of Toxcatl, young people danced with garlands of popcorn, which Graulich interpreted as denoting an abundance of food. According to his interpretation of the Nahua feasts, Toxcatl was originally a celebration of the harvests, and the garlands of popcorn denoted agricultural bounty, especially of maize (Graulich 1999, 354–55). Tezcatlipoca was not primarily a maize god, but Seler (1996, 83) pointed out his connections with Cinteotl-Itztlacoliuhqui, the blind god of frost and punishment, who was also related to maize, vegetation, and sexual transgression. Thelma Sullivan regarded Itztlacoliuhqui as a fertility god, associated with excess and exuberance, while questioning his association with Tezcatlipoca (Sullivan 1976, 260). Olivier's (2003, 214–22) reassessment showed that such associations were not inconsistent, and reaffirmed Itztlacoliuhqui's links with Tezcatlipoca. Graulich (1983, 577) also linked Tezcatlipoca with Piltzintecuhtli, the god who laid with Xochiquetzal and fathered Cinteotl, the Maize God, as told in early colonial sources that include the "Historia de los mexicanos por sus pinturas" (2002, 31) and the "Histoyre du Mechique" (Thévet 2002, 155).

Tezcatlipoca was known as Telpochtli, "youth." According to Olivier (2003, 59), *telpochtli* literally means "he of the obscured promontory," in allusion to puberty. As such, he was the patron of the *telpochcalli*, the houses where young men were educated in the arts of war, singing and dancing. Olivier (2003, 66–68) linked this aspect of the deity with his role as a warrior and his lubricity. In mythical narratives, Tezcatlipoca often participated in passages that involve magical seduction, and the procurement and abduction of women. According to Diego Muñoz Camargo, he abducted Xochiquetzal from the primeval garden of Tamoanchan (Muñoz Camargo 1984, 202–03). In the "Annals of Cuauhtitlan" (1992, 31–35), he was one of the gods who deceived Quetzalcoatl and induced him to forget his ritual duties and get drunk with his sister. While the text is not explicit, this passage suggests that Tezcatlipoca induced his foe to commit sexual transgression and incest. Couples that eat or drink together generally imply sexual cohabitation and marriage in Mesoamerican narratives and pictorial representations (Boone 2000, 56; Carmack 1979, 361).

Tezcatlipoca also induced sexual indulgence and facilitated illicit engagements in the legendary stories of ancient Nahua kings. Taking the aspect of a naked chili seller, he caused the daughter of the Toltec king Huemac to fall ill, lusting for the disguised god's genitals—one of several wrongdoings that eventually led to the fall of Tollan (Sahagún 1989, 1: 210). In another story (where he was named as Yohualli, "night"), he counseled the Mexica king Huitzilihuitl about the way to approach the secluded daughter of the king of Cuauhnahuac by shooting an arrow inside her tightly guarded palace (Chimalpahin 1997, 118–23; Olivier 2003, 67–68). Not surprisingly, Tezcatlipoca was invoked by suitors who needed his favor to obtain amorous rewards (Ruiz de Alarcón 1984, 132–34).

Tezcatlipoca's youthful vigor and his sexual prowess were emphasized in the Toxcatl rituals, when a handsome young man was selected from a group of captives to embody the god for an entire year, and die at the end of the feast. Long paragraphs of the *Florentine Codex* are devoted to describing his qualities, and especially, the defects that he should not have. These are excerpts from his description:

> Indeed, he who was thus chosen was of fair countenance, of good understanding, quick, of clean body, slender, reed-like, long and thin, like a stout cane, like a stone column all over, not of overfed body, not corpulent, nor very small, nor exceedingly tall (*ca iehoatl ic pepenalo, in qualli itlachieliz, in mjmatquj, in mjmatinj, in chipaoac ynacaio, cujllotic, acatic, piaztic, iuhqujn otlatl, ipanoca temjmjltic, amo tlacaçolnacaio, amo tomaoac, amo no tetepiton amo no cenca quauhtic*).

> He was like something smoothed, like a tomato, like a pebble, as if sculptured in wood; he was not curly haired, curly headed; his hair was indeed straight, his hair was long (*iuh-qujn tlachictli, iuhqujn tomatl, iuhqujn telolotli, iuhqujn, quaujtl tlaxixintli, amo quacocototztic, quacolochtic, vel tzōmelaoac, tzompiaztic*). (Sahagún 1950–82, bk 2: 66)

Sahagún's informants went on describing his forehead, his head, his eyes, cheeks, nose, lips, teeth, neck, hands, and stomach. They also added that he spoke well and didn't stutter, nor did he speak a barbarous language. Once selected, he was carefully trained to behave elegantly and play the flute. He went around the city, playing music and smoking, and everywhere people revered him in awe.

Graulich (1999, 349) interpreted Toxcatl as the feast of the Aztec king. At the beginning of the *veintena*, the *tlahtoani* presented Tezcatlipoca's impersonator with costly gifts and arrayed him with pomp because, as stated by Sahagún's informants, "verily he took him to be his beloved god" (*ipampa canel ic ytlaçoteuh ipan qujmati*) (Sahagún 1950–82, bk 2: 69). Graulich concluded that it was the king who presented the victim for sacrifice, and consequently secluded himself in penance during the last four days of the feast. Olivier (2003, 397, 400–02) agreed that the sacrifice of Tezcatlipoca was equated with the sacrifice of the king himself, and pointed out that, in Nahua rhetoric, the king was conceived as an instrument of Tezcatlipoca, comparable to the flute that the god played at will.

The impersonator changed his appearance at the beginning of the *veintena* of Toxcatl (Sahagún 1950–82, bk 2: 70). His hair was shorn and bound like that of a seasoned warrior. At that point, he was married to four women who were named after goddesses: Xochiquetzal, goddess of carnal love; Xilonen, goddess of tender corn; Atlantonan, goddess of waters; and Huixtocihuatl, goddess of salt. He lived in their company for twenty days, sleeping with them and, in Sahagún's words, he "had conversation" with them—a euphemism for sexual intercourse (Sahagún 1989, 1: 117). In the last five days of the feast, they sang and danced with him at several places around the city. The final day, they all embarked on a boat that took them to a place on the lake's eastern shore. The women returned from there, while the *ixiptla* proceeded by foot to a small temple called Tlacochcalco. He broke his flutes while slowly ascending the steps of the temple where he was sacrificed. His heart was offered to the sun and his body was lowered to the foot of the stairway, where it was beheaded. The head was hung in the *tzompantli*. De la Serna (2003, 99) added that the newly chosen youth who would impersonate the god through the following year accompanied his predecessor up the steps of the temple, encouraging him to confront death. The new impersonator also consumed the largest portion of the victim's body, while the rest was given in small pieces to high-ranking people.

Sahagún described another part of the feast, which centered on an amaranth figure of Huitzilopochtli.[7] Young people danced with ropes and garlands of roasted maize around the procession that brought this image to the main temple. The celebrations culminated with the sacrifice of Huitzilopochtli's impersonator, who had lived throughout the year with Tezcatlipoca's *ixiptla* (Sahagún 1950–82, bk 2: 76).

THE YOUNG GODS OF THE MAYA

Coe's (1973, 16) comparison of K'awiil and Tezcatlipoca inspired protracted debate. Taube (1992, 79) took a critical perspective, concluding that "although Tezcatlipoca and God K are perhaps cognate in a general sense, there is not a direct one-to-one correspondence between the deities." In my view, the question is whether the links between the two gods are significant even in the absence of a one-to-one correspondence, which would be unexpected in the first place. Rogelio Valencia Rivera and Susan Milbrath discussed correspondences between Tezcatlipoca and K'awiil that go beyond their shared iconographic attributes—the smoking mirror and the missing foot that are often associated with both deities (Milbrath 2015; Valencia Rivera 2006). For the present argument, the most significant homologies involve their qualities as young gods related with agricultural bounty, wealth, and abundance, and their sexual engagements, which are visibly related to fertility and reproduction.

Figure 1.2. The Maya Maize God. (a) Detail of Late Classic vase K1183. Source: Drawing by Oswaldo Chinchilla Mazariegos. (b) Early Classic graffito from Tikal Structure 5D-Sub3A, showing an ithyphallic portrait of the dancing Maize God. Source: Drawing by Oswaldo Chinchilla Mazariegos, after Trik and Kampen 1983, fig. 83g.

In the following paragraphs, I show that the Maize God shared similar attributes. For one thing, the Maize God paralleled the physical beauty of the young man who impersonated Tezcatlipoca during Toxcatl (Figure 1.2). For Mary Miller and Simon Martin he embodied the epitome of male beauty, and his long profile served as a model for artistic representations of Classic Maya lords (Miller and Martin 2004, 52–53). His glittering appearance was enhanced by elegant attire and abundant jewelry—reminiscent of the finery bestowed upon the impersonator of Tezcatlipoca by the Mexica king himself. Bioarchaeological and iconographic studies suggest that some cranial modifications were intended to replicate the elongated shape of the Maize God's head (Houston et al. 2006, 45; Tiesler 2014, 226–27).

The handsome appearance of the Maya Maize God is markedly different from K'awiil's uncanny, serpentine visage (Figure 1.3a). Yet they have much in common. The iconographic distinction between them is blurred by several traits, including their elongated, tonsured head, often with a chunk of hair on top. Both are young and slender, and they commonly bear marks that denote terse, shiny skin, although some portraits of K'awiil have ventral scales characteristic of snakes. The Maize God does not share K'awiil's serpent foot, but Taube (1992, 48) identified

Figure 1.3. K'awiil and the Maize God with cranial torches. (a) K'awiil. Detail of vase K2970. (b) The Maize God. Detail of vase K5126. Source: Drawings by Oswaldo Chinchilla Mazariegos.

representations in which he was supplied with a cranial torch, a distinctive attribute of K'awiil (Figure 1.3b). Considering their overlapping traits and domains, Martin (2006, 179) characterized them as "partly synonymous entities."

Both deities are strongly associated with agricultural bounty. Eric Thompson noted God K's association with foliage and vegetation, and linked him with the appellative *Kauil*, attested in colonial sources (Thompson 1970, 224–26). He translated *Kauil* as "bountiful harvest" or simply "foodstuff." Both he and Ralph Roys considered deities that used this name in colonial texts—including Uaxac Yol Kauil and Itzamna Kauil—as "representing some aspect of food or crops," and referring to the Maize God (Roys, in *Ritual of the Bacabs* 1965, 155, 159; see also Barrera Vásquez 1991, 387, and Bolles 2001, who agree with these translations). David Stuart's decipherment of God K's hieroglyphic name as K'awiil confirmed Thompson's original inkling, reinforcing his ties with agriculture and sustenance (Stuart 1987, 15–16).

K'awiil's links with wealth and abundance are relevant to understand his connections with royalty and dynastic succession, apparent in the hieroglyphic phrase *u ch'am K'awiil*, "[he/she] receives K'awiil", which commemorated the accession of rulers (Martin 1997, 855). By receiving K'awiil, rulers may have been entrusted as keepers of agricultural bounty and prosperity. They may have also been regarded as capable of mastering the force of lightning. Citing work by Clemency Coggins, Taube (1992, 73–75) pointed out portraits of the storm god Chak wielding K'awiil in the shape of an axe, and suggested that it represented the power to produce lightning. Martin (2006, 172) likened those representations with portraits of kings wielding K'awiil effigies—the so-called manikin scepters—while dancing (Grube 1992, 208–11). The meanings and purposes of those dances were manifold, but they may have cast the rulers as rainmakers, endowed with the capacity of bringing fertility to the earth. In Mesoamerica, lightning is regarded as a powerful fertilizing force that impregnates the earth, allowing the growth of crops and vegetation (Staller and

Stross 2013, 158–60). Summarizing the available evidence, Taube (1992, 79) highlighted K'awiil's association with lightning, rain, and fertile maize, concluding that "God K epitomizes the vital, engendering force from which life comes."

There is no indication that the Maya Maize God was related to lightning, and this was an important distinction between the two gods. Yet it should be noted that maize heroes in Mesoamerican myths are frequently associated with rainmaking, thunder, and lightning (Braakhuis and Hull 2014, 452; Chinchilla Mazariegos 2017, 15). The agricultural metaphors represented by both deities are illustrated on Quirigua Stela H, where a stream of precious liquid flows down from a warrior K'awiil—who emerges from the ruler's ceremonial bar, armed with spear and shield—upon the Maize God who peeks out beneath a mountain glyph at the base (Figure 1.4).

Figure 1.4. Detail of Quirigua Stela H, north side. At the top, K'awiil is armed with shield and spear. A thick flow of liquid descends upon the Maize God, who peeks out at the base of the carving. Source: Photograph by Dmitri Beliaev, Atlas Epigráfico de Petén Project, CEMYK.

K'awiil's associations with the Maize God go beyond the generation of maize. More broadly, both were regarded as gods of abundance. In addition to maize, they were linked with all kinds of wealth, particularly cacao and jade. Martin (2006) noted the close relationship of both deities with cacao. Examples include figurines from Alta Verapaz that show the dancing Maize God sprouting corncobs or cacao pods (Chinchilla Mazariegos 2017, 196), and portraits of K'awiil bringing large bags or baskets full of cacao and other foodstuffs on painted capstones from Campeche and Yucatan (Figure 1.5). Some capstones have hieroglyphic captions that contain the phrase *ox wi'il*, which Martin (2006, 173) translated as "abundance of food."

Figure 1.5. Painted capstones from Dzibilnocac, Campeche, showing K'awiil as a bringer of abundant food and wealth. (a) Capstone 1. Plentiful grains fall from an inverted sack in K'awiil's hand. (b) Capstone 3. K'awiil holds a basket full of grains. The caption includes references to cacao and "abundance of food." Source: Drawings by Christian Prager, Maya Image Archive (mayadictionary.de). License: CC by 4.0.

In ancient Mesoamerica, cacao was not just food; it was an item of wealth, like in kind to jade, quetzal feathers, and other valuables. Taube (2005) showed that the Maize God was frequently portrayed on jade objects, while representations in other media show him covered with jewelry. The display of abundant wealth is one of his more salient characteristics. A painted capstone from the Temple of the Owls at Chichen Itza shows K'awiil bringing a plate full of ear spools—presumably made of jade—with cacao pods and other jewels hanging behind him. Commenting on this capstone, Martin (2006, 174) emphasized the god's probable role in myths about the origin of cacao, and suggested that the jewels represented precious seeds. Cacao grains were indeed precious, and not just in a metaphorical way. They were one of the most important items of material wealth in ancient Mesoamerica, and the Chichen Itza artists portrayed them on a par with jade jewelry and other valuables, not only in this capstone, but also in sculptured columns and friezes where earspools grow together with cacao pods from the trunk of the same trees, and seem to rain down along with headdresses, gold ornaments, and earspools (González de la Mata et al. 2013; Martin 2006, 175–76). The Temple of the Owls capstone portrayed K'awiil as a bringer of wealth, more than cacao per se. Reviewing his representations in the codices, Valencia Rivera (2011) also concluded that more than anything else, the god was related with abundance, a provider of bountiful harvests and wealth of all kinds.

At first glance, the relationship of K'awiil and the Maize God with wealth, abundance, and agricultural fertility casts them as benevolent deities who would bring prosperity and well-being. This impression may be deceptive. In Mesoamerica, interactions between people and deities generally involved compromises and negotiations that were fulfilled through appropiate rituals, prayers and offerings (Monaghan 2000, 36–39). Maize gods are generally regarded as frail, requiring constant attention from farmers and ritualists, just like children do from their parents (Sandstrom 1998, 67). While we are missing detailed information on their personality, the probabilities are that, rather than reliable donors, K'awiil and the Maize God were as fickle as Tezcatlipoca. They bestowed wealth and abundance but could easily withdraw it if not properly maintained and appeased.

A crucial attribute of both K'awiil and the Maize God was their youthfulness. Young age is characteristic of Mesoamerican maize gods, who are often described as children in mythical narratives that recount their birth and the events of their infancy. Invariably, the young heroes overcame older opponents who may include their brothers and their evil grandmother. Moreover, they triumphed where their parents had failed. With good reason, Coe (1973, 13–14) initially used the term "Young Lords" to designate youthful characters that were later identified as representations of the Maya Maize God. He takes the appearance of a baby in some of the well-known scenes that portray his birth. K'awiil's youthfulness is especially apparent at Palenque, where he was represented as a plump baby on the piers of the Temple of the Inscriptions. In his manifestation as GII of the Palenque Triad, his name is read *Unen K'awiil*, "baby K'awiil." The inscriptions show that he was the last-born of the Triad gods. Appropriately, he used the epithet *ch'ok*, "youth," employed by young men in the Maya inscriptions (Martin 2002, 62; Stuart 2005, 174).

Figure 1.6. The Maize God attended by a group of naked young women. The hieroglyphic inscription refers to the god's death. Detail of vase K7268. Source: Drawing by Oswaldo Chinchilla Mazariegos.

Closely related to the gods' youthfulness was their sexual proclivity. K'awiil's sexuality is apparent in codex-style vessels that show an old god emerging from his serpent leg. The old god approaches a young and attractive woman who is usually ensnared in the coils of K'awiil's serpent leg, in ways that suggest lewdness and sexual craving. K'awiil's role appears to be passive but he was, at the very least, an important mediator in the seduction of the lady (García Barrios and Valencia Rivera 2011; Robicsek and Hales 1981, 110). In this context, K'awiil's leg may have phallic connotations. Missing legs and arms are broadly distributed metaphors related to castration, and generally associated with illicit sexuality in Mesoamerica (Galinier 1984; Klein 2001, 234–35; Olivier 2003, 421–23).

An ithyphallic portrait on an Early Classic graffiti from Tikal provides unequivocal expression of the Maize God's sexuality (Figure 1.2b). The theme reappears in more subtle ways in painted scenes that show him surrounded by young, naked or barely dressed women that attend him and accommodate his garments (Figures 1.6 and 1.7). While sometimes described as "dressing scenes" (Quenon and Le Fort 1997, 892), their sexual connotations are apparent, not just from the ladies' seductive appearance, but also from the fact that these encounters happen in watery places. In Mesoamerican myths, streams and ponds are places of choice for amorous encounters, and the characters who enjoy water are also prone to sexual enticement (Chinchilla Mazariegos 2017, 201). But such encounters are not without consequence; Graulich (1997, 177–80) showed that sexual encounters consistently led to the defeat and death of the heroes in Mesoamerican narratives. This outcome is evident in representations of the Maize God's affairs with the ladies, who are sometimes marked with death signs and have nametags that designate them as manifestations of Akan, the god of drunkenness and death (Grube 2004, 70). Rather than legitimate wives, they appear to be temptresses, whose embrace poses as much peril as enjoyment. Indeed, the hieroglyphic captions on some of these vessels recount the death of the Maize God, suggesting that his amorous encounter with the naked ladies was inextricably linked to his demise. Be that as it may, the Maize God's sexual proclivity is implied.

TOXCATL AND THE MAYA MAIZE GOD

The homologies between K'awiil and the Maize God are significant to assess their correspondences with Tezcatlipoca. These Maya gods are not identical to each other, yet they embody partly overlapping attributes related with agricultural bounty, wealth, and abundance. Their youthfulness and sexual proclivity are also significant. In different ways, both overlap with Tezcatlipoca, and the Toxcatl rituals dedicated to Tezcatlipoca are strongly reminiscent of the mythical deeds of the Maya Maize God.

In his analysis of the Nahua feasts, Graulich (1999, 347) commented on the lack of myths that would provide guidance for the interpretation of the Toxcatl rituals. The observation was only partly accurate. While not all components of the feast find correlates in the extant records, Olivier (2003, 386–88) related some of them with the myths of the origin of music. He linked the appearance of

Figure 1.7. Detail of the Vase of the Paddlers (K3033), showing the Maize God in dancing pose, attended by two naked women in an aquatic setting. A turtle carapace appears behind the hips of the squatting woman to the viewer's left. Source: Drawing by Oswaldo Chinchilla Mazariegos.

Tezcatlipoca's impersonator as a flute player and dancer with the god's role in the mythical origin of music and dance, known from versions recorded by Jerónimo de Mendieta and André Thévet (Mendieta 1973, 1: 50–51; Thévet 2002, 157). The myth recounts how the god sent an envoy—the wind, according to Thévet—to the house of the sun, across the sea, to bring music. He instructed the envoy to cross the sea over a bridge formed by a whale, a siren, and a turtle, which, Thévet noted, were Tezcatlipoca's nieces. The envoy succeeded despite the sun's reluctance, and brought musicians and musical instruments, originating the music and dances that were performed to honor the gods.

In contemporary narratives from the Gulf Coast, the maize heroes angered their opponents by making noise while dancing and playing music. In Nahua and Popoluca versions, this occurred after the young heroes crossed the sea or another body of water on the back of a turtle (Blanco Rosas 2006, 73–74; Foster 1944, 192–93; González Cruz and Anguiano 1984, 220–23). While the aim of the journey was different, the manner of crossing and the noise, music, and dance of the maize heroes at the end of the crossing recall the Nahua myth of the origin of music. The ancient Maya Maize God was another consummate dancer, and Taube (2009) suggested that he played a role in the mythical origins of dance. Not by coincidence, the mythical dances of the Gulf Coast maize heroes and those of the Maya god were connected to their respective journeys across water (Chinchilla Mazariegos 2011, 53–71; 2017, 195–202, 207–14).

Figure 1.8. The Nahua goddess Xochiquetzal wearing a turtle shell on the back. Detail of *Codex Fejérváry-Mayer*, pl. 35. Source: Drawing by Oswaldo Chinchilla Mazariegos.

Olivier (2003, 390–96) linked Tezcatlipoca's "nieces"—the turtle, the siren, and the whale that allowed his envoy to cross the sea—with the women who performed as his wives during the *veintena* of Toxcatl. He noted correlates between the names cited by Thévet, and those of the goddesses mentioned by Sahagún's informants in their description of Toxcatl. I suggest another correlation, with the women companions of the Classic Maya Maize God. We know very little about their identity, beyond the erotic and mortuary connotations noted above. But there is an intriguing clue in the Vase of the Paddlers, which shows one of the most elaborate representations of the myth (Figure 1.7) (Chinchilla Mazariegos 2011, 51–53). The woman who kneels behind the Maize God has a turtle shell behind the hips. In highland Mexican codices, the goddess Xochiquetzal sometimes wore a jeweled turtle shell in the same position (Figure 1.8). She was especially associated with Tezcatlipoca, who, according to Muñoz Camargo (1984, 202–03), abducted her from Tamoanchan. While unique in Maya representations of this episode, the turtle behind her hips may qualify the woman on the Vase of the Paddlers as akin to the Aztec goddess of carnal love and to one of the four wives of Tezcatlipoca's impersonator during the Toxcatl feast.

Figure 1.9. The Maize God in his transit to death, riding a canoe manned by the Paddler Gods. Detail of the Vase of the Paddlers (K3033). Source: Drawing by Oswaldo Chinchilla Mazariegos.

Figure 1.10. The Maize God riding a canoe in his transit to death. Detail of vase K5608. Source: Drawing by Oswaldo Chinchilla Mazariegos.

In the Nahua ritual, Tezcatlipoca's impersonator embarked on a canoe together with his four wives, who accompanied him part of the way to the place of his death at Tlacochcalco. Likewise, the episode in which the Maya Maize God received the ladies' attentions was followed by his canoe journey, equated to his death. The Vase of the Paddlers is one of several ceramic vessels in which both scenes are juxtaposed in ways that suggest a temporal sequence. The vase shows the Maize God dancing while attended by comely young women (Figure 1.7). The following scene on the vase shows him riding a canoe and adopting an elegant mourning pose— the wrist raised to the forehead, with the hand extended forward (Figure 1.9). As noted, the hieroglyphic captions on several vases suggest that the god's affairs with women were closely linked to his death (Chinchilla Mazariegos 2017, 194–214). Representations of the death passage of the Maize God in a canoe—sometimes accompanied by other gods or animals—were favorite subjects in Classic Maya art (Figure 1.10)

According to Sahagún's informants, the sacrifice at Tlacochcalco was immediately followed by the selection of a new impersonator that would embody Tezcatlipoca during the following year (Sahagún 1950–82, bk 2: 66). Arguably, this stage of the ritual amounted to a rebirth of the god, perhaps underlined by the new impersonator's consumption of his predecessor's flesh, reported by De la Serna (2003, 99). Tezcatlipoca's yearly re-embodiment finds correspondence in

Table 1.1. Comparison of the Maya Maize God and Tezcatlipoca

Maya Maize God	Tezcatlipoca
Young	Young
Physically perfect	Physically perfect
Dancer	Musician
Associated with wealth, cacao, jade	Associated with abundance and wealth
Associated with maize and agricultural bounty	Related to maize gods (Cinteotl and Itztlacoliuhqui-Ixquimilli)
Attended by young women	Married to four goddesses
Canoe journey	Canoe journey
Death	Sacrifice
Rebirth	New impersonator chosen

the rebirth of the Maize God after his demise in Classic Maya representations. In the Vase of the Paddlers, the portent unfolds below the canoe, where an aquatic serpent lets out the Maize God from its wide-open maw (Figure 1.9). While the serpent may be interpreted as swallowing the baby, the scene is better understood as showing the rebirth of the god who adopts the bodily stance of a baby, beckoning his birth (Martin 2002). The scene can be compared with other representations of the rebirth of the Maize God from the open maws of a serpent, a split water-lily rhizome, or the cracked shell of a turtle (Chinchilla Mazariegos 2011, 72–84; 2017, 214–23; Quenon and Le Fort 1997).

Table 1.1 summarizes the homologies between the Maize God and Tezcatlipoca. The correlations are multiple, and include not only shared attributes of the gods, but perhaps more importantly, parallel mythical and ritual episodes that reappear in recognizably similar ways. These correlates suggest that the Maya and Aztec shared related beliefs about the ordeal of the young god, culminating with his death and rebirth.[8]

FINAL COMMENTS

In his classic overview of Nahua religion, H. B. Nicholson commented on the antiquity of the *veintena* ritual cycle. He suggested that the Postclassic Nahua of the Valley of Mexico built a superstructure of elaborate rituals on an "ancient and fundamental foundation" related to the agricultural cycle (Nicholson 1971, 434). On similar premises, and in support of his interpretation of the seasonal and agricultural correlates of the Nahua feasts, Graulich argued that the *veintena* cycle was "a work of centuries and millennia, of slow growth, transformation, adaptation, of gradual ritualization of simple, ordinary gestures, linked with important moments, first in the life of the hunter-gatherer, then the cultivator" (Graulich 2002b, 51). The origin of the ritual cycle was likely as old as the eighteen *veintena* solar year in Mesoamerica, and the religious beliefs that found expression in the *veintena* rituals were equally old, if not older. The sixteenth-century Nahua feasts reflected the religious imprint of multiple waves of historical change and communication among Mesoamerican peoples. I suggest that rather than discrete translations resulting from distinct cases of contact, the homologies discussed in this chapter resulted from complex and enduring patterns of interaction that stretched across Mesoamerica through millennia. Ultimately, the homologies among Tezcatlipoca, K'awiil, and the Maya Maize God seem to be related to their youthfulness, their sexual proclivity, and their patronage of wealth and abundance. The three deities shared these attributes not only with one another, but also with other young gods in Mesoamerican myths.

The homologies should not obscure the disparities between the Maya and Nahua beliefs and rituals. As mentioned, the impersonator of Tezcatlipoca took the appearance of a warrior at the same time he took wives. This is consonant with the god's manifestation as Yaotl, "Enemy," and his close association with war. While K'awiil was sometime portrayed with weapons, the Maya Maize God had no warlike connotations. Nor did he share much with other entities related to Tezcatlipoca, including Huehuecoyotl, the old coyote, Chalchiuhtotolin, the bejeweled turkey, or Tepeyollotl, the jaguar "heart of the mountain." But those manifestations had little bearing on the Toxcatl rituals, which commemorated only certain aspects of Tezcatlipoca's multiple personalities.

Representations of the Maize God's myths on Classic Maya vessels are usually regarded as reflecting the subjects of mythical narratives. But it is equally plausible that they were modeled after ritual re-enactments that took place in ancient Maya cities, involving human impersonators. The extant artistic representations hint of a mythical drama comprising several key episodes that may have corresponded to stages of ritual re-enactment. From this perspective, the Classic Maya performances of the Maize God myths approximated the ritual actions of Tezcatlipoca and his four wives during Toxcatl. Conversely, the Maya representations hint at mythical beliefs that are not recorded in the extant Nahua sources, and they may help to clarify the connotations of the Toxcatl rituals. The myths that provided paradigms for the Classic Maya representations, and for the Late Postclassic Nahua rituals were embedded in deeply rooted Mesoamerican religious beliefs.

ACKNOWLEDGMENTS

I first presented some of these arguments in 2008, when I had the privilege of sharing the stage with Michael D. Coe in a public talk at the Museo Popol Vuh.

Manuel Aguilar Moreno's invitation to participate in a symposium in honor of Mike at California State University, Los Angeles, allowed me to revisit the topic in 2013. I presented a revised version at the 2016 symposium in honor of Michel Graulich, organized by Élodie Dupey García and Elena Mazzetto at the Instituto de Investigaciones Históricas, Universidad Nacional Autónoma de México. Each venue provided opportunities to discuss these ideas with colleagues and further develop them. I thank the institutional support provided for my research by Yale University and the Museo Popol Vuh, Universidad Francisco Marroquín. I especially thank Guilhem Olivier's stimulating input, but I take full responsibility for the present arguments.

NOTES

1. English translation by the author from the Spanish text: "En esta fiesta mataban un mancebo muy acabado en disposición, al cual habían criado por espacio de un año en deleites. Decían que era la imagen de Tezcatlipoca. En matando al mancebo que estaba de un año criado, luego ponían otro en su lugar ... Escogíanlos entre todos los captivos, los más gentiles hombres, y teníanlos guardados los calpixques. Ponían gran diligencia en que fuesen los más hábiles y más bien dispuestos que se pudiesen haber, y sin tacha ninguna corporal."

2. On K'awiil, see Milbrath 2015; Taube 1992, 69–79; Valencia Rivera 2006, 2011. On the Maya Maize God, see Braakhuis 1990, 2009; Chinchilla Mazariegos 2011, 43–95; 2017, 185–223; Miller and Martin 2004, 56–58; Taube 1985; 1992, 41–50; 2009; Thompson 1970, 282–91.

3. On Tezcatlipoca and the feast of Toxcatl, see Baquedano 2015; Carrasco 1991; Clendinnen 1991, 104–10; Graulich 1999, 339–60; 2002a; Heyden 1989, 1991; Nicholson 1971; Olivier 2003; Seler 1963, 1: 113–17.

4. See Robertson (1985, 299–300) on the processes involved in the movement of artistic styles from one region to another.

5. Olivier (2003) offered extensive discussions of Tezcatlipoca's multiple personalities and their complex connotations. See also other sources listed in note 3.

6. Sources on the mythical deeds of Tezcatlipoca include: "Historia de los mexicanos por sus pinturas" (2002, 31–39), Thévet (2002, 145–57, 161–63), "Leyenda de los Soles" (2002, 177–79; see also "Legend of the Suns," 1992, 144–45), and the works of Sahagún (1950–82, bk 3: 11–31), Chimalpahin (1997, 1: 119–23), Mendieta (1973, 1: 50–52), and Muñoz Camargo (1984, 202–03).

7. On this topic, see Schwaller (Chapter Seven) in this volume.

8. On the death and rebirth of Mesoamerican gods, see also Olivier (Chapter Two) in this volume.

REFERENCES

"Annals of Cuauhtitlan." 1992. In *History and Mythology of the Aztecs: The Codex Chimalpopoca*, edited and translated by John Bierhorst, 1–138. Tucson: University of Arizona Press.

Baquedano, Elizabeth. 2015. *Tezcatlipoca: Trickster and Supreme Deity*. Boulder: University Press of Colorado.

Barrera Vásquez, Alfredo. 1991. *Diccionario Maya: Maya-Español, Español-Maya*. Mexico City: Porrúa.

Blanco Rosas, José Luis. 2006. "Erosión de la agrodiversidad en la milpa de los zoque popoluca de Soteapan: Xutuchincon y Aktevet." PhD diss., Universidad Iberoamericana. http://www.bib.uia. mx/tesis/pdf/014791.

Bolles, David. 2001. *Combined Dictionary-Concordance of the Yucatec Mayan Language*. Report submitted to FAMSI accessed June 17, 2017. http://www.famsi.org/reports/96072/index.html.

Boone, Elizabeth Hill. 2000. *Stories in Red and Black: Pictorial Histories of the Aztecs and Mixtecs*. Austin: University of Texas Press.

Braakhuis, Edwin. 1990. "The Bitter Flour: Birth-scenes of the Tonsured Maize God." In *Mesoamerican Dualism*, edited by Rudolf van Zantwijk, Rob de Ridder, and Edwin Braakhuis, 125–47. Utrecht: ISOR Universiteit Utrecht.

———. 2009. "The Tonsured Maize God and Chicome-Xochitl as Maize Bringers and Culture Heroes: A Gulf Coast Perspective." *Wayeb Notes* 32, accessed February 5, 2015. http://www. wayeb.org/notes/wayeb_notes0032.pdf.

Braakhuis, Edwin, and Kerry Hull. 2014. "Pluvial Aspects of the Mesoamerican Culture Hero." *Anthropos* 109: 449–66.

Carmack, Robert M. 1979. *Historia social de los quichés*. Guatemala City: Seminario de Integración Social Guatemalteca.

Carrasco, Davíd. 1991. "The Sacrifice of Tezcatlipoca: To Change Place." In *To Change Place: Aztec Ceremonial Landscapes*, edited by Davíd Carrasco, 31–57. Boulder: University Press of Colorado.

Chimalpahin, Domingo Francisco de San Antón Muñón. 1997. *Codex Chimalpahin*. Edited by Arthur J. O. Anderson and Susan Schroeder. 2 vols. Norman: University of Oklahoma Press.

Chinchilla Mazariegos, Oswaldo. 2011. *Imágenes de la mitología maya*. Guatemala City: Museo Popol Vuh, Universidad Francisco Marroquín.

———. 2017. *Art and Myth of the Ancient Maya*. New Haven: Yale University Press.

Clendinnen, Inga. 1991. *Aztecs: An Interpretation*. Cambridge: Cambridge University Press.

Coe, Michael D. 1973. *The Maya Scribe and his World*. New York: The Grolier Club.

Covarrubias, Miguel. 1946. "El arte olmeca o de La Venta." *Cuadernos Americanos* 4: 154–79.

De la Serna, Jacinto. 2003. *Tratado de las supersticiones, idolatrías, hechicerías, ritos, y otras costumbres gentílicas de las razas aborígenes de México*. Biblioteca Virtual Universal, accessed September 24, 2019. https://www.biblioteca.org.ar/libros/89972.pdf.

Durán, Diego. 1984. *Historia de las Indias de Nueva España e islas de la Tierra Firme*. Edited by Ángel María Garibay. 2 vols. Mexico City: Porrúa.

Foster, George M. 1944. "Nagualism in Mexico and Guatemala." *Acta Americana* 2, no. 1–2: 85–103.

Galinier, Jacques. 1984. "L'homme sans pied: Métaphores de la castration et imaginaire en Méso-amérique." *L'Homme* 24, no. 2: 41–58.

García Barrios, Ana, and Rogelio Valencia Rivera. 2011. "Relaciones de parentesco en el mito del Dios Viejo y la Señora Dragón en las cerámicas de estilo Códice." In *Texto, imagen e identidad en la pintura maya prehispánica*, edited by Merideth Paxton and Manuel A. Hermann Lejarazu, 63–87. Mexico City: Universidad Nacional Autónoma de México.

González de la Mata, María Rocío, Francisco Pérez Ruiz, and José Osorio León. 2013. "Reflejos de un universo mítico en la iconografía de Chichén Itzá." In *XXVI Simposio de Investigaciones Arqueológicas en Guatemala*, edited by Bárbara Arroyo and Luis Méndez Salinas, 835–45. Guatemala City: Ministerio de Cultura y Deportes, Asociación Tikal.

González Cruz, Genaro, and Marina Anguiano. 1984. "La historia de Tamakastsiin." *Estudios de Cultura Náhuatl* 17: 205–25.

Graulich, Michel. 1983. "Myths of Paradise Lost in Pre-Hispanic Central Mexico." *Current Anthropology* 24: 575–88.

———. 1997. *Myths of Ancient Mexico*. Norman: University of Oklahoma Press.

———. 1999. *Ritos aztecas. Las fiestas de las veintenas*. Mexico City: Instituto Nacional Indigenista.

———. 2002a. "Tezcatlipoca-Omacatl, el comensal imprevisible." *Cuicuilco. Revista de Ciencias Antropológicas* 9, no. 25: 317–26.

———. 2002b. "Acerca del problema de ajustes del año calendárico mesoamericano al año trópico." *Estudios de Cultura Náhuatl* 33: 45–56.

Grube, Nikolai. 1992. "Classic Maya Dance. Evidence from Hieroglyphs and Iconography." *Ancient Mesoamerica* 3: 201–18.

———. 2004. "*Akan*—the God of Drinking, Disease and Death." In *Continuity and Change: Maya Religious Practice in Temporal Perspective*, edited by Daniel Graña Behrens, Nikolai Grube, Christian M. Prager, Frauke Sachse, Stephanie Teufel, and Elizabeth Wagner, 59–76. Acta Mesoamericana 14. Markt Schwaben: Verlag Anton Saurwein.

Heyden, Doris. 1989. "Tezcatlipoca en el mundo náhuatl." *Estudios de Cultura Náhuatl* 19: 83–93.

———. 1991. "Dryness Before the Rains: Toxcatl and Tezcatlipoca." In *To Change Place: Aztec Ceremonial Landscapes*, edited by Davíd Carrasco, 188–202. Boulder: University Press of Colorado.

"Historia de los mexicanos por sus pinturas." 2002. In *Mitos e historias de los antiguos nahuas*, edited by Rafael Tena. Mexico City: Consejo Nacional para la Cultura y las Artes.

Houston, Stephen, Karl Taube, and David Stuart. 2006. *The Memory of Bones: Body, Being, and Experience among Classic Maya*. Austin: University of Texas Press.

Klein, Cecelia F. 2001. "None of the Above: Gender Ambiguity in Nahua Ideology." In *Gender in pre-Hispanic America*, edited by Cecelia F. Klein, 183–253. Washington, DC: Dumbarton Oaks.

"Legend of the Suns." 1992. In *History and Mythology of the Aztecs: The Codex Chimalpopoca*, edited and translated by John Bierhorst, 139–62. Tucson: University of Arizona Press.

"Leyenda de los Soles." 2002. In *Mitos e historia de los antiguos nahuas*, edited and translated by Rafael Tena, 169–205. Mexico City: Consejo Nacional para la Cultura y las Artes.

López Austin, Alfredo. 1993. *The Myths of the Oppossum: Pathways of Mesoamerican Mythology*. Translated by Bernard R. Ortiz de Montellano, and Thelma Ortiz de Montellano. Albuquerque: University of New Mexico Press.

———. 2001. "El núcleo duro, la cosmovisión y la tradición mesoamericana." In *Cosmovisión, ritual e identidad de los pueblos indígenas de México*, edited by Johanna Broda and Félix Báez-Jorge, 47–65. Mexico City: Fondo de Cultura Económica.

———. 2003. "Indigenous Mythology from Present-day Mexico." In *Native Religions and Cultures of Central and South America: Anthropology of the Sacred*, edited by Lawrence E. Sullivan, 33–66. New York: Bloomsbury Academic.

Martin, Simon. 1997. "The Painted King List: A Commentary on Codex-Style Dynastic Vases." In *The Maya Vase Book: A Corpus of Rollout Photographs of Maya Vases*. Vol. 5, compiled by Justin Kerr, 846–67. New York: Kerr Associates.

———. 2002. "The Baby Jaguar: An Exploration of its Identity and Origin in Maya Art and Writing." In *La organización social entre los mayas. Memoria de la Tercera Mesa Redonda de Palenque*. Vol. 1, edited by Vera Tiesler Blos, Rafael Cobos, and Merle Greene Robertson, 49–78. Mexico City: Instituto Nacional de Antropología e Historia.

———. 2006. "Cacao in Ancient Maya Religion: First Fruit from the Maize Tree and other Tales from the Underworld." In *Chocolate in Mesoamerica: A Cultural History of Cacao*, edited by Cameron L. McNeil, 154–83. Gainesville: University Press of Florida.

Mendieta, Jerónimo de. 1973. *Historia eclesiástica indiana*. Edited by Francisco Solano y Pérez-Lila. 2 vols. Biblioteca de Autores Españoles 260–261. Madrid: Ediciones Atlas.

Merriam-Webster. 2019. "Translate." *Merriam-Webster.com*, accessed September 23, 2019. https://www.merriam-webster.com/dictionary/translate.

Milbrath, Susan. 2015. "The Maya Lord of the Smoking Mirror." In *Tezcatlipoca: Trickster and Supreme Deity*, edited by Elizabeth Baquedano, 163–96. Boulder: University Press of Colorado.

Miller, Mary, and Simon Martin. 2004. *Courtly Art of the Ancient Maya*. New York: Thames and Hudson.

Monaghan, John. 2000. "Theology and History in the Study of Mesoamerican Religions." In *Supplement to the Handbook of Middle American Indians*. Vol. 6, *Ethnology*, edited by John D. Monaghan, series editor Robert Wauchope, 24–49. Austin: University of Texas Press.

Muñoz Camargo, Diego. 1984. "Descripción de la ciudad y provincia de Tlaxcala, de la Nueva España e Indias del Mar Océano para el buen gobierno y ennoblecimiento dellas, mandada hacer por la S.C.R.M. del Rey Don Felipe, Nuestro Señor." In *Relaciones geográficas del siglo XVI: Tlaxcala*. Vol. 1, edited by René Acuña. Mexico City: Universidad Nacional Autónoma de México-Instituto de Investigaciones Antropológicas.

Nicholson, Henry B. 1971. "Religion in pre-Hispanic Mexico." In *Handbook of Middle American Indians*. Vol. 10, *The Archaeology of Northern Mesoamerica, part I*, edited by Gordon F. Ekhholm and Ignacio Bernal, series editor Robert Wauchope, 395–446. Austin: University of Texas Press.

Olivier, Guilhem. 2003. *Mockeries and Metamorphoses of an Aztec God: Tezcatlipoca, "Lord of the Smoking Mirror."* Translated by Michel Besson. Niwot: University of Colorado Press.

Olivier, Guilhem, and Roberto Martínez. 2015. "Translating Gods: Tohil and Curicaueri in Mesoamerican Polytheism in the *Popol Vuh* and the *Relación de Michoacán*." *Ancient Mesoamerica* 26: 347–69.

Popol Vuh. The Mayan Book of the Dawn of Life. 1996. Edited and translated by Dennis Tedlock. New York: Touchstone Books.

Quenon, Michel, and Genevieve Le Fort. 1997. "Rebirth and Resurrection in Maize God Iconography." In *The Maya Vase Book: A Corpus of Rollout Photographs of Maya Vases*. Vol. 5, compiled by Justin Kerr, 884–99. New York: Kerr Associates.

Ritual of the Bacabs. 1965. Edited and translated by Ralph L. Roys. Norman: University of Oklahoma Press.

Robertson, Donald. 1985. "The Cacaxtla Murals." In *Fourth Palenque Round Table, 1980*, edited by Elizabeth P. Benson, 291–302. San Francisco: Pre-Columbian Art Research Institute.

Robicsek, Francis, and Donald M. Hales. 1981. *The Maya Book of the Dead: The Ceramic Codex. The Corpus of Codex Style Ceramics of the Late Classic Period*. Charlottesville: University of Virginia Art Museum.

Ruiz de Alarcón, Hernando. 1984. *Treatise on the Heathen Superstitions and Customs that Today Live Among the Indians Native to This New Spain, 1629*. Edited and translated by J. Richard Andrews, and Ross Hassig. Norman: University of Oklahoma Press.

Sahagún, Bernardino de. 1950–82. *Florentine Codex: General History of the Things of New Spain, Fray Bernardino de Sahagún*. Translated with notes and illustrations by Arthur J. O. Anderson, and Charles E. Dibble. 13 vols. Santa Fe: The School of American Research, University of Utah Press.

———. 1989. *Historia General de las Cosas de Nueva España*. 2nd ed. Edited by Alfredo López Austin and Josefina García Quintana. 2 vols. Mexico City: Consejo Nacional para la Cultura y las Artes.

Sandstrom, Alan R. 1998. "El nene lloroso y el espíritu nahua del maíz: el cuerpo humano como símbolo clave en la Huasteca veracruzana." In *Nuevos aportes al conocimiento de la Huasteca: selección de trabajos pertenecientes al VIII Encuentro de Investigadores de la Huasteca*, edited by Jesús Ruvalcaba Mercado, 59–94. Mexico City: Centro de Investigaciones y Estudios Superiores en Antropología Social.

Schellhas, Paul. 1904. *Representations of Deities in the Maya Manuscripts.* Papers of the Peabody Museum of Archaeology and Ethnology 4, no. 1. Cambridge, MA: Harvard University Press.

Seler, Eduard. 1904. "Wall Paintings of Mitla: A Mexican Picture Writing in Fresco." In *Mexican and Central American Antiquities, Calendar Systems, and History*, edited by Charles P. Bowditch, 243–324. Smithsonian Institution Bulletin 28. Washington, DC: Smithsonian Institution.

———. 1963 [1904–06]. *Comentarios al Códice Borgia.* Vols. I and II. In *Códice Borgia y Comentarios de Eduard Seler.* 3 vols. Mexico City: Fondo de Cultura Económica.

———. 1996. *Collected Works in Mesoamerican Linguistics and Archaeology.* Vol. 5, edited by Frank Comparato. Lancaster: Labyrinthos.

Staller, John E., and Brian Stross. 2013. *Lightning in the Andes and Mesoamerica: Pre-Columbian, Colonial, and Contemporary Perspectives.* Oxford: Oxford University Press.

Stuart, David. 1987. *Ten Phonetic Syllables.* Research Reports on Ancient Maya Writing 14. Washington, DC: Center for Maya Research.

———. 2000. "'The Arrival of Strangers': Teotihuacan and Tollan in Classic Maya History." In *Mesoamerica's Classic Heritage: From Teotihuacan to the Aztecs*, edited by Davíd Carrasco, Lindsay Jones, and Scott Sessions, 465–514. Boulder: University Press of Colorado.

———. 2005. *The Inscriptions from Temple XIX at Palenque.* San Francisco: The Pre-Columbian Art Research Institute.

Sullivan, Thelma D. 1976. "The Mask of Itztlacoliuhqui." In *Actas del XLI Congreso Internacional de Americanistas, México 1974*, 252–62. Mexico City: Instituto Nacional de Antropología e Historia.

Taube, Karl. 1985. "The Classic Maya Maize God: A Reappraisal." In *Fifth Palenque Round Table, 1983*, edited by Virginia M. Fields, 171–290. San Francisco: Pre-Columbian Art Research Institute.

———. 1992. *The Major Gods of Ancient Yucatan.* Studies in Pre-Columbian Art and Archaeology 32. Washington, DC: Dumbarton Oaks.

———. 1996. "The Olmec Maize God: The Face of Corn in Formative Mesoamerica." *Res: Anthropology and Aesthetics* 29–30: 39–81.

———. 2004. *Olmec Art at Dumbarton Oaks.* Washington, DC: Dumbarton Oaks.

———. 2005. "The Symbolism of Jade in Classic Maya Religion." *Ancient Mesoamerica* 16: 23–50.

———. 2009. "The Maya Maize God and the Mythic Origins of Dance." In *The Maya and their Sacred Narratives: Text and Context in Maya Mythologies.* Acta Mesoamericana 20, edited by Geneviève Le Fort, Raphaël Gardiol, Sebastian Matteo, and Christophe Helmke, 41–52. Markt Schwaben: Verlag Anton Saurwein.

Taube, Karl, and Bonnie L. Bade. 1991. *An Appearance of Xiuhtecuhtli in the Dresden Venus Pages.* Research Reports on Ancient Maya Writing 35. Washington, DC: Center for Maya Research.

Thévet, André. 2002. "Histoire du Mechique." In *Mitos e historia de los antiguos nahuas*, edited by Rafael Tena, 115–65. Mexico City: Consejo Nacional para la Cultura y las Artes.

Thompson, J. Eric S. 1934. *Sky Bearers, Colors, and Directions in Maya and Mexican Religion.* Contributions to American Archaeology 10. Washington, DC: Carnegie Institution.

———. 1939. *The Moon Goddess in Mesoamerica with Notes on Related Deities.* Contributions to American Anthropology and History 29. Washington, DC: Carnegie Institution.

———. 1970. *Maya History and Religion.* 3rd ed. Norman: University of Oklahoma Press.

Tiesler Blos, Vera. 2014. *The Bioarchaeology of Artificial Cranial Modifications: New Approaches to Head Shaping and its Meanings in Pre-Columbian Mesoamerica and Beyond.* New York: Springer.

Valencia Rivera, Rogelio. 2006. "Tezcatlipoca y K'awiil: algo más que un parecido." *Revista del Museo de América* 15: 45–60.

———. 2011. "La abundancia y el poder real: El dios K'awiil en el Posclásico." In *De hombres y dioses: creencias y rituales mesoamericanos y sus supervivencias,* edited by Katarzyna Mikulska Dabrowska and José Contel, 67–96. Warsaw: University of Warsaw-Instituto de Estudios Ibéricos e Iberoamericanos.

Van der Loo, Peter L. 1987. *Códices, costumbres, continuidad: un estudio de la religión mesoamericana.* Leiden: Archeologisch Centrum R. U. Leiden.

Whittaker, Gordon. 1986. "The Mexican Names of Three Venus Gods in the Dresden Codex." *Mexicon* 8: 56–60.

CHAPTER TWO

The Re-enactment of the Birth of the Gods in Mexica *Veintena* Celebrations

Some Observations

GUILHEM OLIVIER

CALENDAR AND BIRTH OF THE GODS

Although the Nahua collaborators of *fray* Bernardino de Sahagún (1950–82, bk 3: 1) state, "How the gods had their beginning, where they had their beginning, cannot be known" (*In quenin tzintique in teteuh in canpa tzintique amo vel macho*), we have various Mesoamerican mythical accounts that tell of the birth of the gods. One of the most renowned is the myth of the birth of Huitzilopochtli, who emerged fully armed from the womb of his mother Coatlicue to annihilate his sister Coyolxauhqui and his brothers, the Centzon Huitznahua or "Four Hundred Southerners" (Sahagún 1950–82, bk 3: 1–5). Similarly, we have scenes of divine births depicted in pictographic manuscripts; for example the central part of the *Codex Borgia* shows the birth of five Tezcatlipoca of different colors and of Quetzalcoatl who emerge from an earth goddess with sacrificial attributes (*Códice Borgia* 1993, pl. 32; see also Boone 2007, 183–85) (Figure 2.1). Birth dates reaching back into ancient antiquity were even recorded on Classic period Maya stelae, for example those of the three deities that epigraphers refer to as GI, GII, and GIII, which form the famed "Palenque Triad" (Berlin 1963). In magnificent bas-reliefs, the ancient Maya recorded the dates of their birth: October 21, 2360 B.C. for GI; October 25, 2360 B.C. for GII; and November 8, 2360 B.C. for GIII (Schele and Miller 1986, 60; Stuart 2005, 67, 79–80, 158).[1]

Figure 2.1. The birth of five Tezcatlipoca of different colors and of Quetzalcoatl, who emerge from an earth goddess with sacrificial attributes. Detail of *Codex Borgia*, pl. 32. Source: Drawing courtesy of Elbis Domínguez.

As a whole, these diverse sources shed light on the origin and stories of the gods, as well as some of their characteristics, as in the case of the deities from Central Mexico and the Mixtec area, whose calendrical names—which correspond to the dates of their birth—have special connotations that reflect their personalities (Caso 1961). In this regard, it is enlightening to recall the case of the Mixtec god 9 Wind, whose birth was depicted in the *Codex Vindobonensis*, where we see him with his umbilical cord emerging from a flint knife in the year 10 House on the day 9 Wind (*Códice Vindobonensis* 1992, pl. 49) (Figure 2.2). What is striking about this date is that 9 Ik'—the Maya equivalent of 9 Wind—is the birth date of god GI at Palenque, whereas in Central Mexico, it is said that Quetzalcoatl was also born on the day 9 Wind (*Codex Telleriano-Remensis* 1995, f. 8v; Graulich 1994–95, 34–35; Stuart 2005, 67). An enduring tradition surrounding the sacred nature of this date can be traced through its broad geographical dissemination in Mesoamerica, as well as its extensive temporal distribution, beginning in the Classic period among the Maya to the present, supported by the remarkable ethnographic data collected by Guy Stresser-Péan among the Totonacs today in Tepetzintla, in the Sierra de Puebla. The Totonacs say that their patron god Ak' Najatza Yun—9 Wind—was born on this day in the divinatory calendar, at a crossroads, from a long, flat red rock (Stresser-Péan 2005, 319, 372–73). This latter detail coincides perfectly with

Figure 2.2. The Mixtec god 9 Wind is born from a flint knife in the year 10 House. Detail of *Codex Vindobonensis*, pl. 49. Source: Drawing courtesy of Elbis Domínguez.

the depiction of the birth of 9 Wind in the *Codex Vindobonensis* mentioned above. Significantly, to celebrate the annual fiesta in his honor, the Totonacs of Tepetzintla chose December 12, the feast day of the Virgin of Guadalupe that also—in 1991—happened to coincide with the day 9 Wind in the 260-day ritual calendar, when their patron god was born (Stresser-Péan 2005, 159).

Other important sources that speak to us of the origin of the gods are the descriptions of rituals conducted to commemorate and at times recreate their birth through its symbolic re-enactment. Among the Mexica, the "anniversaries" of the gods were celebrated principally during the twenty "movable" feast days[2] in the 260-day divinatory calendar (Caso 1961; Graulich 1990–91, 1993–94, 1994–95). Our knowledge of these festivals is limited; the most important information is found in the work of *fray* Bernardino de Sahagún. On the one hand, his Nahua collaborators described eighteen movable feast days of different kinds in a summary in Spanish included in Book II of the *Florentine Codex* and—in more detail—fourteen movable feast days in Book IV of the same manuscript (Sahagún 1950–82, bk 2: 35–41; bk 4: 1–133; see also Graulich 1990–91, 32).[3] On the other hand, we have more complete documentation, both in Sahagún's work and in other written and iconographic sources, concerning the eighteen *veintena* festivals, celebrated during the 365-day solar year. Also in these ritual contexts albeit not systematically, the birth of some deities was re-enacted as discussed below. Although some of these commemorations are based on well-known myths, others allude to accounts that were only partially recorded, but that can be reconstructed precisely on the basis of their ritual staging. Finally, the purpose of this chapter is to study how mortals actively participated in the birth/creation of their own gods.

THE *VEINTENA* OF OCHPANIZTLI AND THE BIRTH OF THE MAIZE GOD

According to an in-depth study by Michel Graulich, Ochpaniztli was originally the first *veintena* of the Mexica solar calendar year (Graulich 1999, 89–143)—composed of eighteen "months" (*veintenas*) of twenty days plus five unlucky days, the *nemontemi*.[4] The fertilization of the Earth Goddess and the birth of the Maize God—mythical events that had taken place in Tamoanchan—were re-enacted in these celebrations. In fact, various accounts explain how a god—Huehuecoyotl, Tezcatlipoca, or Piltzintecuhtli—seduced a goddess—Xochiquetzal, Toci-Tlazolteotl, or Cihuacoatl—who gave birth to Cinteotl-Itztlacoliuhqui, the Maize God (Graulich 1987, 62–68).

During the *veintena* of Ochpaniztli, a 40-to-45-year-old slave woman was chosen to represent Toci, the Earth Goddess. Accompanied by midwives, the *ixiptla* or impersonator of Toci attended playful ritual skirmishes between prostitutes and women healers who threw balls shaped from plant material at each other as a means of diversion. After that, the personification of Toci wove cloth, went to the marketplace, and scattered cornmeal on the ground. When she was taken to the temple of the goddess, it was important for her to be in good spirits, without a trace of sorrow, so she was told she would spend the night with the king. The unfortunate and unsuspecting woman had her throat slit as a priest was carrying her on his back.

Scholars such as Eduard Seler (1963, 1: 119–20) and Graulich (1999, 91, 94–95, 112) have interpreted this posture as a reference to the way brides were carried by old ladies during weddings (*Codex Mendoza* 1992, 3: f. 61r). However, Diego Durán (1971, 233) mentioned that: "A priest took her on his back, carrying her face upward. And so, as she was held thus by the arms on the man's back the sacrificer appeared" (*tomandola vn sacerdote a cuestas boca arriba y teniendola assida por los braços echada ella boca arriba en las espaldas del yndio*; Durán 1995, 2: 151).[5] As a consequence, Elena Mazzetto (forthcoming) understands this type of ritual death as a re-enactment of the sacrifice of Tlalteotl's, the Earth Goddess who was cut apart as a prelude to the appearance of plants (Thévet 1905, 28–29).

Once sacrificed, the representative of Toci was flayed and a strong, tall priest donned her skin and became the new image of the goddess. Then this priest, armed with bloody brooms, accompanied by Huastecs and other priests, confronted armed warriors and nobles. When he reached the foot of the Templo Mayor, the new representative of Toci stood with arms and legs stretched wide open facing the temple of Huitzilopochtli (Durán 1995, 2: 148–54; Sahagún 1950–82, bk 2: 118–26). From the studies of Seler (1963, 1: 120) and Konrad Theodor Preuss (1904, 136–37), we know that this position meant that the Earth Goddess was fertilized by the Mexica tutelary god, probably assimilated with Tezcatlipoca, the father of maize in the myth. Then, Cinteotl-Itztlacoliuhqui, the god of maize and frost, appeared beside Toci and:

> … she placed herself by her son, Cinteotl. Here this one had been waiting. He had with him his thigh[-skin] mask, and he had put on his peaked cap, curved back and serrated. And this cap was given the name Itztlacoliuhqui, "curved obsidian knife." This [Itztlacoliuhqui is the god of] frost (*itlan oalmoquetza in jconeuh in Cinteutl: in vncan oqujchixticaca, imexaia*

Figure 2.3 (a & b). Mimixcoa and Huastecs with enormous false phalluses approach the goddess Toci to fertilize her. Detail of *Codex Borbonicus*, pl. 30. Source: Drawings by Rodolfo Ávila.

Figure 2.4. Toci-Tlazolteotl gives birth to Cinteotl, the Maize God. Detail of *Codex Borbonicus*, pl. 13. Source: Photograph courtesy of Bibliothèque de l'Assemblée nationale, Paris.

ietivitz: yoan cōmaquja, icopil, quacoltic, yoan tzitziqujltic: auh inin motocaiotiaia, itztlacoli-uhqj: iehoatl in çetl). (Sahagún 1950–82, bk 2: 121)

According to Graulich (1999, 116), this sudden appearance of the maize and frost god "evidently signified his birth." Although in Durán's account (1995, 2: 153) the Maize God is not mentioned, this author asserted that at some moment the priest who personified the goddess "… thus bent over … moaned eerily. And it is said that the earth moved and quaked at that moment" (… *ynclinado empeçaua a gemir dolorossamente … y dicen que la tierra haçia sentimiento y tenblaua en aquel ynstante*) (Durán 1971, 235), which could simulate giving birth (Graulich 1999, 116).

In a plate illustrating the *veintena* festival of Ochpaniztli in the *Codex Borbonicus*, we see the Mimixcoa and Huastecs carrying enormous detachable phalluses walking toward the goddess Toci to fertilize her (*Códice Borbónico* 1991, pl. 30) (Figure 2.3 a & b). Another representation in the same *Codex Borbonicus* in the section on the *trecenas* (13-day period in the 260-day calendar) that has been related to the *veintena* of Ochpaniztli shows Toci-Tlazolteotl giving birth to Cinteotl (*Códice Borbónico* 1991, pl. 13; Graulich 1997, 211–14) (Figure 2.4). Facing the goddess is Tezcatlipoca disguised as a vulture, in other words, the god who seduced the goddess in Tamoanchan, the father of maize (Olivier 2003, 112–14). It is worth adding that Tezcatlipoca can also be seen in pictographic codices as Itztlacoliuhqui, which shows we have a process of fusion between father and son also expressed in the god Xochipilli, who can be identified with Cinteotl, as well as with Piltzintecuhtli, the father of maize (Olivier 2003, 214; Seler 1963, 1: 155–56).

Returning to the *veintena* of Ochpaniztli, a final argument can be gleaned from a passage about the representative of Toci, which says that after the sacrifice of the captives, "Then she went where [earlier] she had gone to get [capture] her son; she went to bring her son, Cinteotl or Itztlacoliuhqui (*Mec iauh in vmpa ocanato iconeuh; qujvicatiuh in iconeuh, in cinteutl ano itztlacoliuhqui*)" (Sahagún 1950–82, bk 2: 122). As insightfully noted by Mazzetto (2014, 223), by using the verb *ana*, "capture," "grasp someone with force," to describe Toci's interaction with Cinteotl-Itztlacoliuhqui, Sahagún's Nahua collaborators expressed the idea that the woman who gives birth has captured an enemy, which corresponds in this ritual context to the birth of the Maize God (Olivier 2014–15).

ARRIVAL OR BIRTH OF THE GODS IN TEOTL ECO?

After Ochpaniztli came the *veintena* of Teotl Eco or Teteo Eco, "The God Arrives" or "The Gods Arrive" (Sahagún 1950–82, bk 2: 127–30). The arrival of the gods on earth was awaited at that time. As Graulich (1999, 149) explained, after Ochpaniztli which reenacted the transgression in Tamoachan, the sacrifice of Toci, the Mother of the Gods, and the birth of Cinteotl-Itztlacoliuhqui, it was logical to commemorate the arrival of the gods on earth, the sons of the primordial goddess, cast out from Tamoanchan. In fact, a variant of the myth of the paradise of Tamoanchan tells how Citlalicue—who, in this case, is the Mother of the Gods—gave birth to a flint knife in the sky, which fell to earth, precisely at Teotihuacan. From this flint knife, 1600 gods were born (Mendieta 1980, 77–78).

During the *veintena* of Teotl Eco the arrival of the gods was expected; it was said that young gods, such as Huitzilopochtli and Tezcatlipoca,[6] would arrive first and old gods such as Ixcozauhqui—the numen of fire—and Yacatecuhtli—the tutelary god of merchants—who came from far away would appear later (Sahagún 1950–82, bk 2: 127–29). The ritual significance of the "birth" attributed to this "arrival" might seem forced, but there are elements that confirm it.

In the first place, the idea that the gods arrived or descended from the sky came from the myth cited above that mentions the expulsion from the sky of the flint knife, from which the gods were born in Teotihuacan (Mendieta 1980, 77–78). In fact, in the hymn of the Mimixcoa where the descent of these divine beings armed with bows and arrows is described, the Nahua commentator explains that the verb *temo*, "to descend," also means "to be born": "I descended" means "I came down, I was born with my cactus arrow, I was only born with my bow and arrow" (*onitemoc onitlacat ipan notzivac miuh onitemoc ipan in notzivac miuh zan niman ipan nitlacat in notlavitol in momiuh*) (Sahagún 1950–82, bk 2: 230; 1958, 93–94; see also Preuss 1905a, 136; Seler 1963, 1: 138).

Apparently, this equivalence of "to descend" and "to be born" is not limited to the Nahuatl language; for example, Maarten Jansen points out that in the Mixtec language, "Apart from *cacu* 'to be born,' there are other verbs in *fray* Francisco de Alvarado's dictionary that have the same meaning: *quevui* 'to enter,' *ndacu* 'to descend,' *tuvui yuhu nuu* 'to appear with a mouth and face'" (Jansen 1982, 58). A Maya glyph could also be included in this semantic field of birth; it reads U-TAL-KAB, "it is his earth-touching," represented by a hand over the glyph for the earth, which is associated with the birth of the gods in the inscriptions of the Cross Group at Palenque (Stuart 2005, 78–79) (Figure 2.5). Stephen Houston, David Stuart and Karl Taube explain the expression, "'touching the earth' with the hands, perhaps in reference to the fact that, in traditional birthing practices, Maya babies fell out of the uterine channel while their mothers stood" (Houston et al. 2006, 141).[7] From this the possibility arises of interpreting the "descent of

Figure 2.5. Represented by a hand over the glyph for the earth, the Maya glyph U-TAL-KAB, "it is his earth-touching," is associated with the birth of the gods in the inscriptions of the Cross Group at Palenque. Source: Drawing courtesy of Elbis Domínguez, after Stuart 2005, 78.

Kukulcan"—the Yucatec-Maya equivalent of Quetzalcoatl—during the *veintena* of Yaxkin (Landa 1941, 158), as the celebration of his birth (Graulich 1999, 193).[8] Returning to the Mexica, to witness the arrival of Huitzilopochtli during Teotl Eco, a priest watched for a child's footprint in a large tray filled with dough (Durán 1995, 2: 157–58; 1971, 241). According to Sahagún's Nahua collaborators, it was Tezcatlipoca, in his guise as Telpochtli, "Youth," who arrived first and left a small footprint in maize flour (*iotextli*) placed on a woven mat (Sahagún 1950–82, bk 2: 127). This "arrival" of the gods can be equated to a birth, so much so that Durán (1995, 2: 157–58) states that the divine footprint that appeared was that of "a newborn." That said, according to the description of the same feast in the *Codex Tudela* a priest took

> ... some fragrant herbs called *ya[u]htli* and they were ground and dried and placed in a gourd in front of the image of the devil, where at midnight the priest was there watching until dawn or until day or midday, and all the people were silent and waiting and this priest who was watching the gourd did not eat a thing nor did he take his gaze away from it until he saw there the feet of roosters and lions and many other animals; and seeing them together and in seeing them he raised a cry and shouted "*oatzico!*" which means, they have arrived (... *unas yerbas olorosas que llaman ya[u]htli y estavan molidas y secas y puestas en la xicara delante de la ymagen del demonio, dende media noche estaba allí el sacerdote mirando hasta la madrugada o hasta el día o medio día, y todo el pueblo estava callado y aguardando y este sacerdote que estaba mirando en la xicara no comía bocado ni se quitava de mirar en ella hasta que via allí pies de gallos y de leones y de otros munchos animales; y víalos juntamente y en viéndolos daba grandes boces y dezia: ¡oatzico! que quiere dezir, ya an llegado*). (*Códice Tudela* 2002, f. 22r)

The footprints here reveal the arrival of the gods through their animal doubles, an episode in the feast of Teotl Eco that can be related to rituals to seek the *nahual* or animal double of newborns. Historical sources on the subject are scarce, but we can cite a fascinating account—dated 1671—by a French pirate known as Exquemelin, who was familiar with the coasts of Yucatan and Belize:

> It is a manner of admiration how they use a child newly born, as soon as he comes into the world, they carry it to the temple, here they make a hole which they fill with ashes only, on which they place the child naked, leaving it there alone a whole night, not without great danger, nobody daring to come near it; meanwhile the temple is open on all sides, that all sorts of beasts may freely come in and out; next day the father and relatives of the infant return to see if the track or step of any animal appears in the ashes; not finding any they leave the child there till some beast has approached the infant and left behind him the mark of his feet; to this animal, whatsoever it be, they consecrate the creature newly born as to its god, which he is bound to worship all his life, esteeming the said beast his patron and protector ... (in Foster 1944, 94)

This remarkable testimony speaks to us of a ritual that was carried out in a temple where a naked newborn was placed in a hole filled with ashes to await an animal, whose footprints reveal its identity to the child's parents. Numerous ethnographic accounts of the Mixe, Zapotecs, Mixtecs, Chatino, Triqui, Totonacs, and Nahua tell us of this custom of scattering ashes after the birth of a child, ashes on which an animal, the double of the newborn, would leave its mark (Martínez González 2011, 118–25; Olivier 2018, 360-62).

In short, the ritual described in the *Codex Tudela* that refers to the footprints of animals that reflect the arrival of the gods during Teotl Eco confirms the idea that this arrival was similar to a birth, the gods revealing their animal doubles, just as occurred following the birth of infants.

QUECHOLLI AND PANQUETZALIZTLI: THE GENERATION AND BIRTH OF HUITZILOPOCHTLI

Now our focus will shift to two extremely important *veintenas* in the Mexica annual calendar: Quecholli and Panquetzaliztli. They were of supreme significance, because they involved staging nothing less than the generation and birth of Huitzilopochtli, the patron god of the Mexica.

In the *veintena* of Quecholli, the principal episode was a great collective hunt headed by the king carried out on Zacatepec hill (Sahagún 1950–82, bk 2: 134–40). Arrows were made, shooting competitions were held, and later, during the collective hunt, both the prey from the hunt and war captives were sacrificed, in which both groups of victims were equated through a logic that compared warfare with the hunting of men (Olivier 2015a, 314–22). Thus, the deer were sacrificed "in the same way as the men" (*al mesmo modo que de los hombres*) (Durán 1995, 2: 84) by heart extraction, while war captives were bound by the hands and feet and hung on poles, as if hunting prey (Sahagún 1950–82, bk 2: 139). During Quecholli, slaves who represented pulque gods and impersonators of the Hunting God, Mixcoatl, and the Earth Goddess, Coatlicue, were also sacrificed (Sahagún 1950–82, bk 2: 137–38).

In this regard, we might mention a pertinent observation made by Francisco del Paso y Troncoso (1898, 207), in his commentary on plate 33 of the *Codex Borbonicus* that represents the *veintena* of Quecholli:

> Finally, for being drawn on page XXXIII of our Codex the two deities Mixcoatl and Coatlicue; the latter confused with Chimalman and recognized as the mother of Huitzilopochtli; and the former as the husband of one or the other, and according this, probably the father of the War God, we might say that here the two progenitors of the patron god of Mexico appear; and that the solemnity of the month Quecholli comes to be the precursor of the birth of Huitzilopochtli, which can be inferred to have occurred in the next month [Panquetzaliztli], for the ceremonies held in it (*Finalmente, por estar dibujados en la pág. XXXIII de nuestro Códice los dos númenes Mixcóatl y Coatlicue; confundida ésta con Chimalman, y reconocida como madre de Huitzilopochtli; y marido aquel de una ó de otra, y, según esto, probablemente padre del dios de la guerra, podemos decir que aquí figuran los dos genitores del patrono de México;*

y que la solemnidad del mes quecholli viene á ser precursora del nacimiento de Huitzilopochtli, que se infiere ocurrió en el siguiente mes [panquetzaliztli], por las ceremonias que en él se celebraban).

Following Paso y Troncoso's observation, Graulich (1999, 188–90) interpreted the feast of Quecholli as the re-enactment of the fertilization of Chimalman-Coatlicue by Mixcoatl, a prelude to the birth of Quetzalcoatl in the next fiesta. The same author clarifies that the Mexica had replaced Quetzalcoatl with Huitzilopochtli, their patron deity (Graulich 1987, 347–49).[9] So, by referring to Coatlicue as the wife of Mixcoatl, the Mexica were very opportunely confusing the mother of Quetzalcoatl and that of Huitzilopochtli. In fact, what is striking is that the author from Tlaxcala, Diego Muñoz Camargo (1998, 84) stated:

> ... here they wanted to shoot with arrows and kill a female cacique by the name of Cohuatlicue, a ruler of this province, whom they did not shoot, first they made friends with her and Mixcohuatl Camaxtle had her as his wife, and from this Cohuatlicue and Mixcohuatl Camaxtle was born Quetzalcohuatl (*... aquí quisieron flechar y matar a una señora cacica que se llamaba Cohuatlicue, señora de esta provincia, a la cual no flecharon, antes hicieron amistades con ella y la hubo por mujer Mixcohuatl Camaxtle, y de esta Cohuatlicue y Mixcohuatl Camaxtle nació Quetzalcohuatl).*

In other versions, Chimalman is the wife of Mixcoatl and the mother of Quetzalcoatl ("Legend of the Suns" 1992a, 153; 1992b, 94; Mendieta 1980, 82–83; Motolinía 1971, 52; Thévet 1905, 34). That said, in the tradition recorded by Mendieta (1980, 82–83), Chimalman conceived Quetzalcoatl after swallowing a greenstone that she had found when she was sweeping; that is, she was performing the same task as Coatlicue when she became pregnant with Huitzilopochtli (Sahagún 1950–82, bk 3: 1–2, see also Gillespie 1993, 192–93).

Without doubt Coatlicue and Chimalman can be regarded as different names for the Earth Goddess (Gillespie 1993, 109, 193; Graulich 1987, 175–78). Finally, in the case of the Mexica, the mythological traditions that are staged during the feast of Quecholli undoubtedly reflect a type of political-religious strategy: by substituting their patron god Huitzilopochtli as the son of Coatlicue, the Mexica were appropriating the prestigious Toltec legacy symbolized by Quetzalcoatl (López Luján and López Austin 2007; Olivier 2015a, 417–21). Therefore, it is possible that they accorded Mixcoatl the role of father to Huitzilopochtli.

We shall explore in greater detail the development of the *veintena* of Panquetzaliztli, above all concerning the re-enactment of the birth of Huitzilopochtli. Although most experts have assigned this meaning to the *veintena* (Broda 1987, 76; Brundage 1982, 179; González Torres 1985, 134; Matos Moctezuma 1987, 57; Paso y Troncoso 1898, 213–14; Schwaller 2019, 17–20, 140–45; among others), it is necessary to point out that our principal sources do not seem to highlight the very episode of the ritual that would stage the birth of the Mexica patron god.[10] For example, in the *Florentine Codex* and Durán's work, the descriptions of

Panquetzaliztli include the re-enactment of the struggle between Huitzilopochtli and the Centzon Huitznahua, and they confirm the identification of the Templo Mayor with Coatepec hill, the place of Huitzilopochtli's birth in the myth (Durán 1995, 2: 25–46, 282–84; Sahagún 1950–82, bk 2: 141–50, 175–76; 2000, 162–63, 247–53). That said, instead of emphasizing the birth of the god, these sources insist on the ritual death of Huitzilopochtli, through slaves that have been bathed who represented him and also of a statue of the god made of amaranth dough and seeds.[11] This statue was ritually killed with an arrow with a flint arrowhead that was shot by a priest who represented Quetzalcoatl; after that the statue was distributed to be eaten by the king and the people of the city (Durán 1995, 2: 43–44; Sahagún 1950–82, bk 3: 5–6). It should also be mentioned that the ritual death of Huitzilo-pochtli—whether represented by the sacrifice of slaves that have been bathed or shooting a statue with arrows—is absent in the rich corpus of myths that have come down to us concerning the heroic deed of the Mexica god. This suggests the possibility that some mythical events were only expressed through ritual and that, perhaps, other mythical events—for instance, in this case, the sacrifice of Coyolx-auhqui[12]—were not staged in the ritual.

Be that as it may, it can be proposed that the making of the amaranth dough and seed statue of Huitzilopochtli was equated with a birth. Indeed, the list of buildings in the sacred precinct of Tenochtitlan in the appendix of Book II of the *Florentine Codex* includes the description of various places associated with the *veintena* of Panquetzaliztli. Among them two stand out: Tilocan or Xilo-can,[13] where it is said: "they cooked the [amaranth seed dough for] the image of Huitzilopochtli" (*ycucia in vitzilopuchtli ijxiptla*) (Sahagún 1950–82, bk 2: 192); this is followed by a description of the structure called Itepeyoc,[14] where Sahagún's Nahua collaborators explain that "there [the image of] Huitzilopochtli took form" (*vncan tlacatia in vitzilopuchtli*).[15] The Spanish text for this section reads: "This was a house where the satraps [religious officials] made the dough for the image of Huitzilopochtli" (*Este era una casa donde hacían de masa la imagen de Huitzilo-pochtli los sátrapas*) (Sahagún 2000, 281). The Nahuatl text uses the verb *tlacati*, which means "to be born"; this would explain the translation proposed by Alfredo López Austin (1965, 99): "there was born Huitzilopochtli." At the same time, the verb *tlacatilia*—which has the same root as *tlacati* "to be born"—means "to beget something," but also "to shape or reduce to a certain shape," which corresponds to the act of making the statue of a deity (Molina 1970, part I: f. 63v; part II: f. 115v). Similarly, when translating the beginning of the description of the *veintena* of Panquetzaliztli in the *Primeros Memoriales*—"*Panquetzaliztli, iquac tlacatia in vitzilopuchtli*"—Wigberto Jiménez Moreno (1974, 57) proposed, "Panquetzaliz-tli, when Huitzilopochtli was born," whereas Thelma Sullivan (in Sahagún 1997, 64) translated it as, "Panquetzaliztli, 'Raising of banners,' was when [the figure of] Huitzilopochtli was fashioned."

Confirmation for the interpretation that the creation of the Huitzilopochtli statue was equated to a birth can be found in the description of the feast of Panquetzaliztli in the *Codex Tudela*:

> ... and [when] the stick or stone [was] brought to the temple on which they assembled a figure like this of dough made of amaranth, which is a seed that they call *çouale* and in this way they assembled it on the stick and with paper and maguey points or thorns until it was the size they wished, which, when it was made, everyone ate the dough of which it was made, I mean the priests, and they took it to the top of the temple and they said that Ochilopochtli had been born (... *y traydo el palo o piedra al templo ençima del armavan una figura como esta de una masa de huahtle ques una semilla que llaman çouale y desta masa armavan sobre el palo y con papel y con puntas o espinas de maguey hasta le poner de el tamaño que querian el qual hecho comian todos de la masa que se hizo digo los saçerdotes y subianle a lo alto del tenplo y dezian que ya avia naçido ochilopochtli). (Códice Tudela* 2002, f. 25r; Batalla Rosado 2002, 416)

Similarly, *fray* Toribio de Benavente or Motolinía (1971, 53) described the *veintena* of Panquetzaliztli as: "This feast was the birth of Uchilobus of the Virgin and they made Uchilobus of seeds" (*Esta fiesta era el nacimiento de Uchilobus de la virgen, y hacían a Uchilobus de semillas*). Finally, the author of the "Historia de los mexicanos por sus pinturas" (1941, 221), when narrating the myth of the birth of Huitzilopochtli, clearly established the connection with the celebration of the *veintena* of Panquetzaliztli, which is described as, "the feast of the birth of Uchilogos and of the four hundred men that he killed" (*fiesta del nacimiento de Uchilogos y de los cuatrocientos hombres que mató*).

It is important to emphasize the role of the *tlatoani* or king in these celebrations. During the *veintena* of Quecholli, the interpreter of the *Codex Tudela* explains that "Motençuma went with all the people ... and Motençuma went dressed in the attire of Mizcohual [Mixcoatl] whom they sacrificed" (*yba Motençuma con toda la jente ... y yba Motençuma vestido de la vestidura como el Mizcohual que sacrificaban*) (*Códice Tudela* 2002, f. 24r) (Figure 2.6). Also, we saw that during this *veintena* the fertilization of Chimalman-Coatlicue by Mixcoatl was re-enacted as a prelude to the birth of Quetzalcoatl in Panquetzaliztli in the next *veintena* (Graulich 1999, 188–90; Paso y Troncoso 1898, 207). We also saw how by referring to Coatlicue as the wife of Mixcoatl, the Mexica very opportunely identified the mother of Quetzalcoatl with that of Huitzilopochtli (Gillespie 1993, 109, 193; Graulich 1987, 175–78). As a logical consequence of this, the Mexica sovereign, as the *ixiptla* of Mixcoatl, staged the fertilization of Chimalman-Coatlicue, who would give birth to Quetzalcoatl-Huitzilopochtli. We also saw that during Ochpaniztli, it was said that the personification of Toci was going to spend the night with the king, so that symbolically the fertilization of Toci in front of the temple of Huitzilopochtli was carried out by the king, the representative of Huitzilopochtli and Tezcatlipoca on earth (Sahagún 1950–82,

Figure 2.6. King Motecuhzoma II wore the insignia of Mixcoatl when he headed the collective hunt during the *veintena* of Quecholli. Detail of *Codex Tudela*, fol. 24r. Source: Drawing courtesy of Elbis Domínguez.

bk 2: 119). Returning to the feast of Quecholli, it is worth highlighting that all of those who accompanied the *tlatoani*—men, women, and even children—were dressed as Mixcoatl and the Mimixcoa, participating collectively, which is fairly unusual, in the process of identification with the fertilizing deity (Olivier 2015b, 428–29).

Digressing a moment, it is significant that the Mexica *tlatoani* adopted the identity of Mixcoatl-Camaxtli, patron god of the inhabitants of the Puebla-Tlax-cala Valley, their principal foes, to ritually engendrate Huitzilopochtli, the Mex-ica patron god. Without going into further detail, it can be said that one of the names of Huitzilopochtli was Yaotl, which means "Enemy" (Durán 1995, 2: 158). That said, weren't all the offspring produced by the warriors as well as those born to Mexica mothers also enemies? We should bear in mind that newborns were referred to as "enemies" and that it was believed that their mothers, by giving birth, had captured war captives (Sahagún 1950–82, bk 6: 167, 204). This explains why, in the case of death during childbirth, these women shared with warriors, fallen in battle or killed on the sacrificial stone, the dwelling place of the Sun as their final resting place (Sahagún 1950–82, bk 4: 162–63; see also Olivier 2014–15).

We also saw that in the description of the *veintena* of Ochpaniztli, it was said that Toci-Tlazolteotl—a goddess considered to be of Huastec origin—had "captured" Cinteotl-Itztlacoliuhqui, a way of saying that she had given birth to him.

In sum, it can be proposed that enemies were an essential part of the formation of Mexica identity and also that of their patron gods (Olivier 2015a, 635–53). When interpreting the feast of Quecholli as the re-enactment of the fertilization of the Earth Goddess who would give birth to Huitzilopochtli in Panquetzaliztli, we saw how the king and the Mexica people were ritually granted the role of progenitors of their own patron god. The participation of the entire community in the ritual process, which led to the birth of the tutelary god is again expressed through the process of making the statue of Huitzilopochtli from amaranth dough and seeds; in fact, after describing the distribution and consumption of the "body" of the Mexica patron god, Durán (1971, 95; 1995, 2: 44) adds that, "All those who received the communion were obliged to give tithes of the same seed which had formed the dough of the flesh and the bones of the god" (*todos los que comulgauan quedauan obligados á dar diezmo de aquella semilla de que se hacia aquella massa para la carne y guessos de aquel dios*). In other words, the whole of the Mexica people provided the constituent elements for the making/birth of Huitzilopochtli. At the same time that the gods were fed through the sacrifice of the *ixiptla* or deity representatives, these ritual processes led to their cyclic rebirth.

The attentive reader will have noticed that the birth of gods such as Huitzilopochtli was re-enacted during various *veintenas* (Teotl Eco, Panquetzaliztli, Toxcatl), without overlooking the celebrations of the "anniversaries" of the gods during the "movable" feasts which were mentioned at the beginning of this chapter. In fact, we find in the sources various dates that appear as the "calendrical names" of the gods—for example Tezcatlipoca is called "1 Death" and "2 Reed," Quetzalcoatl, "9 Wind," "1 Reed," and "7 Reed," etc.—which would imply that they were born several times. Until it is possible to return to this topic, we can cite the commentary of Alfonso Caso (1961, 78–79) in which he states, "The large number of calendrical names that can be related to the gods suggests that all the days of the *tonalpohualli* must have been regarded as names of some divinity, or at least of some of their attributions, or of those animals that served them as *nahual* or disguises, or of the plants with which they were connected." We also recall the somewhat disconcerting comment of the author of the "Historia de los mexicanos por sus pinturas" (1941, 220–21) on the "new" birth of Huitzilopochtli in Coatepec: "and Uchilogos was born from her again, beyond the other times that he had been born, because as he was god he did and could do whatever he pleased" (*y nasció della Uchilogos otra vez, allende de las otras veces que avía nacido, porque como era dios hacía y podía lo que quería*). In this regard, it will be important to take into account the fact that, as among the ancient Maya, "The ritual summoning of supernatural beings into the human realm was considered as a process of birth" (Taube 1994, 660), which could explain the numerous ritual births of the gods. Finally, the information brought together here confirm the fundamental role of mortals in the functioning of the universe and most of all in the very process of the creation of their own gods.

ACKNOWLEDGMENTS

I would like to thank Debra Nagao for her translation, Elbis Domínguez and Rodolfo Ávila for preparing the drawings that illustrate this chapter, and Élodie Dupey García, Elena Mazzetto, and the anonymous reviewer for their valuable comments.

NOTES

1. Recently David Stuart specified: "I believe the mythical narrative at Palenque suggests that the appearance of the Palenque Triad gods was not a literal 'birth,' but perhaps a creative act performed by the ritual bloodletting of the Progenitor God himself. In the case of GI, this act was a rebirth, a re-creation of an established cosmological deity into a new form and within the three-part structure seemingly necessary for community patrons in the Classic lowlands" (Stuart 2005, 183).
2. These were referred to as "movable" because they were not tied to the solar calendar and could occur at different times of the year.
3. Additional data appear in the works of Diego Durán (1995), Jacinto de la Serna (1987), and in the glosses of the *Codex Telleriano-Remensis* (1995), among other sources.
4. Concerning this *veintena*, see also Neurath in this volume (Chapter Four).
5. Inga Clendinnen (1998, 267) and Caroline Dodds Pennock (2007, 50) have analyzed the face-upward posture of Toci's impersonator during the sacrifice; the latter suggested there was almost "a unification of identity between the priest and the victim as if they are fused at the moment of death," and also proposed that this priest could have been the one that afterward wore the victim's skin.
6. Concerning the youth of the gods, see also Chinchilla Mazariegos in this volume (Chapter One).
7. Interestingly, among the Guayaki of Paraguay, the verb *waa*, "to be born," also means "to fall" (Clastres 1972, 10–11).
8. We already mentioned the representation of the birth of Quetzalcoatl 9 Wind from a flint knife in the year 10 House, portrayed in the *Codex Vindobonensis* (*Códice Vindobonensis* 1992, 49). In the next plate (*Códice Vindobonensis* 1992, 48), in the year 6 Rabbit, on the day 7 Flower—that is, nine years later—we see a small naked 9 Wind in the sky as he receives diverse accoutrements from the supreme couple; in the same year, but on the day 5 Reed—193 days after the earlier episode—the same deity, now attired and an adult, descends to earth by means of a feathered cord (Jansen 1982, 140–47). In this Mixtec version of the life of 9 Wind Quetzalcoatl, the "descent" of the god is therefore much later than his birth.
9. Concerning the substitution of Quetzalcoatl by Huitzilopochtli, see also Dupey García in this volume (Chapter Three).

10. John Schwaller (2019, 144–45) proposes that: "Symbolically, during the final Panquetzaliztli ritual, the *ixiptla* coming down with the *xiuhcoatl* was Huitzilopochtli reborn, just as his amaranth *ixiptla* was 'killed'."

11. Concerning the amaranth dough and seed statues of the gods, see the detailed studies by Mazzetto (2017) and Schwaller in this volume (Chapter Seven).

12. Graulich (1999, 203) proposed the hypothesis that the sacrifice of a slave personifying a pulque god—Cuatlapanqui—in Panquetzaliztli could have served as a substitute for the sacrifice of Coyolxauhqui, which was re-enacted 40 days later during the *veintena* of Tititl. The importance of the death of Coyolxauhqui in the myth—and even her prominent iconographic presence at the base of the Templo Mayor—calls into doubt the role of a little known pulque god as a substitute for the sister of Huitzilopochtli in the re-enactment of such a significant mythical event. Other interpretations of the absence of Coyolxauhqui in the Panquetzaliztli festival and the possibility of a substitute for her sacrifice are discussed in Schwaller (2019, 145).

13. This is a *calmecac*, a temple school, located near the Templo Mayor, where young priestesses lived who prepared the dough to make the statue of Huitzilopochtli (Mazzetto 2014, 262–64).

14. This is a building associated with the Tlacatecco, in the House of the Eagles near the Templo Mayor, where the rites of enthronement were carried out (López Luján 2006, 1: 287–91; Mazzetto 2014, 263–64).

15. In another passage from Book II of the *Florentine Codex*—in an appendix that describes the temple of Huitzilopochtli—the making of a statue of the god at night in the place called Itepeyoc is mentioned: "And the image of Huitzilopochtli was [made] only of amaranth seed [dough]. It was very large; it was as tall as a man" (*auh yn ixiptla catca vitzilobuchtli, çan tzoalli, cenca vuey, cennequetzalli*) (Sahagún 1950–82, bk 2: 175). The most detailed description of the making of the statue of Huitzilopochtli is in Book XII of the *Florentine Codex*, but this occurs during the *veintena* of Toxcatl (Sahagún 1950–82, bk 12: 51–53).

REFERENCES

Batalla Rosado, Juan José. 2002. *El Códice Tudela y el Grupo Magliabechiano: la tradición medieval europea de copia de códices en América*. Madrid: Ministerio de Educación, Cultura y Deportes, Agencia Española de Cooperación Internacional, Testimonio Compañía Editorial.

Berlin, Heinrich. 1963. "The Palenque Triad." *Journal de la Société des Américanistes* 52: 91–99.

Boone, Elizabeth H. 2007. *Cycles of Time and Meaning in the Mexican Books of Fate*. Austin: University of Texas Press.

Broda, Johanna (de Casas). 1987. "Templo Mayor as Ritual Space." In *The Great Temple of Tenochtitlan: Center and Periphery in the Aztec World*, edited by Johanna Broda, Davíd Carrasco, and Eduardo Matos Moctezuma, 61–123. Berkeley, Los Angeles, London: University of California Press.

Brundage, Burr Cartwright. 1982. *El Quinto Sol. Dioses y mundo azteca*. Translated by R. Quijano R. Mexico City: Diana.

Caso, Alfonso. 1961. "Nombres Calendáricos de los Dioses." *El México Antiguo* 9: 77–100.

Clastres, Pierre. 1972. *Chronique des Indiens Guayaki*. Paris: Plon.

Clendinnen, Inga. 1998. *Los aztecas. Una interpretación*. Translated by A. Usigli. Mexico City: Nueva Imagen.

Codex Mendoza. 1992. Edited by Frances Berdan and Patricia R. Anawalt. 4 vols. Berkeley: University of California Press.

Codex Telleriano Remensis. Ritual, Divination, and History in a Pictorial Aztec Manuscript. 1995. Edited by Eloise Quiñones Keber. Austin: University of Texas Press.

Códice Borbónico. 1991. Edited by Ferdinand Anders, Maarten Jansen, and Luis Reyes García. Graz, Madrid, Mexico City: ADEVA, Sociedad Estatal Quinto Centenario, Fondo de Cultura Económica.

Códice Borgia. 1993. Edited by Ferdinand Anders, Maarten Jansen, and Luis Reyes García. Graz, Madrid, Mexico City: ADEVA, Sociedad Estatal Quinto Centenario, Fondo de Cultura Económica.

Códice Tudela. 2002. Edited by Juan José Batalla Rosado. Madrid: Ministerio de Educación, Cultura y Deportes, Agencia Española de Cooperación Internacional, Testimonio Compañía Editorial.

Códice Vindobonensis. 1992. Edited by Ferdinand Anders, Maarten Jansen, and Gabina Aurora Pérez Jiménez. Graz, Madrid, Mexico City: ADEVA, Sociedad Estatal Quinto Centenario, Fondo de Cultura Económica.

Dodds Pennock, Caroline. 2007. "Female Dismemberment and Decapitation: Gendered Understandings of Power in Aztec Ritual." In *Cultures of Violence: Interpersonal Violence in Historical Perspective*, edited by Carroll Stuart, 47–73. Basingstoke: Palgrave Macmillan.

Durán, Diego. 1971. *Book of the Gods and Rites and the Ancient Calendar.* Translated and edited by Fernando Horcasitas and Doris Heyden. Norman: University of Oklahoma Press.

———. 1995. *Historia de las Indias de Nueva España e islas de Tierra Firme.* Edited by José Rubén Romero and Rosa Camelo. 2 vols. Mexico City: Consejo Nacional para la Cultura y las Artes.

Foster, George M. 1944. "Nagualism in Mexico and Guatemala." *Acta Americana* 2, no. 1–2: 85–103.

Gillespie, Susan D. 1993. *Los reyes aztecas. La construcción del gobierno en la historia mexica.* Translated by Stella Mastrangelo. Mexico City: Siglo XXI.

González Torres, Yolotl. 1985. *El sacrificio humano entre los mexicas.* Mexico City: Fondo de Cultura Económica.

Graulich, Michel. 1987. *Mythes et rituels du Mexique ancien préhispanique.* Brussels: Académie Royale de Belgique.

———. 1990–91. "Fêtes mobiles et occasionnelles des Aztèques." *Annuaire de l'École Pratique des Hautes Études, Section des Sciences Religieuses* 99: 31–37.

———. 1993–94. "Fêtes mobiles et occasionnelles des Aztèques (suite)." *Annuaire de l'École Pratique des Hautes Études, Section des Sciences Religieuses* 102: 25–31.

———. 1994–95. "Fêtes mobiles et occasionnelles des Aztèques (suite et fin)." *Annuaire de l'École Pratique des Hautes Études, Section des Sciences Religieuses* 103: 33–39.

———. 1997. "Elementos de las fiestas de las veintenas en las trecenas del *Códice Borbónico.*" In *Códices y documentos sobre México. Segundo simposio.* Vol. 2, edited by Salvador Rueda Smithers, Constanza Vega Sosa, and Rodrigo Martínez Baracs, 205–20. Mexico City: Instituto Nacional de Antropología e Historia, Consejo Nacional para la Cultura y las Artes.

———. 1999. *Ritos aztecas. Las fiestas de las veintenas.* Mexico City: Instituto Nacional Indigenista.

"Historia de los mexicanos por sus pinturas." 1941. In *Nueva colección de documentos para la historia de México*, edited by Joaquín García Icazbalceta, 209–40. Mexico City: Salvador Chavez Hayhoe.

Houston, Stephen, Karl Taube, and David Stuart. 2006. *The Memory of Bones: Body, Being, and Experience among Classic Maya.* Austin: University of Texas Press.

Jansen, Maarten. 1982. *Huisi Tacu. Estudio interpretativo de un libro mixteco antiguo: Codex Vindobonensis Mexicanus I.* Amsterdam: Centro de Estudios y Documentación Latinoamericanos.

Landa, Diego de. 1941. *Landa's Relación de las Cosas de Yucatán: A Translation.* Edited and translated by Alfred M. Tozzer. Papers of the Peabody Museum of American Archaeology and Ethnology 18. Cambridge, MA: Harvard University Press.

"Legend of the Suns." 1992a. In *History and Mythology of the Aztecs: The Codex Chimalpopoca*, edited and translated by John Bierhorst, 139–62. Tucson: University of Arizona Press.

"Legend of the Suns." 1992b. In *Códice Chimalpopoca: The Text in Nahuatl with a Glossary and Grammatical Notes*, edited by John Bierhorst, 85–100. Tucson: University of Arizona Press.

López Austin, Alfredo. 1965. "El Templo Mayor según los informantes indígenas." *Estudios de Cultura Náhuatl* 5: 75–102.

López Luján, Leonardo. 2006. *La Casa de las Águilas: un ejemplo de la arquitectura religiosa de Tenochtitlan*. 2 vols. Mexico City: Harvard University-Mesoamerican Archive and Research Project, Instituto Nacional de Antropología e Historia, Fondo de Cultura Económica.

López Luján, Leonardo, and Alfredo López Austin. 2007. "Los mexicas en Tula y Tula en México-Tenochtitlan." *Estudios de Cultura Náhuatl* 38: 33–83.

Martínez González, Roberto. 2011. *El nahualismo*. Mexico City: Universidad Nacional Autónoma de México-Instituto de Investigaciones Históricas.

Matos Moctezuma, Eduardo. 1987. "The Templo Mayor of Tenochtitlan: History and Interpretation." In *The Great Temple of Tenochtitlan. Center and Periphery in the Aztec World*, edited by Johanna Broda, Davíd Carrasco, and Eduardo Matos Moctezuma, 15–60. Berkeley, Los Angeles, London: University of California Press.

Mazzetto, Elena. 2014. *Lieux de culte et parcours cérémoniels dans les fêtes des vingtaines à Mexico-Tenochtitlan*. International Series 2661. Oxford: BAR Publishing.

———. 2017. "¿Miel o sangre? Nuevas problemáticas acerca de la elaboración de las efigies de *tzoalli* de las divinidades nahuas." *Estudios de Cultura Náhuatl* 53: 73–118.

———. Forthcoming. "Cuando la tierra ríe. Apuntes sobre el humor ritual entre los nahuas prehispánicos." *Revista Española de Antropología Americana*.

Mendieta, Gerónimo de. 1980. *Historia eclesiástica indiana*. Edited by Joaquín García Icazbalceta. Mexico City: Porrúa.

Molina, Alonso de. 1970. *Vocabulario en lengua castellana y mexicana y mexicana y castellana*. Edited by Miguel León-Portilla. Mexico City: Porrúa.

Motolinía, or Benavente, Toribio de. 1971. *Memoriales o libro de las cosas de la Nueva España y de los naturales de ella*. Edited by Edmundo O'Gorman. Mexico City: Universidad Nacional Autónoma de México-Instituto de Investigaciones Históricas.

Muñoz Camargo, Diego. 1998. *Historia de Tlaxcala. Ms. 210 de la Biblioteca Nacional de París*. Edited by Luis Reyes García. Mexico City, Tlaxcala: Gobierno del Estado de Tlaxcala, Centro de Investigaciones y Estudios Superiores en Antropología Social, Universidad Autónoma de Tlaxcala.

Olivier, Guilhem. 2003. *Mockeries and Metamorphoses of an Aztec God: Tezcatlipoca, "Lord of the Smoking Mirror."* Translated by Michel Besson. Niwat: University of Colorado Press.

———. 2014–15. "Why Give Birth to Enemies? The Warrior Aspects of the Aztec Goddess Tlazolteotl-Ixcuina." *RES. Anthropology and Aesthetics* 65–66: 54–71.

———. 2015a. *Cacería, sacrificio y poder en Mesoamérica. Tras las huellas de Mixcóatl, "Serpiente de Nube."* Mexico City: Fondo de Cultura Económica, Universidad Nacional Autónoma de México, Centro de Estudios Mexicanos y Centroamericanos.

———. 2015b. "Enemy Brothers or Divine Twins? A Comparative Approach Between Tezcatlipoca and Quetzalcoatl, Two Major Deities from Ancient Mexico." In *Tezcatlipoca: Trickster and Supreme Deity*, edited by ElizabethBaquedano, 59–82. Boulder: University Press of Colorado.

———. 2018. "Relics, Divination, and Regeneration: The Symbolism of Ashes in Mesoamerica." In *Smoke, Flames, and the Human Body in Mesoamerican Ritual Practice*, edited by Vera Tiesler, and Andrew Scherer, 347–78. Washington, DC: Dumbarton Oaks.

Paso y Troncoso, Francisco del. 1898. *Descripción, historia y exposición del códice pictórico de los antiguos náuas que se conserva en la biblioteca de la cámara de diputados de París (antiguo Palais Bourbon)*. Florence: Tipografía de Salvador Landi.

Preuss, Konrad Theodor. 1904. "Phallische Fruchtbarkeits-Dämonen als Träger des altmexikanischen Dramas. Ein Beitrag zur Urgeschichte des mimischen Weltdramas." *Archiv für Anthropologie. Organ der Deutschen Gesellschaft für Anthropologie, Ethnologie und Urgeschichte*, Neue Folge 1, no. 3: 129–88.

———. 1905. "Der Kampf der Sonne mit den Sternen in Mexiko." *Globus. Illustrierte Zeitschrift für Länder- und Völkerkunde* 87, no. 7: 136–40.

Sahagún, Bernardino de. 1950–82. *Florentine Codex: General History of the Things of New Spain, Fray Bernardino de Sahagún*. Translated with notes and illustrations by Arthur J. O. Anderson, and Charles E. Dibble. 13 vols. Santa Fe: The School of American Research, University of Utah Press.

———. 1958. *Veinte himnos sacros de los nahuas*. Edited and translated by Ángel María Garibay K. Mexico City: Universidad Nacional Autónoma de México, Instituto de Investigaciones Históricas.

———. 1974. *"Primeros Memoriales" de fray Bernardino de Sahagún*. Edited and translated by Wigberto Jiménez Moreno. Mexico City: Instituto Nacional de Antropología e Historia, Secretaría de Educación Pública.

———. 1997. *Primeros Memoriales*. Edited and translated by Thelma D. Sullivan. Completed and revised, with additions, by Henry B. Nicholson, Arthur J. O. Anderson, Charles E. Dibble, Eloise Quiñones Keber, and Wayne Ruwet. Norman: University of Oklahoma Press.

———. 2000. *Historia general de las cosas de Nueva España*. Edited by Alfredo López Austin and Josefina García Quintana. 3 vols. Mexico City: Consejo Nacional para la Cultura y las Artes.

Schele, Linda, and Mary Ellen Miller. 1986. *The Blood of Kings: Dynasty and Ritual in Maya Art*. New York, Fort Worth: George Braziller, Kimbell Art Museum.

Schwaller, John F. 2019. *The Fifteenth Month. Aztec History in the Rituals of Panquetzaliztli*. Norman: University of Oklahoma Press.

Seler, Eduard. 1963 [1904–06]. *Comentarios al Códice Borgia*. Vols. I and II. In *Códice Borgia y comentarios de Eduard Seler*. 3 vols. Mexico City: Fondo de Cultura Económica.

Serna, Jacinto de la. 1987. "Manual de ministros de indios para el conocimiento de sus idolatrías, supersticiones, dioses, ritos, hechicerías y otras costumbres gentílicas de las razas aborígenes de México." In *El Alma encantada*, edited by Fernando Benítez, 261–475. Mexico City: Fondo de Cultura Económica.

Stresser-Péan, Guy. 2005. *Le Soleil-Dieu et le Christ. La christianisation des Indiens du Mexique vue de la Sierra de Puebla*. Paris: L'Harmattan.

Stuart, David. 2005. *The Inscriptions from Temple XIX at Palenque*. San Francisco: The Pre-Columbian Art Research Institute.

Taube, Karl. 1994. "The Birth Vase: Natal Imaginary in Ancient Maya Myth and Ritual." In *The Maya Vase Book*. Vol. 4, compiled by Justin Kerr, 650–85. New York: Kerr Associates.

Thévet, André. 1905. "Histoyre du Mechique, manuscrit français inédit du XVI siècle." Edited by Edouard de Jonghe. *Journal de la Société des Américanistes* 2: 1–41.

CHAPTER THREE

Quetzalcoatl in Nahua Myths and Rituals

Inconspicuous or Omnipresent Protagonist?

ÉLODIE DUPEY GARCÍA

The Nahua of Late Postclassic Central Mexico (A.D. 1200–1521) worshipped a complex pantheon of divinities, which included a wind god that bore multiple names, among which were Ehecatl "Wind" and Chicnahui Ehecatl "9 Wind"—after the day of his birth—, but also Quetzalcoatl, an appellation that can be translated as "Feathered Serpent," among other possible interpretations. Ehecatl also split into four varicolored avatars, known as Ehecatotontin or "Little Winds," following the principles of fission and fusion that characterized the Mesoamerican gods (López Austin 1983; see also Dupey García 2010).

The data about the Nahua Wind God, Quetzalcoatl-Ehecatl, conveyed in colonial records emphasizes his role in cosmogonic myths. As a consequence, this deity has been intensely investigated by experts in Nahua mythology and religion. Another mythical aspect of Quetzalcoatl has also attracted much attention, namely Topiltzin Quetzalcoatl, the hero of the Tollan epic story, who was inextricably linked to the deity Quetzalcoatl-Ehecatl (Nicholson 1979). In contrast, the involvement of Quetzalcoatl in Nahua religious practices is a research field where there are still many gaps to fill, particularly regarding the ritual cycle of the *veintenas*. In these festivals, the inconspicuous participation of Quetzalcoatl captures the attention, because it differs from Quetzalcoatl's central place in the Nahua pantheon and omnipresent role in the mythical adventures, which were often re-enacted or at least alluded to during the festivals of the solar year, as stressed by renowned Americanist scholars (López Austin 1998, 117; Mazzetto and Dupey García, in this volume).

The aim of this chapter is to explore the seeming contradiction between the role of Quetzalcoatl in myths and rituals, in particular through an analysis of the *veintena* Huey Tecuilhuitl. Here the subtle participation of our protagonist, as well as of specific figures of Nahua society, evoke Quetzalcoatl's role as transgressor in mythology. This inquiry will also lead me to reflect on the complexity of the relationship between rites and myths. Concretely, I will propose that a specific mythical theme or motif could be referenced in diverse ritual contexts, while a myth was not necessarily performed in its entirety in a particular festival.

QUETZALCOATL IN NAHUA MYTHOLOGY

In order to facilitate the comparison of myths and rites, a brief outline of the roles of Quetzalcoatl-Ehecatl in the cosmogonic narrative and of Topiltzin Quetzalcoatl in the mythical cycle of Tollan is in order. Before proceeding further with the actual participation of these characters in mythology, however, it is important to stress that, for the Nahua, breath and wind were closely related and both were associated with the concepts of origin and dynamism (Dupey García 2020; Olivier 2003; Taube 2001). Quetzalcoatl was said to be born from the breath of the primordial god, Tonacatecuhtli (*Codex Telleriano-Remensis* 1995, fol. 8v). In turn, Ehecatl blew through his beak-shaped mask and his breath transformed into wind pushed the sun and the moon that were recently created in Teotihuacan across the sky ("Costumbres ..." 1945, 55; Sahagún 1950–82, bk 7: 8). From then on, these celestial bodies began to move in the sky and the succession of days and nights started. The Wind God put the cosmos in motion.

What is more, the Nahua myths tell that by himself or together with other gods—for instance, Tezcatlipoca and Huitzilopochtli—Quetzalcoatl-Ehecatl took charge of the entire genesis or participated in major creations, especially that of the sky, earth, fire, and the day-count (e.g. "Historia de los mexicanos por sus pinturas" 1941; Thévet 1905). He was also said to have brought divine belongings to humans, in particular, maize and music (e.g. "Leyenda de los Soles" 1992, 146–47; Thévet 1905, 27–28). Quetzalcoatl was, as well, the creator of a humanity which he formed with ground bones from the ancestors and blood from his own penis ("Leyenda de los Soles" 1992, 145–46). In everyday life, too, he was responsible for human beings' existence, because he was one of the divinities who produced the sparks that caused women to conceive when these were introduced into their wombs (Sahagún 1950–82, bk 6: 141, 181, 202; see also Graulich 1992, 34–35). Furthermore, according to the myth that described the creation of flowers, Quetzalcoatl, in the form of a bat, introduced female fertility, because he broke the hymen of the goddess Xochiquetzal, or he produced her first menstruation

(*Codex Magliabechiano* 1970, fol. 61v; see also Boone 2007, 204; Dupey García 2013; Graulich 1986, 1990; Olivier 2015a: 566–82). Mythology also emphasizes the role of Quetzalcoatl in the conservation of the cosmos, because he secured the separation of the sky and the earth as one of the "columns" that supported the canopy of heaven (e.g. *Códice Borgia* 1993, pl. 51; "Historia de los mexicanos por sus pinturas" 1941, 213). Interestingly, though, the Nahua thought that the gods who had created the world were also those who ruined it after a certain time. Chief among these was the Wind God. In particular, he was accused of having destroyed the Sun of Wind, an age in which he himself acted as the sun. After being defeated by Tezcatlipoca, Quetzalcoatl drove furious winds that at one extreme annihilated humankind and at the other converted men into monkeys (e.g. *Códice Vaticano A* 1996, fol. 6r). More generally, his battle against his brother-enemy Tezcatlipoca led to the destruction—always followed by a new creation—of the successive ages that preceded the epoch in which the Nahua of the Late Postclassic believed they were living (Dupey García 2018; Graulich 1987, 72–98).

As for the mythical cycle of Tollan, it began with the birth of Topiltzin Quetzalcoatl from the couple formed by Mixcoatl and Chimalman. As an adult, Quetzalcoatl became a warrior and a conqueror, and he ruled the Toltecs of Tollan (e.g. "Leyenda de los Soles" 1992, 153–54). In Quetzalcoatl's days, Tollan existed in a golden age, to the point that the mythical city became a model for the urban and refined Nahua elites of the Late Postclassic, as well as the source of their political power (López Luján and López Austin 2007; Olivier 2015a, 417–21). The inhabitants of Tollan were great builders of palaces and pyramids, and its master farmers obtained exceptional crops. The subjects of Quetzalcoatl also discovered and accumulated precious materials and then went on to create unparalleled art pieces (e.g. "Annals of Cuauhtitlan" 1992, 28–31; Sahagún 1950–82, bk 3: 13–15, bk 10: 165–70).

Additionally, the mythological literature narrates the decadence of Tollan and the downfall of Quetzalcoatl (e.g. "Annals of Cuauhtitlan" 1992, 30–33; Durán 1995, 2: 19–20, 23; Sahagún 1950–82, bk 3: 17–18; Thévet 1905, 36–37). Although several accounts tell this story, one of their common traits is the link between the collapse of Tollan and the transgressions of Quetzalcoatl, in particular his inappropriate sexual behavior and drunkenness. It is worth adding that, in this context, the battle between Quetzalcoatl and Tezcatlipoca resurfaces, in which the latter contributes to the ruin of the Toltec king. This mythical motif led Michel Graulich (1987, 185–205) to convincingly propose that the myth of Tollan refers to the fourth cosmic age or Fourth Sun, in which Quetzalcoatl acts as the sun. When he was defeated by Tezcatlipoca, he was replaced by Huitzilopochtli, who became the sun of the fifth era, the Mexica Fifth Sun.

QUETZALCOATL IN THE *VEINTENAS* CYCLE

Although brief, this synopsis of Quetzalcoatl-Ehecatl's mythological actions demonstrates that this complex figure occupied a key position in the pantheon as well as the foundation stories of the Nahua. In the *veintena* festivals that celebrated the gods and often evoked the myths, however, our protagonist was rather inconspicuous. Even if the iconographic and written sources do allude to Quetzalcoatl, Ehecatl, and the Ehecatotontin when they describe or depict twelve of the eighteen *veintenas*, their participation in this religious cycle was often limited to the seemingly minor involvement of their embodiments (*ixiptla* in Nahuatl) in specific contexts. In Tlacaxipehualiztli, Toxcatl, and Panquetzaliztli, for example, these divine figures are mentioned as part of groups of divinities that were revered as a whole (Durán 1995, 2: 49–50, 105–06), or participated in processions by way of their human embodiments or priests (*Códice Borbónico* 1991, pl. 34).

In other instances, Quetzalcoatl does not even appear, but we witness characters, objects, and spaces that make reference to him. This was the case in Toxcatl, as demonstrated by Elena Mazzetto (2014, 89, 95–96), when two ceremonies occurred in places that are reminiscent of the life of Topiltzin Quetzalcoatl: first, the *tzoalli* image of Huitzilopochtli[1] was carried on a litter called "a serpent bed," as the raft used by Quetzalcoatl to flee in the Toltec epic; second, a sacrifice was performed in a temple named after the *teccizcalli* ("house of shells") of Quetzalcoatl in Tollan (Sahagún 1950–82, bk 3: 14, 38; bk 10: 166). Similarly, at the end of Tepeilhuitl or the beginning of Quecholli, the ritual death of an impersonator of Totoltecatl occurred in a place called Tollan and, thus, recalled the downfall of Topiltzin Quetzalcoatl, because Toltecatl was one of the accomplices of Tezcatlipoca when this god orchestrated the decadence of the Toltecs (Graulich 1999, 187–88; Mazzetto 2014, 248–49). So, in these *veintenas*, Quetzalcoatl was evoked but through subtle allusions to places, objects and his enemies; he, himself, was absent.

The references to four *veintena* feasts mainly devoted to the cult of the water divinities confer on Quetzalcoatl-Ehecatl a more significant role in this Nahua ritual cycle. The *Codex Magliabechiano* (1970, fol. 33v) tells that during Etzalcualiztli—commonly considered the principal feast of Tlaloc, the Rain God—the deity who was at the heart of the ceremonies was, in fact, Quetzalcoatl, the "Air God," who is defined as the "friend or parent of another [god] who was named Tlaloc and brother of another who was named Xolotl" (*amigo o pariente de otro q sellamaua tlaloc y hermano de otro q sellamaua xulotl*). This account finds confirmation in the *Codex Borbonicus*, where Quetzalcoatl, Xolotl, and Tlaloc are painted together in the iconographic composition that represents Etzalcualiztli (*Códice Borbónico* 1991, pl. 26) (Figure 3.1).

Figure 3.1. The celebration of the patrons of the *veintena* Etzalcualiztli: Quetzalcoatl, Tlaloc, and Xolotl. Detail of *Codex Borbonicus*, pl. 26. Source: Photograph courtesy of Bibliothèque de l'Assemblée nationale, Paris.

Sahagún's informants say something similar about Atlcahualo, defining it as

a feast in honor—according to some—of the Tlaloque gods, whom they held to be gods of rain; and—according to others—of their sister, the goddess of water, Chalchiuhtlicue; and—according to [still] others—in honor of the great priest or god of the winds, Quetzalcoatl. And we may say that [they celebrated the feast] in honor of all of these (*vna fiesta a honra (segun algunos) de los dioses tlaloques, que los tenjan por dioses de la pluuja: y segun otros de su hermana, la diosa del agua, chalchiuhtli ycue: y segun otros a honrra del gran sacerdote, o dios de los vientos quetzalcoatl: y podemos dezir que a honrra de todos estos*). (Sahagún 1950–82, bk 2: 1)

Furthermore, they say that in Atlcahualo occurred the sacrifice of an embodiment of the Wind God—under the name of 9 Wind—and they add that the offering of life was done in honor of this divinity (Rodríguez Figueroa 2010, 136–38; see also Sahagún 1950–82, bk 2: 187). Likewise, in Atemoztli and Tepeilhuitl, the mountain gods were celebrated and their *tzoalli* images ritually killed, among them Ehecatl and the Ehecatotonti (Durán 1995, 2: 279; Sahagún 1950–82, bk 2: 23, 152–53).

Although brief, the mention of Quetzalcoatl-Ehecatl in these contexts comes as no surprise, since the Wind God played an important function in the arrival of the wet season (Dupey García 2020; Graulich 1999, 368). Sahagún's informants eloquently describe Quetzalcoatl as "the wind, the guide, the roadsweeper of the rain gods, of the masters of the water, of those who brought rain" (*yn ehecatl ynteiacancauh yntlachpancauh in tlaloque, yn aoaque, yn qujqujiauhti*) (Sahagún 1950–82, bk 1: 9). This could also explain why the Wind God and his avatars participated in the feast of Ochpaniztli (*Códice Borbónico* 1991, pl. 30; Sahagún 1993, fol. 251v), while a human embodiment of Quetzalcoatl was sacrificed in Huey Tozoztli ("Costumbres ..." 1945, 41). These two *veintenas* respectively celebrated the birth of corn and its ripeness (Graulich 1999, 327–34), and, for obvious reasons, the cults of the Maize God—in its diverse expression—and of the aquatic divinities were closely related in Nahua religion. Finally, concerning the exegesis relative to Etzalcualiztli as the festival of "the great priest or god of the winds, Quetzalcoatl," it worth recalling that Alfredo López Austin and Leonardo López Luján (2004) have identified in its rituals references to the myth of the origin of corn, in which Quetzalcoatl played a major role.

The parallel *veintenas* of Huey Tecuilhuitl and Tititl also saw the sacrifice of human embodiments of Quetzalcoatl, although in different religious traditions.[2] Building on Durán's (1995, 2: 70, 72–73) account, Graulich (1999, 250) has proposed that Tititl was the major festival in Cholula and Quetzalcoatl was honored as the tutelary god of the city. A human embodiment was provided by the merchants, a dominant group in the Cholulteca society who hosted the feast. The embodiment of Quetzalcoatl was sacrificed at midnight and his heart presented to the moon. Later, his body was cooked in different manners in the house of the principal merchant, and eaten in an anthropophagous banquet attended by all the members of this guild. The celebration of Huey Tecuilhuitl in Mexico, in turn, included the ritual death of a human embodiment of Quetzalcoat-Ehecatl, which happened in the Temple of Tezcatlipoca:

> The god Ehecatl was commemorated on this same feast. He is also the one known as Quetzalcoatl ... A man was sacrificed on this day, and this sacrifice was performed in the name of the Wind and in the honor of this deity ... This feast took place in the Temple of Tezcatlipoca, honoring the latter in this manner, [but] the ceremony honored Quetzalcoatl, god of the wind, and the manner in which he had been persecuted, plus the victory which

had been achieved over this holy man (Durán 1971, 437) (*En este dia celebraban la fiesta del ídolo Ehecatl que por otro nombre llaman Quetzalcoatl ... Haciase este dia sacrificio de un hombre y este sacrificio era en nombre del viento y á honra suya ... Hacía esta fiesta en el templo de Tezcatlipoca al cual daban aquella honra haciendo conmemoracion de Quetzalcoatl que era el dios del viento en memoria de aquella persecucion que hicieron y victoria que tuvieron contra aquel baron*). (Durán 1995, 2: 265–66)

In light of this brief review of the data on the *veintenas*, how can the participation of Quetzalcoatl and his avatars in this religious cycle be defined? It would be improper to claim that these figures were absent, since, in different Nahua societies, their *tzoalli* and human embodiments were ritually killed in at least five festivals—Atemoztli, Atlcahualo, Huey Tecuilhuitl, Huey Tozoztli, Tepeilhuitl—and possibly in Tititl too. But the colonial descriptions or depictions of these sacrifices and, in general, of the participation of these characters in the *veintenas*, are succinct, fragmentary and, in the case of the images, poorly understood, even when Quetzalcoatl was supposed to be at the heart of some celebrations, as in Etzalcualiztli according to the *Codex Magliabechiano*. In other words, even when the Wind God was worshipped, he was never put under the spotlight in the historical sources; with the exception of the account of the *veintena* dedicated to Quetzalcoatl-Ehecatl in Cholula provided by Durán (1995, 2: 70–78), which accurately portrays the embodiment of the god and describes various of the rituals. In contrast, the documentation from the Valley of Mexico—and more specifically from the city of Mexico—does not provide information about a major festival offered to Quetzalcoatl-Ehecatl.

This lack of ceremonial focus was previously noticed by Durán, who explained it adducing that Quetzalcoatl was among the "... main deities of the natives, and thus the temple in which he stood was of supreme importance, especially the one in Cholula. In the city of Mexico, since [Quetzalcoatl] was not the patron of the city, [the people] did not pay so much heed to his glorification as in Cholula" (... *principales diosses de los yndios y assi el tenplo en que estaua era de mucha autoridad especialmente el de Chollolan en la ciudad de mexico como no era la abocacion de la ciudad tenia no tanta cuenta de hacelle fiesta como en Cholollan*) (Durán 1971, 133; 1995, 2: 73–74). Regardless of what the Dominican friar affirms, the *veintenas* cycle in the city of Mexico not only focused on the Mexica patron, Huitzilopochtli, but also included feasts dedicated to the principal divinities of the pantheon, with the exception of Quetzalcoatl-Ehecatl. There is no doubt, however, that the Wind God was among the principal gods—as Durán says—as illustrated by the position of his shrine in the sacred precinct of Tenochtitlan and Tlatelolco: it was facing the Great Temple shared by Huitzilopochtli and Tlaloc (Matos Moctezuma and Barrera Rodríguez 2011). It is equally significant that he was, in Tenochtitlan, the patron of the priesthood, an institution headed by two supreme priests who bore the name of Quetzalcoatl (Contel and Mikulska Dąbrowska 2011, 32–35; López Austin 1985, 57).[3]

Moreover, the lack of detailed information about rituals revolving around Quetzalcoatl in the Valley and the city of Mexico is noteworthy because of the crucial role he played in Nahua mythology. Leading figures in Mesoamerican studies such as Graulich (1987, 1999), López Austin (1998; see also López Austin and López Luján 2004), and Guilhem Olivier (2003, 2015a) have reflected on and discussed the connection between myths and rites in Nahua culture. These and other scholars have shown how the mythic adventures could be evoked or re-enacted, in diverse and complex ways, during the feasts of the solar year or, as Emile Durkheim (1968, 262–63, 355) put it, how the myths were set in motion during the religious festivals. So, if myths and rites could be intimately linked, on the one hand, and if Quetzalcoatl was a main character of the Nahua mythology, on the other hand, how do we explain that scarcity and opaqueness dominate the corpus of data about his participation in the major ritual cycle celebrated by the ancient Nahua?

While this paradox has long been perceived by Americanists (e.g. Réville 1885), Graulich (1999, 2001) is, to my knowledge, the only scholar to have developed an elaborate theory to answer this question. As the researcher that has systematically studied the Nahua *veintena* festivals, Graulich did not fail to detect the inconspicuousness of Quetzalcoatl in this religious cycle. In order to explain it, he formed the idea of the substitution of Quetzalcoatl by Huitzilopochtli, which he based on two main arguments, one archeological, the other, philological. In the first place, the Belgian historian evoked the excavations at the Great Temple of Tenochtitlan, which have revealed sculptures of feathered serpents—that is, of *quetzalcoatl*—at the foot of the stairs that ascended to Huitzilopochtli's shrine (Figure 3.2 [a & b]). For Graulich (2001, 11–12), these artworks could refer to Quetzalcoatl of Tollan

Figure 3.2 (a & b). Sculptures of feathered serpents or *quetzalcoatl* at the foot of the stairs that ascended to Huitzilopochtli's shrine in the Templo Mayor of Mexico-Tenochtitlan.
Source: Photographs by Élodie Dupey García, published with the authorization of Proyecto Templo Mayor, INAH, Mexico City.

as the source of authority in Late Postclassic Nahua societies and, therefore, their function could have been to legitimize the power of the Mexica of Tenochtitlan. Yet, they could also indicate that the Great Temple was, first, devoted to the god Quetzalcoatl, who was originally the protector of the city, before being replaced by the Mexica's patron, Huitzilopochtli. Or, in Graulich's own words:

> The building resting on feathered serpents is ambiguous: it legitimates the power of the Mexica, but, at the same time, it shows that the new god Huitzilopochtli surpassed and substituted the ancient one, as he did, too, in the *veintena* festivals, in which Quetzalcoatl was systematically replaced by the left-handed hummingbird (*El hecho de que el edificio descanse sobre serpientes emplumadas es ambiguo: legitima el poder mexica, pero al mismo tiempo expresa cómo el nuevo dios Huitzilopochtli sobrepasó y sustituyó al antiguo, como lo hizo también en las fiestas de las veintenas, en donde Quetzalcóatl fue sistemáticamente reemplazado por el colibrí zurdo*). (Graulich 2001, 12)

In order to support his proposal, Graulich also relied on the chronicles of Fernando de Alvarado Tezozómoc (1998, 42–43; 2001, 62), which tell that the foundational act of Tenochtitlan was linked to the ancient throne of Quetzalcoatl, while the god's temple was the first to be built in the emerging city. Based on this historical evidence, along with other archaeological data, Graulich (1994, 35–36; 1999, 10) suggested that, originally, Quetzalcoatl was the patron of the city built on the Lake of Texcoco, which had existed since Toltec and even Teotihuacan times (Vega 1979, cited in Mazzetto 2014, 180). The Mexica only took over after the victorious rebellion of 1428 against the Tepanecs of Azcapotzalco. As a consequence, they imposed, in the religious domain, the patronage of their tutelary god and they started to eradicate the cult of Quetzalcoatl, at least in the solar-cycle liturgy.

Last but not least, Graulich's theory of the substitution of Quetzalcoatl by Huitzilopochtli rested upon the widely accepted understanding of Panquetzaliztli as the feast in which the Mexica re-enacted the mythical birth of Huitzilopochtli as the Sun God. However, the connection between Panquetzaliztli and the immediately preceding *veintena*, Quecholli, would have us expect something different. As Francisco del Paso y Troncoso (1898, 207) highlighted at the end of the nineteenth century, the rites of Quecholli involved the divine couple Mixcoatl and Chimalman, whose mythical union resulted—as I pointed out above—in the birth of Topiltzin Quetzalcoatl. Interestingly, the following *veintena*, Panquetzaliztli, celebrated the birth of a god, nevertheless it was not that of Quetzalcoatl, but that of Huitzilopochtli, suggesting once again that the Mexica superimposed the cult of their patron on an original worship of Quetzalcoatl (Graulich 1987, 347–49; 1999, 191–224).[4]

However—as emphasized by Graulich (1999, 191–93), first, and Olivier (2015b, 66), afterwards—the Mexica did not subjugate all Mesoamerica and in several regions the veneration of Quetzalcoatl in the *veintenas* cycle survived. As said above, Durán (1995, 2: 70) recounts that Quetzalcoatl was the tutelary god of Cholula, a city in the Valley of Puebla-Tlaxcala where his cult had not disappeared at all. Further south, Graulich (1999, 193) refers to the ancient Maya expecting the arrival of their Feathered Serpent God, Kukulcan, during the *veintena* Xul—the Yucatec counterpart of Quecholli—while his descent from the sky occurred in the first day of Yaxkin (Landa 1994, 178–79), the following *veintena* that corresponded to Panquetzaliztli. In this volume, Olivier demonstrates that this "descent of Kukulcan" could be interpreted as the celebration of the god's birth. Concerning the confusing relationship of Quetzalcoatl and Huitzilopochtli, Olivier (2015b, 70; in this volume) also pointed out that these gods were sometimes said to have the same mother, Coatlicue (Muñoz Camargo 1998, 84; Sahagún 1950–82, bk 3: 1–5), while the "Historia de los mexicanos por sus pinturas" (1941, 209–10) reveals their closeness in a description of the children of the primordial couple that connects them in pairs.

In the rest of this chapter, I won't discuss Graulich's theory of the substitution of Quetzalcoatl by Huitzilopochtli further, although some of the adduced evidence will contribute to supporting the idea of the substitution. Rather, I will return to the relationship between mythology and the solar-cycle rituals, in order to show that a specific *veintena* in which Quetzalcoatl participated, according to the scarce data available in the sources, evoked mythical adventures that involved Quetzalcoatl-Ehecatl and Topiltzin Quetzalcoatl. More specifically, the focus will be on myths in which our protagonists were transgressors and, as such, were the agents responsible for the rupture of the established order, at the same time that they orchestrated the transition to another epoch.

HUEY TECUILHUITL AND THE TRANSGRESSIONS IN TOLLAN

A common thread linked several of the *veintenas* in which the Wind God was worshipped. Indeed, the festivals of Etzalcualiztli, Huey Tecuilhuitl, and also Tititl shared in common interesting ties with the Nahua myth of the successive Suns. Precisely, these feasts all evoked the end of the Suns created by Quetzalcoatl-Ehecatl, periods in which the god sometimes acted as the Sun. As we have seen, Etzalcualiztli celebrated Quetzalcoatl together with Tlaloc and Xolotl, but it was also the time when the Nahua commemorated the end of the Sun of Water, an age that was destroyed by a flood:

> In this [festival], they sacrificed some men and they offered them to their awful god [Tlaloc], asking for a good year … They also say that they sacrificed these men to him and they made this festival to this god in memory of when [he] destroyed the world with water

(*in essa sacrificavano alcuni huomeni e' l'offerivano à questo suo miserabil dio dimandandoli buon anno ... ancora dicono che sacrificavano quelli huomeni e' facevano questa festa à questo dio in memoria de quando destrusse il mondo con aqua*). (*Códice Vaticano A* 1996, fol. 45r; Anders and Jansen 1996, 212–13)

Even when our protagonist is not mentioned, the "Historia de los mexicanos por sus pinturas" (1941, 213–14) narrates that the fourth era, the Sun of Water, was established by Quetzalcoatl when he transformed the goddess Chalchiuhtlicue into the sun.

Similarly, the collapse of a Sun was recorded in Tititl, when the Cholulteca devoted a great feast to Quetzalcoatl according to Graulich's analysis. In the words of some Spanish chroniclers, in particular Durán (1995, 2: 287), the name of the *veintena* referred to a stretch or a pull; an incorrect translation from the view point of etymology (Graulich 1999, 235),[5] but a logical interpretation if we consider that some of the rituals executed in Tititl included two children pulling each other's arms (Durán 1995, 2: 287), as well as the stretching of a cord. In particular, Tovar's *Calendar* shows a man performing this act, while the glosses say: "this way the gods stretch and support the cosmic machine against the great violence of the winds, for them not to destroy it" (*así estiran y sustentan los dioses la machina del mundo contra la gran violencia de los vientos porque no lo destruyan*) (*Tovar Calendar* 1951, fol. 155v). As Graulich (1999, 235) highlighted, this ritual that seeks to avoid the destruction of the world by wind evidently refers to the collapse of the Sun of Wind, an era that came to an end when, defeated by Tezcatlipoca, Quetzalcoatl cast furious winds against humanity. This was why, according to the Belgian scholar, the sacrifice of Quetzalcoatl's embodiment in Tititl was offered to the moon, whose masculine personification was Tezcatlipoca, because this ritual death re-enacted the victory of the Lord of the Smoking Mirror over the Feathered Serpent at the end of the Sun of Wind (Graulich 1999, 250–51).

Additionally, Graulich connected the sacrifice of Quetzalcoatl's embodiment in Tititl with what happened in the parallel *veintena*, Huey Tecuilhuitl. As previously mentioned, this feast also saw the sacrifice of a human embodiment of Quetzalcoatl-Ehecatl, this time in the temple of Tezcatlipoca at Mexico-Tenochtitlan. Durán (1995, 2: 265–66) says that the ceremony was performed in memory of "the manner in which he [Quetzalcoatl] had been persecuted, plus the victory which had been achieved over this holy man when he lived in this land" (Durán 1971, 437). These words unequivocally connect the rituals of Huey Tecuilhuitl with the myth of the decline of Tollan (Graulich 1999; Mazzetto 2014). In this festival, thus, was evoked again the mythical fight between Tezcatlipoca and Quetzalcoatl, as well as the destruction of a cosmic era during which the latter has been the sun. As recorded above, the cycle of Tollan and the epic of Topiltzin Quetzalcoatl were, for the Nahua of the Late Postclassic, the story of the Fourth Sun.

But, beyond the evocation of the downfall of Topiltzin Quetzalcoatl in Huey Tecuilhuitl, the participation of Quetzalcoatl in this *veintena* and the profound meaning of the sacrifice of his embodiment deserves further thought and discussion. Concerning Huey Tecuilhuitl, Graulich (1999, 381) has written that the liturgy takes us—via subtle allusions—to the original paradise of Tamoanchan. His proposal rests upon a comparative analysis of the rites that revolved around the Maize Goddess Xilonen in Huey Tecuilhuitl and the ceremonies of Ochpaniztli that celebrated the Telluric Goddess Toci—also known as Xochiquetzal—in order to recreate, through ritual, the fertilization of the Earth and the birth of the Maize God (Graulich 1999, 379–89). In mythology, indeed, the stories of the maize's birth tell that it originated in Tamoanchan from the illicit sexual relation that the goddess Xochiquetzal had with a god identified as or associated with Tezcatlipoca. This sexual transgression unleashed the rupture between the original couple and their divine children, whose sentence was banishment from Tamoanchan (Graulich 1987, 62–68). There was a compensation, though: maize appeared in order to feed humankind (e.g. Thévet 1905, 31–32).

The resemblance that Graulich detected between the myth of Tamoanchan and the festival of Huey Tecuilhuitl led him to suggest that the role played by the masculine transgressor in the mythical tale was performed during the *veintena* by an embodiment of Xochipilli, the tutelary god of the nobles (Graulich 1999, 392–401). Mazzetto (2014, 144–45) went further, as she delved into the propinquity between the goddesses Xilonen and Xochiquetzal, and the gods Xochipilli and Tezcatlipoca. Furthermore, Mazzetto has interpreted the ritual death of an impersonator of Xilonen in a temple devoted to Tezcatlipoca as a re-enactment of the illicit intercourse of Xochiquetzal and Tezcatlipoca in Tamoanchan.

In associating the rites of Huey Tecuilhuitl with the story of Tamoanchan, Graulich (1999, 399–401) was also able to offer an explanation for the sacrifice of Quetzalcoatl's embodiment during the feast: the end of the Toltec era—in which Quetzalcoatl was the sinner—echoed the story of Tamoanchan, which was the archetypal myth of the end of an age. Mazzetto (2014, 146) has supported this theory, as she emphasizes that Tezcatlipoca's temple being the theater of the death of Quetzalcoatl was an efficient way to ritually recreate the decline of Tollan and, by extension, the rupture of Tamoanchan. She concludes that Huey Tecuilhuitl was characterized by a liturgical redundancy, for the rites performed in this *veintena* refer, in a variety of manners, to the collapse of an epoch, a change of era as a consequence of transgressions, among which are those of Quetzalcoatl (Mazzetto 2014, 163).

There are no doubts that Graulich's and Mazzetto's arguments are well constructed and based on solid evidence. However, my own research suggests that these analyses perhaps tend to overly accentuate the role of mythical transgressor assigned to Tezcatlipoca—a god that, strictly speaking, was not present in Huey

Tecuilhuitl—while I believe the role of Quetzalcoatl as a transgressor in mythology deserves a more thorough analysis. He is indeed a transgressor in several episodes of the mythical adventure—sharing this role with Tezcatlipoca—because an alternating logic guided the actions of these two gods in the myth of the cosmic eras. At the end of Tollan's mythical tale, in particular, Tezcatlipoca is the instigator, whereas Quetzalcoatl is indisputably the sinner: he gets himself drunk and has inappropriate sexual relations. Thus, I believe it is worth considering that if a myth was evoked in Huey Tecuilhuitl, it was actually not that of Tamoanchan, but specifically the collapse of the Sun of Tollan. In other words, if some illicit intercourse was re-enacted in Huey Tecuilhuitl, it may not have been that of Tamoanchan, but rather what happened in Tollan and led to the decline of Toltec civilization; and the male author of the transgressions was perhaps not Tezcatlipoca but rather Quetzalcoatl.

A consistent body of data shows deep ties between the corpus of myths that narrate the fall of Tollan and Huey Tecuilhuitl. As demonstrated by Mazzetto (2014, 144–46), not only did the principal protagonist of the mythical account, Quetzalcoatl, take part in the ritual activity and was sacrificed in the temple of his enemy, Tezcatlipoca, but the goddess Xilonen—who was also honored during this *veintena*—has much in common with Xochiquetzal. Now, Xochiquetzal is a main character of the mythical cycle of Tollan, in which she is—as in the myth of Tamoanchan—the woman who breaks the rule of appropriate sexual behavior. According to Durán's version of the story, the decadence of Tollan started when Quetzalcoatl was accused of having intercourse with a prostitute called Xochiquetzal (Durán 1995, 2: 23).

In Huey Tecuilhuitl, though, Xilonen substituted for Xochiquetzal, probably because, as a maize goddess, her identity was more in line with the mood of the *veintena*. Besides being the major festival of the lords, Huey Tecuilhuitl was part of an extensive celebration of food abundance that took place during this phase of the ritual cycle, in particular during the group of *veintenas* formed by Etzalcualiztli, Tecuilhuitontli, and Huey Tecuilhuitl (Graulich 1999). Significantly, one of the principal rites of Etzalcualiztli—for which the *veintena* was named—consisted of preparing and eating *etzalli*, a dish that symbolized surplus for it combined corn and beans (Durán 1995, 2: 260). In Tecuilhuitontli and Huey Tecuilhuitl, people celebrated by sharing different dishes and, more generally, exchange and distribution of food occurred (Durán 1995, 2: 267; Motolinía 1971, 52; Sahagún 1950–82, bk 2: 14, 95, 98). This reference to alimentary abundance and generosity as common features of the complex of *veintenas* under consideration inevitably recalls that wealth was one of the characteristic traits of the golden age of Tollan. In particular, Sahagún's informants say that, for the Toltecs

Of no value were food and all sustenance. It is said that all the squashes were very large, and some were quite round. And the ears of maize were as large as hand grinding stones, and long. They could hardly be embraced in one's arms … And these Toltecs enjoyed great wealth; they were rich; never were they poor. Nothing did they lack in their homes. Never was there want. And the small ears of maize were of no use to them; they only [burned them to] heat the sweat baths (*hatlaçotli catca, in qualoni, in ixq'ch in tonacaiutl, qujlmach in aiotetl, cenca vevejtepopol catca, cequi çan mamalacachtic: auh in cintli vel memetlapiltic, vivitlatztic, çan quimalcochovaia …Auh in iehoantin in tolteca, cenca mocujltonovaia, motlacamatia, aic motolinjaia, atle monectoca in jnchan aic maianaia: auh in molquitl, amo intech monequja, çan jc temazcallatiaia*). (Sahagún 1950–82, bk 3: 14)

Another component reveals that the ambiance of the fall of Tollan and the transition between two ages were recreated during the double Festival of the Lords.

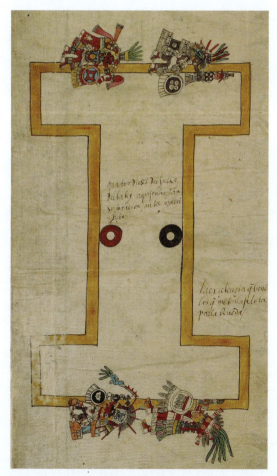

Figure 3.3. Four gods participate in a ballgame in the depiction of the *veintena* Tecuilhuitontli. Quetzalcoatl is one of them and appears in the lower left corner of the court. Detail of *Codex Borbonicus*, pl. 27. Source: Photograph courtesy of Bibliothèque de l'Assemblée nationale, Paris.

This involves the depiction of a ballgame court in a plate from the *Codex Borbonicus* that represents Tecuilhuitontli and Huey Tecuilhuitl. Furthermore, in this rather enigmatic scene, Quetzalcoatl is one of the four gods that participates in the game that occurs on the court (*Códice Borbónico* 1991, pl. 27) (Figure 3.3). Although imbued with complex meanings, the Mesoamerican ballgame has been analyzed as a symbol of the alternating between night and day, created by the movement of the celestial bodies (Krickeberg 1966). By extension, it could also symbolize the transition between greater cycles of time, because the paradigm of the day was inherent in the Nahua conception of time (Graulich 1987). It is not surprising, then, that the fall of Tollan and the transition to the Mexica age are sometimes said to have originated in a ballgame that opposed the rain gods and Huemac ("Leyenda de los Soles" 1992, 156), a character of the mythical cycle of Tollan who merges with Quetzalcoatl, according to Durán (1995, 2: 16). Another version of the Toltec decadence tells us that while Tezcatlipoca was playing a game in the ball court with Quetzalcoatl, he changed into a jaguar and frightened the Toltecs so much that they drowned in a river as they tried to escape (Mendieta 1980, 82).

Finally, two ritual activities performed in Huey Tecuilhuitl evoked the transgressions of Quetzalcoatl in Tollan through the exhibition and punishment of drunkenness and inappropriate sexual conduct. As mentioned above, Nahua mythology associated the decadence of Toltec civilization with sexual behaviors that offended morality. According to an indigenous testimony, however, Quetzalcoatl's departure from Tollan resulted from one of Tezcatlipoca's trickeries that tarnished the hero's reputation, while he was, in fact, innocent of the accusation brought against him. Durán, who gathered the testimony, explains that while the hero—here called Huemac and Topiltzin—was absent from his cell, Tezcatlipoca and his accomplices

> had secretly introduced a harlot called Xochiquetzal, who lived a whorish life in those times. When Topiltzin returned to his cell, ignorant of the harlot's presence, the evil wizards spread rumors about Xochiquetzal, who was lying in the cell of Topiltzin. This they did in order to spoil the priest's reputation and that of his disciples (Durán 1971, 68) (*con mucho secreto le avian metido dentro á una ramera, que entonces bivia, muy desonesta, que avia nombre Xochiquetzal, y que bolviendo Topiltzin á su celda, inorando lo que dentro avia, abiendo aquellos malvados publicado como Xochiquetzal estava en la celda de Topiltzin, para hacer perder la opinion que del se tenia y de sus dicipulos*). (Durán 1995, 2: 23)

In Huey Tecuilhuitl the figure of the prostitute also appeared. Specifically, these women took part in dances along with the warriors and the nobles. According to the *Florentine Codex*, the implicit aim of these dances was to test the men's morality. Several youths who had fasted for twenty days were in charge of providing light to the dancers, but also of keeping a close watch on the people. When these custodians detected inappropriate conduct, they punished the culprit some days later, beating him with "pine boughs which went burning. Verily, they left him for dead" (*ocoquauhtica, tlatlatlatiuh, ca micquj in qujcacoa*) (Sahagún 1950–82, bk 2: 101). Further explanations provided by Sahagún's informants reveal, however, that the men who danced with the prostitute were not really expected to behave virtuously or to resist temptation, but they had to take care of their reputation and be discreet in order for their transgressions to remain hidden. As in the case of Quetzalcoatl, some were discovered and punished, as illustrated in the following extract that speaks about the warriors in charge of the education of the youths, who

> asked for the women only in secret, not before others ... And the woman came forth only at night; she spent only the night [with him]; she departed when it was well into the night. But if one was noted living in concubinage, there was anger because of it, there was concern over it ... There, before everyone, they punished him. For this they cut off his warrior's hair dress; they took from him all his possessions, his adornment, his lip pendant. Thereafter they beat him repeatedly with a pine stick; they verily caused him to swoon. They singed his head with fire; his body smoked; it blistered (*çan ichtaca in qujnnaoatia cioa ... Auh in cioatl, çan oaliooalqujça, çan moiooalpoloa, oc ueca ioan in qujça: auh intla aca ittoz, in momecatitinemj, ic tlaqualanjaia, ic tlaiolitlacoaia ... vncan teixpan qujtlatzacujltia, ic qujtzotzocoltequj, muchi qujcujlia in ixqujch ytlatquj, yn inechichioal, yn itempilol: çatepan qujujujtequj, ocoquauhtica, vel qujhiiocaoaltia, qujquatlechichinoa, tlêtlecaleoa, haaquaqualaca, yn inacaio*). (Sahagún 1950–82, bk 2: 102)[6]

Additionally, Huey Tecuilhuitl was a festival during which the resistance of individuals in the face of pulque consumption was tested, at the same time that drunkenness was severely punished. In this context, Sahagún's informants recall that drunkenness was an exclusive privilege of the elders and they offer a detailed description of what happened if the youths, the offering priests, and the maidens were discovered drinking pulque. A council was held and rendered a judgment, which, in case of culpability, was a death sentence. The condemned was executed in the market place and the judges took the opportunity to admonish the people, causing, in opinion of Sahagún's informants, the wise and the clear thinker to be terrified (Sahagún 1950–82, bk 2: 106–07).

Besides evoking the two mythical motifs—inappropriate drunkenness and sexual relations—that were said to have led to the fall of Tollan, a specific rite during Huey Tecuilhuitl, the "flower race (*xochipayina*)," constitutes another allusion to the transgressions of Quetzalcoatl, associated, in this case, with the role he played in the fertilization of women. This was how the *xochipayina* in this *veintena* happened: after a dance in which the lords and some young virgins adorned with flower garlands participated, these were offered in front of Huitzilopochtli's statue in the Great Temple. As soon as the offering was made, the youths that belonged to the *calmecac* of the Great Temple raced to the bottom in order to seize the garlands. The first youths to reach this goal were allowed to make licentious comments to the virgins who had worn these floral adornments (Durán 1995, 2: 266). For Graulich (1986; 1990; 1999, 114–15, 238–43), this last part of the ritual race occurred because, for the Nahua, the flower was a metaphor for the female sex. The race, thus, signified the virgins' fertilization and alluded, again, to the sexual transgression of Tamoanchan. The Belgian scholar's interpretation rests on the mythical episode of the creation of flowers that relates—as I mentioned earlier—how the first flowers were created from a fragment of Xochiquetzal's genitals.

Without going into detail, it is worthwhile recalling that, according to the only surviving account of this myth, the creation of flowers resulted from a *sui generis* sexual relation Xochiquetzal had with a bat that originated from the semen of Quetzalcoatl. The god changed into this animal and got inside Xochiquetzal's body and pulled off a piece of her genitals, an act that signifies the rupture of the hymen of this virgin goddess and, hence, amounts to intercourse (Dupey García 2013). In sum, the analysis of Huey Tecuilhuitl's ritual practices—the sacrifice of a human embodiment of Quetzalcoatl, the dance of the male elites with the prostitutes, the punishment of the drunks, and the "flower race"—suggests that the transgressions evoked in this *veintena* were those of Quetzalcoatl. Quetzalcoatl who got drunk and was accused of having sexual relations with a prostitute in the myth of Tollan; Quetzalcoatl who, in another mythical narration, penetrated the virgin Xochiquetzal and thus propiciated the creation of flowers. Notably, the *veintena* that immediately followed Huey Tecuilhuitl was Tlaxochimaco, whose principal rite was a massive offering of flowers dedicated to Huitzilopochtli (e.g. Sahagún 1950–82, bk 2: 105, 108–09), the god that, according to Graulich, replaced Quetzalcoatl in the solar cycle.

FINAL REMARKS

The myth of the creation of flowers also found echoes in Ochpaniztli (Dupey García 2013). As the cornerstone of his study of the *veintenas*, Ochpaniztli has been interpreted by Graulich as the festival that inaugurated the ritual cycle and that re-enacted the first acts of cosmogony, that is, the creation of the Earth, its fertilization, and the birth of the Maize God. The fertilization of the Earth, in particular, was suggested in multiple ritual ways, for example when the participants in the feast spat and threw flowers on the Earth Goddess. In Mesoamerica, spittle often alludes to semen, while flowers could symbolize the feminine sex (Graulich 1999, 114–15). Without hesitation, the associations of spittle-semen and flower-sex bring us back to the myth of the creation of flowers that saw the transformation of Quetzalcoatl's semen into a bat and of Xochiquetzal's hymen into flowers. It is worth adding that, in the rite as in the myth, the symbolic intercourse was followed by skin being stripped: a piece of Xochiquetzal genitals was pulled off in the myth, while the human embodiment of the Earth Goddess was sacrificed and flayed in Ochpaniztli (Dupey García 2013). Interestingly, Quetzalcoatl participated—although we do not know how—in the rituals of Ochpaniztli

(Sahagún 1993, fol. 251v), while a bat was part of the group of males that fertilized the Earth Goddess in a depiction of this festival (*Códice Borbónico* 1991, pl. 30).

This set of data reveals that the same mythical story could be evoked in diverse ritual contexts, which emphasized different aspects of a myth. Likewise, all the episodes of a mythical narrative were not necessarily performed together in a particular festival; rather, they may appear in different moments of the ritual sequence. Through the examples examined we see that, in Ochpaniztli, an aspect of the myth of the creation of flowers was alluded to—specifically the penetration and stripping of Xochiquetzal's genitals—as part of a multifaceted re-enactment of the transgressive fertilization of the Earth that brought to mankind the divine belongings: maize and flowers. As detailed here, Huey Tecuilhuitl too recalled this mythical account, but as part of a broad evocation of Quetzalcoatl's transgressions—that included inappropriate sexual behavior—which had led to the decline of Tollan and the transition to the Mexica Fifth Sun. As I have shown elsewhere, another part of the myth that narrates how the first malodourous flowers were taken to the underworld and converted into fragrant ones was re-enacted in another period of the ritual cycle, during the consecutive *veintenas* of Tlacaxipehualiztli and Tozoztontli (Dupey García 2013).

These final ideas reached through the analysis of apparently unrelated rituals performed in different *veintenas* converge with the reflections on the relationship between myth and ritual expressed by López Austin (1998, 110–19) in his masterful study of mythology in the Mesoamerican tradition, which he explained on the basis of two interrelated nuclei, *mito-creencia* (myth-belief) and *mito-narración* (myth-narration):

> Mythic expression occurs in two very different forms. One is the text, a formalized, structured, complete act. It is the face of the myth. The other is a scattered, omnipresent, often diffuse expression, comprised of words, gestures, attitudes, and visual images, often scarcely perceptible ... (López Austin 1993, 81)

When considering ritual, López Austin has theorized that this complex cultural and social manifestation cannot be reduced to a mere expression nor an uninterrupted re-enactment of the myths, but rather is an autonomous system with its own function, structure, and laws (López Austin 1998, 117), whose relationship with mythology can be summarized as follows:

> We need to consider that [a festival] was not strictly a theatrical performance of a unique, uninterrupted piece, a dramatic representation, but rather ritual acts that recalled, for their actions, protagonists, and metaphorical meanings, fundamental episodes of a mythical tale (*Debemos tener en cuenta que no se trataba estrictamente de una teatralización como pieza unitaria, ininterrumpida, de representación dramática, sino de actos rituales que rememoran, por sus acciones, personajes y significados metafóricos, episodios fundamentales de un relato mítico*). (López Austin and López Luján 2004, 438)

These considerations confirm that while Quetzalcoatl seems to be the figure notable for his absence in Nahua *veintenas*, the search for this essential protagonist of mythology in this ritual cycle proves to be fruitful to deepen our understanding of the complex relationship between myth and rite in Mesoamerica. It definitely invites us to continue reflecting on the repetition and continuity of themes and motifs in the mythical kaleidoscope that lives quietly under the surface of Meso-american ritual practices.

ACKNOWLEDGMENTS

I sincerely acknowledge Gabrielle Vail, John Monaghan, Elena Mazzetto, and the anonymous reader selected by Peter Lang for their insightful review of this chapter and their help in improving it in both style and substance. I am also grateful to Guilhem Olivier and Mirjana Danilović for their assistance in locating specific information and references.

NOTES

1. On the *tzoalli* images of Huitzilopochtli, see Schwaller in this volume (Chapter Seven).
2. On the parallel *veintenas*, see Mazzetto and Dupey García in this volume (Introduction).
3. On this topic, see also Peperstraete in this volume (Chapter Eight).
4. On this topic, see also Olivier in this volume (Chapter Two).
5. From the etymological point of view, it seems that the word *tititl* had more to do with the idea of shrinking or something wrinkled. On this etymology are based the interpretations of this name in several sources and historical studies (see a synthetic revision of the debated meaning of *tititl*, in Graulich 1999, 233–36).
6. Regarding the prostitute, she was also rejected from her community. In contrast with the ending of the myth, however, in real life things often concluded quite peacefully and the man who had been castigated sometimes married the woman.

REFERENCES

Anders, Ferdinand, and Maarten Jansen. 1996. *Religión, costumbres et historia de los antiguos mexicanos. Libro explicativo del llamado Códice Vaticano A*. Graz, Mexico City: ADEVA, Fondo de Cultura Económica.

"Annals of Cuauhtitlan." 1992. In *History and Mythology of the Aztecs: The Codex Chimalpopoca*, edited and translated by John Bierhorst, 1–138. Tucson: University of Arizona Press.

Boone, Elizabeth H. 2007. *Cycles of Time and Meaning in the Mexican Books of Fate*. Austin: University of Texas Press.

Codex Magliabechiano Cl. XIII. 3 (B. R. 232). 1970. Edited by Ferdinand Anders. Graz: ADEVA.

Codex Telleriano-Remensis: Ritual, Divination, and History in a Pictorial Aztec Manuscript. 1995. Edited by Eloise Quiñones Keber. Austin: University of Texas Press.

Códice Borbónico. 1991. Edited by Ferdinand Anders, Maarten Jansen, and Luis Reyes García. Graz, Madrid, Mexico City: ADEVA, Sociedad Estatal Quinto Centenario, Fondo de Cultura Económica.

Códice Borgia. 1993. Edited by Ferdinand Anders, Maarten Jansen, and Luis Reyes García. Graz, Madrid, Mexico City: ADEVA, Sociedad Estatal Quinto Centenario, Fondo de Cultura Económica.

Códice Vaticano A 3738. 1996. Edited by Ferdinand Anders and Maarten Jansen. Graz, Mexico City: ADEVA, Fondo de Cultura Económica.

Contel, José, and Katarzyna Mikulska Dąbrowska. 2011. "'Mas nosotros que somos dioses nunca morimos.' Ensayo sobre *Tlamacazqui*: ¿*Dios, sacerdote o qué otro demonio?*" In *De dioses y hombres: Creencias y rituales mesoamericanos y sus supervivencias*, edited by Katarzyna Mikulska Dąbrowska and José Contel, 23–65. Warsaw: University of Warsaw.

"Costumbres, fiestas, enterramientos y diversas formas de proceder de los indios de Nueva España." 1945. Edited by Federico Gómez de Orozco. *Tlalocan* 2, no. 1: 37–63.

Dupey García, Élodie. 2010. "Les métamorphoses chromatiques des dieux mésoaméricains: un nouvel éclairage par l'analyse de leur identité et de leurs fonctions." *Studi e Materiali di Storia delle Religioni* 76, no. 2: 351–71.

———. 2013. "De pieles hediondas y perfumes florales. La reactualización del mito de creación de las flores en las fiestas de las veintenas de los antiguos nahuas." *Estudios de Cultura Náhuatl* 45: 7–36.

———. 2018. "Vientos de creación, vientos de destrucción. Los dioses del aire en las mitologías náhuatl y maya." *Arqueología mexicana* 153: 40–45.

———. 2020. "Creating the Wind. Color, Materiality, and the Senses in the Images of a Mesoamerican Deity." *Latin American and Latinx Visual Culture* 2, no. 4: in press.

Durán, Diego. 1971. *Book of the Gods and Rites and the Ancient Calendar.* Translated and edited by Fernando Horcasitas and Doris Heyden. Norman: University of Oklahoma Press.

———. 1995. *Historia de las Indias de Nueva España e islas de Tierra Firme.* Edited by José Rubén Romero and Rosa Camelo. 2 vols. Mexico City: Consejo Nacional para la Cultura y las Artes.

Durkheim, Émile. 1968 [1912]. *Les formes élémentaires de la vie religieuse. Le système totémique en Australie.* 5th ed. Paris: Presses Universitaires de France.

Graulich, Michel. 1986. "El problema del bisiesto mexicano y las *xochipaina* de *Tititl* y de *Huey Tecuilhuitl.*" *Revista Española de Antropología Americana* 16: 19–33.

———. 1987. *Mythes et rituels du Mexique ancien préhispanique.* Brussels: Académie Royale de Belgique.

———. 1990. "La fleur défendue. Interdits sexuels en Mésoamérique." In *Problèmes d'histoire des religions.* Vol. 1, *Religion et tabou sexuel*, edited by Jacques Marx, 105–16. Brussels: Éditions de l'Université de Bruxelles.

———. 1992. "Quetzalcoatl-Ehecatl, the Bringer of Life." In *Ancient America. Contributions to New World Archaeology*, edited by Nicholas J. Saunders, 33–38. Oxford: Oxbow Books.

———. 1994. *Montezuma ou l'apogée et la chute de l'empire aztèque.* Paris: Fayard.

———. 1999. *Ritos aztecas. Las fiestas de las veintenas.* Mexico City: Instituto Nacional Indigenista.

———. 2001. "El simbolismo del Templo Mayor de México y sus relaciones con Cacaxtla y Teotihuacan." *Anales del Instituto de Investigaciones Estéticas* 79: 5–28.

"Historia de los mxicanos por sus pinturas." 1941. In *Nueva colección de documentos para la historia de México*, edited by Joaquín García Icazbalceta, 209–40. Mexico City: Salvador Chavez Hayhoe.

Krickeberg, Walter. 1966. "El juego de pelota mesoamericano y su simbolismo religioso." In *Traducciones mesoamericanistas*. Vol. 1, edited by Barbro Dahlgren de Jordan, 191–313. Mexico City: Sociedad Mexicana de Antropología.

Landa, Diego de. 1994. *Relación de las cosas de Yucatán*. Edited by María del Carmen León Cázares. Mexico City: Consejo Nacional para la Cultura y las Artes.

"Leyenda de los Soles." 1992. In *History and Mythology of the Aztecs: The Codex Chimalpopoca*, edited and translated by John Bierhorst, 139–62. Tucson: University of Arizona Press.

López Austin, Alfredo. 1983. "Nota sobre la fusión y fisión de los dioses en el panteón mexica." *Anales de Antropología* 20, no. 2: 75–87.

———. 1985. *Educación mexica. Antología de textos sahaguntinos*. Mexico City: Universidad Nacional Autónoma de México-Instituto de Investigaciones Antropológicas.

———. 1993. *The Myth of the Opossum. Pathways of Mesoamerican Mythology*. Translated by Bernard R. Ortiz de Montellano, and Thelma Ortiz de Montellano. Albuquerque: University of New Mexico Press.

———. 1998 [1990]. *Los mitos del tlacuache. Caminos de la mitología mesoamericana*. 4th ed. Mexico City: Universidad Nacional Autónoma de México-Instituto de Investigaciones Antropológicas.

López Austin, Alfredo, and Leonardo López Luján. 2004. "El Templo Mayor de Tenochtitlan, El Tonacatépetl y el mito del robo del maíz." In *Acercarse y mirar. Homenaje a Beatriz de la Fuente*, edited by María Teresa Uriarte and Leticia Staines Cicero, 403–55. Mexico City: Universidad Nacional Autónoma de México-Instituto de Investigaciones Estéticas.

López Luján, Leonardo, and Alfredo López Austin. 2007. "Los mexicas en Tula y Tula en México-Tenochtitlan." *Estudios de Cultura Náhuatl* 38: 33–83.

Matos Moctezuma, Eduardo, and Raúl Barrera Rodríguez. 2011. "El templo de Ehécatl-Quetzalcóatl del recinto sagrado de México-Tenochtitlan." *Arqueología mexicana* 18, no. 108: 72–77.

Mazzetto, Elena. 2014. *Lieux de culte et parcours cérémoniels dans les fêtes des vingtaines à Mexico-Tenochtitlan*. Oxford: British Archaeological Reports.

Mendieta, Gerónimo de. 1980. *Historia eclesiástica indiana*. Edited by Joaquín García Icazbalceta. Mexico City: Porrúa.

Motolinía, or Benavente, Toribio de. 1971. *Memoriales o Libro de las cosas de la Nueva España y de los naturales de ella*. Edited by Edmundo O'Gorman. Mexico City: Universidad Nacional Autónoma de México-Instituto de Investigaciones Históricas.

Muñoz Camargo, Diego. 1998. *Historia de Tlaxcala. Ms. 210 de la Biblioteca Nacional de París*. Edited by Luis Reyes García. Tlaxcala, Mexico City: Gobierno del Estado de Tlaxcala, Centro de Investigaciones y Estudios Superiores en Antropología Social, Universidad Autónoma de Tlaxcala.

Nicholson, Henry B. 1979. "Ehecatl Quetzalcoatl vs. Topiltzin Quetzalcoatl of Tollan: A Problem in Mesoamerican Religion and History." In *Actes du XLII° Congrès International des Américanistes, Congrès du Centenaire, Paris, 2–9 septembre 1976*. Vol. 6, 35–47. Paris: Société des Américanistes.

Olivier, Guilhem. 2003. *Mockeries and Metamorphoses of an Aztec God: Tezcatlipoca, "Lord of the Smoking Mirror."* Translated by Michel Besson. Niwot: University Press of Colorado.

———. 2015a. *Cacería, sacrificio y poder en Mesoamérica. Tras las huellas de Mixcóatl, "Serpiente de Nube."* Mexico City: Fondo de Cultura Económica, Universidad Nacional Autónoma de México, Centro de Estudios Mexicanos y Centroamericanos.

———. 2015b. "Enemy Brothers or Divine Twins? A Comparative Approach Between Tezcatlipoca and Quetzalcoatl, Two Major Deities from Ancient Mexico." In *Tezcatlipoca: Trickster and Supreme Deity*, edited by Elizabeth Baquedano, 59–82. Boulder: University Press of Colorado.

Paso y Troncoso, Francisco del. 1898. *Descripción, historia y exposición del códice pictórico de los antiguos náuas que se conserva en la biblioteca de la cámara de diputados de París (antiguo Palais Bourbon)*. Florence: Tipografía de Salvador Landi.

Réville, Albert. 1885. *Les religions du Mexique, de l'Amérique centrale et du Pérou*. Paris: Librairie Fischbacher.

Rodríguez Figueroa, Andrea Berenice. 2010. "Paisaje e imaginario colectivo del altiplano central mesoamericano: el paisaje ritual en *atl cahualo* o *cuahuitl ehua* según las fuentes sahaguntinas." MA thesis, Universidad Nacional Autónoma de México.

Sahagún, Bernardino de. 1950–82. *Florentine Codex: General History of the Things of New Spain, Fray Bernardino de Sahagún*. Translated with notes and illustrations by Arthur J. O. Anderson and Charles E. Dibble. 13 vols. Santa Fe: The School of American Research, University of Utah Press.

———. 1993. *Primeros Memoriales: Facsimile Edition*. Norman: University of Oklahoma Press.

Taube, Karl. 2001. "The Breath of Life. The Symbolism of Wind in Mesoamerica and the American Southwest." In *The Road to Aztlan: Art from a Mythic Homeland*, edited by Virginia M. Fields and Victor Zamudio-Taylor, 102–23. Los Angeles: Los Angeles County Museum of Art.

Tezozómoc, Hernando de Alvarado. 1998. *Crónica mexicáyotl*. Translated by Adrián de León. Mexico City: Universidad Nacional Autónoma de México-Instituto de Investigaciones Históricas.

Tezozómoc, Fernando de Alvarado. 2001. *Crónica mexicana*. Madrid: Dastin.

Thévet, André. 1905. "Histoyre du Mechique, manuscrit français inédit du xvie siècle." Edited by Edouard de Jonghe. *Journal de la Société des Américanistes* 2: 1–41.

Tovar Calendar (The). 1951. Edited by George Kubler and Charles Gibson. New Haven: Memoirs of the Connecticut Academy of Arts and Sciences.

Vega Sosa, Constanza. 1979. *El recinto sagrado de México-Tenochtitlan. Excavaciones 1968–1969 y 1975–1976*. Mexico City: Instituto Nacional de Antropología e Historia.

CHAPTER FOUR

Beyond Nature and Mythology

Relational Complexity in Contemporary and Ancient Mesoamerican Rituals

JOHANNES NEURATH

MIMESIS, MAGIC, AND THE REPRESENTATION OF NATURAL CYCLES

Ever since studies on Aztec *veintena* festivals and similar ritual cycles of pre-Columbian Mesoamerica began to be published in the late nineteenth century, it has been assumed that these ceremonies were closely related to the agricultural cycle. This approach is not only based on the information on calendar rituals given by Bernardino de Sahagún, Diego Durán, and in other available historical sources from the decades immediately following the Spanish Conquest, it is also inherited from nineteenth-century authors studying European folklore and Indo-European philology. As part of what is known in German as *Naturmythologische Schule*, "School of Nature-Mythology," scholars like Wilhelm Mannhardt (1868, 1875, 1877) and Friedrich Max Müller (1879, 1907) focused on what they considered pagan or polytheistic tribal religions of Early Europe, in which, according to their analyses, elements or forces of nature were (first) personified and (then) ritually enacted.

Frequently, no further questions were raised about why tribal people would bother to perform rituals. "People of nature"—as German ethnologists used to call them—were part of nature, so their religions were determined by nature. But even though those early studies were often rather tautological (Kohl 1988–2001, 4: 229), the approach was quickly adopted by many of the emerging philological disciplines (Pöge-Alder 2007). As mythology based on the personification of natural phenomena became a universalist anthropological paradigm, early German Mexicanists, like Eduard Seler (1899) and Konrad Theodor Preuss (1904a, 1904b, 1905a, 1905b, 1906), were busy elaborating a Mannhardtian framework for Aztec rituals, including the *veintena* cycle. They were particularly close to the astralist branch of "Nature-Mythology," stressing mythological battles between deities of light and darkness, although they quarreled about the relative pre-eminence of Moon or Venus (Preuss 1905b, 1910; Seler 1905, 1907, 1923).

Preuss traveled among Cora, Huichols and Mexicaneros between 1905 and 1907, this being the reason why I am particularly interested in his work (Neurath 2007; Neurath and Jáuregui 1998). In his writings on the natural foundations of mythology, he was explicit in rejecting any notions of causality. Rather, he reflected on the non-dualist character of Indigenous thought and ritual practices. For him, magic was based on a type of synecdoche or, rather, on a pragmatic, as well as synthetic, mode of thought he called *komplexe Vorstellung*, "complex concept" (Preuss 1914, 9–13). Studying Cora rituals, he concluded that for the Cora whatever happens on the ritual ground also happens in nature (Preuss 1912; 1998, 403–19). Signifiers and significants, representations and real things are not distinguished; this is why events on the small scale of ritual are not understood as simply "influencing" the events on the macrocosmic level. In a way, he got pretty close to contemporary ideas about non-dualism in anthropology (Scott 2013). Although Preuss was later forgotten, during certain time he was quite influential. He is quoted in Hermann Usener's *Die heilige Handlung* (1904), in Aby Warburg's *Schlangenritual*,[1] in Ernst Cassirer's *Theory of Symbolic Forms* (2010; see also Alcocer 2006), as well as in Maurice Leenhardt's *Do Kamo* (1997).

Later "Nature-Mythologists" were more inclined toward evolutionism and functionalism. Hunters had dances imitating the movements of animals, but among agriculturalists, mimetic rituals featured regular natural events, like the growth of cereals, the change of seasons, the movements of heavenly bodies, or the arrival of migratory birds (Preuss 1930). Sir James Frazer popularized a theory of magic where rituals imitating natural processes are understood as attempts of "primitive people"—defined as populations lacking any advanced technology— to manipulate nature (Frazer 1920, 52). Even though this whole line of thought has been denounced as completely inadequate (Douglas 1966; Tambiah 1990; Wittgenstein 1996), this idea has somehow become stuck in the imaginary of scholars of pre-Columbian cultures. Materialist and Marxist scholars incorporated the Frazerian version of "Nature-Mythology" in their ultra-functionalist framework, interpreting it as propaganda. They believed that priestly elites at places like Tenochtitlan actually manipulated the masses, making them believe that the continuity of natural cycles depended on violent ritual performances like human sacrifices (Erdheim 1978; Soustelle 1955, 102; Wolf 1999, 154). With the rise of the state or the "Asiatic mode of production", "Nature-Mythology" became part of an ideology "created by cynical rulers who deliberately invent subtle and totally convincing mystifying devices for the domination of others" (Bloch 1986, 6).

In recent decades, emphasis shifted to *cosmovisión* (worldview), based on the idea of pre-Modern societies living in harmony with nature, and sharing "collective representations." While binary classification of nature is seen as the *raison d'être* of pre-Columbian religions, ritual tends to be understood as an effort to connect or to separate elements of nature and, therefore, to maintain a fragile cosmic order (López Austin 1980; see also Descola 2005, 288–307). Rather than talking about "false consciences," scholars stress *cosmovisiones* as relatively adequate symbolizations of nature, partly based on correct observation, but also influenced by untruthful mythology. Eventually, rituals were understood as having the function of producing a merger of both aspects in a shared "social reality" (Broda 1987, 212; 1991, 462).

As we see, "Nature-Mythology" has been oscillating between functionalist and more phenomenological, non-functionalist approaches, as well as between non-dualist mimesis and symbolic representation, but the existence of a direct correspondence between ritual and natural cycles, and the importance of this correspondence, are seldom put into question. I think it is useful to take several steps back and to start asking whether people like the Aztecs actually performed ceremonies in order to foster fertility. Were deities actually personifications of the forces of nature? And if they were, did people "pray" to them in order to obtain rain or the regeneration of nature? Or how did they relate to those entities? In what sense did they celebrate seasonal changes, sowing and harvest?

Once we stop assuming certain things, it seems useful to turn to the works of a recent generation of scholars that focus on ritual action. Rediscovering Gregory Bateson's study of the *Naven* festivals of the Iatmul in New Guinea (Bateson 1958), they came to understand ritual as a type of necessarily complex and "condensed" action that defies any simple notion of purposefulness (Houseman and Severi 1998; Severi 2001, 2002). Simultaneously, ritual action is able to express several incompatible or contradictory social relations (Houseman and Severi 1998). Moreover, distinct ritual actors do not need to agree on the meaning of what they perform (Humphrey and Laidlaw 1994). What one person sees as acts of reciprocal exchange, might be understood as a free gift by another (Rio 2007). "Ritual condensation" explains why ritual action is often so "strange" and, in a way, quite unlike to how dramatic play or theatrical representation is usually understood.

At the same time, authors belonging to the so-called "ontological turn" in anthropology (Henare et al. 2007; Holbraad and Pedersen 2017; Wagner 1972) began rejecting anthropological theories based on Western naturalism. They question the whole idea of representation in ritual, and consequently disapprove of any judgments of other peoples' ideas and practices as "just symbolic" or irrational. The goal is to produce an anthropology that actively avoids disqualifications of any kind (Goldman 2016). Even Marx's theory on the "fetishism of commodities" was not spared. People who criticize irrational aspects of capitalism should not compare those to so-called magical practices of non-European or pre-Modern people (Viveiros de Castro 2015).

When I began to document the ritual cycles of the Tuapuritari Huichols in the early 1990s, I was still unaware of many of those approaches, but Preuss, who had conducted field research in the region, helped me to appreciate the non-representationality of ritual objects and actions. Huichols practicing initiation become their own ancestors, so what they do is not just a metaphoric enactment of cosmogonic myths. As they are the original ancestors turning into the ancestral deities, every time the initiation ritual takes place, it happens for the first time. The content of those rituals is its own origin (Preuss 1933, 9; see also Neurath 2002).

On the other hand, elements of "Nature-Mythology" were easy to find: Huichol ceremonies, as those of neighboring Cora, Southern Tepehuans, and Mexicaneros, actually celebrate the three main phases of the corn's life: the sowing of the seed, the development of the green corncob (*elote*) and the storage of the dry corncob (*esquite*). Additionally, the cycle of corn is linked to the stages of human life cycle (Valdovinos 2008) and to stages of the cosmogony (Neurath 2002). In this sense, "Nature-Mythology" definitely has its place. But I also found many asymmetries and paradoxes that did not fit that well into the frameworks of either traditional "Nature-Mythology," nor *cosmovisión* studies. Little by little, I came to understand ritual complexity. It was pretty obvious that rituals always have more than one meaning. In terms of Victor Turner's symbolic anthropology, this could be called "polysemy" or "symbolic condensation" (Turner 1967, 29), but in Huichol ritual there were not just several levels of meaning; ritual action could actually be contradictory. Therefore, I prefer "ritual condensation" in Michael Houseman and Carlo Severi's (1998) terms.

What I found out is that relations to ancestral deities (or animals) are always ambiguous. Nobody desires to get in touch with those beings, but it is necessary, as they are the source of life and authority. When initiates become the ancestor deities, they create rain, daylight, knowledge, but they also inspire fear to common people. They are actually seen as pathological agents. Such ambiguities are not an isolated phenomenon documented among the Huichols, as similar things have been documented in Amazonia (Barcelos Neto 2008; Déléage 2009a; Fausto 2000, 2007; Kopenawa and Albert 2010), but also in ethnographic accounts of Mesoamerican people. At least among the Nahua of Puebla (Questa Rebolledo 2013, 2016; Romero 2011), Mazatecs of Oaxaca (Rodríguez Venegas 2014), and Tepehuans of Durango (Reyes 2015), alterity may also be defined as the realm of ambivalent ancestral beings that can be one's enemy or ally.

"Antagonist identification" is a term that seems to be appropriate to describe the relationship between people and spirits, or deities. Huichol ancestors are relatives, but they are also enemies. Animal deities are often hunters trying to kill humans, but *cargo* holders (members of the community's traditional government) identify with them and turn into them. Some gods are worse than others, but all deities are sources of both life and disgrace. Moreover, it is virtually impossible to comply with the gods. Humans always will have ritual debts. In some rituals, people fight against deities, or try to control or domesticate them. They also negotiate, and try to forge alliances with them. Due to the complexity of the relations between humans and beings of alterity, ritual action expresses a variety of possibilities that range from fighting to negotiating, from transformation to gift exchange, from identification to marriage.

While documenting contemporary Huichol rituals, I recalled the discussions of the *veintenas* and the scholars trying to determine the precise meaning of each of the ceremonies. In particular, I remembered long discussions I had with Gustavo Torres about Michel Graulich's thesis concerning the shift between the ritual cycle and the seasonal cycle due to a lack of calendrical adjustments among the Aztecs, which lead to an inversion of the seasons associated with the *veintenas* (Graulich 1987, 1999; Torres Cisneros 2001). Other scholars sought to explain apparent calendrical incongruities too. For example, they pointed out that the Aztecs had more than one ritual cycle, so not all ceremonies mentioned by the chroniclers were part of the festivals of the tropical year (Broda 1983). Furthermore, a whole range of agricultural methods was practiced, so it is quite plausible that crucial moments like sowing and harvesting were celebrated several times a year.

The concepts of ritual complexity and ritual condensation offer even more possibilities to shift attention away from the unilateral emphasis on (simply) reconstructing the correspondences between specific ceremonies and seasonal events. But trying to be fair, it has to be said that some Mesoamericanists had paid attention to ritual complexity. Karl Anton Nowotny (1961, 198) was critical of Seler's oversimplifications and refuted the idea of an astral religion. In her chapter on the Aztec Templo Mayor, Johanna Broda (1987) mentions an interesting contrast between reciprocal exchange as evidenced by the numerous excavated offerings, and sacrificial rites emphasized by written sources. I believe this line of analysis should be followed up. Gordon Brotherston's analysis of the *Popol Vuh* highlights the complexity of the interactions between people on the surface of the Earth and of the underworld Xibalba. The hero twins not only fight against the beings of darkness, they also forge an alliance with them, and the result of this ambiguous relationship is the appearance of corn (Brotherston 1992, 1994, 2008). Graulich (1999), too, offers clues to understand ritual condensation. In his interpretation of Aztec ritual, there is an alternation between cosmic battles and ceremonies celebrating "sin" or transgression. The only thing he never considered was a simultaneous occurrence of both. In this sense, ritual condensation is still a new approach for Mesoamerican studies.

Antagonist identification seems to be a topic that is growing in importance among scholars studying Mesoamerica. In some of the most fascinating chapters of his new book, Guilhem Olivier explains how the Aztecs had this kind of relationship with many of their deities. Pregnant women were identified with Tlazolteotl, a goddess giving birth to enemy warriors. The great *tlatoani* was an ambivalent being, too, identified with Huitzilopochtli-Yaotl, their patron deity as well as "the enemy" (Olivier 2015, 653; in this volume). Human sacrifice, too, is more and more understood as expressing relational ambiguity in dealing with others (Fujigaki Lares 2015).

ANIMISM AND AMBIGUITY IN AMERINDIAN RELATIONS TO ALTERITY

In any study of Mesoamerican or Amerindian ritual, the best point of departure seems to be analyzing how people relate to alterity. According to recent studies, many or most Amerindian ontologies are defined as animist (Descola 2005) or multinaturalist (Viveiros de Castro 1998). Maybe those authors are overgeneralizing a bit, but one of the reasons why these ontologies were "discovered" was the easiness of transformation into the other that characterized them. In many Amerindian groups, shamans or other ritual specialists put on a special dress or headdress and, almost immediately, they can report quite seriously that they have gone through a transformation. Now, they are not just behaving like an animal, or pretending to be a spirit, they actually *are* that animal or spirit.[2]

Although I would not go as far as considering all ritual action as non-representational (Neurath 2013), at least during a certain phase, it can be quite clear that certain protagonists of ritual processes are not just acting. Studies on shamanic enunciation show the special use of linguistic forms, like evidentiality, to express the non-representational character of such performances, that is, the reality of transformation (Déléage 2009b). In other contexts, spatial markers are used to express the enunciator's shifting identities (Valdovinos 2008). But often, the most surprising discovery is that animist transformation is actually not that difficult. As Viveiros de Castro (1992, 1998) and Philippe Descola (2005) argue, those transformations do not affect the human "souls." All living beings (at least important and powerful ones) share a human interiority. The diversity of natures is defined by exterior traits, like the patterns of fur, the color of skin or feathers, the presence or absence of horns, and the like. As everybody is essentially human, transformation is mainly a modification of exteriority (Descola 2005; Viveros de Castro 1998). Ritual dress should be understood to be equivalent to a special gear to survive in an alien world. "The animal clothes that shamans use to travel the cosmos are not fantasies, but instruments; they are akin to diving equipment, or space suits, and not carnival masks" (Viveiros de Castro 1998, 482).

In Huichol multinaturalist animism, shared humanity is a very important feature that, as a matter of fact, was already observed in the late nineteenth century by pioneer ethnographer Carl S. Lumholtz (1900, 1902). Many animals, some plants and important elements of nature, such as fire and rain, are addressed with kinship terms: Tatewarí, "Our Grandfather," is the fire; Tayau, "Our Father," is the Sun; Tatei, "Our Mother," can be the rain, the corn, the sea, or the sky; Tamatsi, "Our Elder Brother," is *maxa*, white-tailed deer (*Odocoileus virginianus*) or *hikuri* (peyote, the psychotropic cactus *Lophophora williamsii*); Tamuta, "Our Younger Brother," is the rabbit, and so on. All those *relatives* are truly human beings, not just metaphorically speaking. In dreams, even uninitiated people are able to perceive them as humans, but for a shaman it is much easier to see them as what they actually are. The same group of ancestors also appears as mountains, rocks, lakes, waterholes, and other features of landscape (Neurath 2002). They are "ancestors-toponyms," as Regina Lira (2014, 179) puts it, located in geography, but also part of the social hierarchy. The use of kinship terms denotes closeness and respect, but the relationship to those *humans of other natures* should not be understood as purely harmonious. Kinship does not preclude all kinds of antagonisms between humans and ancestors. Approaching the realms of alterity, for example, visiting "sacred places," is a "delicate," or dangerous affair. Animal and ancestral spirits are feared for many reasons. Some of them may be animals that hunt humans. One of the most common forms of shamanic healing is extracting arrows and other projectiles from the bodies of patients who were shot by such ancestral deities.

The ease of transformation means that it is not too difficult to establish contact with those beings, but it is very important to learn how to control situations involving otherness. During Huichol rituals, deities are constantly asked to "rest," to "sit down" on little stools, or to "lie down" on mats or beds offered to them. This may be seen as treating them as honorable visitors or elders, but it can also be seen as an effort to keep gods from moving around in an uncontrolled way. During dreams, at least three situations are considered very dangerous for uninitiated people, who do not know "how to dream". When somebody offers you food and you accept it, you may transform into the species that offered you food. During dreams, you perceive animals such as deer as humans and fail to notice that they are offering you grass, and not tortillas. In other situations, a dreamer may be seduced by a beautiful woman, and may end up being devoured by her—eventually by her toothed vagina (*vagina dentada*). As it turns out, she is actually a female cannibal monster. But even answering questions can be dangerous. To engage in a conversation with spirits entails the risk of being captured by them.

Among the Nahua studied by Laura Romero (2011), a sick person is someone who is not able to control transformation. Against his or her will, this person turns into an animal or an ancestor. Symptoms indicate into which animal the patient is transforming: people who lose weight are turning into a deer; people with stomachaches have the god of fire sitting inside their navel using it as a fireplace (Neurath 2015b). Any irreversible transformation equals death in the human world. Healing implies a negotiation with the spirits who may agree to accept a substitute for their human victim, such as special offerings that include blood from animal sacrifices. But when ritual promises are not kept, spirits attack again. Controlled transformation requires a considerable effort, practicing what is called *yeiyari*, "following the [straight] trails of the ancestors," or *costumbre*, which includes: taking *cargos* of the community, visiting the ancestors at their sacred spots, participating in ritual deer hunts, and practicing animal sacrifices and ritual purification through practices of austerity, such as abstaining from eating salt and sleep deprivation.[3]

Among the Huichols, as in many Amerindian life-worlds, the realms of alterity are the source of life, power, and wealth, but also of sickness and disgrace. It is impossible to keep positive and negative aspects apart. As Anne-Christine Taylor notes in one of her articles on the Achuar of Ecuador, relations to alterity are best characterized as simultaneity of identification and antagonism (Taylor 2003). Generalizing a bit, we may say that the Amerindian fundament of authority is the knowledge of an ontologically complex world, and the capacity to relate to all the other powerful beings that inhabit the cosmos and also to control them. Therefore, ritual specialists need to have a talent for cosmopolitical diplomacy: the ability to negotiate across different realms of existence, to be able to manipulate, and not to be manipulated by the others. In the end, ritual is often nothing more than trying to maintain a fragile *status quo*. But the main reason why the realms of alterity are perceived as attractive is that, again, they are a main source of wealth and power. In his classic study of the Nahua underworld, Tim Knab describes the interior of the mountains (Tlalocan) as inhabited by skeletonized dead people who grow abundant crops, and own all the riches of the world (Knab 1991). Alessandro Questa Rebolledo (2016), working in another community of Highland Puebla, adds that mountains [or mountain deities] are actually "the true peasants in the highlands, devotedly growing forests, *milpas* [corn fields] and people." They are not giants, but for them ordinary humans are like dwarfs. Mountains are "filled with grain, and can additionally be crammed with chickens, turkeys, pigs, and oxen, while others may even contain cars, computers, and airplanes."

It is important to note that the ambiguity in the relationship between contemporary Mesoamerican communities and alterity is more or less the same as between Indigenous people and the non-Indigenous world. Realms of alterity are often described in terms of abundance and ancientness, but also in terms of rural Mestizo culture, or urban cityscapes. The Huichol underworld is populated by cannibal giants, prehistoric animals like mammoths, vampires, goatsuckers (*chupacabras*), and Christian saints—beings who are all very old, but own the latest technology (Neurath 2002, 95, 231). In Tzeltal speaking Cancuc, Chiapas, ancestors are imagined as light skinned middle class Mexicans, driving around in shiny new cars, constantly going to the bank, or to the gas station, and afterwards having drinks, and listening to the loud music that is popular in towns (Pitarch 2010, 2012, 2013). Among the Southern Tepehuans of Santa María de Ocotán, Durango, sick people live in the underworld like rural Mestizos herding calves (Reyes 2015, 251). Among the villagers of Nahua descent living on the slopes of Mexico's great volcanoes Popocatepetl and Iztaccihuatl, the spirit of the volcano is an urban *güero* (White). Part of the offering they give to the mountain deity are suits like those used by lawyers and government officials (*licenciados*) (Glockner 1996, 98, 203). According to David Lorente's ethnography of the Nahua of the Sierra de Texcoco, the insides of waterholes, caves and mountains (the underworld) are conceived of as a modern city full of high rises, and metro lines (Lorente 2011). Similarly, according to Romero's research among the Nahua of the Sierra Negra, Puebla, the deities of the underworld are slick bureaucrats, sitting in well-equipped offices, and monitoring common people on flat-screen TV sets (Romero 2011, 57).

In any case, the "others" are tricky to deal with. In Highland Chiapas, spirits preside over Kafkaesque tribunals located in the interior of sacred mountains. Usually, they are unwilling to receive shamans who are trying to file their complaints, but they accept gifts (*regalitos*) offered to them by the ritual specialists (Pitarch 2013, 125). In some cases, shamans actually blackmail deities in order to recover the souls of their human patients (Severi 1996, 263–66).

LOSING THE COSMIC BATTLE

Having discussed some of the relational complexities of Huichol, and more broadly Mesoamerican, and Amerindian cosmopolitics, let us see how all this ambiguity is expressed in ritual. But why should we compare contemporary and ancient ceremonial practices?

As a matter of fact, available information on Huichol and Cora ritual cycles has been widely used as a tool to understand aspects of pre-Columbian religion, including calendar festivals (Graulich 1999; López Austin 1994; Preuss 1912; Seler 1901, 1923). As we shall see, sacrificial practices focused on animist transformation into deities and ritual personifications of them are key elements of Wixarika (Huichol) ritual. Without doubt this whole ritual complex is comparable to what Aztecs did during *veintena* festivals, where gods and goddesses were impersonated by *ixiptla*, victims of human sacrifice wearing all the attributes of specific deities. In a way, therefore, although I cannot consider myself a specialist on pre-Columbian cultures, I feel entitled to draw from my own ethnographic experience in order to discuss how ancient Mesoamerican rituals may be understood. But I do not want to look just for similarities in symbolism, which clearly exist, but at how relational complexity may be useful in reframing the study of Mesoamerican and Amerindian ritual in general.

Preuss insisted on the Sun's fight against the stars (or against the great snake of darkness) as a central motif of Mexican religions.[4] According to his theory, this myth must be seen as an organizing principle, not only among the Cora, Huichols and Mexicaneros, but also among the ancient Mexicans and many other groups of North and Middle America (Preuss 1905a, 1905b, 1912, 1929; see also Alcocer 2008; Neurath 2004). Lumholtz had already documented a Huichol story about the first sunrise provoking a cosmic battle, not unlike the well-known Mexica legend of Huitzilopochtli's birth on the Coatepec mountain (Lumholtz 1902, 107–08). Preuss (1998, 134) soon confirmed the importance of such myths. He had not yet spent much time in the Sierra when he started to write reports on how happy he was to realize that his fieldwork had proven his theories on Mexican astral religion to be true.

The cosmic battle eventually became a well-accepted line of interpretation among Mesoamericanists (Caso 1953, 47–54; Graulich 1999, 40–43; Seler 1923). Returning to the Huichols, it is true that initiates identify with the rising sun (or first sunrise), and they are suspected—like the Sun Father of the creation story— of trying to kill everybody who is not able to finish initiation. Likewise, Philip E. Coyle (2001) documented how incoming Cora *cargo* holders identify with the newborn Sun after the winter solstice and New Year ceremonies. What Preuss missed is that in the Huichol ceremony of the homecoming of peyote pilgrims, it is actually the group of non-initiates identified with darkness that wins the cosmic battle. Unwilling to recognize the divinity of the initiates, they obligate them to renounce their special status (Neurath 2015a).

Before continuing with Aztec calendar festivals, let us consider some more information on Huichol initiation, because I believe it helps to increase our understanding of the antagonist identifications involved in ritual relations between humans and beings of alterity. Ceremonial centers called *tukipa* organize a pilgrimage to the desert of Wirikuta, where peyote is collected by the members of the group of gourd cup holders (*xukuri'+kate, jicareros*). In a perspectivist framework, eating peyote enables pilgrims to become "peyote-persons" (*hikuritamete*), and to see as well, and to perceive as much light as a peyote. This is how they obtain visions of sunrise. During the same trip, each member of the group also transforms (or should transform) into one of the ancestral deities. The one who is in charge of the gourd of Father Sun becomes the Sun, the one who holds the gourd of Fire, becomes the fire, and so on. Circles of white turkey feathers attached to the hats of the *peyoteros* are peyote flowers, meaning the homecoming pilgrims are flowering cacti. Later, during the peyote dance (Hikuri Neixa), the peyote-people collectively transform into the Cloud Snake (Haiku), now using the white feathers as part of their dress.

Haiku is composed of 25 to 35 homecoming *peyoteros*, and its arrival at the dance ground is considered, in the ritual, to be the arrival of the first rains. At the same time, great amounts of peyote, as well as corn and calabash seeds, are given out to members of the community. As each member of the group of *peyoteros* also personifies a specific ancestral deity, the Cloud Snake is a composite being which contains all of the assembled ancestors. Throughout this dance, they frequently assemble in order to form a giant snakehead, which attacks imprudent bystanders. Based on the fact that all deified ancestors are also conceived of as deer, during certain parts of the choreography the *peyoteros* jump around in imitation of deer— they mimic fighting like stags and other aspects of this animal's behavior.

However, transformation and multiplication of identity are not the main issues. The real challenge is to be an ancestor, but also to continue to be a normal human. In a way, coming back from Wirikuta is more difficult than going there. This is why rituals of homecoming are longer and more complicated than initiation itself. Mythological narratives mainly talk about the voyage to the Place of Sunrise, but the climax of the ritual year is the reintegration of the peyote-people into the community. For the people who did not participate in the peyote pilgrimage, the homecoming peyote-people are dangerous like the rattlesnake of their dance. They can make you sick just by looking at you, so the gifts they distribute are not fully appreciated. Having obtained the visionary ability (*nierika*) of shamans (*mara'akate*), the peyote-people now *are* the ancestral deities. As such they create and invent the world through their own self-sacrifice. But they are able to destroy it, too. They have managed to obtain visions *and* to transform themselves into the objects of their visions, like peyote and deer, Rain Snake and sunlight. Giving out peyote and seeds during the final peyote dance is part of this generous giveaway of themselves.

But things do not turn out as neatly as Maurice Bloch's theory of "rebounding violence" in initiation rituals might suggest (Bloch 1986). Initiates do not triumph over non-initiates. The *peyoteros*, now turned ancestors, are unable to re-conquer the community they had left as ordinary human beings. The people of the village, those who remained at home, deny the free gift to initiated pilgrims. In fact, they do not treat them with much respect, but rather make fun of them. Certain dances consist of non-*peyoteros* hunting *peyoteros* down like deer. The deer paradigmatically gives itself to the shamanic hunter, but now not much respect is shown for the captured deer gods. Even though the *peyoteros* actually *became* the ancestors, they are treated like impostors, as ordinary people pretending to be something special. "Conflicting modes of relationship" (in the sense of Houseman's and Severi's theory of ritual condensation) is best expressed when non-*peyoteros* receive the returning pilgrims' gifts, but obligate them to accept tiny *tamales*, cigarettes or small coins as "payment." They do so partly to neutralize the *peyoteros'* dangerousness, and partly because initiated people tend to become all too powerful in communities. Religious and political power has to be brought under communal control (Neurath 2015a). On the one hand, free gift is generative. The world, knowledge, light and time, only exist because of the initiates' visionary experience. But as the creators of everything important, shamans have an enormous potential to accumulate power and to abuse it.[5]

Following Perig Pitrou (2015, 101), such situations truly deserves to be called "cosmopolitical," as it is the ontological status of things and beings that are subject to tensions and negotiations. It is understandable that under normal conditions nobody really desires close or direct contact with deities or impersonators of deities. Offerings, therefore, are not so much for establishing relations with divine beings, but part of diplomatic *etiquette* in order to maintain a *status quo*. In my studies of Huichol art, I describe the dangerous nature of sculptures identified with deities. They are kept hidden inside ritual pits because people do not want to be seen, and therefore harmed, by the statues. Offerings are deposited on top of circular lids made of stone that keep the pits closed (Neurath 2013, 66–73; 2015b).

TO MARRY AND TO KILL: FROM NAMAWITA NEIXA TO OCHPANIZTLI

In Huichol rituals, direct and indirect relations to deities, gift and exchange, predation and alliance, always coexist. Common ritual deposits of gourd bowls, arrows and other ceremonial objects are examples of ritual condensation in which ritual actions of reciprocal exchange and free gift actually coincide. Gourds are given in order to oblige deities to re-tribute, while arrows are projectiles shot at deities who are identified with prey animals who voluntarily offer themselves to the hunters (Neurath 2013).

During all major rituals, emphasis shifts from reciprocity to the free gift and back again. Ceremonies start with the preparation of items for reciprocal exchange with the deities, but singing shamans inevitably enter into the dynamics of cosmogonic self-sacrifice. Any ritual killing of animals (deer, cattle, goats, sheep, roosters) requires the consent of the animal, which only the singing shaman is normally able to obtain through an experience of ritual identification with the victim. Sacrificial blood is a free gift. But once the animal is dead, and its blood sprinkled over the offerings, ritual dynamics switch back to the existential principles dominated by values of reciprocity. Sacrificial blood is traded for rain, life, and the like.

When considering the annual ritual cycle, a similar shift can be observed. Ceremonies of the rainy season emphasize reciprocity (alliance), whereas rituals of the dry season focus on the free gift, sacrifice and predation. The Hikuri Neixa festival I described, marks a seasonal transit, a shift from gift to exchange. But ceremonies of the dry season cannot be reduced to gift, nor can rituals of the rainy season be reduced to exchange. Regardless, the transition from reciprocity to free gift and back to exchange is always a problematic process, and "conflicting modes of relationship" are most clearly to be observed.

The perpetual shifting between an emphasis on free gift and one on exchange is related to the ambiguity of the Huichols' attitude toward Mestizos (*teiwarixi*). During most of the year, Huichol discourse and ritual practice is rather anti-Mestizo: non-Indians are lazy, less developed human beings, who lost the way of initiation and, therefore, lack social and shamanic skills. However, during one particular time of the year, an alliance with the Mestizos is celebrated. In this context, the devaluation of the Mestizo world is relativized.

This particular moment is known as Namawita Neixa, the circular "*Mitote* dance of the coverings of rain" (*neixa*: "dance" or "mitote," *wita(ri)*, "rain," *nama*, "coverings," similar to *itarite*, "beds"). Celebrated only a couple of weeks after Hikuri Neixa, it is the festival of sowing. It has to be celebrated when the rainy season actually starts, but it is conceptually related to the summer solstice. Sun arrives at the Northern extreme of his annual trip, becomes a bit lazy, and decides to rest. A pretty girl seduces him and then devours him with her *vagina dentata*. Sun Father dies and transforms into the female monster that devoured him. He becomes his own nemesis and enemy alter ego: the goddess Takutsi Nakawe, "Our Great Grandmother," the primordial female monster.

During Namawita Neixa, Takutsi Nakawe appears as a young male dancer dressed like an old Huichol lady and wearing a wooden mask with a Mestizo-style beard. This event is actually a return. She had been the original shaman of the Huichols, but because she was abusive, always drunk, and cannibalistic, she was demoted in a revolution guided by Morning Star. However, in the rainy season, Takutsi regains her power. It is a dark season, with clouded skies and not much sun, and without solar, paternal authority. Nobody can be arrested, rules of ritual austerity can be neglected, and no sacrifice is celebrated. Instead, planters marry the five corn maidens, and an alliance between humans and the beings of the underworld is celebrated. This is not just a "ritual inversion," because during Namawita Neixa women and corn are actually treated as they always should be treated, according to the rules established when Watakame, the first agriculturalist, a failed hunter, acquired corn from a Mestizo lady.

Identified with Takutsi Nakawé or the Virgin of Guadalupe, the Mother of Corn lived in a ranch deep inside a canyon (that is, in the underworld). Watakame wanted to buy corn, but ended up marrying the five corn maidens (Niwetsika). The condition was to never put the corn maidens to work, never to make them suffer, and to treat them well, but Watakame and his family did not keep this promise.

At least during the celebration of Namawita Neixa, corn cannot be burned. It has to be prepared without the addition of lime and salt, and cannot be cooked on a *comal* (hearth), but inside an earth-oven. Furthermore, as they are identified with Niwetsika, women do not work during Namawita Neixa, so on this day cooking and sweeping are male tasks. Again, an interesting contrast between myth and ritual can be observed. Creation stories usually focus on the death of Takutsi and how her reign came to an end, but ritual emphasizes her return.

In a dramatic nocturnal dance, five male impersonators of a group of female "Messengers" or "Angels" of rain (the Nia'ariwamete) extinguish and destroy a burning torch made of pine pitch. This is not just any torch, but the pillar that sustains the sky. When Preuss visited the Huichols over 110 years ago, the same festival was celebrated as a phallic dance around a long pole (Preuss 1998, 284). According to what has been explained to me, the festival is a celebration of the marriage and sexual relation between the agriculturalist and the corn field. On the other hand, a big "doll" (*muñeca*) made of corncobs and dressed as the corn deity Niwetiska is ritually killed. Her corncobs are threshed and the kernels distributed to all the members of the community to be used on the corn fields they are about to plant (Neurath 2002, 267–82).

Again, we can see that the ritual cycle of the Huichol is a syntagmatic sequence that can be related to the change of seasons, but there is a relational ambiguity in each of the festivals. First the peyote-people are not allowed to triumph, even when they just have created the world of light. What follows is an ambiguous celebration, featuring the marriage and killing of the corn deity. The same festival establishes a set of laws only obeyed on one day of the year, and throws the world back into the original state of ethnic and cosmological lack of differentiation.

Now, some elements of Namawita Neixa invite us to have a look at Ochpaniztli, one of the *veintena* festivals of the Aztecs often interpreted by Nature-Mythologists (including Frazer 1920). Scholars habitually struggle with the confusing accounts in the sources (*Códice Borbónico* 1991; Durán 1971; Sahagún 1950–82), so it might be a good case study to determine what an approach highlighting relational complexity can do for pre-Columbian studies.

Preuss saw the "Festival of Sweeping" as the Aztec harvest festival in which Teteo Innan, the Mother of the Gods, has to be rejuvenated. The festival is actually focused on several female deities, but Preuss postulated that Chicome Coatl, the corn deity, and Teteo Innan, the Earth Goddess, were aspects of one and the same Mannhardtian "daemon of vegetation" (Preuss 1904a, 129). In previous rituals, the Aztec goddess of corn was represented as a young girl, but in Ochpaniztli, Teteo Innan was personified by a 40-to-45-year-old mature woman, who was dressed in all the iconographic attributes of the deity. This transformation resembled the course of the agricultural cycle. The elderly deity had to go through a rebirth (Preuss 1904a, 136). The tall and strong male priest who decapitated the deity was anointed with her blood—and possibly also dressed with her skin—and assumed her identity (Preuss 1904a, 140). Rejuvenated (s)he stood at the foot of the Great Pyramid, opened his/her legs, and married the solar god. Immediately a young corn deity was born. There has been a lot of discussion about who exactly was the child born out of her sexual relation with Huitzilopochtli: Cinteotl, "God of the Corncob," Itztlacoliuhqui, "Curved Obsidian Knife" (Olivier 2003, 117), the god of frost, or the Morning Star (Graulich 1999, 95; see also Brown 1984; DiCesare 2009)?

Elements of page 30 of the Codex Borbonicus offer more arguments for Preuss' rather classic nature-mythologist interpretation, for it shows a corn deity standing on a pyramid in the middle of a group of four rain or corn deities (*Códice Borbónico* 1991, pl. 30). A row of ithyphallic Huastecs dance around the pyramid. According to Preuss, this festival not only celebrated fertility and harvest, but it was also associated with "sin." Abundant crops are the result of the gods' frenetic sexual activity (Preuss 1904a, 154–57). Preuss underscores that many Aztec goddesses were called "prostitutes" or "sinners," like Tlazolteotl, the goddess of filth (Preuss 1904a, 150). He considered Xochiquetzal to be an equivalent of the Roman deity Flora (Preuss 1904a, 154). It is also the case that in old Germanic cults, the "great prostitute" was the goddess of grains (Mannhardt 1868, 22, quoted in Preuss 1904a, 138). In this rather universalist framework, Preuss thought it was obvious that Aztec vegetation deities would be sexual transgressors and sick with syphilis (Preuss 1904a, 157).[6]

Graulich's interpretation of Ochpaniztli follows Preuss in some respects, but he emphasizes that this festival was a celebration of spring, originally scheduled in April. Due to a lack of calendric adjustments, at the time of the Spanish Conquest the festival was celebrated in September (Graulich 1999, 63–69). As Graulich shows, in Ochpaniztli there was a whole range of female deities who were personified and sacrificed: Toci-Teteo Innan, Chicomecoatl, and Atlatonan. Perhaps the "fixed personae notion" of Aztec deities is a misapprehension (Clendinnen 1991, 248), but this is not what I want to focus on here. Graulich called attention to an interesting case of relational ambiguity that is clearly connected to an important episode of Aztec mythical history. When the Aztecs were vassals of the Lord of Culhuacan, Huitzilopochtli, their patron deity, asked to marry a young princess, daughter of Achitometl, but there was no proper wedding, as the Aztecs sacrificed the bride and flayed her— just as what they did with the woman who was the personification or embodiment (*ixiptla*) of Toci during the Ochpaniztli festival (Durán 1984, 2: 39–43; see also Brown 1984, 195–209). Similarly, according to Sahagún (1988, 1: 148), in Ochpaniztli, the king was said to spend the night with the *ixiptla* of Toci, but then she was killed (Graulich 1999, 91). Also, Graulich (1999, 114) underscores that Toci was simultaneously loved and hated. Some people spit at the priest wearing her skin, while others threw flowers at him. In fact, the male priest putting on the skin and the dress of the sacrificed woman acquired a strange gender-ambiguity (Clendinnen 1991, 201), not unlike the Huichol character of Takutsi Nakawé.

The *ixiptla* of Chicomecoatl, Seven Serpent, was a 12- or 13-year-old female slave. She wore a green feather, possibly identifying her as the deity of green corn (Graulich 1999, 90), even though she is otherwise better understood as the deity of mature corn (Dupey García 2015; Mazzetto 2016; Ragot 2016). According to Durán, the rite during which she climbs to the summit of the temple of Huitzilopochtli was actually the "essence of the ceremony" (Durán 1984, 1: 138). As in the case of Toci, Preuss and Graulich (1999, 90) understood this rite as a "marriage." It is not completely clear if this interpretation is correct, but for Graulich it was important to establish a relation between this ritual and the above-mentioned scene where the *ixiptla* of Toci was deceived by the king and killed.

Written sources clearly talk about cleaning. After all, Ochpaniztli means "Sweeping." But it is clear that there was some kind of sexual transgression involved. A somewhat controversial translation of a passage of the *Primeros Memoriales* may indicate that the *ixiptla* of Chicomecoatl had sex with young Huastecs or people dressed like ones. The Nahuatl word *macuexyecoaya*, mentioned in the *Primeros Memoriales*, has been translated as "having sexual relations with Huaxtecs [Huastecs]" (Graulich 1999, 114), but it is probably better read as "battle of the armlets (*maxcuextli*)" (Sullivan in Sahagún 1997, 63). In any case, sexual transgression is not just a misinterpretation of scholars like Preuss and Graulich. As we have already pointed out, in Ochpaniztli ithyphallic Huastecs did appear to impregnate Toci, according to the Codex Borbonicus (Graulich 1999, 94), and Sahagún mentioned that the king would spend the night with a female victim (Sahagún 1988, 1: 148).

FINAL REMARKS

Ochpaniztli features several more rites, like the arrow sacrifice *tlacacaliztli*, probably also expressing a ritual condensation of hunt, war and marriage. This ritual can be compared to the famous sacrifice to the Morning Star still practiced by the Skidi-Pawnee of Nebraska in the nineteenth century (Neurath 2008). There, too, the ritual focuses on how to relate to an ambiguous deity who is an enemy princess, as well as a corn goddess. Finally, we should take into account other *veintenas*, like Huey Tecuilhuitl, focused on Xilonen, the deity of tender green corn (*xilotl*). Graulich (1999, 382–89) pointed out a great deal of parallelism and other similarities to Ochpaniztli. There are also rites that can be interpreted as marriage that turns into a sacrifice. A priest carried the *ixiptla* of Xilonen on his back, and then he killed her. Toxcatl, too, famously features the marriage between a god and four female deities, one of them being a corn goddess, but in this case the deities were not killed (Olivier 2003).[7]

As we have seen, "ritual condensation" is a useful conceptual tool to analyze Huichol ceremonies. We also wanted to find out to what extent *veintena* festivals like Ochpaniztli can be understood as ritual actions expressing relational complexity. Maybe it is possible to understand Ochpaniztli as a ritual celebrating the fertilization of the earth (as in Graulich's interpretation), and simultaneously as a ceremony of harvest or of the first fruits (as most other scholars say). And above all, rather than only focusing on agricultural symbolism, which without doubt existed, Ochpaniztli could be seen as a celebration of a brief and unstable alliance with one's enemies.

Antagonist identification emerges as a key concept, not only in contemporary ethnography of Amerindian people, but also in Pre-Columbian studies. In this sense, I think it is worthwhile to point out certain parallels between Huichol and Aztec rituals, above all how women personifying enemies and otherness have to be treated exceptionally well; they marry, but they are also killed. This chapter cannot offer a comprehensive study of Aztec ritual, but I would like to refer again to Olivier (2015), who provides a variety of material to help understand the relational complexity involved with rulers or kings. As we have seen, even corn often comes from the "others," or the enemies. In the case of the Aztecs, Toci-Teteo Innan as mother of corn was represented by an enemy woman, the daughter of a foreign ruler (Declercq 2018, 225, 459). Before, we mentioned the Huichol, and briefly referred to the *Popol Vuh* and the Skidi-Pawnee.

In any case, agricultural rites show the same relational complexity as sacrifice, hunt, and initiation. Here, the argument is more about showing the potential of new approaches and encouraging one to explore them more systematically. The time has come for Mesoamericanists to finally leave behind the sole focus on "Nature-Mythology." As we have seen, this school was not totally erroneous, but it is important and worthwhile to venture into experimenting with more recent anthropological approaches. Ritual complexity will not substitute for mimesis or symbolic representation, but it offers an important complement.

ACKNOWLEDGMENTS

I want to express my gratitude to both editors of this volume; without their invaluable feedback this chapter wouldn't be the same.

NOTES

1. This is finally acknowledged in the most recent edition (Warburg 2010, 563).
2. Eduardo Viveiros de Castro (1998) systematized available ethnographic information from the South American Lowlands. A similar synthesis still needs to be elaborated for Mesoamerica, but the same ease of transformation has been documented among Nahua from different regions (Lorente 2011; Questa Rebolledo 2013; Romero 2011), Highland Maya (Pitarch 2010, 2013), and Huichols (Lira 2014; Neurath 2013, 2015a).

3. In other indigenous societies of Mesoamerica, Northern Mexico, and other regions of the Americas, souls are stolen or lost, and healers are busy retrieving them (Lorente 2011; Severi 1996). Among the Tarahumara, bodies and multiple souls tend to disintegrate. A constant ritual effort is required to keep them all together (Fujigaki Lares 2015). Among the people of the Nahua tradition living in the region of Texcoco (Lorente 2011), and among the Tzeltal of Highland Chiapas (Pitarch 2010, 2013), souls are vagabonds. They want to leave the human world, because they are attracted by the lifestyle of the spirits. In order to recover lost souls, healers work hard to lure them back to human society (Lorente 2011, 167).

4. Today we would say Mesoamerican religions.

5. To make sense of this situation, Knut Rio's study of the island of Ambrym in the archipelago of Vanuatu (South Pacific Ocean) was key (Rio 2007). There, too, rituals emphasizing non-reciprocity clash with more conventional forms of ritual exchange.

6. Preuss extended this line of interpretation to the Pueblo Southwest. A polychrome ceramic bowl from the Hopi town of Awatovi, Arizona, at Berlin's *Museum für Ethnologie* (Kat.-Nr. IV, B. 3252. Collection Keam, 1902), shows 12 ithyphallic "daemons" dancing in a row. They are Koyemshi, Mud Heads, or ritual clowns. A female figure who seems to be a corn deity throws water at the dancers (Preuss 1904a, 129–30).

7. On this topic, see also Chinchilla Mazariegos in this volume (Chapter One).

REFERENCES

Alcocer, Paulina. 2006. "La forme interne de la conscience mythique, apport de K. Th. Preuss à la *Philosophie des formes symboliques* de Ernst Cassirer." *L'Homme. Revue française d'anthropologie* 180: 139–70.

———. 2008. "Lucha cósmica y agricultura del maíz. La etnología comparativa de K. Th. Preuss." In *Por los caminos del maíz. Mito y ritual en la periferia septentrional de Mesoamérica*, edited by Johannes Neurath, 30–84. Mexico City: Consejo Nacional para la Cultura y las Artes, Fondo de Cultura Económica.

Barcelos Neto, Aristoteles. 2008. *Apapaatai: rituais de máscaras no Alto Xingu*. São Paulo: Editora da Universidade de São Paulo.

Bateson, Gregory. 1958. *Naven. The Culture of the Iatmul People of New Guinea as Revealed Through a Study of the "Naven" Ceremonial*. Palo Alto: Stanford University Press.

Bloch, Maurice. 1986. *From Blessing to Violence. History and Ideology in the Circumcision Ritual of the Merina of Madagascar*. Cambridge Studies in Social Anthropology. Cambridge: Cambridge University Press.

Broda, Johanna (de Casas). 1983. "Ciclos agrícolas en el culto: un problema de correlación del calendario mexica." In *Calendars in Mesoamerica and Peru. Native American Computations of Time, Proceedings of the 44th International Congress of Americanists, Manchester 1982*, International Series 174, edited by Anthony F. Aveni and Gordon Brotherston, 145–64. Oxford: British Archaeological Reports.

———. 1987. "The Provenience of the Offerings: Tribute and Cosmovision." In *The Aztec Templo Mayor*, edited by Elizabeth H. Boone, 211–56. Washington, DC: Dumbarton Oaks.

———. 1991. "Cosmovisión y observación de la naturaleza: el ejemplo del culto a los cerros en Mesoamérica." In *Arqueoastronomía y etnoastronomía en Mesoamérica*, edited by Johanna Broda,

Stanislaw Iwaniszewski, and Lucrecia Maupomé, 461–500. Mexico City: Universidad Nacional Autónoma de México- Instituto de Investigaciones Históricas.

Brotherston, Gordon. 1992. *Book of the Fourth World. Reading the Native Americas through their Literature*. Cambridge: Cambridge University Press.

———. 1994. "Huesos de muerte, huesos de vida: la compleja figura de Mictlantecuhtli." *Cuicuilco*, nueva época 1, no. 1: 85–98.

———. 2008. "El guajolote provee las semillas: el sustento en las creencias anasazi y mexicanas." In *Mito y ritual en la periferia septentrional de Mesoamérica*, edited by Johannes Neurath, 273–93. Mexico City: Consejo Nacional para la Cultura y las Artes, Fondo de Cultura Económica.

Brown, Betty Ann. 1984. "Ochpaniztli in Historical Perspective." In *Sacrifice in Mesoamerica*, edited by Elizabeth H. Boone, 195–209. Washington, DC: Dumbarton Oaks.

Caso, Alfonso. 1953. *El pueblo del Sol*. Mexico City: Fondo de Cultura Económica.

Cassirer, Ernst. 2010. *Philosophie der Symbolischen Formen 2. Das mythische Denken*. Hamburg: Meiner.

Clendinnen, Inga. 1991. *Aztecs: An Interpretation*. Cambridge: Cambridge University Press.

Códice Borbónico. 1991. Edited by Ferdinand Anders, Maarten Jansen, and Luis Reyes García. Graz, Madrid, Mexico City: ADEVA, Sociedad Estatal Quinto Centenario, Fondo de Cultura Económica.

Coyle, Philip E. 2001. *From Flowers to Ash: Náyari History, Politics, and Violence*. Tucson: University of Arizona Press.

Declercq, Stan. 2018. *'In mecitin inic tlacanacaquani:* 'los mecitin (mexicas): comedores de carne humana.' Canibalismo y guerra ritual en el México Antiguo." PhD diss., Universidad Nacional Autónoma de México.

Déléage, Pierre. 2009a. *Le chant de l'anaconda. L'apprentissage du chamanisme chez les Sharanahua (Amazonie occidentale)*. Paris: Société d'Éthnologie.

———. 2009b. "Epistemología del saber tradicional." *Dimensión Antropológica* 46: 69–79.

Descola, Philippe. 2005. *Par-delà nature et culture*. Paris: Gallimard.

DiCesare, Catherine. 2009. *Sweeping the Way. Divine Transformation in the Aztec Festival of Ochpaniztli*. Boulder: University Press of Colorado.

Douglas, Mary. 1966. *Purity and Danger. An Analysis of Concepts of Pollution and Taboo*. London: Routledge and Keagan.

Dupey García, Élodie. 2015. "The Materiality of Color in the Body Ornamentation of Aztec Gods." *RES. Anthropology and Aesthetics* 65–66: 72–88.

Durán, Diego. 1971. *Book of the Gods and Rites and the Ancient Calendar*. Translated and edited by Fernando Horcasitas and Doris Heyden. Norman: University of Oklahoma Press.

———. 1984. *Historia de las Indias de Nueva España e islas de Tierra Firme*. 2 vols. Edited by Ángel M. Garibay. Mexico City: Porrúa.

Erdheim, Mario. 1978. "Transformaciones de la ideología mexica en realidad social." In *Economía política e ideología en el México prehispánico*, edited by Pedro Carrasco and Johanna Broda, 195–220. Mexico City: Centro de Investigaciones Superiores del Instituto Nacional de Antropología e Historia, Editorial Nueva Imagen.

Fausto, Carlo. 2000. "Of Enemies and Pets: Warfare and Shamanism in Amazonia." *American Ethnologist* 26, no. 4: 933–56.

———. 2007. "Feasting on People. Eating Animals and Humans in Amazonia." *Current Anthropology* 48, no. 4: 497–530.

Frazer, James George. 1920. *The Golden Bough: A Study in Magic and Religion*. Vol. 1, *The Magic Art and the Evolution of Kings*. 3rd ed. London: MacMillan.

Fujigaki Lares, Alejandro. 2015. "La disolución de la muerte y el sacrificio. Contrastes de las máquinas de transformaciones y mediaciones de los rarámuri y los mexicas." PhD diss., Universidad Nacional Autónoma de México.

Glockner, Julio. 1996. *Los volcanes sagrados: mitos y rituales en Popocatépetl y la Iztaccíhuatl*. Mexico City: Grijalbo.

Goldman, Marcio. 2016. "Cosmopolíticas, etno-ontologías y otras epistemologías." *Cuadernos de Antropología Social* 44: 27–35.

Graulich, Michel. 1987. *Mythes et rituels du Mexique ancien préhispanique*. Brussels: Académie Royale de Belgique.

———. 1999. *Ritos aztecas. Las fiestas de las veintenas*. Mexico City: Instituto Nacional Indigenista.

Henare, Amiria, Martin Holbraad, and Sari Wastell. 2007. "Introduction." In *Thinking Through Things. Theorizing Artefacts Ethnographically*, edited by AmiriaHenare, Martin Holbraad, and Sari Wastell. London, New York: Routledge.

Holbraad, Martin and Morten Axel Pedersen. 2017. *The Ontological Turn, An Anthropological Exposition*. Cambridge: Cambridge University Press.

Houseman, Michael, and Carlo Severi. 1998. *Naven or the Other Self. A Relational Approach to Ritual Action*. Leiden: Brill.

Humphrey, Carolyn, and James Laidlaw. 1994. *The Archetypal Actions of Ritual. A Theory of Ritual Illustrated by the Jain Rite of Worship*. Oxford: Clarendon Press.

Knab, Tim J. 1991. "Geografía del inframundo." *Estudios de Cultura Náhuatl* 21: 31–57.

Kohl, Karl-Heinz. 1988–2001. "Naturmythologie." In *Handbuch religionswissenschaftlicher Grundbegriffe*. Vol. 4, edited by Hubert Cancik, Burkhard Gladigow, and Matthias Samuel Laubscher. Stuttgart: Kohlhammer.

Kopenawa, Davi, and Bruce Albert. 2010. *The Falling Sky. Words of a Yanomami Shaman*. Cambridge, MA: Harvard University Press.

Leenhardt, Maurice. 1997. *Do kamo. La persona y el mito en el mundo melanesio*. Barcelona: Paidós.

Lira, Regina. 2014. "L'alliance entre la Mère Maïs et le Frère Aîné Cerf: action, chant et image dans un rituel wixárika (huichol) du Mexique." PhD diss., École des Hautes Études en Sciences Sociales.

López Austin, Alfredo. 1980. *Cuerpo humano e ideología. Las concepciones de los antiguos nahuas*. Mexico City: Universidad Nacional Autónoma de México- Instituto de Investigaciones Antropológicas.

———. 1994. *Tamoanchan y Tlalocan*. Mexico City: Fondo de Cultura Económica.

Lorente, David. 2011. *La razzia cósmica. Una concepción nahua sobre el clima*. Mexico City: Centro de Investigaciones y Estudios Superiores en Antropología Social.

Lumholtz, Carl S. 1900. "Symbolism of the Huichol Indians." *Memoirs of the American Museum of Natural History* 3, no. 1: 1–291.

———. 1902. *Unknown Mexico. A Record of Five Year's Exploration Among the Tribes of the Western Sierra Madre; in the Tierra Caliente of Tepic and Jalisco; and Among the Tarascos of Michoacan*. 2 vols. New York: Charles Scribner's Sons.

Mannhardt, Wilhelm. 1868. *Die Korndämonen. Beitrag zur germanischen Sittenkunde*. Berlin: Ferdinand Dümmler's Verlagsbuchhandlung.

———. 1875. *Wald- und Feldkulte 1. Der Baumkultus der Germanen und ihrer Nachbarstämme. Mythologische Untersuchung*. Berlin: Gebrüder Borntraeger.

———. 1877. *Wald- und Feldkulte 2. Antike Wald- und Feldkulte aus nordeuropäicher Überlieferung*. Berlin: Gebrüder Borntraeger.

Mazzetto, Elena. 2016. "La veintena de Ochpaniztli. Una posible metáfora de crecimiento del maíz en los espacios del Templo Mayor de México-Tenochtitlan." In *El maíz nativo en México. Una aproximación desde los estudios rurales*, edited by Ignacio López Moreno and Ivonne Vizcarra Bordi, 65–92. Mexico City: Universidad Autónoma Metropolitana.

Müller, Friedrich Max. 1879. *Lectures on the Origin and Growth of Religion as Illustrated by the Religions of India*. New York: Charles Scribner's Sons.

———. 1907. *Natural Religion: the Gifford Lectures Delivered before the University of Glasgow in 1888*. London and New York: Longmans, Green.

Neurath, Johannes. 2002. *Las fiestas de la Casa Grande: procesos rituales, cosmovisión y estructura social en una comunidad huichola*. Mexico City: Universidad de Guadalajara, Instituto Nacional de Antropología e Historia.

———. 2004. "El doble personaje del planeta Venus en las religiones indígenas del Gran Nayar: mitología, ritual agrícola y sacrificio." *Journal de la Société des Américanistes* 90, no. 1: 93–118.

———. 2007. *Arte antiguo cora y huichol. La colección de Konrad T. Preuss, Artes de México* 85. México: Artes de México.

———. 2008. "La iconografía del complejo ceremonial del sureste y el sacrificio de flechamiento pawnee: contribuciones analíticas desde la perspectiva mesoamericanista." In *Por los caminos del maíz. Mito, ritual y cosmovisión en la periferia septentrional de Mesoamérica*, Biblioteca Mexicana, edited by JohannesNeurath, 173–214. Mexico City: Consejo Nacional para la Cultura y las Artes, Fondo de Cultura Económica.

———. 2013. *La vida de las imágenes. Arte huichol*. Mexico City: Consejo Nacional para la Cultura y las Artes, Artes de México.

———. 2015a. "Shifting Ontologies in Huichol Ritual and Art." *Anthropology and Humanism* 40, no. 1: 58–70.

———. 2015b. "Complex Relations and Modifications of Visibility. Ceremonial Pits and Sacrificial Stones among the Huichols." *Cahiers d'anthropologie sociale* 11: 70–83.

Neurath, Johannes, and Jesús Jáuregui. 1998. "La expedición de Konrad Theodor Preuss al Nayarit (1905–1907) y su contribución a la mexicanística." In *Fiestas, literatura y magia en el Nayarit. Ensayos sobre coras, huicholes y mexicaneros de Konrad Theodor Preuss*, edited by Jesús Jáuregui and Johannes Neurath, 15–60. Mexico City: Centro de Estudios Mexicanos y Centroamericanos, Instituto Nacional Indigenista.

Nowotny, Karl A. 1961. *Tlacuilolli. Die mexikanischen Bilderhandschriften*. Berlin: Gebrüder Mann Verlag.

Olivier, Guilhem. 2003. *Mockeries and Metamorphoses of an Aztec God: Tezcatlipoca, "Lord of the Smoking Mirror."* Translated by Michel Besson. Niwat: University of Colorado Press.

———. 2015. *Cacería, sacrificio y poder en Mesoamérica. Tras las huellas de Mixcóatl, "Serpiente de Nube."* Mexico City: Fondo de Cultura Económica, Universidad Nacional Autónoma de México, Centro de Estudios Mexicanos y Centroamericanos.

Pitarch, Pedro. 2010. *The Jaguar and the Priest. An Ethnography of Tzeltal Souls*. Austin: University of Texas Press.

———. 2012. "La ciudad de los espíritus europeos. Notas sobre la modernidad de los mundos virtuales indígenas." In *Modernidades indígenas*, edited by Pedro Pitarch and Gemma Orobitg, 61–87. Madrid: Iberomericana Vervuert.

———. 2013. *La cara oculta del pliegue. Ensayos en antropología indígena*. Mexico City: Consejo Nacional para la Cultura y las Artes, Artes de México.

Pitrou, Perig. 2015. "Life as a Process of Making in the Mixe Highlands (Oaxaca, Mexico): Towards a 'General Pragmatics' of Life." *Journal of the Royal Anthropological Institute* 21, no. 1: 86–105.

Pöge-Alder, Kathrin. 2007. *Märchenforschung: Theorien, Methoden, Interpretationen.* Tübingen: Günter Narr Verlag.

Preuss, Konrad Theodor. 1904a. "Phallische Fruchtbarkeits-Dämonen als Träger des altmexikanischen Dramas. Ein Beitrag zur Urgeschichte des mimischen Weltdramas." *Archiv für Anthropologie. Organ der Deutschen Gesellschaft für Anthropologie, Ethnologie und Urgeschichte,* Neue Folge 1, no. 3: 129–88.

———. 1904b. "Der Ursprung des Menschenopfers in Mexiko." *Globus. Illustrierte Zeitschrift für Länder- und Völkerkunde* 86, no. 7: 108–19.

———. 1905a. "Der Kampf der Sonne mit den Sternen in Mexiko." *Globus. Illustrierte Zeitschrift für Länder- und Völkerkunde* 87, no. 7: 136–40.

———. 1905b. "Der Einfluß der Natur auf die Religion in Mexiko und den Vereinigten Staaten." *Zeitschrift der Gesellschaft für Erdkunde Berlin* 5–6: 361–80, 433–60.

———. 1906. "Der dämonische Ursprung des griechischen Dramas erläutert durch mexikanische Parallelen." *Neue Jahrbücher für das klassische Alterthum, Geschichte und deutsche Literatur und für Pädagogik,* B. G. Teubner, Leipzig, Jahrgang 1906, 2. *Abteilung,* 18, no. 3: 161–93.

———. 1910. "Naturbeobachtungen in den Religionen des mexikanischen Kulturkreises." *Zeitschrift für Ethnologie* 42, no. 5: 793–804.

———. 1912. *Die Nayarit-Expedition. Textaufnahmen und Beobachtungen unter mexikanischen Indianern 1. Die Religion der Cora-Indianer in Texten nebst Wörterbuch Cora-Deutsch.* Leipzig: B. G. Teubner.

———. 1914. *Die geistige Kultur der Naturvölker.* Leipzig: B.G. Teubner.

———. 1929. "Das Frühlingsfest im Alten Mexiko und bei den Mandan Indianern der Vereinigten Staaten von Nordamerika." In *Donum Natalicum Schrijnen. Verzameling van opstellen door oud-leerlingen en bevriende vakgenooten opgedragen aan Mgr. Prof. Dr. Jos. Schrijnen bij Gelegenheid van zijn zestigsten verjaardag 3 Mei 1929,* 825–37. Chartres: Imprimerie Durand.

———. 1930. *Der Unterbau des Dramas.* Vorträge der Bibliothek Warburg VII. Leipzig: B. G. Teubner.

———. 1933. *Der religiöse Gehalt der Mythen.* Tübingen: J.C.B. Mohr.

———. 1998. *Fiesta, literatura y magia en el Nayarit. Ensayos sobre coras, huicholes y mexicaneros de Konrad Theodor Preuss,* edited by Jesús Jáuregui and Johannes Neurath. Mexico City: Centro de Estudios Mexicanos y Centroamericanos, Instituto Nacional Indigenista.

Questa Rebolledo, Alessandro. 2013. "Visible Dancers and Invisible Hunters. Divination, Dancing and Masking among the Highland Nawa of Eastern Mexico." Paper presented at the conference *The culture of invention in the Americas,* May 21–23, 2013, Ex-convento de la Coria, Trujillo (Spain).

———. 2016. "Mining Spirits. An Ethnographic Account of Modernity and Indigenous Knowledge in the Northern Highlands of Puebla, Mexico." Paper presented at the *115th Annual Meeting of the American Anthropological Association,* November 16–20, 2016, Minneapolis.

Ragot, Nathalie. 2016. "Chicomecóatl. La diosa del maíz en los códices del Centro de México." In *Los códices mesoamericanos. Registros de religión, política y sociedad,* edited by Miguel Ángel Ruz Barrio and Juan José Batalla Rosado, 137–50. Toluca: El Colegio Mexiquense.

Reyes, J. Antonio, 2015. "The Perpetual Return of the Ancestors: An Ethnographic Account." PhD diss., University of St. Andrew's.

Rio, Knut. 2007. "Denying the Gift: Aspects of Ceremonial Exchange and Sacrifice on Ambrym Island, Vanuatu." *Anthropological Theory* 7, no. 4: 449–70.

Rodríguez Venegas, Citlali. 2014. "La ilusión turística: mazatecos, niños santos y güeros en Huautla de Jiménez, Oaxaca." Master's thesis, Universidad Nacional Autónoma de México.

Romero, Laura. 2011. "Ser humano y hacer el mundo: La terapéutica nahua en la Sierra Negra de Puebla." PhD diss., Universidad Nacional Autónoma de México.

Sahagún, Bernardino de. 1950–82. *Florentine Codex: General History of the Things of New Spain, Fray Bernardino de Sahagún.* Translated with notes and illustrations by Arthur J. O. Anderson and Charles E. Dibble. 13 vols. Monographs of The School of American Research and the Museum of New Mexico 14. Santa Fe: The School of American Research, University of Utah Press.

————. 1988. *Historia general de las cosas de Nueva España.* Edited by Alfredo López Austin and Josefina García Quintana. 2 vols. Madrid: Alianza editorial.

————. 1997. *Primeros Memoriales.* Edited and translated by Thelma Sullivan. Completed and revised, with additions, by Henry B. Nicholson, Arthur J. O. Anderson, Charles E. Dibble, Eloise Quiñones Keber, and Wayne Ruwet. Norman: University of Oklahoma Press.

Scott, Michael. 2013. "Nondualism is Philosophy Not Ethnography: For the Motion. Steps to a Methodological Nondualism." In *Critique of Anthropology* "The 2011 annual debate—non-dualism is philosophy not ethnography," edited by Soumaya Venkatesan, Keir Martin, Michael W. Scott, Christopher Pinney, Nikolai Ssorin-Chaikov, Joanna Cook, and Marilyn Strathern (The Group for Debates in Anthropological Theory (GDAT), The University of Manchester), 33, no. 3: 300–60.

Seler, Eduard. 1899. "Die Achtzehn Jahresfeste der Mexikaner (Erste Hälfte)." *Veröffentlichungen aus dem Kgl. Museum für Völkerkunde* 6: 67–209.

————. 1901. "Die Huichol-Indianer des Staates Jalisco in Mexiko." *Mitteilungen der Anthropologischen Gesellschaft in Wien* 31: 138–63.

————. 1905. "Einige Bemerkungen zu dem Aufsatze Dr. K. Th. Preuss über den Einfluss der Natur auf die Religionen in Mexiko und in den Vereinigten Staaten." *Zeitschrift der Gesellschaft für Erdkunde zu Berlin* 5: 461–63.

————. 1907. "Einiges über die natürlichen Grundlagen der mexikanischen Mythen." *Zeitschrift für Ethnologie. Organ der Berliner Gessellschaft für Anthropologie, Ethnologie und Urgeschichte* 39: 1–41.

————. 1923. "Mythos und Religion der alten Mexikaner." In *Gesammelte Abhandlungen zur Amerikanischen Sprach- und Alterthumskunde* 4, edited by Caecilie Seler-Sachs, 1–156. Berlin: Behrend.

Severi, Carlo. 1996. *La memoria ritual. Locura e imagen del blanco en una tradición chamánica amerindia.* Quito: Ediciones Abya-Yala.

————. 2001. "Cosmology, Crisis, and Paradox: On the White Spirit in the Kuna Shamanic Tradition." In *Disturbing Remains: Memory, History, and Crisis in the Twentieth Century,* edited by Michael S. Roth and Charles G. Salas, 178–206. Los Angeles: Getty Research Institute.

————. 2002. "Memory, Reflexivity and Belief. Reflexions on the Ritual Use of Language." *Social Anthropology* 10, no. 1: 23–40.

Soustelle, Jacques. 1955. *La vida cotidiana de los aztecas en vísperas de la Conquista.* Mexico City: Fondo de Cultura Económica.

Tambiah, Stanley J. 1990. *Magic, Science, Religion, and the Scope of Rationality.* Cambridge: Cambridge University Press.

Taylor, Anne-Christine. 2003. "Les masques de la mémoire. Essai sur la fonction des peintures corporelles jivaro." *L'Homme. Revue française d'anthropologie* 165: 223–48.

Torres Cisneros, Gustavo. 2001. "Les visages de Soleil el Lune (Xëën po'o yë' ajkxy ywiinjëjp): configurations calendaires, mythiques et rituels du temps chez les Mixes de l'Oaxaca, Mexique." PhD diss., École Pratique des Hautes Études.

Turner, Victor. 1967. *The Forest of Symbols. Aspects of Ndembu Ritual.* Ithaca, NY: Cornell University Press.

Usener, Hermann. 1904. "Heilige Handlung." *Archiv für Religionswissenschaft* 7: 281–339.

Valdovinos, Margarita. 2008. "Les chants de *mitote náyeri*. Une pratique discursive au sein de l'action rituelle." PhD diss., Université Paris X.

Viveiros de Castro, Eduardo. 1992. *From the Enemy's Point of View: Humanity and Divinity in an Amazonian Society*. Chicago: University of Chicago Press.

———. 1998. "Cosmological Deixis and Amerindian Perspectivism." *Journal of the Royal Anthropological Institute* N.S. 4: 469–88.

———. 2015. "Who's Afraid of the Ontological Wolf? Some Comments on an Ongoing Anthropological Debate." *Cambridge Anthropology* 33, no. 1: 2–17.

Wagner, Roy. 1972. *Habu: The Innovation of Meaning in Daribi Religion*. Chicago: University of Chicago Press.

Warburg, Aby. 2010. *Werke*. Frankfurt: Suhrkamp.

Wittgenstein, Ludwig. 1996. *Observaciones a La Rama Dorada de Frazer*. Madrid: Tecnos.

Wolf, Eric W. 1999. *Envisiong Power. Ideologies of Dominance and Crisis*. Berkeley: University of California Press.

PART II

Ritual Actors and Activities in the *Veintena* Festivals

CHAPTER FIVE

Haab' Festivals among the Postclassic Maya

Evidence from Ethnohistoric Sources and the Madrid Codex

GABRIELLE VAIL

Ethnohistoric materials from the Maya area clearly point to the importance of a festival calendar based on the *haab'*, or 365-day year. Among the Maya, like the highland Mexican cultures, this 365-day period was divided into 18 units of 20 days (which are called "months" in the literature), and a five-day period of transition ending one year and initiating the next.

Descriptions of the monthly festivals appear in the compilation of writings known to us today as the *Relación de las cosas de Yucatán*, attributed to Diego de Landa, the second bishop of Yucatan (Gates 1978; Landa 1941). Thanks to the penetrating research of Matthew Restall and John Chuchiak, we now know that the texts brought together as the *Relación* were compiled from multiple sources in the years leading up to the mid-sixteenth century (Restall and Chuchiak 2002). The Late Postclassic Maya codices, written perhaps 100 to 150 years before the texts in Landa's *Relación*, provide an earlier source of information about the monthly *haab'* festivals (Vail 2002). It is interesting that they, too, were painted by many hands and represent a compilation of texts (or in this case, almanacs), rather than a single-authored work.

As detailed in what I will call Landa's *Relación* for the sake of simplicity, the festival calendar began with 1 Pop, a day referenced in the *Relación* as New Year's day. This marks the conclusion of a five-day period preceding it known as Wayeb', in which a series of termination rituals were performed, as well as a transfer of power from one "yearbearer" to another. In the mid-sixteenth century, the year-bearers were the days K'an, Muluk, Ix, and Kawak in the 260-day *tzolk'in* calendar (in other words, these four days were the only ones that could correspond with 1 Pop in successive years). This yearbearer set is represented in various almanacs in the Madrid Codex, including that on pages 34–37 (see Bricker 1997).

An earlier set, corresponding to the days B'en, Etz'nab', Ak'b'al, and Lamat, is highlighted in a number of different contexts in the Paris and Dresden codices, such as the yearbearer pages on Dresden 25–28 and Paris 19–20; it also occurs in certain Classic period texts, including a mural from the northern lowland site of Ek' Balam (Lacadena 2004; Taube 1988; Vail and Looper 2015). Because these latter texts were generally concerned with dynastic matters, however, there is little emphasis on rituals pertaining to the *haab'* calendar in Classic period contexts.

The 18 months of the Maya *haab'* are illustrated in Figure 5.1, where the date 1 Pop is followed 20 days later by 1 Wo; after another 20 days, one arrives at 1 Sip, then 1 Sotz', and so forth. To my knowledge, there is only one text from the Classic period that provides a *haab'* count. This is a mural text painted in a

Figure 5.1. Glyphs representing the 18 months of the *haab'*, plus the five-day period of Wayeb'. Source: Morley 1975, Fig. 20.

beautiful calligraphic hand from Room 22 of the Acropolis of Ek' Balam, a Classic period site located in the eastern Yucatan peninsula (Lacadena 2004, 63–67).

Ek' Balam differs from most other Classic period sites in that the majority of its texts are painted (on murals and capstones), rather than being carved on stone monuments (although it does have several of those as well). It appears to have ties to sites in the southern and western lowlands, rather than strictly with sites in its more immediate vicinity. There is a strong emphasis on Classic period dynastic traditions similar to those emphasized in the southern Maya lowlands. Nevertheless, Ek' Balam's texts also have certain elements that very clearly tie them to later traditions from the northern lowland region, such as serpent-style numbers and an emphasis on recording counts in the *haab'* calendar (Lacadena 2004, personal communication, in H. Bricker and V. Bricker 2011, 508).

The mural text in question highlights the beginning of nine months at 20-day intervals, which are linked to the completion of a *tun*, or 360-day period, on 9.17.13.0.0, or November 13, AD 783. This encompasses the end of a Lamat year, with the *haab'* dates 1 Pax, 1 K'ayab', and 1 Kumk'u recorded, and the beginning of a B'en year 25 days later (Wayeb' is not mentioned). The start of the *haab'* on 1 Pop corresponds with 8 B'en in the *tzolk'in* calendar (Lacadena 2004). This date is also referenced on the Dresden yearbearer pages (25–28), where it is associated with the patron of the outgoing year K'awiil, the god of sustenance, and the patron of the incoming year K'in Ahaw, or Lord Sun. The prophecies for B'en years are extremely negative, including "misfortune to the maize" and predictions of drought. The rituals done to appease the deities include offerings of food and incense to both the outgoing and incoming yearbearer patrons and the sacrifice of a turkey.

What we see pictured in the Dresden almanac matches descriptions from ethnohistoric sources (in particular, Landa's *Relación de las cosas de Yucatán*) in a number of respects, including processions along roads, ceremonies performed in the "temple" or house of the *principal,* and others at the entrance to the community. Landa does not describe the setting up of a tree, however, which is an important element on all four of the Dresden yearbearer pages (Taube 1988, 239). The reason for such discrepancies is not clear, but it is interesting to note that the colonial-period Yucatec manuscripts called the *Books of Chilam Balam* describe the setting up of world trees at each of the four quarters in order to hold up the sky following a great flood. Birds are said to have perched on the trees to initiate the new creation (Knowlton 2010, 65). Although not shown in the Dresden almanac, these birds may be referenced in the hieroglyphic caption to the lower register on the Dresden yearbearer pages, where we are told that "The first [or great] *itzam(na) muut?/ kokaaj? te'* [tree] was set up in the east," or north, west, or south, depending on the year. The name of the tree has been read in a variety of ways—often just as Itzamna, the name of the male Yucatec Maya creator deity, but some scholars believe this is an avian form of the deity, known as Itzam Muut or Kokaaj, who is sometimes referred to as the Principal Bird Deity. This being is commonly associated with world trees in iconographic compositions from the Late Preclassic period, such as the San Bartolo murals, to Classic period Palenque and the Postclassic codices (Saturno et al. 2010). This clearly reflects a broader Mesoamerican mythological tradition, as evidenced by page 1 of the Mexican *Codex Fejérváry-Mayer*, with its depictions of the four world trees with birds perched on top (*Códice Fejérváry-Mayer* 1994, pl. 1; see http://www.famsi.org/research/graz/fejervary_mayer/img_page01.html). This scene takes place following the sacrifice of the god Tezcatlipoca, who is associated with the first of five creations in the central Mexican calendar (Graulich 1997, 65, citing "Historia de los mexicanos por sus pinturas").

Unfortunately, the Ek' Balam text makes no mention of the events that took place on the *haab'* dates recorded, but ethnohistoric sources clearly identify Pop as a period of renewal (e.g. Gates 1978, 70–71). Subsequent dates highlighted in the mural include the beginnings of the following months: 1 Wo, 1 Sip, 1 Sotz', 1 Tzek, and 1 Xul. Ethnohistoric sources describe the particulars of the festivals celebrated in these months (Table 5.1), but a question immediately comes to mind when we consider the temporal differences between the timing of the initiation of each "month" in the Late Classic period (when 1 Pop corresponds with late January) and in the mid-sixteenth century, when Landa's account was written (when 1 Pop corresponds with late July in the Gregorian calendar). Significantly, there is a half-year difference in the timing, which raises the question of whether the festivals were shifted over time so that they were seasonally significant, or whether they were fossilized and always performed in the same month. If they were fossilized, there must have been substantial seasonal disparities between the festivals as originally practiced and those recorded in ethnohistoric sources. Evidence presented by Harvey and Victoria Bricker suggests that this was the case, as they find that the halfway point of the *haab'*—0 Yax—was measured against the summer solstice to determine the movement of the former against the latter over time (H. Bricker and V. Bricker 2011, 682–83; also V. Bricker and H. Bricker 1988). If their interpretation is correct, then this indicates that, among the Postclassic Maya at least, corrections were not made to keep *haab'* rituals aligned with seasonal events.

While an interesting topic for consideration, this is not the primary focus of my discussion. Instead, I provide an overview of the *haab'* festivals referenced in ethnohistoric sources and their potential correlates in the Late Postclassic Maya codices, which were likely produced within approximately 100 or 150 years of when Landa's *Relación* was compiled.

Table 5.1. *Haab'* festivals recorded in Landa's *Relación*

Month	Festival	Principal Activities	Notes
Pop	General festival Renewal of household items Purification ritual	– fasting; cleansing – stretching of rope (purification ceremony) – offerings of food and drink – prayers – lighting new fire; burning incense – feast	Priest assisted by four "chaaks"
Wo	Purification of books For priests, "physicians," and "sorcerers"	Ritual preparations (rope ceremony, offerings, prayers, lighting new fire, burning incense) – anointing of books – prognostications (from books) – feast	Invoked deity K'inich-ahaw Itzamna (Itzamna in aspect as sun god)
Sip	Purification of implements	Ritual preparations (see above)	
	(a) For physicians and sorcerers	(a) casting lots (prognostications) – invoking gods of medicine – amulets and idols covered with blue bitumen – feast	
	(b) For hunters	(b) invoking gods of hunt – arrow, skull of deer anointed with blue pitch – dancing; bloodletting ritual – feast	
	(c) For fishermen	(c) invoking gods of fishing – anointing fishing tackle with blue bitumen – bloodletting ritual and dance – blessing and setting up tree trunk – journey to coast to fish	
Sotz'	For beehive owners	– fasting	Preparation for Tzek festival

Continued

Table 5.1. Continued

Month	Festival	Principal Activities	Notes
Tzek	For beehive owners	– offerings to four Chaaks (platters with balls of incense; rims painted with images of honey) – feast	Bakabs/Hobnil as patrons
Xul	In honor of K'uk'ulkan	– fasting – general procession; included "comedians" – gathering at temple of K'uk'ulkan – ritual preparations; incense burned to idols – dances and offerings	Five-day festival beginning on 16th of Xul; held at Maní
Yaxk'in	Preparation for Mol festival Purification of implements Initiation ceremony	– ritual preparations – implements, house posts anointed with blue pitch – nine blows given to children by priestess Ixmol	Blows given to children so they would grow up to be excellent craftsmen
Mol	For beehive owners Preparation of wooden images of deities	– fasting – acquiring cedar wood – building of thatched hut – burning incense to Akantun deities; letting blood	Intended for gods to provide flowers for bees.
Ch'en	Conclusion of making of wooden deity images	– cleansing – ritual preparations as per other ceremonies – delivery of images to owner – feasting	
Yax	Renovation of temple (ok nah), terra cotta deity images, and their braziers	– consulted predictions of Bakabs – renewed terra cotta figures and braziers – built a new house [for the "idols"?] or renovated the old one – recorded text on wall of these events	Celebrated in either Ch'en or Yax Similar to rituals performed by Lacandón Maya to renew incense burners
Sak	For hunters		To appease gods
Keh			Nothing listed

Table 5.1. Continued

Month	Festival	Principal Activities	Notes
Mak	Festival to the Chaaks and Itzamna	– cleaning and arraying of temple – assembly in courtyard – ritual preparations as per other ceremonies – lower step spread with mud from well – upper steps decorated with blue pitch – feasting	
K'ank'in			Nothing listed
Muwan	For owners of cacao plantations	– gathering at one of plantations – sacrifice of a spotted dog; burning of incense – offerings of blue iguanas, birds' feathers, and game – feasting	In honor of gods Ek' Chuwah, Chaak, and Hobnil
Pax	For war chief	– conducting of war chief to temple – offerings and gifts of incense – war dances – feasting	Lasted over a five-day period
K'ayab'			Nothing listed
Kumk'u		– fasting – preparation of offerings	Preparations for Wayeb'

The discussion of the festival calendar in Landa's text begins with a description of the renewal rituals associated with the start of the year. At the time, 1 Pop fell on July 16th in the Julian calendar then in use (corresponding to July 26th in the Gregorian calendar). This was a period of renewal of household utensils and other items, and involved sweeping the houses and leaving all of the debris on a waste heap outside of town, where it was left untouched. Particular emphasis was placed on the sanctification of ritual space (by stretching a cord around the perimeter of a temple courtyard), and the lighting of a new fire. These two activities were performed at the start of many of the monthly festivals, which were held by practitioners of various professions, including healers, hunters, beekeepers, cacao growers, and so forth. Other commonalities among the ceremonies included the burning of incense and offerings of food to the deities. Additionally, a great many of the *haab'* ceremonies referenced in the *Relación* were focused on the renewal of various items, which involved structures, images of deities, household items, pottery vessels, etc. (Gates 1978, 70–81). Beginning with the earliest investigations (Förstemann 1902; Thomas 1882), codical researchers have suggested connections between the descriptions of *haab'* rituals included in Landa's *Relación* and almanacs from the Maya codices, in particular the Madrid Codex. Although the majority of discussions focus on the Wayeb' and Pop ceremonies (e.g. H. Bricker and V. Bricker 2011, 120–42; Förstemann 1902; Taube 1988; Thomas 1882; Tozzer in Landa 1941), connections have also been drawn to a number of other possible *haab'* rituals, including Sip festivals focusing on deer and deer hunters (Bill 1997); the *ok nah* ceremony (renovation of the temple) celebrated in Yax or Ch'en (Vail 2002); festivals performed by beekeepers in Tzek or Mol (Vail 1994); and the renovation of wooden images of the deities in Mol and Ch'en (Ciaramella 2004).

Before proceeding, it is important to emphasize that *haab'* dates are rarely recorded in Maya codical almanacs; in most cases, therefore, the assignment of an almanac to a particular festival is based on iconographic and hieroglyphic evidence, rather than calendrical information provided by the scribe. This is the case, for example, with the almanacs on Madrid 50b and 51c (Figure 5.2a), which have been attributed to the Sip ceremony (Bill 1997) based on Landa's description: "The next day the hunters gathered in the house of one of them ... The hunters invoked the gods of the chase ... ; they distributed the incense, which they then threw in the brazier; while it burned each one took an arrow and the skull of a deer, which the assistants anointed with blue pitch; some then danced with these ..." (Gates 1978, 72). The correspondences between the textual description and what is depicted in the almanacs (the arrow and the skull of a deer) are incontrovertible, and the figure pictured in the two almanacs can be clearly identified as the god Ah Sip, who is associated with the hunt. The same deity appears as the base of a tree in an almanac which shows a deer being trapped by a snare (Figure 5.2b), and he wears the skin of a peccary in another almanac (Figure 5.2c), where he stands in front of an incense burner in which rubber incense is being burned. Each of these almanacs may concern a different aspect of the Sip hunters' festival.

Drilling new fire, as we have seen, is a common component of many of the *haab'* rituals. This act is represented in several of the Madrid almanacs, in two cases immediately following the yearbearer almanacs (suggesting the possibility of a Pop date), although the fact that these almanacs occur within the section related to deer hunting and trapping suggests that this is another possible association. The third almanac picturing the drilling of new fire occurs in the same section as the two almanacs discussed previously showing the Sip ritual dance. Again, it is difficult to know if it was meant to represent the Pop or Sip ritual, or whether it could have had both associations. There is nothing specific to the almanacs that would allow us to make an assignment to one *haab'* ceremony over another.

Figure 5.2. (a) Sip ceremony on Madrid 50b; (b) Sip deity as base of tree on Madrid 45c; (c) Sip deity in costume of peccary on Madrid 39c. Source: *Codex Tro-Cortesianus* 1967, pl. 39, 45, 50 (details). With permission of Museo de América, Madrid.

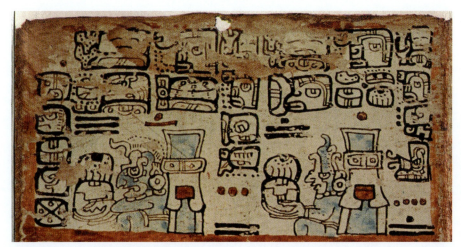

Figure 5.3. Renewal ceremony on Madrid 16a. Source: *Codex Tro-Cortesianus* 1967, pl. 16 (detail). With permission of Museo de América, Madrid.

In the case of the almanac on page 16a of the Madrid Codex (Figure 5.3), however, a renovation ceremony involving the presentation of offerings and painting structures blue that could have a number of different correlates in the *haab'* can be limited more specifically by its hieroglyphic caption. The reference in each of the almanac's four frames to *ok nah* provides a clue that the ritual represented is the ceremony described in Landa's *Relación* as falling in Mol or Ch'en. He refers to this very specifically as the *ok nah* ceremony, which he interprets as renovation of the temple dedicated to the maize gods (Gates 1978, 77). In this context, *ok nah* likely means "to renovate the house," as suggested by the term *ok nabil* in the Colonial Vienna dictionary (V. Bricker 2002, personal communication). Deities pictured or referenced on Madrid 16a include the creator Itzamna, the Death God, the maize deity, and the god of sustenance K'awiil, each of whom is commonly depicted or named in renewal almanacs.

Madrid 19b also illustrates what appears to be a ceremony associated with renewing a community structure, although it is much more complex than the previous example (Figure 5.4). Its format is substantially different from that of more standard almanacs, as it is rendered in a circular format, and it also includes several deities who are not commonly depicted in this context, including the underworld deity God A' and the merchant deity God M. This almanac integrates elements suggesting the conflation of several different activities or ceremonies, including the purification of the structure by stretching a rope around its perimeter, the painting of the structure with blue and red/brown materials, and a bloodletting ritual (the rope is shown passing through the five deities' genitals). Also of interest are the *k'in* "sun" glyph on the rope, the turtle at the apex of the

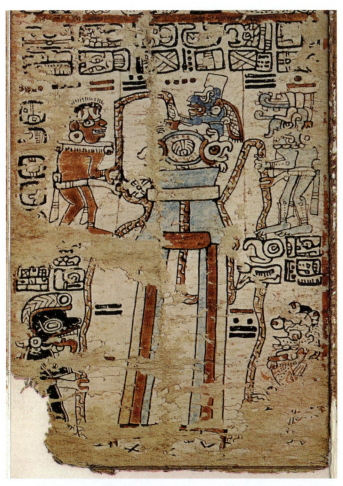

Figure 5.4. Renewal ceremony on Madrid 19b. Source: *Codex Tro-Cortesianus* 1967, pl. 19 (detail). With permission of Museo de América, Madrid.

structure, and the *yax* "first" or "blue/green" glyph on its back. As we have seen, the ceremony for purifying the temple courtyard, in which a rope was stretched around the perimeter by the priest's four assistants, was performed at the start of many ceremonies, including those initiating the new year in Pop. The Pop ceremony is described as follows: "When all were congregated ..., the priest purified the temple, seated in pontifical garments in the middle of the court ... The chacs [rain deities, here identified specifically as the priest's assistants] seated themselves in the four corners, and stretched from one to the other a new rope, inside of which all who had fasted had to enter, in order to drive out the evil spirit" (Gates 1978, 70). A similar description occurs in relation to at least five other monthly festivals and may have played a part in the others as well, although it is not always explicitly mentioned.

Timothy Knowlton and I have previously commented on the turtle with the *yax* glyph on its carapace, which is next to an image of the creator Itzamna (Knowlton and Vail 2010). One of the terms for "turtle" listed in colonial-period sources is *coc* [*kok*], and Landa notes that an "idol" called Yaxcocahmut was associated with the Muluk yearbearer ceremonies. Paired with the *yax* glyph, the whole can be read as "first turtle is Itzamna's prognostication." In this respect, then, we see the turtle man-ifestation of the creator (also highlighted in the name of the K'iche' creator Xpiya*coc*), in place of the bird manifestation seen in the Dresden yearbearer almanacs.

Other interpretations of the turtle appearing in this almanac have been pro-posed, suggesting that it was "read" in this instance as *mak*, one of the meanings of which is "turtle." Kerry Hull and Michael Carrasco favor this interpretation, suggesting that *mak* "turtle" is here serving as a rebus for *mak* "to cover" (Hull and Carrasco 2004). They note that the turtle appears at the apex of the temple, in the same place a capstone would appear to seal off the building when it was being constructed. This is of interest in relation to a series of capstones from Ek' Balam which document the covering or sealing (*mak*) of the chambers in which they were placed (Lacadena 2004; Vail 2019).

Mak is also the name of one of the eighteen months in the *haab'*, suggesting still another possible interpretation of the scene on Madrid 19b. In this case, it is interesting to compare Landa's description of the Mak ritual with what is depicted in the Madrid almanac. He notes that, for the festival, a pyramid was constructed in the center of the court; its lower portion was covered with "mud from the well" (Gates 1978, 78) and the upper levels with blue pitch, similar to what we see depicted in the almanac (with the brown color likely signifying the mud). If the turtle does indeed have a polyvalent reading, then the *yax* glyph on its carapace, meaning "first," may allude to the fact that this is the "founding" event which served as the basis for future Mak ceremonies.

The possibility that the almanac does refer to a foundational ritual receives support from the bloodletting ceremony depicted, in which the five deities each draw a rope through their genitals to provide blood for the sun. This is represented by the *k'in* glyph highlighted in the illustration, which appears to be traveling on the rope. The rope may signify the ecliptic (the path of the sun through the sky), as Susan Milbrath (1999, 76–77, Fig. 3.4b) originally proposed. This imag-ery recalls a myth prevalent in the highland region of central Mexico, recounted in the *Leyenda de los Soles*, in which the deities had to sacrifice themselves in the time before human creation in order to feed the sun so that it could follow its path through the celestial realm ("Legend of the Suns" 1992, 147–49, "The Fifth Sun"; see also Graulich 1997, 131–32). It is plausible to suggest that other Meso-american cultures had a similar mythology, especially in light of stories collected by ethnographers such as Alfonso Villa Rojas from contemporary Yucatec Maya speakers, which tell of a rope that formerly ran through the sky to provide sustenance to the gods (Villa Rojas 1945; see also Miller 1982).

DISCUSSION AND CONCLUSIONS

Ethnohistoric and codical sources detail the intimate relationship between myth and ritual as played out in the *haab'* festivals, a topic exemplified in the work of Graulich (1997, 1999). In the Maya codices, dozens of other almanacs remain to be explored with this relationship in mind. Of interest in this respect are several depicting what appears to be a power struggle being played out by the maize deity (who is seated in the temple as the reigning yearbearer patron) and the black merchant deity who is grasping his fan/emblem of office and holds a flint point at his side, perhaps preparing to strike (Figure 5.5). Might this be a pre-Hispanic version of the events that take place during Semana Santa in parts of the Maya area today (see, e.g. Christenson 2001), where the Mam (representing the forces of chaos) vanquishes the maize deity (Jesus Christ) for the five days of Holy Week

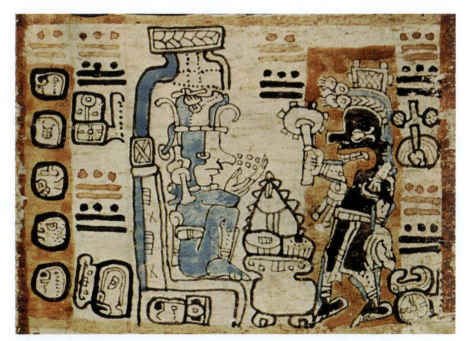

Figure 5.5. Possible yearbearer ceremony on Madrid 51b. Source: *Codex Tro-Cortesianus* 1967, pl. 51 (detail). With permission of Museo de América, Madrid.

(equivalent to the pre-Hispanic Wayeb')? These types of connections seem likely and form the subject of an ongoing investigation.

In recent years, codical specialists have begun the process of decoding the underlying meaning of dozens of almanacs found in the Maya codices, like that depicted in Figure 5.5, which have so far eluded interpretation. Substantial progress has been made, arguing for the utility of a conjunctive approach to analyzing the Maya codical almanacs, based on an evaluation of the calendrical, epigraphic, and iconographic components as an integrated unit tied to activities and rituals that often have correlates in the ethnohistoric literature.

REFERENCES

Bill, Cassandra. 1997. "The Roles and Relationships of God M and Other Black Gods in the Codices, with Specific Reference to Pages 50–56 of the Madrid Codex." In *Papers on the Madrid Codex*, edited by Victoria R. Bricker and Gabrielle Vail, 111–45. New Orleans: Tulane University.

Brasseur de Bourbourg, Charles E. 1869–70. *Manuscrit Troano: études sur le système graphique et la langue des Mayas*. Paris: Imprimerie Impériale.

Bricker, Harvey M., and Victoria R. Bricker. 2011. *Astronomy in the Maya Codices*. Philadelphia: American Philosophical Society.

Bricker, Victoria R. 1997. "The Structure of Almanacs in the Madrid Codex." In *Papers on the Madrid Codex*, edited by Victoria R. Bricker and Gabrielle Vail, 1–25. New Orleans: Tulane University.

Bricker, Victoria R., and Harvey M. Bricker. 1988. "The Seasonal Table in the Dresden Codex and Related Almanacs." *Archaeoastronomy* 12, *JHA* 19: S1–S62.

Christenson, Allen. 2001. *Art and Society in a Highland Maya Community: The Altarpiece of Santiago Atitlan*. Austin: University of Texas Press.

Ciaramella, Mary. 2004. *The Idol-Makers in the Madrid Codex*. Research Reports on Ancient Maya Writing 54. Washington, DC: Center for Maya Research.

Codex Tro-Cortesianus (Codex Madrid). 1967. Commentary by Ferdinand Anders. Graz: ADEVA.

Códice Fejérváry-Mayer. 1994. Edited by Ferdinand Anders, Maarten Jansen, and Luis Reyes García. Graz, Mexico City: ADEVA, Fondo de Cultura Económica.

Förstemann, Ernst. 1902. *Commentar zur Madrider Mayahandscrift: Codex Tro-Cortesianus*. Verlag von L. Danzig: Sauniers Buchandlung.

Gates, William, ed. 1978. *Yucatan Before and After the Conquest by Diego de Landa*. New York: Dover.

Graulich, Michel. 1997. *Myths of Ancient Mexico*. Norman: University of Oklahoma Press.

———. 1999. *Ritos aztecas. Las fiestas de las veintenas*. Mexico City: Instituto Nacional Indigenista.

Hull, Kerry, and Michael Davíd Carrasco. 2004. "'MAK-'Portal' Rituals Uncovered: An Approach to Interpreting Symbolic Architecture and the Creation of Sacred Space among the Maya." In *Continuity and Change: Maya Religious Practices in Temporal Perspective*, edited by Daniel Graña Behrens, Nikolai Grube, Christian M. Prager, Frauke Sachse, Stefanie Teufel, and Elisabeth Wagner, 131–42. Markt Schwaben: Verlag Anton Saurwein.

Knowlton, Timothy. 2010. *Maya Creation Myths: Words and Worlds of the Chilam Balam*. Boulder: University Press of Colorado.

Knowlton, Timothy, and Gabrielle Vail. 2010. "Hybrid Cosmologies in Mesoamerica: A Reevaluation of the Yax Cheel Cab, a Maya World Tree." *Ethnohistory* 37, no. 4: 709–39.

Lacadena, Alfonso. 2004. "The Glyphic Corpus from Ek' Balam, Yucatán, México." FAMSI report, 09 September 2017, http://www.famsi.org/reports/01057/01057LacadenaGarciaGallo01.pdf.

Landa, Diego de. 1941. *Landa's Relación de las Cosas de Yucatán: A Translation.* Edited and translated by Alfred M. Tozzer. Papers of the Peabody Museum of American Archaeology and Ethnology, XVIII. Cambridge, MA: Harvard University Press.

"Legend of the Suns." 1992. In *History and Mythology of the Aztecs: The Codex Chimalpopoca*, edited and translated by John Bierhorst, 139–62. Tucson: University of Arizona Press.

Milbrath, Susan. 1999. *Star Gods of the Maya: Astronomy in Art, Folklore, and Calendars.* Austin: University of Texas Press.

Miller, Arthur G. 1982. *On the Edge of the Sea: Mural Painting at Tancah-Tulum, Quintana Roo, Mexico.* Washington, DC: Dumbarton Oaks.

Morley, Sylvanus G. 1975. *An Introduction to the Study of the Maya Hieroglyphs.* New York: Dover.

Restall, Matthew, and John F. Chuchiak IV. 2002. "Special Commentary: A Reevaluation of the Authenticity of Fray Diego de Landa's Relación de las cosas de Yucatán." *Ethnohistory* 49, no. 3: 651–69.

Saturno, William A., Karl A. Taube, and David Stuart. 2010. *The Murals of San Bartolo, El Petén, Guatemala. Part 2: The West Wall.* Ancient America 10. Barnardsville, NC: Boundary End Archaeology Research Center.

Taube, Karl A. 1988. "The Ancient Yucatec New Year Festival: The Liminal Period in Maya Ritual and Cosmology." PhD diss., Yale University.

Thomas, Cyrus. 1882. *A Study of the Manuscript Troano.* U.S. Department of the Interior, Contributions to North American Ethnology 5. Washington, DC: Government Printing Office.

Vail, Gabrielle. 1994. "A Commentary on the Bee Almanacs in Codex Madrid." In *Códices y documentos sobre México: primer simposio*, edited by Constanza Vega Sosa, 37–68. Mexico City: Instituto Nacional de Antropología e Historia.

———. 2002. *Haab' Rituals in the Maya Codices and the Structure of Maya Almanacs.* Research Reports on Ancient Maya Writing 53. Washington, DC: Center for Maya Research.

———. 2019. "Reconstruyendo rituales de la élite maya en las Tierras Bajas del norte. Una mirada desde los códices mayas y Ek' Balam." *Revista Española de Antropología Americana* 49: 241–63.

Vail, Gabrielle, and Matthew G. Looper. 2015. "World Renewal Rituals among the Postclassic Yucatec Maya and Contemporary Ch'orti' Maya." *Estudios de Cultura Maya* 45: 121–40.

Villa Rojas, Alfonso. 1945. *The Maya of East Central Quintana Roo.* Washington, DC: Carnegie Institution.

CHAPTER SIX

Maize and Flaying in Aztec Rituals

ELENA MAZZETTO

INTRODUCTION

In disciplines like the history of religion and anthropology, models have been frequently applied and interpretations devised regarding rituals specific cultural groups have carried out, based on methodologies different schools have thought to have elaborated. In the case of Mesoamerica, specialists' analyses of the full complement of world creation myth narratives are clearly a branch of Adolph E. Jensen's so-called Morphological-Cultural school. In his studies on sacrifice, the German ethnologist coined the notion of "Dema divinity,"[1] that is, figures present in the mythologies of cultures considered "primitive" and related to the agricultural cycle that were responsible for endowing cultures with land and useful plants. In some of the cases Jensen analyzed, the necessary conditions for this creation were dismembering the bodies and scattering the blood of these supernatural beings (Jensen 1963). Based on this notion of Dema divinity, historians such as Michel Graulich (2000 [1987], 60–61; 2005, 68) and Yolotl González Torres (1990, 105–08) interpreted the famed "rending" myth of the earthly monster Tlalteotl, described in the "Histoyre du Mechique" (Thévet 2002, 151), whose rending led to the creation of the earth's surface.[2]

Another fundamental work for understanding interpretive approaches applied to Mesoamerican religious phenomena is James Frazer's *The Golden Bough*. Its theory of magic as a rudimentary attempt to exert control over nature was based on a principle of imitation, by which if man imitated nature's cycles, nature must do the same. As such, the function of rite was to manipulate plant cycles, entreating their successful development (Frazer 1981, 23–25). The importance ascribed to this annual repetition of symbolic gestures whose end was to imitate natural events is also found in work by Mircea Eliade (2014, 331), for whom man was able to intervene both in the sacred dimension as well as the agricultural cycle through manipulation and conjuration. For Eliade (2014, 344), the significance of agricultural sacrifice coincided with the periodic regeneration of sacred forces, where the act of slaying (i.e. violent death) repeated the act that had occurred at the beginning of time.[3]

The nature-cycle imitation ritual and sacrifice as regeneration are two concepts frequently employed to interpret rites the peoples of the Valley of Mexico realized throughout the *veintena* festival cycles. Some of these ceremonies were interpreted as metaphors for plants' birth and growth processes. The rites recreated and commemorated time's passage as well as rhythms that seasonal changes dictated, like the arrival, and cessation, of rains and winds. In the present study, I shall focus on an analysis of one ceremony (among a number) thought to be nature-imitative, specifically flaying, a practice applied to the bodies of sacrificial victims which occurred at different times throughout the festival cycle that, starting in the nineteenth century, was interpreted as a ritual reproduction of the effects of seasonal changes on the earth.

I shall present the historiography that underlies the study of flaying, revealing how the interpretation of this specific form of human body processing has changed. Despite the fact a close relationship to the agricultural cycle has been maintained, a much more polysemous reading of this religious act has been achieved. I shall particularly focus on the hypothesis that the act of peeling away human skin is a metaphor for peeling away cornhusks. First suggested in the 1940s by Eric Thompson, the theory continues to be favored among specialists in pre-Hispanic Nahua religion. That said, most who have written on the issue identified husking as an action that characterized corn-planting, including the planting that in the sixteenth century took place around March. Based on readings of sixteenth-century colonial-era chronicles, the goal of the present chapter is to apply a critical perspective to that hypothesis. I shall emphasize how the search for exact correspondences among phases relevant to the plant's preparation and the described ritual's staging can lead us to underestimate various significant factors in the natural environment. Temperature and geographical latitude played a highly relevant role in which grain-cultivation techniques were practiced in each of the plant's growth stages.

FLAYING: AGRARIAN METAPHOR OR WAR-RELATED DISPLAY?

One of the Mesoamerican religious practices for which a relationship with corn-growing phases was established is a particular *post-mortem* body treatment applied to certain sacrificial victims, specifically, flaying. Throughout the Mexica solar calendar, the circumstances under which this rite was carried out were distinct and involved both *ixiptla* as well as prisoners of war. During the observance of the solar year cycle, the two main celebrations at which the rite was practiced were Tlacaxipehualiztli, "the flaying of men," and Ochpaniztli, "Sweeping." In 1519, the former took place in March—the annual planting season—whereas the latter occurred in September, a little more than a month before the start of the harvest.

Tlacaxipehualiztli was a *veintena* given over to Huitzilopochtli and Xipe Totec, two deities closely related to war and, in the case Xipe Totec, to corn (Broda 1970; González González 2011; Nicholson 1972). The finest warriors captured on the battlefield were offered up by their overlords and participated in a rite known as *tlahuahuanaliztli*, that is, "scratching" or "scoring." Every prisoner of war, a future sacrificial victim, equipped with mock-weaponry, was made to fight against some of the most distinguished Mexica warriors atop a round stone known as *temalacatl* that featured a central hole. After suffering repeated injuries, the prisoner was sacrificed by having his heart removed (cardiectomy), followed by decapitation and flaying. At this point, victims' skins formed the key element in a series of rites involving a number of social actors. Those suffering from skin or eye diseases pledged to wear the hides for twenty days, as a penance and in the hopes of recovering from their illnesses. Additionally, the captive's overlord (thus the owner of the captive's skin) was the recipient of goods the xipeme-penitents[4] amassed during a collective alms-gathering made throughout the city (Durán 1984, 1: 103–12, 248–50; Sahagún 1950–82, bk 2: 47–60; see also González González 2011, 371–90, Graulich 1999, 279–320;).

Ochpaniztli was a *veintena* dedicated to a number of feminine deities: Toci-Teteo Innan, "Our Grandmother," "Mother of the Gods," an earth goddess; Chicomecoatl or "Seven-Serpent," goddess of sustenance and, especially, of ripe corn; and Atlatonan, a water goddess. In this religious context, these deities' *ixiptla* were sliced open at the throat and flayed. Priests, representing the goddesses, wore the skins. Following the death and rebirth processes brought on by sacrifice, these goddesses participated in different ceremonies (Durán 1984, 1: 131–40, 274–75; Sahagún 1950–82, bk 2: 118–26; see also Brown 1984; Carrasco 2002; DiCesare 2009; Graulich 1999, 89–143). Thus, two opposing yet complementary festivals were undertaken: male victims sacrificed by cardiectomy, in the case of Tlacaxipehualiztli; and female victims' throats slit in the case of Ochpaniztli. The former was a daytime sacrifice, the latter nocturnal.

In an attempt to relate rites carried out during these two months with the agricultural cycle and the seasons in which the two observances took place, authors such as Albert Réville, James Frazer, Eduard Seler, Konrad Theodor Preuss, and John Eric Sidney Thompson compared the rites' different actions with gestures typical of land preparation and corn-growing cycles. In particular, an historiographic review of these intellectuals' work shows how the telluric nature of the goddesses celebrated in the "sweeping" festival, Ochpaniztli, led to the establishment of an association between flaying and the earth's surface. On the other hand, the same rite celebrated in Tlacaxipehualiztli, the parallel *veintena*, having also been seen as related to seasonal changes on the earth's surface, was quickly, and more specifically, linked to corn-plant preparation phases for future agricultural cycles.

In his book *Les religions du Mexique, de l'Amérique centrale et du Pérou*, Réville declares with respect to the Ochpaniztli *veintena* that

> The importance here afforded the victim's flaying appears related to cultivating the soils, whose surfaces must be flayed to plant the next crop (*Cette importance donnée ici à l'écorchement de la victime nous paraît en rapport avec la culture du sol dont il faut écorcher la surface pour y semer la moisson prochaine*). (Réville 1885, 100)

Additionally, according to the French historian, the goddess Toci's flayed skin represented planted soils, while the skin from her thigh, transformed into a mask worn by the *ixiptla* of the corn deity Cinteotl, the goddess's son in the rite, represented completely developed and ripened corn. Thus, the union of the two skins, Toci's and her son Cinteotl's, was critical to achieving a good harvest (Réville 1885, 100). Analyzing flaying as part of a symbolic framework of "deity slaying," Frazer believed the Ochpaniztli's victims were skinned to allow their immediate rebirth after death (Frazer 1981, 666). According to Preuss, the goddess's flaying signified the earth's rejuvenation following harvest (Preuss 1904, cited by Graulich 1999, 106; Seler 1963, 1: 119). In his *Comentarios al Códice Borgia*, Seler detailed the need for a detailed study on this post-sacrifice practice in the overall festival cycle as a means of understanding its true significance:

> The victim's flaying in the autumnal festival, Ochpaniztli, the priest's donning her skin and portraying the goddess in subsequent festival observances, are ceremonies also celebrated in the major spring festival, Tlacaxipehualiztli. In my study of the Mexicans' solar year's eighteen festivals, I assert that the victim's flaying in the spring festival, and another person wearing his skin […] must necessarily mean the earth, as it were, puts on a new skin; it once again is covered in vegetation, rejuvenates […]. But a previous and careful study will be necessary to affirm the autumnal festival can be interpreted in that way as well. To resolve this problem, in my opinion, we must separate two festival elements. First, we have to verify the sacrifice's symbolism and then what, in this case, flaying and the priest's donning the victim's skin mean (*La desolladura de la víctima en esta fiesta de otoño, Ochpaniztli, el ponerse el sacerdote su piel de ésta y representar a la diosa en las siguientes partes de la fiesta, son ceremonias que se celebraban igualmente en la gran fiesta de primavera, Tlacaxipehualiztli. En mi estudio sobre las dieciocho fiestas del año solar de los mexicanos opino que la desolladura de la víctima en esta fiesta de primavera, y el ponerse otra persona su piel ... forzosamente ha de significar que la tierra, valga la frase, se pone una nueva piel, que vuelve a cubrirse de vegetación, que se rejuvenece ... Pero para afirmar que también puede interpretarse de esta manera la fiesta de otoño, hace falta un previo estudio detenido. Para dilucidar este problema, hay que separar, a mi ver, los dos aspectos*

de la fiesta: primero hay que averiguar el simbolismo del sacrificio y luego lo que significa en este caso la desolladura y el ponerse el sacerdote la piel de la víctima). (Seler 1963, 1: 119)

In the case of Tlacaxipehualiztli, given its position in the calendar, rites were interpreted as related to "spring" and nature's renovation. According to Seler (1963, 1: 130), the victim's skin represented the dry season's old hide. *Xipeme* dressed in flayed captives' skins were an image of the countryside's dry conditions. For Preuss, Xipe was the land that was dying and changing skin, like a sown kernel of corn. The *tlahuahuanaliztli*, "scratching" or "scoring," corresponded to carving furrows in the earth in preparation for sowing. Additionally, the sacrifice on the *temalacatl*, the monolith characterized by its round opening, was the metaphorical representation of corn kernels placed into the earth's womb. Flaying, according to Preuss, was a metaphor for stripping corncobs of their kernels (Preuss 1903, in Graulich 1999, 293).

Numerous specialists across successive generations continued to consider Seler's interpretation valid, including Carlos Margáin Araujo (1945, 165), who believed that in Tlacaxipehualiztli the earth is covered in a new, vernal skin. However, as Carlos González González (2011, 249) rightly noted, Margáin Araujo emphasizes that the same *post-mortem* bodily practice in Ochpaniztli could not have the same significance since it was performed in the agricultural cycle's opposite season. Other authors that were partisans of the Selerian interpretation included Walter Krickeberg (1961), Jacques Soustelle (1983), Martha Ilia Nájera Coronado (2014, 215–16), and George Vaillant (1988), among others.

Several researchers, notably Johanna Broda (1970, 257–58), Henry Nicholson (1972, 216), Michel Graulich (1999, 293), and Leonardo López Luján (2005, 218), have pointed out how these interpretations are the product of a nineteenth century mentality, when major differences between growing seasons and techniques both known and employed in Europe and Mesoamerica were not considered. The four seasons seen in Europe are absent in the latter geographical-cultural area. As well, corn-planting agricultural techniques did not call for creating furrows; holes were made in the ground (Hernández 2015, bk 6; Ruiz de Alarcón 1953, 131–33; Sahagún 1950–82, bk 11: 283). Broda (1970, 261–62) emphasized the difference between flayed skin as an element effectively associated with fertility and the act of wearing skin as a metaphor of new earth covered in vegetation (i.e. Seler's theory). The fact that flayed captives' skin was used as an object that could predict a rainy, fertile season is borne out; for example, the *Tovar Calendar* (1951, 22) says that, in Tlacaxipehualiztli, a flayed skin was hung from a temple and a great deal of fat dripping down augured a rainy year.

Henry Nicholson (1972, 216) also encouraged reflection on the possibility that such human body processing, in Xipe Totec observances, might well be linked to a fertility-propitiation rite. This American researcher was the first to note that flaying rites were not exclusive to the aforementioned *veintenas,* nor were they always related to an agricultural imaginary, since other divinities were flayed from time to time. For example, in Tecuilhuitontli an *ixiptla* of Xochipilli was flayed (Batalla Rosado 2009, 95; *Costumbres* 1945, 44; Durán 1984, 1: 155). Sahagún described the deity as "a naked man, flayed" (*un hombre desnudo que está desollado*) (Sahagún 1969, 1: 60; see also González González 2011, 250). During Xocotl Huetzi, a war prisoner was placed for the rite on a mast known as *xocotl,* and after the fall of the pole, his head was flayed (*Códice Magliabechiano,* fol. 37v., see Anders and Jansen 1996, 173).[5] According to Bernardo Ortiz de Montellano, flaying and the practice of wearing flayed skins was meant to bring therapeutic relief for those ill with skin and eye diseases. Such penitents vowed to wear the skin for the 20-day *veintena* that came after Tlacaxipehualiztli (i.e. Tozoztontli), hoping to cure these illnesses (Ortiz de Montellano 1990, 163).

Tlacaxipehualiztli victims' skins were taken from publically vanquished and sacrificed prisoners of war while Toci-Teteo Innan's skin, during Ochpaniztli, was involved in numerous ritual combats. In light of the above, other specialists have not hesitated to consider flaying a rite closely linked to the sphere of warfare. Davíd Carrasco drew attention to the major role of Toci-Teteo Innan's skin as it related to Mexica warfare, forming the center of ritualized war games (Carrasco 2002, 212–18). Her thigh skin, worn by the Cinteotl *ixiptla,* was left behind in enemy territory, an action that unleashed real fighting between rival groups (Sahagún 1950–82, bk 2: 122). Anne-Marie Vié Wohrer followed Miguel Acosta Saignes's methodology to look for the "Tlacaxipehualiztli complex" made up of sacrifice by arrow (*tlacacaliztli*) and body processing via flaying, in other New World geographic locations (Acosta Saignes 1950). While Acosta Saignes looked more to the hemisphere's southern areas, the French investigator compared a number of customs on the part of indigenous people in the southern United States with the sacrificial ceremonies associated with the Mexica veintenas. Similarities she saw led her to postulate that Tlacaxipehualiztli expressed war- and hunting-related values, which in the southern United States were related to appropriating the bodies of animals that were consumed and slain enemies. Far from being an exclusively agrarian metaphor, flaying would therefore also correspond to the body processing typically carried out by hunting groups (Vié-Wohrer 2008).[6] More recently, Claude-F. Baudez (2010, 2012) shed new light on this rite, interpreting the act of covering oneself in the skin of another as a transformation, or, put another way, that the flayed enemy turned into a Mexica. The same transition was realized in Ochpaniztli, when a domestic woman became a warrior woman by taking on Toci's appearance and donning her skin.

Finally, we cannot leave out skins' expiatory functions in the above-mentioned rites; skins were periodically displayed in public space. In fact, Graulich (1999, 142) draws attention to the fact that it was not the skin that changed but rather its wearer. All skin wearers were penitents and the skin represented the stain of their transgression. Getting rid of the skin at the beginning of every season drove away the filth that had built up during half a year.[7] As the Belgian researcher has made clear, the skin's ultimate destiny was to be discarded, hidden in underground areas, such as the foundations of structures, and at crossroads. They were also left out on temporary structures, like the *tocititlan*, at the outer limits of Mexico-Tenochtitlan, cast out of the urban milieu as something filthy that should be moved away from the ceremonial center (Durán 1984, 1: 154; Sahagún 1950–82, bk 2: 125; see also DiCesare 2009, 99; Mazzetto 2014, 197–204).

To conclude this lengthy historiographic review, I assert my patent agreement with González Torres (1985, 274–76), who considered the act of wearing skin a highly polysemous ritual expression. According to that Mexican scholar, the meaning of the act is in itself related to five factors: the skin's origins, the identity of the sacrificial victim, that of its wearer, the ceremony in which the rite was carried out and the skin's final end.

Regarding other Mesoamerican cultural areas, Diego de Landa's colonial-era chronicle, *Relación de las cosas de Yucatán*, documents the existence of a ritual the postclassic Maya realized that in certain senses seems to be a mixture of Tlacaxipe-hualiztli and Ochpaniztli rites. The sacrificed body's treatment recalls the *veintena* dedicated to Xipe Totec, since the body was cast down to the foot of the pyramid and it was flayed at the base of that structure. Overlords' anthropophagous feasting and ritual use of the captives' bones also affords an efficacious comparison to Tlacaxipehualiztli. Nevertheless, the fact that it was priests who wore the victims' skins was a typical custom related to female Ochpaniztli flayings (Landa 1985, 91). Unfortunately, that document does not specify at what time of year this ritual took place, nor is there further mention in descriptions of solar-calendar *haab'* festivals that are discussed in the book's second section takes up,[8] making it impossible to place this flaying rite in relationship with seasonal changes in the agricultural cycle.[9]

EHUATL, IZHUATL, OF SKIN AND LEAVES: FLAYING AND HUSKING

Preuss's interpretation was not entirely forgotten. In fact, Thompson specifically took up the parallelism between treatment techniques for sacrificial victims' bodies and for corn. Yet instead of kernel stripping, he compared them to another agrarian phase, specifically the maize ear's husking: "As we know that [Xipe Totec] was originally connected with agriculture, it does seem improbable in view of our knowledge of other symbolic sacrifices that the flaying of the victim represented the husking of the corn. This did not take place when the crop was gathered, for the ears were stored with their coverings of leaves in special granaries until required" (Thompson 1940, 145).

In his analysis of the ancient Nahua' festival cycle, Graulich proposed a lapse among the eighteen solar-calendar festivals due to the absence of adjustments (as, for instance, our leap years) between the 365-day calendar's duration and that of the actual year (Graulich 1999, 71–84; 2000, 293–305).[10] As a consequence, this 209-day gap would mean ceremonies performed during the *veintena* festivals would not be related to annual agricultural cycles, but rather, would be displaced by more or less half a year. This gap—that ancient Mesoamericans carried out voluntarily—had to do with the fact that it allowed the two time-calculating systems, the solar and the ritual, to continue to coincide, a position taken by authors such as Alfonso Caso (1967). Graulich posited that previous to the presumed calendar gap, Tlacaxipehualiztli fell in October, at the start of the dry season, the season in which war was made and corn plants completed their development prior to harvest. He interpreted *tlahuahuanaliztli* as a re-actualization of the sacred war undertaken to nourish the Sun and the Earth, as described in the "Leyenda de los Soles" (2002, 185–87). The Mimixcoa, the protagonists of this mythic adventure and, by extension, prototypes of sacrificial victims, would correspond, on a ritual level, to the numerous warriors sacrificed on the *temalacatl*, while at the same time, they would become metaphors for the very corn plants gathered in the fields. Thus, there was a double harvest: a corn harvest undertaken by men, and a culling of victims the gods carried out. War prisoner victims would correspond to corn kernels. As such, according to Graulich (1999, 314), Thompson's theory is not to be ruled out. In effect, the researcher highlights how two huskings of the maize ears could exist: one at harvest time and another at the time of planting. I shall take up this notion below.

Almost seventy years after Thompson wrote the lines cited above, and some thirty years after Graulich's research, González González revisited and further developed Thompson's comparative thesis. He established another clear connection between the warrior's body sacrificed at Tlacaxipehualiztli—torn apart to be eaten by the captor's relatives—and the corn kernels boiled alongside the captive's flesh, a preparation known as *tlacatlaolli*, "shelled man-corn." González González attributed flaying to a twofold relationship with the grain. On the one hand, this post-sacrificial treatment corresponded to the act of cooking the kernels with lime (the so-called *nixtamalización* process), designed to facilitate removing the kernels' pericarp (i.e. its skin). On the other hand, he cogently points out that the Nahuatl verb *xipehua*, that is, "to strip bark," "husk," or "flay" (Molina 1970, part I: fol. 39v, 41v, part II: fol. 159r) was used to describe the victims' flaying process as well as that of stripping off cornhusks, an action that González—as does Thompson—identifies as occurring before planting (González González 2011, 286–87; 2016, 120–24).[11] In a review of González González's book, Guilhem Olivier (2013, 1750) accurately points out that it is necessary to understand the exact moment of the agricultural cycle in which the maize leaves were stripped, since this action is referenced for both sowing and harvesting among different indigenous groups. Two reflections must be underscored. The first is that researchers have not sustained their interpretation of the "flaying-husking-sowing" connection when performing an overall analysis of the Nahuatl-language descriptions of the corn cycle presented in sixteenth-century documents. Second, there is no generalized information about the corn planting, harvest, and storage processes, because elements such as climate, temperature, the type of structure used to store the maize ears, and cultural customs represent factors subject to extreme fluctuation based on the geographical area in question.

CORN STORAGE METHODS

In his proposal, Thompson did not consider that when we are discussing the treatment of the corn cob after harvest, we must take into account not one, but two processes: storing the cobs, and preparing the seeds that have been selected for the next sowing. In tropical areas today, climate conditions prevent kernels from being stripped from cobs immediately after harvest; ears must be put away where they can dry out and rid themselves of moisture for proper long-term storage. As Teresa Rojas Rabiela and Michael Smith explain, the method used to preserve grains determines, above all, how much time they will last before decomposition sets in (Rojas Rabiela 1985, 101–05; Smith 1991, 17–26). In a hot, humid area like Yucatán, stored, husked corn cannot last longer than six months, whereas very dry kernels can last up to a year. For that reason, in this climate zone, unhusked maize storage represents the best conservation strategy (Smith 1991, 22). Also for that reason, storage of unhusked maize is practiced among Chiapas's Mochó people, as well as in the Chol Serrana region in Chiapas and Tabasco (Mariaca García et al. 2014; Petrich 1985, 86).[12] The same storage methods are found in Oaxaca's Sierra Mixe; in certain parts of Veracruz, like San Pedro Tziltzacuapan (Hernández González 2009, 158); among the Copaltitla Nahua in the Veracruz Huasteca (Argüelles Santiago 2008, 114); as well as in the Ixhuatlan de Madero municipal district among Nahua communities in the north of Veracruz (Sandstrom 2010, 183–84), and at Coatzonco, Huautla, Hidalgo (Alfonso Vite Hernández 2019, personal communication). In fact, in these communities, the husking is known as *tlaxipehualiztli* (Sandstrom 2010, 185; Alfonso Vite Hernández 2019, personal communication). In Huehuetenango, Guatemala, the presence or absence of corn husks in the household trough is strongly related to temperature; for this reason, wrapping corn ears in their bracts can protect the grain from pest attacks as it undergoes the drying process (*Almacenamiento de granos* ...). In contrast, among the Huautepec Mazatecs, ears of corn are not stored in troughs, but rather, are hung whole from household ceiling beams, almost completely husked yet bound by the husks as well (Carrera García et al. 2012, 467). They are left to dry and the kernels are stripped off based on family food needs. The same technique has been adopted in the state of Chihuahua (Minnis and Whalen 2012, 155). Among the Mayos (state of Sonora), ears of corn are stored unhusked (Beals 2016, 103).

The storage technique changes completely when we analyze data from the Basin of Mexico, as well as that from other Mexican states. In Santa Ana Tlacotenco, in Mexico City's Milpa Alta borough, ears are harvested with husks in place. Once in the household, the ears are husked and left to dry, as are the husks themselves, later to be used for tamale making (Galarza and López Ávila 1995, 52; Guilhem Olivier 2019, personal communication). Among the Huauhchinango Nahua, in Puebla, ears are husked in the milpa as soon as they are harvested. The maize ear's dried cornhusk (called a *totomochtli* in Nahuatl) is cut, bare-handed, with a copper awl to avoid injuring fingernails, but left hanging on the plant (Chamoux 1981, 174). In Tetimpa, in the Atlixco Valley on the eastern slopes of Popocatepetl volcano, the husking also takes place at the time of harvest; the ears are then laid out under the sun for five to seven days and are stored once dry (Uruñuela Ladrón de Guevara et al. 2012, 224). The same thing occurs in San Juan Ixtenco, in Tlaxcala state (Alaya Johnson 2018, personal communication), as well as in various areas in the state of Guerrero, as for example in Tlapa (López and Alvarado 2009, 24) and Acatlan, where the act of stripping the ears of their husks is called "*quitarle la ropa al maíz*" (i.e. undressing the corn). At San Juan Tetelcingo, the verb *pixca* not only means "to harvest" but also "to husk the ears" since the two actions are synonymous (González Torres 2013). In relation to preparing the seeds to be saved for sowing, in Central Mexico generally the biggest, most attractive ears are selected and stored, complete with their bracts (Chamoux 1981, 174). Although no longer a common practice, traditionally husking was realized step by step after the harvest. The corncobs freed of their *totomoxtle* and this last one was used to tie up the ears in bundles that were hung from the roof of the house in order to dry. With respect to the Mexicas, Durán mentions this was done during the month of Tlacaxipehualiztli, when he describes "bunches of ears hanging on the roofs" (Durán 1984, 2: 248).

HARVEST GESTURES IN THE *FLORENTINE CODEX*

The *Florentine Codex* is the primary source for approaching the rhythms that characterize the life cycle of corn. The collaborators of Franciscan friar Bernardino de Sahagún provided highly valuable information on harvest phases. In Book 10, where the qualities of a good farmer are described, we find this quite intriguing passage:

Plant, sow beans, make holes ... fill the hole and push the earth back into place, remove the undeveloped ears from the stalk, strip away the spoilt ears, cut and break the corn stalks, pull out the stalks, remove the baby ears that are not developing (*xilotl*) by breaking them off, remove the baby ears that grow next to the main ears (*cacamatl*), by breaking them off, gather the corn, gather the dried cornstalks, break off the ears from the stalk, gather the green ears, gather the ears, *harvest, flay, strip off the husks*,[13] *tie up the ears*,[14] bind the ears, knot the ears of corn, make a chain with the ears, move them, fill up the troughs, plant by spreading the seeds, scatter them ... cut, break, tear up, strip the kernels with force, crush them, toss them away, hurl them, cast them to the wind (*tlapixoa, hetlaça, tlatzotzopitza ... tlatacaxtlaloa, tlatlaluia, tlaxilotlapana, tlacincuecuextlaça, ohoapuztequi, oacui, xilotzaiana, cacamatzaiana, tlaâquetzaltia, tlacotzana, miiaoacui, elocui, tlacinpoztequi, pixca, tlaxipeoa, tlazoayotlaça, ochoa, tlaochoa, tlaochollalia, mocincozcatia tlaçaça, tlacuezcomatema, tlapixoa, tlachaiaoa ... tlatequi, tlapuztequi, tlacotona tlauitequi, tlaquequeça, tlaacana tlahecaquetza, tlahecamotla*). (Náhuatl: Sahagún 1950–82, bk 10: 41–42; the author's translation)

The Spanish-language text confirms what the document's Nahuatl passages make plain:

The laborer ... toils greatly at his office, to wit ... piercing the earth to sow beans, filling in the holes where the corn is planted, earthing up, or bringing the dirt to the sprouts, stripping away the ryegrass weed, pulling out the stalks and breaking them, and extracting the ears, stripping away the baby ears, pulling up the stalks so the seedling grows well and, in time, harvesting the green ears, and breaking up the stalks by ripping them out at harvest time, picking the corn when it's good and seasoned; flaying, denuding the ears and tying the ears together, knotting the husks together; making corn-ear chains, tying one to another; carrying off everything you picked and putting it into a silo; breaking down the empty stalks with a club; threshing and cleaning them, scattering the chaff (and) casting it into the wind (*El labrador ... trabaja mucho en su oficio, a saber ... agujerar la tierra para sembrar los frijoles, cegar los hoyos donde está el maíz sembrado, acohombrar, o allegar la tierra a lo nacido, quitar el vallico, entresacar las cañas quebrándolas, y entresacar las mazorquillas, y quitar los hijos de las mazorcas, y quitar los tallos porque crezca bien lo nacido, entresacar a su tiempo las mazorcas verdes, y al tiempo de la cosecha quebrar las cañas cogiéndolas y coger el maíz cuando está ya bien sazonado; desollar o desnudar las mazorcas y atar las mazorcas unas con otras, añudando las camisillas unas con otras; y hacer sártales de mazorcas, atando unas con otras, y acarrear a casa lo cogido y ensilarlo; quebrar las cañas que tienen nada, aporreándolas; trillar, limpiar, aventar (y) levantar al viento lo trillado*). (Sahagún 1969, 3: 122–23)

Another suggestive passage is found in Book 11, where corn is described, as are its different varieties and growing techniques: "I harvest, I cut at the base, I collect the mature ears, I tie them together, I form a bundle, I make them look like a bundle, I throw out the stalks, I seize the husks, I pull the husks off, I gather the ears, I cut them, I flay them, I throw out the seed stems ..." (*Njpixca, njtlatzinpoztequj, njçincuj, nochoa, nocholoa, njtlaocholteuhtlalia, njtlavaiotlaça, njtlazoacuj, njtlatzicueoa, njtlaquechcuj: njtlacotona, njtlaxipeoa, njtlaxilotzontlaça ...*) (Náhuatl: Sahagún 1950–82, bk 11: 279; the author's translation).

These two passages describe the harvest cycle, by phases, to ultimately take up the sowing process. Nahua collaborators speak of gathering the corn, husking the ears and of the technique—still practiced today in numerous parts of Mexico—of tying ears set aside for planting to roof beams in the house, storing the ears and then planting their seeds in *milpa* fields when the time to begin a new growing cycle arrives. Unfortunately, in the second passage, it is impossible to make a comparison with the Spanish-language text, since Bernardino de Sahagún did not translate this description of different corn varieties and limited himself—in *Florentine Codex* folios 246r to 249v—to setting down a long, evangelizing sermon. Be that as it may, these two excerpts attest to the fact that stripping the ears took place at harvest, not planting time. Once most ears had been harvested and husked, those selected to be used in future planting were hung from household roof beams in clusters, almost entirely husked (Durán 1984, 1: 248). Iconography supports my interpretation since storage of husked ears is clearly portrayed in at least two illustrations from the Sahagún text (Figure 6.1) (Batalla Rosado 2012; Olivier 2013, 1750).

Figure 6.1. Corn storage. Detail of Ms. Med. Palat. 219, bk 7: fol. 16r. Source: Photograph courtesy of Biblioteca Medicea Laurenziana, Florence. By concession of the MiBACT. Any further reproduction by any means is prohibited.

Figure 6.2. Offering of *ocholli* maize ears in Tlacaxipehualiztli. Detail of Ms. Med. Palat. 219, bk 9: fol. 49v. Source: Photograph courtesy of Biblioteca Medicea Laurenziana, Florence. By concession of the MiBACT. Any further reproduction by any means is prohibited.

Ocholli ears—those that were hung from household ceiling beams to be used for planting and that played an important role in Tlacaxipehualiztli (*Códice Magliabechiano*, 1996, fol. 90r.) —are also portrayed as husked (Figure 6.2).

Representations of ears still wrapped in their bracts can be found when the plant is represented whole (*Códice Borbónico* 1991, pl. 29; *Códice Borgia*, 1963, pl. 24) and also when the ears are represented as an attribute of agriculture and rain deities, like tender ears, *xilotl* (*Códice Magliabechiano*, 1996, fol. 29r) or ripe cobs (*Códice Borbónico* 1991, pl. 29). Ears wrapped in their bracts, in the form of *xilotl* or of ears separated for sowing, can be also a religious offering (*Códice Borbónico* 1991, pl. 23; Sahagún 1979, bk 2: fol. 28r) (Figures 6.3, 6.4 and 6.5).[15]

Despite the fact he did not develop his position further, Graulich's proposal is correct: husking could take place at different points in the agricultural cycle, depending on a variety of factors. By suggesting an exclusive link between husking/flaying and sowing, Thompson ignored the complexity of the preparation cycle and uses of corn and its geographical variants. Storage of corn ears for consumption, for example, can be done with or without *totomoxtle*. Therefore, husking can be

Figure 6.3. Maize ear wrapped in its bracts as an attribute of agriculture and rain deities. Detail of *Codex Magliabechiano*, fol. 29r. Source: Drawing by Elena Mazzetto.

Figure 6.4. Maize ears wrapped in their bracts as a religious offering. Detail of *Codex Borbonicus*, pl. 23. Source: Photograph courtesy of Bibliothèque de l'Assemblée nationale, Paris.

Figure 6.5. Maize ears wrapped in their bracts as a religious offering. Detail of Ms. Med. Palat. 218, bk 2: fol. 29r. Source: Photograph courtesy of Biblioteca Medicea Laurenziana, Florence. By concession of the MiBACT. Any further reproduction by any means is prohibited.

undertaken at harvest time, but also just before consumption. Husking corn ears selected for sowing, on the other hand, can be done step by step by taking of the *totomoxtle* after the harvest, but never completely before sowing (Danièle Dehouve 2019, personal communication). Sixteenth-century documents specifically mention husking/flaying and tying the ears in bundles as being related to the harvest phase, the activity that took place after cutting ears from cornstalks in the *milpa* fields.

CONCLUSIONS

In the present chapter I have examined the relationship between corn plants and their cultivation phases, and with flaying, the *post-mortem* technique to which sacrificial victims' bodies were subject, employed in a number of pre-Hispanic Nahua solar-cycle ceremonies and above all during the Tlacaxipehualiztli and Ochpaniztli *veintenas*, two moments every year that marked a change of seasons.

Specifically, I have undertaken an historiographic review of interpretations specialists have published on the religious significance of flaying, highlighting a variety of approaches undertaken throughout these studies' history. In particular, I have focused on interpretations that, beginning in the nineteenth century, posit the existence of an imitative link between natural cycles—as well as agricultural labors—and ritual considerations. According to that school of thought, skinning victims was a metaphor for seasonal changes that affected the "skin" of the earth. A more recent and specific symbolic reading has related this way of processing the human body with the sowing and harvest cycles of maize, such that stripping away a victim's skin was related to the act of husking corn ears before new planting. Based on a painstaking study of sixteenth-century Nahua sources and iconography, alongside contemporary farming methods practice by various indigenous groups, I have shown, first, what the interpretative limits are when it comes to the search for a perfect, ideal correspondence between grain-cultivation technique and religious ceremonies. Corn's growth and storage cycle is a complex issue, linked to highly variable climatic and cultural factors. This means corn-husking for food use will take place after harvest or before consumption depending on outdoor temperatures and geographic placement. Secondly, I have indicated how, in Nahua culture, husking did not correspond to sowing, but was rather related to the harvest, since the action of stripping the maize's leaves to be stored or for the preparation of bundles meant to future sowing is listed among the tasks farmers undertook when they collected ears from the *milpa*. Although husking could have been done at different moments after the harvest, it was never completely done before sowing.

With absolutely no pretense of conclusively determining the complex polysemy of the act of flaying in pre-Hispanic Nahua religion, I do assert that if we consider its performance a highly detailed agricultural metaphor for corn-husking, we have to move away from the automatic association of "flaying-husking-sowing." Indeed, we will need to reformulate the overall interpretative theory both in the light of Nahua documents and ethnographic evidences.

ACKNOWLEDGMENTS

I would like to thank Gabrielle Vail, Michael Parker, Wendy Aguilar, and Stan Declercq for the translation of this chapter and Guilhem Olivier, Danièle Dehouve, and Élodie Dupey García for sharing information and for their helpful remarks.

NOTES

1. The term comes from New Guinea's Marind-Anim language.
2. See Botta (2009) for a critique of this concept applied to indigenous mythology.
3. See Neurath, in this volume (Chapter 4), for a deeper understanding of different schools of thought that influenced the development of studies of Mesoamerican religion.

4. *Xipeme* means "the Xipes." *Xipe* is the divine name of the supernatural entity venerated as part of Tlacaxipehualiztli; *-me* is one of the plural indicators for animate nouns.

5. We must add to these cases the periodic flaying of sacrificial victims' heads, where skin was removed from the skull before being incorporated into the *tzompantli* (Durán 1984, 1: 31–32; see also Chávez Balderas 2017, 192–93).

6. Vié-Wohrer (2008) largely attributes flaying's agricultural symbolism to agricultural deities like Chicomecoatl and Cinteotl. Nevertheless, she emphasizes this post-sacrificial process's war- and hunting-related functions, as in the case of deities like Xipe Totec and Camaxtli.

7. In his article on the Ochpaniztli *veintena*, Luis Grave Tirado follows Graulich's interpretation, which considers flaying a rite for soil regeneration and expulsion of evils (Grave Tirado 2004, 168).

8. Concerning that calendar and its rituals, see Vail in this volume (Chapter Five).

9. Advances in sacrificial victim bone analysis have led to the discovery of marks indicative of flaying at Classic period Maya sites. This is the case of markings on bone found in materials from collapses and fill from Becán's Structure X, in Mexico's Campeche State (Tiesler Blos 2004, 44). Study of bone remains from sacrificial victims from the Aztec Templo Mayor revealed victims of flaying were not just humans but animals as well. This is the case at Offering 126, where five wolf cubs and a number of birds that had been flayed were discovered (Chávez Balderas 2017, 146). For an in-depth study of skeletal remains associated with victims of flaying from the Templo Mayor, see Cortés Meléndez (forthcoming).

10. For more on this notion, see this volume's Introduction.

11. Husking corn is an action that has also been compared to ritual acts in the Maya area, particularly phallic piercing. Karl Taube demonstrates how, among the Yucatec Maya, various tools used to husk maize ears are made of buckhorn, sharpened bone and wood. They are used to pierce and separate the husks and expose kernels on the cob. Taube believes that if these instruments were found in Classic period elite tombs, it is quite probable they were identified with bleeding devices similar to those used in phallic perforation rites (Taube 1985, 180).

12. Nevertheless, this is not the case with the Zinacantec people, who gather, husk and strip kernels off ears beside the *milpa* fields, so they only need carry the kernels to troughs (Vogt 1979, 93).

13. I would like to thank Gabriel Kruell for the translation of this verb.

14. Italics mine.

15. In Guerrero, the *totomoxtle* of the cobs called "owners of the cornfield" ("*dueños de la milpa*," a maize bush with a double cob), is preserved until the ritual consumption of its grains (Dehouve 2008).

REFERENCES

Acosta Saignes, Miguel. 1950. *Tlacaxipehualiztli, un complejo mesoamericano entre los caribes*. Caracas: Universidad Central-Facultad de Filosofía y Letras-Instituto de Antropología y Geografía.

Almacenamiento de granos a nivel rural. Oficina regional de la FAO para América latina y el Caribe. Serie: Tecnologia Postcosecha 1. April 2018, http://www.fao.org/docrep/X5050S/x5050S00. htm.

Anders, Ferdinand, and Maarten Jansen. 1996. *Libro de la vida. Texto explicativo del llamado Códice Magliabechiano CL XIII 3 (BR232)*. Graz, Mexico City: ADEVA, Fondo de Cultura Económica.

Argüelles Santiago, Jazmín Nallely. 2008. "El maíz en la identidad cultural de la Huasteca Veracruzana." MA thesis, Universidad Mayor de San Simón.

Batalla Rosado, Juan José. 2009. "El Libro Escrito Europeo del 'Códice Tudela' o 'Códice del Museo de América', Madrid." *Itinerarios* 9: 83–115.

———. 2012. "Análisis de la representación de depósitos de almacenamiento en los códices." In *Almacenamiento prehispánico, del Norte de México al Altiplano Central*, edited by Séverine Bortot, Dominique Michelet, and Véronique Darras, 187–202. Paris, San Luis Potosí, Mexico City: Université de Paris I Panthéon-Sorbonne, Universidad Autónoma de San Luis Potosí, Centro de Estudios Mexicanos y Centroamericanos.

Baudez, Claude-François. 2010. "Sacrificio de sí, sacrificio del 'otro'." In *El sacrificio humano en la tradición religiosa mesoamericana*, edited by Guilhem Olivier and Leonardo López Luján, 431–51. Mexico City: Instituto Nacional de Antropología e Historia, Universidad Nacional Autónoma de México.

Baudez, Claude-François. 2012. *La douleur rédemptrice. L'autosacrifice précolombien*. Paris: Riveneuve.

Beals, Ralph. 2016. "La cultura contemporánea de los indios cahitas." In *Etnografía del Noroeste de México*, edited by Jaime Labastida, vol. 2, 93–365. Mexico City: Siglo XXI.

Botta, Sergio. 2009. "De la tierra al territorio. Límites interpretativos del naturismo y aspectos políticos del culto a Tláloc." *Estudios de Cultura Náhuatl* 40: 175–99.

Broda, Johanna (de Casas). 1970. "Tlacaxipehualiztli: A Reconstruction of an Aztec Calendar Festival from 16th Century Sources." *Revista Española de Antropología Americana* 5: 197–274.

Brown, Betty Ann. 1984. "Ochpaniztli in Historical Perspective." In *Sacrifice in Mesoamerica*, edited by Elizabeth H. Boone, 195–209. Washington, DC: Dumbarton Oaks.

Carrasco, David. 2002. "The Sacrifice of Women in the *Florentine Codex*. The Hearts of Plants and Players in War Games." In *Representing Aztec Ritual: Performance, Text, and Image in the Work of Sahagún*, edited by Eloise Quiñones Keber, 197–225. Boulder: University Press of Colorado.

Carrera García, Silvia, Hermilio Navarro Garza, Ma. Antonia Pérez Olvera, and Bernardino Mata García. 2012. "Calendario agrícola mazateco, milpa y estrategia alimentaria campesina en territorio de Huauhtepec, Oaxaca." *Agricultura, Sociedad y Desarrollo* 9, no. 4: 455–75.

Caso, Alfonso. 1967. *Los calendarios prehispánicos*. Mexico City: Universidad Nacional Autónoma de México-Instituto de Investigaciones Históricas.

Chamoux, Marie-Noëlle. 1981. *Indiens de la Sierra, la communauté paysanne au Mexique*. Paris: L'Harmattan.

Chávez Balderas, Ximena. 2017. *Sacrificio humano y tratamientos postsacrificiales en el Templo Mayor de Tenochtitlan*. Mexico City: Instituto Nacional de Antropología e Historia.

Códice Borbónico. 1991. Edited by Ferdinand Anders, Maarten Jansen, and Luis Reyes García. Graz, Madrid, Mexico City: ADEVA, Sociedad Estatal Quinto Centenario, Fondo de Cultura Económica.

Códice Magliabechiano CL XIII 3 (BR232). 1996. Edited by Ferdinand Anders and Maarten Jansen. Graz, Mexico City: ADEVA, Fondo de Cultura Económica.

Cortés Meléndez, Víctor. Forthcoming. *El desollamiento humano entre los mexicas*. Mexico City: Instituto Nacional de Antropología e Historia, Ancient Culture Institute.

"Costumbres, fiestas, enterramientos y diversas formas de proceder de los Indios de Nueva España." 1945. Edited by Federico Gómez de Orozco. *Tlalocan* 2, no. 1: 37–63.

Dehouve, Danièle. 2008. "El venado, el maíz y el sacrificado." *Diario de Campo. Cuadernos de Etnología* 4: 1–39.

DiCesare, Catherine. 2009. *Sweeping the Way. Divine Transformation in the Aztec Festival of Ochpaniztli*. Boulder: University Press of Colorado.

Durán, Diego. 1984. *Historia de las Indias de Nueva España e islas de la Tierra Firme.* Edited by Ángel M. Garibay. 2 vols. Mexico City: Porrúa.

Eliade, Mircea. 2014. *Traité d'histoire des religions.* Paris: Éditions Payot.

Frazer, James. 1981. *La Rama Dorada.* Mexico City: Fondo de Cultura Económica.

Galarza, Joaquín, and Carlos López Ávila. 1995. *Tlacotenco Tonantzin Santa Ana. Tradiciones: toponimia, técnicas, fiestas, canciones, versos y danzas.* Mexico City: Centro de Investigaciones y Estudios Superiores en Antropología Social.

González González, Carlos. 2011. *Xipe Tótec. Guerra y regeneración del maíz en la religión mexica.* Mexico City: Instituto Nacional de Antropología e Historia, Fondo de Cultura Económica.

———. 2016. "Xipe Tótec, el portador de la guerra y el maíz." In *Xipe Tótec y la regeneración de la vida*, edited by Carlos González, 23–198. Mexico City: Secretaría de Cultura, Instituto Nacional de Antropología e Historia.

González Torres, Yolotl. 1985. *El sacrificio humano entre los mexicas.* Mexico City: Fondo de Cultura Económica.

———. 1990. "Las deidades Dema y los ritos de despedazamiento en Mesoamérica." In *Historia de la religión en Mesoamérica y áreas afines. II Coloquio*, edited by Barbro Dahlgren, 105–12. Mexico City: Universidad Nacional Autónoma de México.

———. 2013. "Etnografía del maíz: variedades, tipos de suelo y rituales en treinta monografías." In *Etnografía de los confines. Las andanzas de Anne Chapman*, edited by Andrés Medina and Ángela Ochoa, 179–219. Mexico City: Centro de Estudios Mexicanos y Centroamericanos.

Graulich, Michel. 1999. *Ritos aztecas. Las fiestas de las veintenas.* Mexico City: Instituto Nacional Indigenista.

———. 2000 [1987]. *Mythes et rituels du Mexique ancien préhispanique.* Brussels: Académie Royale de Belgique.

———. 2005. *Le sacrifice humain chez les Aztèques.* Paris: Fayard.

Grave Tirado, Luis Alfonso. 2004. "Barriendo en lo ya barrido. Un nuevo repaso a Ochpaniztli." *Estudios de Cultura Náhuatl* 35: 157–77.

Hernández, Francisco. 2015. *Obras Completas de Francisco Hernández.* April 2018, http://www.francishohernandez.unam.mx/home.html

Hernández González, María Isabel. 2009. "El complejo cerro-agua-maíz-ancestros en San Pedro Cholula." *Diario de Campo*, Tercera Época, 52: 154–165.

Jensen, Adolf E. 1963. *Myth and Cult Among Primitive Peoples.* Chicago: University of Chicago Press.

Krickeberg, Walter. 1961. *Las antiguas culturas mexicanas.* Mexico City: Fondo de Cultura Económica.

Landa, Diego de. 1985. *Relación de las cosas de Yucatán.* Edited by Miguel Rivera Dorado. Madrid: Historia 16.

"Leyenda de los Soles". 2002. In *Mitos e historia de los antiguos nahuas*, edited by Rafael Tena, 174–206. Mexico City: Consejo Nacional para la Cultura y las Artes.

López, María Susana Xelhuantzi, and José Luis Alvarado. 2009. "Teozintli actual en el Cerro de la Estrella. Reflexiones y consideraciones en torno a esta planta ancestral." *Diario de Campo,* Tercera Época, 52: 18–25.

López Luján, Leonardo. 2005. *The Offerings of the Templo Mayor of Tenochtitlan.* Albuquerque: University of New Mexico Press.

Margáin Araujo, Carlos. 1945. "La fiesta azteca de la cosecha Ochpanistli." *Anales del Instituto Nacional de Antropología e Historia* 1: 157–74.

Mariaca Méndez, Ramón, Juanita E. Cano Contreras, Guadalupe Morales Valenzuela, and Mauricio Hernández Sánchez. 2014. "La milpa en la región serrana Chiapas-Tabasco de Huitiupán-Tacotalpa". In *Montañas, pueblos y agua. Dimensiones y realidades de la Cuenca Grijalva*, 2 vols., edited by Mario González-Espinoza and Marie Claude Brunel Manse, 323–59. Mexico City: El Colegio de la Frontera Sur, Juan Pablo Editor.

Mazzetto, Elena. 2014. *Lieux de culte et parcours cérémoniels dans les fêtes des vingtaines à Mexico-Tenochtitlan*. Oxford: British Archaeological Reports.

Minnis, Paul E., and Michael E. Whalen. 2012. "Comercio y tributo de bienes locales y exóticos: economía política y almacenamiento en Casas Grandes, Chihuahua, México." In *Almacenamiento prehispánico, del Norte de México al Altiplano Central*, edited by Séverine Bortot, Dominique Michelet, and Véronique Darras, 151–57. Paris, San Luis Potosí, Mexico City: Université de Paris I Panthéon-Sorbonne, Universidad Autónoma de San Luis Potosí, Centro de Estudios Mexicanos y Centroamericanos.

Molina, Alonso de. 1970. *Vocabulario en Lengua Castellana y Mexicana y Mexicana y Castellana*. Edited by Miguel León-Portilla. Mexico City: Porrúa.

Nájera Coronado, Martha Ilia. 2014. *El don de la sangre en el equilibrio cósmico. El sacrificio y el autosacrificio sangriento entre los antiguos mayas*. Mexico City: Universidad Nacional Autónoma de México.

Nicholson, Henry B. 1972. "The Cult of Xipe Totec in Mesoamerica." In *Religión en Mesoamerica. XII Mesa Redonda*, edited by Jaime Litvak King and Noemi Castillo Tejero, 213–17. Mexico City: Sociedad Mexicana de Antropología.

Olivier, Guilhem. 2013. "Carlos Javier González González, Xipe Tótec. Guerra y regeneración del maíz en la religión mexica." *Historia Mexicana* 248: 1741–51.

Ortiz de Montellano, Bernardo. 1990. *Aztec Medicine, Health and Nutrition*. New Brunswick: Rutgers University Press.

Petrich, Perla. 1985. *La alimentación mochó. Acto y palabra*. San Cristóbal de las Casas: Universidad Autónoma de Chiapas.

Réville, Albert. 1885. *Les religions du Mexique, de l'Amérique Centrale et du Pérou*. Paris: Librairie Fischbacher.

Rojas Rabiela, Teresa. 1985. *La cosecha del agua: Pesca, caza de aves y recolección de otros productos biológicos acuáticos de la cuenca de México*. Mexico City: Secretaría de Educación Pública, Centro de Investigaciones y Estudios Superiores en Antropología Social.

Ruiz de Alarcón, Hernando. 1953. *Tratado de las idolatrías, supersticiones, dioses, ritos, hechicerías y otras costumbres gentílicas de las razas aborígenes de México*. Mexico City: Fuente Cultural.

Sahagún, Bernardino de. 1950–82. *Florentine Codex: General History of the Things of New Spain, Fray Bernardino de Sahagún*. Translated with notes and illustrations by Arthur J. O. Anderson and Charles E. Dibble. 13 vols. Santa Fe: The School of American Research, University of Utah Press.

———. 1969. *Historia general de las cosas de Nueva España*. Edited by Ángel M. Garibay. 4 vols. Mexico City: Porrúa.

———. 1979. *Códice Florentino. Manuscrito 218–20 de la Colección Palatina de la Biblioteca Medicea Laurenziana*. 3 vols. Mexico City: Secretaría de Gobernación, Archivo General de la Nación.

Sandstrom, Alan R. 2010. *El maíz es nuestra sangre: cultura e identidad étnica en un pueblo indio azteca contemporáneo*. Mexico City: Centro de Estudios Mexicanos y Centroamericanos.

Seler, Eduard. 1963. *Comentarios al Códice Borgia*. Vols. I and II. In *Códice Borgia y Comentarios de Eduard Seler*. 3 vols. Mexico City: Fondo de Cultura Económica.

Smith, Michael. 1991. *Modern Maya Storage Behavior. Ethnoarchaeological Case Examples from the Puuc Region of Yucatan*. Pittsburgh: University of Pittsburgh, Latin American Archaeology Publications.

Soustelle, Jacques. 1983. *El universo de los aztecas*. Mexico City: Fondo de Cultura Económica.

Taube, Karl. 1985. "The Classic Maya Maize God: A Reappraisal." In *Fifth Palenque Round Table, 1983*, edited by Virginia M. Fields, 171–290. San Francisco: Pre-Columbian Art Research Institute.

Thévet, André. 2002. "Histoire du Mechique." In *Mitos e historia de los antiguos nahuas*, edited by Rafael Tena, 115–65. Mexico City: Consejo Nacional para la Cultura y las Artes.

Thompson, J. Eric S. 1940. *Mexico Before Cortez. An Account of the Daily Life, Religion, and Ritual of the Aztec and Kindred Peoples*. New York: Charles Scribner's Sons.

Tiesler Blos, Vera. 2004. "Sacrificio y tratamiento ritual del cuerpo humano en la antigua sociedad maya: el caso del Depósito E-1003 de Becán, Campeche." *Arqueología*, Segunda Época, 33: 32–46.

Tovar Calendar (The). 1951. Edited by George Kubler and Charles Gibson. New Haven: Memoirs of the Connecticut Academy of Arts and Sciences.

Uruñuela y Ladrón de Guevara, Gabriela, Patricia Plunket, and Olegario Batalla Coeto. 2012. "Notas e imágenes sobre depósitos tradicionales de almacenamiento en la falda oriental del Popocatepetl." In *Almacenamiento prehispánico, del Norte de México al Altiplano Central*, edited by Séverine Bortot, Dominique Michelet, and Véronique Darras, 221–27. Paris, San Luis Potosí, Mexico City: Université de Paris I Panthéon-Sorbonne, Universidad Autónoma de San Luis Potosí, Centro de Estudios Mexicanos y Centroamericanos.

Vaillant, George C. 1988. *La civilización azteca. Origen, grandeza y decadencia*. Mexico City: Fondo de Cultura Económica.

Vié-Wohrer, Anne-Marie. 2008. "Hypothèses sur l'origine et la diffusion du complexe rituel du *tlacaxipehualiztli*." *Journal de la Société des Américanistes* 94, no. 2. https://journals.openedition.org/jsa/10602

Vogt, Evon Z. 1979. *Ofrendas para los dioses: análisis simbólico de rituales zinacantecos*. Mexico City: Fondo de Cultura Económica.

CHAPTER SEVEN

The Toxcatl and Panquetzaliztli Figurines

JOHN F. SCHWALLER

In her groundbreaking study on the depiction of the Mexica god Huitzilopochtli, Elizabeth Boone noted that at least in the descriptions of the dough figurines of the god used in Panquetzaliztli and Toxcatl, the Franciscan author, Bernardino de Sahagún, manifests a great deal of confusion, and may have conflated the images used in the two celebrations (Boone 1989, 34–35). This study will look at the use of dough images in these two festivals of the Mexica annual cycle, the *xiuhpohualli*, and consider their manufacture and presentation. It will then look at exactly how these images were used in the feasts. Lastly some general observations will attempt to determine the use and character of the distinct images. Various Nahua polities made different choices in terms of the 20-day month that began their solar cycle and also followed a different order and name system for the festivals. This chapter follows the system outlined by Sahagún and Durán for Tenochtitlan and Tlatelolco (Sahagún 1950–82, bk 2: 1–34; Caso 1967, 33–39).

Images made of *huauhtli* (amaranth) played an important role in many of the celebrations of the *xiuhpohualli* or vague solar year. The solar year was divided into eighteen months of twenty days each, called *veintenas*, with five days, the *nemontemi*, left over. Each of the months was characterized by a series of specialized rituals dedicated to a particular god, or to a select set of gods. Two of the months, Toxcatl, generally considered the fifth month, occurring in late spring, and Panquetzaliztli, considered the sixteenth month, occurring in December, featured figurines created with a special dough made from *huauhtli*. In both instances, the deity represented was Huitzilopochtli, the particular Mexica god.

Central to understanding the rituals of Toxcatl and Panquetzaliztli is the Mexica notion of *ixiptlah*. Taken at its basic level, an *ixiptlah* was a symbolic representation of something. This could be an object that stood to represent some cosmic force or deity, or it could be a person costumed like a deity. Generally, the crucial examples considered here were objects or people who represented deities. Since in Nahuatl things cannot exist in the abstract, but must be possessed, owned, or part of someone or something, someone's *ixiptlah* would be known as a *teixiptlah*, someone's impersonator or symbolic representation. Molly Bassett has called the *teixiptlah*, "the localized embodiment."[1] The essence of the *ixiptlah* is that it embodies the essence of the thing being represented, even though externally it might not much resemble the deity or person. On the other hand, many of the *teixiptlahuan* (pl.) did look like the thing they represented.

Tzoalli, amaranth dough, played a central role in the manufacture of these images. *Tzoalli* dough employed for the gods' images used in Toxcatl and Panquetzaliztli was different from what in modern Mexico is now called *alegría*, wherein the amaranth seeds are made into candy (Boone 1989, 35–36; Mazzetto 2017; Reyes Equiguas 2005, 81). Friar Diego Durán provided a detailed account of the manufacture of *tzoalli*. It consisted of several ingredients. The main item was ground amaranth seeds mixed with toasted corn. Dark maguey syrup was then added to make the paste used for the image. To give the image a bit more realism, green, blue, and white beads were inserted to make the eyes, while white corn kernels represented his teeth (Durán 1971, 86–89). Two days before the ceremony in which the *tzoalli* image was to play a part, young women, aged twelve to thirteen, who were dedicated to the god, made his image. The young women, called "Maidens of Penance," lived in a cloister near the temple of Huitzilopochtli. When they entered the cloister, their hair was cut but thereafter they allowed it to grow. They only served the god for a year, after which they left the order to marry (Durán 1971, 83–84).

Unlike the detailed description of the manufacture of the dough image provided by Durán, Bernardino de Sahagún did not inform the reader that the image he described in his writing on the feast of Panquetzaliztli was even made of amaranth seed until the very end of his narrative of the ritual.[2] In Book III of the *Florentine Codex*, Sahagún (1950–82, bk 3: 5–6) held that *tzoalli* was made of *michioauhtzoalli* [*michihuauhtzoalli*] (fish amaranth), also called *chicalotl*. The process of making the final dough was complex. First, the priests charged with making the dough image ground the amaranth seed. It was moistened, divided into pieces, and then kneaded in bowls. In the process of kneading they were careful to remove any bits of rubbish, chaff, or other foreign material. They were also looking for bits of a related type of amaranth, *petzicatl*, known as mirror-stone amaranth, which would have imparted a speckled look to the dough. Sahagún did note that once the dough was completed it was quite firm, even hard, like pine resin or like the *axin*, a substance from some insects (*coccus axin*) that was used as a body color, as a varnish and probably as a binder for pigments as well. The manufacturing process was extremely important because it was the means through which the *ixiptlah* became animate; it became the local embodiment of the deity. Sahagún was very specific about where and when the image became animate. The image, as an *ixiptlah*, no longer existed as an inanimate object, but rather took on the vital life force (Bassett 2015, 132).[3]

Some of the early Spanish sources reported that virgins' blood or other victims' blood was an essential part of the *tzoalli* used in the figures such as those found in Toxcatl and Panquetzaliztli. This seems to be part of a Spanish tendency to ascribe even more ghastly behaviors to the Mexica than they actually practiced. Elena Mazzetto has studied this particular claim in some depth and concluded that there was no basis in reality for it. At worst the images may have been sprinkled with blood from self-sacrifice on the part of the priests or others involved in the manufacture, but there is no evidence that blood was a major constituent part of the images (Mazzetto 2017).

As noted above, the images studied here are part of a large category of objects considered *teixiptlah*. They were considered the local embodiment of the divine. Although they represented the divine, these objects were made in order to be destroyed. While they were objects of veneration for a period, an essential part of the ritual involving the *tzoalli* images was that they were eventually consumed. Certainly, the consumption of the object provided some nutritional value to the person who ate them. Amaranth is widely reported to be a good source of a broad spectrum of nutrients. There are also reports of the curative benefits to its ingestion (Reyes Equiguas 2005, 148–72). Yet, in its ritual use the *tzoalli* was not consumed as an ordinary food, nor as a specific or general cure, but rather it had undergone a spiritual transformation from a commonplace (food) into a divine thing (*teixiptlah*) (Morán 2016, 61).

Bassett (2015, 139–40) has shown that the *teixiplahuan* after construction had to be ritually destroyed in order to pass power to the deity. This created a life cycle and an element for power transfer. The *teixiptlah* gained power in its manufacture, becoming a localized embodiment of the deity. The figurine, or deity-impersonator, or other *teixiptlah*, then became a mechanism for the accumulation of spiritual power through the ceremonies and rituals through which it passed during the *veintena*. At the end of the month, or at some critical juncture in the month, the image, human impersonator, or other *teixiptlah* was sacrificed. This did not mean the loss of power or the destruction of the deity, but rather the transfer of that power *to* the deity, a spiritual and non-corporeal entity.

TOXCATL

Ironically, some of the information that scholars have about the use of amaranth dough images come from the observations of the conquerors and natives involved in the military conquest of Tenochtitlan, the Mexica capital. Some of these describe amaranth images placed in the sanctuaries atop the Templo Mayor. This also is particularly true about the *tzoalli* images that figured as part of the celebrations of Toxcatl ("Dryness"), since this festival occurred during a critical moment of the Spaniard's first occupation of Tenochtitlan. In 1520, while the Spanish were residing in the city, word arrived that an expeditionary force had been sent to capture Hernán Cortés and take him back to Cuba for having violated the license under which he had originally left the island. Cortés took half of his troops to the coast to meet the opposition, leaving half in Tenochtitlan under the leadership of Pedro de Alvarado. During Cortés' absence, Alvarado ordered his men to attack the Mexica nobility while they celebrated Toxcatl, thus forever burning memories of that celebration into the minds of participants, both native and Spanish.

The descriptions of the dough images from the sanctuary of Huitzilopochtli on the Templo Mayor come principally from Cortés and from Andrés de Tapia (Boone 1989, 46–54). Their descriptions are very similar. These two Spaniards describe a figure the size of a man, but made of dough mixed with the blood of sacrificial victims, or of young children. Of course, as seen above, the addition of sacrificial blood to the mixture has been refuted. In addition to the dough image, the sanctuary also contained stone images of the deities. But the identification of these images is problematic. All of them were adorned with jewelry. In one instance, it was described as wrapped in thin cloth, like a bundle. The assumption is that the image described by Cortés (1963, 75) was that of Huitzilopochtli, whereas Tapia's is more definitive (Fuentes 1963, 41). Bernal Díaz del Castillo also offers a description of the deity images from the Templo Mayor. He recalled several as being made of stone, but at least one made of seeds from the land (Díaz del Castillo 1977, 1: 281–82).

In general, the feast of Toxcatl celebrated Tezcatlipoca, another of the major Mexica deities. The festivities of the month fell into two parts. The first part of the month focused on the ritual associated with an *ixiptlah* of Tezcatlipoca, in the form of a man chosen to impersonate the deity for a year as the physical embodiment of the deity.[4] In this festival, the *ixiptlah* was called Titlacahuan ("We, His People") (Olivier 2003, 44). Titlacahuan was an aspect or avatar of Tezcatlipoca. Several of the early colonial authors used the two names almost interchangeably in their descriptions of Tezcatlipoca. Sahagún, in Book II of the *Florentine Codex*, described the selection of the *ixiptlah* in painful detail (Sahagún 1950–82, bk 2: 66–68). The friar devoted scores of words in listing all of the possible physical defects that should be avoided in the selection of the imitator. He also commented that in every respect people treated the *ixiptlah* as the deity. The *ixiptlah* was given wives, the best food, drink, and clothing, and generally treated as the local embodiment of the deity. An important ritual in Toxcatl was the peregrination of the god-impersonator to various important sites. The travel required over four days and occurred five days before the end of the month. At a site called Tlapitzauhcan, the *ixiptlah* eventually met his death by sacrifice at the temple called the Tlalcochcalco. This site has been described as near Chalco Atenco, to the southeast of Tenochtitlan (Sahagún 1950–82, bk 2: 70–71).

Sahagún discussed the Toxcatl festival both in Book II of the *Florentine Codex*, wherein he described all of the other *veintena* ceremonies, and in Book XII, he shared the descriptions of the Toxcatl festival that occurred during the conquest. These accounts, written in Nahuatl with a parallel version in Spanish, come from the elders and others interviewed by Sahagún and his native assistants some forty years after the conquest. These accounts focus on the events of the second half of the month and especially the role played by the amaranth images of the deities, principally that of Huitzilopochtli, in the final ceremonies. Certain aspects of the description are at odds with information found in other parts of the *Florentine Codex*. In particular, in Book XII, Sahagún writes that the feast of Toxcatl was dedicated to Huitzilopochtli, or also known as his feast. But in Book II, Sahagún clearly notes that Toxcatl was dedicated to Tezcatlipoca (Sahagún 1950–82, bk 2: 66, bk 12: 51). The cause of this confusion might well have been that the image that was the focus of the second part of the month was, indeed, of Huitzilopochtli. In spite of this initial discrepancy, the detailed description of the amaranth image and the rituals surrounding it were consistent between these two parts of the *Florentine Codex*.

The descriptions of the dough image of Huitzilopochtli from the two sections of the work align very closely with one another. The image was made at the temple of Huitzilopochtli in the Huitznahuac neighborhood. The basic form was made of mesquite wood that was then covered with dough made from a specific type of amaranth, *michiuauhtli* [*michihuautli*] (fish amaranth), known as *michiuauhtzoalli* [*michihuautzoalli*] when converted into dough. The dough was placed on a mesquite frame, with some dough being made into bones. Once the figure was made, the persons charged with its manufacture then adorned it with the traditional garb of Huitzilopochtli, including the *anecuyotl*, his special headdress, the *tlaquaqualo*, his cape, and the *tehuehuelli*, his shield. He also had face painting, a breechclout, short vest or jacket, a banner, flint knife, and a handful of arrows. Once the image was adorned, it was then placed on a special bier or platform called a *coapechco*, "serpent bench." Four young seasoned warriors then carried the platform from the Huitznahuac temple to the Templo Mayor. Upon arrival at the Templo Mayor, it was then raised using ropes attached to each of the four corners, taking care not to twist or tilt the bench for fear of losing its precious cargo (Sahagún 1950–82, bk 2: 71–73, bk 12: 51–53).

The *Florentine Codex* consists of three texts: the Nahuatl portion, already mentioned, a Spanish version, and the illustrations to accompany the text. The Spanish version of the description of Toxcatl, both in the book on the monthly festivals and in the section on the conquest, does not differ substantially in terms of content from the Nahuatl version, with the exception that in the section on the conquest, the Spanish text is quite brief and lacks any of the extensive details provided in the Nahuatl. The illustrations especially for the section on the conquest are particularly detailed and reaffirm much of what occurs in the text regarding the elaboration of the dough image of Huitzilopochtli. In some ways the illustration from Book II on the monthly festivals offers less information. In Book II the only illustration of the dough image shows a large figure standing before the *huey tlahtoani*. Unfortunately, the image is not dressed in the array of Huitzilopochtli, and so it confuses rather than assists. But clearly, the figure is a standing one, as large as a man. The drawings from Book XII on the conquest, however, are quite helpful, showing the construction and decoration of the figure. A total of six images depict the manufacture, array, and offerings made to the dough figurine. In these drawings the image is, again, the size of a man, but seated rather than standing. In three of the pictures, the *ixiptlah* is seated in front of the Templo Mayor (Sahagún 1979, 3, bk 12: fol. 30v, 31r). In the last image, the *ixiptlah* seems to be seated on the steps of the Temple rather than in the forecourt (Sahagún 1979, 3, bk 12: fol. 32r). The paintings do not clearly show the *anecuyotl* headdress, or the short jacket, but do illustrate the cape, *tehuehuelli* shield, arrows, banner, breechclout, and flint knife.

Friar Diego Durán also provided quite a good deal of information about both the *tzoalli* dough images and about the festivities associated with Toxcatl and Panquetzaliztli. In his description of the Toxcatl rituals, Durán neither mentions the *ixiptlah* of Tezcatlipoca nor the use of a *tzoalli* image, but rather discusses blessings of household goods that were performed by minor priests using incense. Various dances and other rituals accompanied the month. But in the section discussing rituals performed in honor of Tezcatlipoca, Durán mentions something that might be construed as similar to the Toxcatl use of a wooden or *tzoalli* image of the deity. Durán described a ritual during Toxcatl in which either a wooden image of Tezcatlipoca or a human *ixiptlah* was carried on a bier or platform from one neighborhood to the Templo Mayor, where more rituals ensued. Because Durán clarifies that this occurred in Toxcatl and then detailed the wooden framework being carried on a bier or platform and a destination of the Templo Mayor, this must refer to the same ritual that Sahagún described (Durán 1971, 102–04, 426–29). At one point in his description of the *tzoalli* dough image of Huitzilopochtli, Durán suggested that the figure was somewhat large, as large as the actual figure of the god housed in the sacred cell atop the Templo Mayor. The figure was elaborated by a group of young women but it was dressed by a group of noble lords. The figure was placed on a blue bench or litter with handles to be carried by four people.[5]

Just as Sahagún provided images to illustrate the *Florentine Codex*, so Durán included some images in his treatise on native deities and rituals. Two illustrations seem to address the *tzoalli* image used in Toxcatl. The illustration for the month itself is damaged. What remains shows the bottom half of a figure walking from a temple. In spite of the damage, the figure seems to be an *ixiptlah* of Huitzilopochtli. He carries the *tehuehuelli* shield in his left hand, and in his right what seems to be a representation of his signature weapon, the *xiuhcoatl* or "fire snake." Nonetheless, in the legend on that page, Durán explains that the month was dedicated to Tezcatlipoca.

In the illustration of Huitzilopochtli in the section of the work that considers the deities, Durán presents the god as a male figure, seated on a platform. It shows a man wearing the array of the god, Huitzilopochtli, seated on a low platform. He has a gold stripe on his face and one on his forehead. He wears a hummingbird headdress with a golden beak associated with the god. In addition, the figure wears a feather headdress that may or may not be part of the *anecuyotl*. He has a feather cape around his body. In his right hand, he holds the snake staff, iconic of the god. In his left hand, he has the shield with tufts of eagle feathers along with darts without points and a flag. Another flag is tacked on to his back. This is part of a larger image that also includes the symbol for Tenochtitlan, along with aquatic beasts found in the lake, and another seated figure.

Another chronicler to consider the celebrations of the Mexica *xiuhpohualli* was Friar Juan de Torquemada. Torquemada clearly drew heavily from Sahagún for his description of the Toxcatl festivities. Together they provide an extensive description of the construction of the figure of the god made for Toxcatl. Torquemada agreed that the figurine was placed on a litter, like a table or platform, decorated with serpents on each of the four legs. The framework for the figurine was made of mesquite sticks, in the manner of bones. Torquemada offered the most complete description of the adornment of the figure. He reported that it wore a cloth jacket or vest decorated with an image of human bones. He wore a distinctive hat made of paper, wider at the top than at the brim, such that it looked like a bowl. The hat was decorated with feathers and a flint knife. Torquemada was unclear as to whether the flint was a real one or merely feathers made to look like a bloody knife. On his shoulders, the *ixiptlah* of the deity wore a blanket or cloak, the *tlacuacuallo*, made of feathers and held in place with a golden clasp. At the base of the figure, bones made of *tzoalli* were placed, called *teomimilli* [*teumjmjlli*] that represented the god's power over death (Sahagún 1950–82, bk 2: 71–72; Torquemada 1975–83, 3: 380–81).

Torquemada, drawing partially from Sahagún and partially from other sources, explained that the image and litter were carried on the shoulders of men, whom he described as the bravest war captains. On the last night of Toxcatl, the warriors carried the litter to the temple and it was then lifted by means of ropes to keep it level. In front of the litter, there was a large banner made of paper, over 30 meters long and about 1.5 meters wide. It was decorated with the epithets and exploits of the god. Once the litter and image were installed in the god's sanctuary some special rituals were performed. The ruler beheaded four quail in sacrifice and threw them at the base of the god. The warriors who accompanied the ruler collected the quails, which were then salted and prepared for the monarch's meal. The god was also venerated with incense from clay censers. The censer was shaped like a hollow spoon or gourd. Bits of clay were intentionally left in the clay body so that after the firing the censer would rattle (Sahagún 1950–82, bk 2: 72–73; Torquemada 1975–83, 3: 381–82).

Gleaning common information from these sources, one can summarize that the *tzoalli* dough image of Huitzilopochtli used in the Toxcatl festival was the size of a man. It was made on top of a frame of mesquite wood. The image was placed on a platform or bier. It was carried from Huitznahuac to the Templo Mayor. It was dressed in the array of Huitzilopochtli, including his signature headdress, cape, jacket, and shield. In the case of Durán, the association of this figure with Toxcatl is more tenuous. Although he has detailed descriptions of the *tzoalli* and other items, he does not clearly associate it with Toxcatl.

PANQUETZALIZTLI

Panquetzaliztli ("The Raising of Banners") was the fifteenth month of the *xiuhpohualli* and was dedicated to Huitzilopochtli, the principal deity of the Mexica.[6] It occurred in late November and into mid-December of the European calendar. The month was celebrated with singing the hymn dedicated to Huitzilopochtli, the *tlaxotecayotl*, every night, along with dancing. The leading participants in many of the other rituals of the month were seasoned warriors and wealthy merchants. The warriors had captured enemies on the battlefield, while the merchants had purchased slaves. The captured enemies and slaves would be sacrificed in a major ritual at the end of the month. The daily celebrations of the month for the warriors and merchants consisted of minor rites along with banquets to prepare the sacrificial victims for the events of the final day.

The high point of the festivities of Panquetzaliztli occurred on the last day of the month. Spectators would witness a dizzying blur of ceremonies and rituals as the celebrations came to their inevitable end in human sacrifice atop the Templo Mayor and then a *dénouement* that continued into the subsequent month. The logistics of the final day were exceedingly complex, as three different sets of rituals were enacted, all coming together for the final sacrifice. The events of the day began with the emergence of a dough figure of Huitzilopochtli from his sanctuary on the Templo Mayor. This *ixiptlah* was carried on a ritual run through part of Tenochtitlan and the Valley of Mexico called *ipaina Huitzilopochtli*, Huitzilopochtli's swiftness (Durán 1971, 458; see also Sahagún 1950–82, bk 2: 145–47). The dough figure was called variously Painal, Painalton ("Little Painal"), or Painaltzin ("Honored Painal").[7] It was a representation of Huitzilopochtli and thus considered an *ixiptlah*. This local embodiment of the divinity, the dough figurine, would figure as the key element that linked all of the day's ceremonies and performances. Painal was considered a distinct manifestation, or avatar, of Huitzilopochtli. There were three levels of symbolism at work in this ritual. The figurine was an *ixiptlah* of Huitzilopochtli, but called Painal. A bit further on, Sahagún contradicts himself and notes that the figurine representing Painal was made of wood.[8] In a different section, Sahagún also notes that the deity called Painal was an *ixiptlah* of Huitzilopochtli, his deputy or vicar. The priest who carried the Huitzilopochtli figurine had the title of Topiltzin Quetzalcoatl. Not only was the priest called by that title, he was also considered an *ixiptlah* of the god named Quetzalcoatl. Yet in this ceremony he was also an *ixiptlah* of Huitzilopochtli (Bassett 2015, 130–31; Hvidtfeldt 1958, 128, 138–39).[9] The human localized embodiment of Huitzilopochtli carried a dough image that represented Painal that was also a localized embodiment of the same deity.

As a result of this complexity, the sources become somewhat confused as to whether there were one or two images. Some contexts seem to indicate that there were two figurines, one of Huitzilopochtli made of amaranth dough and another of Painal made of wood. Potentially there were three *ixiptlahuan* (pl.): the two figurines and the priest-impersonator.

According to Sahagún, the figurine image of the god that emerged on the last day of Panquetzaliztli was dressed in the raiment of Huitzilopochtli. It wore a feather devise from its shoulder to its waist. It carried the *anecuyotl*, also uniquely related to Huitzilopochtli. It had a golden banner that was the emblem of the month of Panquetzaliztli, along with a green stone necklace. It had a mirror devise on his back and other adornments of turquoise. Lastly, there seems to have been a herald who preceded the god, carrying the deity's unique weapon the *xiuhcoatl*, or fire snake. These were all markers specifically of the god Huitzilopochtli (Sahagún 1950–82, bk 2: 175–76; see also Bassett 2015, 130–31).

In the section on Huitzilopochtli, Durán gave a description of the image: "[The priest] descended from the summit of the temple carrying a dough image made of *tzoalli* dough, which is made of amaranth seeds and maize kneaded with honey. The priest brought down an idol made of this dough. Its eyes were small green beads, and its teeth were grains of corn" (Durán 1971, 80). "The dough was dressed in the form of the god. On it was placed the bird's beak of shining, burnished gold; the feather headdress on his head; his apron of plumes; his shield, staff, bracelets,

and anklets, his splendid sandals; and his breechcloth, a magnificent piece of nee-
dlework and feathers" (Durán 1971, 86).

In Nahua thought, Painal was considered a captain for Huitzilopochtli. In
some stories that tell of a time when both gods were men, Huitzilopochtli would
send Painal in the vanguard. Because Painal was swift, he would lead the troops
into battle. He thus represented the speed that was necessary in war. Sahagún
noted that Painal represented Huitzilopochtli in processions and was his *ixiptlah*
(Sahagún 1950–82, bk 1: 1; see also Torquemada 1975–83, 3: 76). Painal was also
a messenger of the gods, and of Huitzilopochtli in particular. Thus, the Europeans
associated him with the Greco-Roman god Mercury.[10] He carried sticks used for
making fire and a golden banner in his hands (Sahagún 1997, 94–95). The banner
carried by the god is related to the name of the month of Panquetzaliztli, "Raising
of Banners." He credited the name of the ceremony (*ipaina Huitzilopochtli*—the
"swiftness of Huitzilopochtli") to the legend that the god was never taken captive,
always defeated his enemies, and was so fast that his foes could never catch him,
but rather he caught them (Durán 1971, 458). The relationship between Painal
and Huitzilopochtli in Mexica thought must have been so close that they became
largely indistinguishable. When discussing the Panquetzaliztli ritual in the context
of describing the god Huitzilopochtli in Book III of the *Florentine Codex*, Sahagún
(1950–82, bk 3: 5–6) ceased to call the dough figurine Painal, but rather always
referred to it as Huitzilopochtli.[11]

There is confusion about the size, number, and construction of the images.
Durán (1971, 86–87) asserts that the principal image was made of *tzoalli*. In the
chapter on the veneration of Huitzilopochtli, he implies that the figure was rather
large, being carried to the Templo Mayor on a litter by four men, and then lifted
ceremoniously to the sanctuary on top with ropes. But later, in his account of the
ceremonies of Panquetzaliztli, he observed that, "It was about as large as a man
could carry in his arms while fleeing so swiftly that others could not catch up with
him" (Durán 1971, 458).

In the Appendix to Book II, Sahagún again discussed the images used in
Panquetzaliztli but that description matches what was already described earlier in
Book II. In the Appendix, he wrote that there were two images: one of Huitzilopochtli and the other of Tlacauepan Cuexcotzin (or Tlacahuepan Cuexcotzin). The
Huitzilopochtli image was the size of a man, made only of amaranth seed, but carried by a contingent of youths and priests. Tlacahuepan Cuexcotzin was an aspect
of Tezcatlipoca. The figurine was smaller and also made of *tzoalli*. According to the
legend, Tlacahuepan-Tezcatlipoca appeared in the market of the semi-mythical
city of Tula with a little child dancing in his hand. The child was none other than
Huitzilopochtli. Guilhem Olivier also suggests that Tlacahuepan was the patron
god of the Tepanecs, one of the members of the Aztec Triple Alliance (Olivier

2003, 155–56). The fact that Tlacahuepan appeared with a child dancing in his hand, however, also argues that the Huitzilopochtli figure would have been small enough to carry in one's hands. The Nahuatl text implies that both images (Huitzilopochtli and Tlacahuepan) were made or became animated in different places. The verb used in Sahagún is *tlacatia*, meaning to give birth, while *tlacatilia* means to take on human form (Kartunnen 1992, 253).[12] Sahagún indicated that the figure of Huitzilopochtli was made, or became animated, at the place called Itepeyoc ("His Hill"). The corresponding ceremony for the Tlacauepan Cuexcotzin occurred in the Huitznahuac neighborhood of Tenochtitlan. In these ceremonies, the *teixiptlah* became animate during the course of the night of the eighteenth of the month.[13] At morning, the images were revealed and gifts were given to them. In the afternoon, there was a procession that continued until sunset. At that point, the image (or images) was returned to the Templo Mayor. A priest called Yiopoch (Yopoch) guarded the images all night.

As Sahagún continues in the Appendix to Book II, he described the image of Painal, there called Painaltzin. This image was carried in the arms of the priest, and made only of wood, unlike the other *teixiptlah* that was of amaranth. This tends to contradict what he had written earlier in the main portion of Book II. Boone (1989, 37), in her study of Huitzilopochtli, noted that the amaranth images were built upon a wooden framework, and so possibly this image might have been finished in the same way. In all respects, this image of Painal from the Appendix to Book II seems to be the same as the one described elsewhere in the *Florentine Codex*, except for the issue of wood versus amaranth, or a combination of the two. Consequently, Sahagún suggested in the Appendix that there could be three images: two of *tzoalli* (one large, one small), the other of wood. The issue of Painal being made of wood seems to contradict what Sahagún reported elsewhere and what other authors, such as Durán reported, at least for the Panquetzaliztli celebration of *ipaina Huitzilopochtli*. Although, Sahagún (1950–82, bk 2: 175–76) explicitly noted that these figures were used in the celebration of Panquetzaliztli in the Appendix to Book II, they seem to correspond more closely to the feast of Toxcatl. Nonetheless, the remainder of the discussion in the Appendix to Book II deals with the "swiftness of Huitzilopochtli."

Once the image of Huitzilopochtli had been constructed, it was ritually bathed. Yopoch, the local embodiment of Huitzilopochtli, a *teixiptlah*, had undergone a year of fasting and penance in preparation for this moment. He danced when he began his penance, putting on the array of the god, which he wore throughout the course of the year. Similarly, once the *tzoalli* image was completed, Yopoch put on the regalia of the god and danced. A procession began with one dancer leading Yopoch. The master of the young men from the Huitznahua neighborhood served as the guide. Next in the order of the procession came the leaders of the other youth groups, the young seasoned warriors, and all the eagle and ocelot warriors. Since this was the night before the final ceremonies of Panquetzaliztli, pine torches carried along illuminated the way. Adding solemnity to the procession, some participants provided incense and others played flutes (Sahagún 1950–82, bk 3: 7).

The procession wound its way through the southern part of Tenochtitlan to the sanctuary called the House of Mist, *Aiauhcalco* (Ayauhcalco), in the Huitzilopochco neighborhood (Sahagún 1950–82, bk 2: 142; *cf.* Mazzetto 2014, 151). The sanctuary was located on the shores of the lake, a place where ritual bathing had occurred and where the ashes of sacrificial victims were frequently deposited. In the sanctuary, the *tzoalli* image was set down in preparation for the ritual bathing. The *ixiptlah* took off the raiment of the god in anticipation of the ritual. The high priest of Huitzilopochtli collected some water in a blue gourd, which he placed in front of the image, also an *ixiptlah*. He then picked up four fresh, green reeds that he dipped in the gourd bowl of water and then bathed the face of the image four times. At the same time, he also ritually bathed Yopoch, the god-impersonator. This bathing ritual had a cognate ritual when the sacrificial victims were prepared for the final sacrifice.

At the conclusion of the bath, the impersonator dressed again in the raiment of the god and picked up the *tzoalli* image in his arms to the accompaniment of flute playing. From the House of Mist, the procession then went to Itepeyoc, which was the name of one of the other buildings in the sacred precinct of Tenochtitlan. The *tzoalli* image was stored there until the following morning. Many of the men who had done penance returned home to await the final acts of the celebration (Sahagún 1950–82, bk 3: 7–8).

Durán wrote that before dawn on the ceremonial day, the young women who had originally worked on the dough image emerged from their cloister to escort the god to his temple. As his escorts, they were called the *ipilhuan Huitzilopochtli* ("Huitzilopochtli's children") (Durán 1971, 86). The girls wore new white skirts and blouses, adorned with garlands of toasted corn (or popped corn), called *momochitl*, around their heads, as necklaces, and over their left arm. They also wore red paint on their cheeks and red parrot feathers on their forearms. The chosen girls lifted the litter and carried the amaranth image to the temple. As they entered the courtyard, the boys from the religious school attached to the temple, the *telpochcalli*, took over carrying the litter. The boys too were adorned with garlands and necklaces of toasted corn. The boys carried the image to the foot of the Templo Mayor. There the assembled multitude paid honor to the image of the god in the traditional manner by bowing down, touching the ground, and bringing dirt to their lips (Durán 1971, 86–87). Although it was carried on a litter, the context argues that this *ixiptlah* was the small, handheld image of the deity.

THE *TZOALLI IXIPTLAHUAN* OF HUITZILOPOCHTLI

Two different months, Toxcatl and Panquetzaliztli, witnessed celebrations in which *tzoalli* images of Huitzilopochtli figured prominently. As noted earlier, the use of *tzoalli* was nearly ubiquitous in the celebration of the feasts of the *xiuhpohualli*, but only in Toxcatl and Panquetzaliztli were there figurines of Huitzilopochtli. In the case of Toxcatl, the figurine seems to have been carried on a platform, while in Panquetzaliztli the signature ritual, *ipaina Huitzilopochtli*, required that a priest carry the image of the deity while running a circuit that was possibly as long as some twenty-three miles.

Many commentators could not understand why ceremonies to Huitzilopochtli figured so prominently in Toxcatl, a month ostensibly dedicated to Tezcatlipoca. Moreover, the Toxcatl celebration, while it has some similarities to other devotions to Huitzilopochtli, differed from the Panquetzaliztli celebrations particularly in that the participants did not run with the image of the god. Nonetheless, the Spanish who witnessed Toxcatl remembered very well the dancing and other celebrations that were part of the feast. One explanation held that the amaranth image was actually that of Tezcatlipoca and that the Spaniards were mistaken. But this is not a detail that would have confused Sahagún's informants. Olivier (2003, 226) has provided the most cogent explanation. He posited that both gods were honored during these festivities. There were amaranth figurines of both, both had their own unique processions, and then were worshipped together. An eye witness, Diego Holguin, wrote after the conquest that: "that idol Uchilobos [Huitzilopochtli] had an Indian tied on its back with a rope and another idol was in front of him with an Indian in the same manner" (Martínez 1990–92, 1: 207). For Olivier, the other idol was undoubtedly Tezcatlipoca. Obviously, the Spaniards were not fluent in Mexica symbolism and had difficulty telling one god from the other. They might well have known of the tradition of making a dough image of Huitzilopochtli during Panquetzaliztli. When another dough image was used in Toxcatl, the assumption was that it must have been Huitzilopochtli as well. Nevertheless, Olivier's explanation that both gods were honored in this way resolves the confusion and validates the observations of the conquistadors.

Reviewing the sources, two very different images of Huitzilopochtli were used in festivals. One was small, small enough to be carried by one person. It was almost certainly made of *tzoalli*, with additional colored seeds used for various features. It also wore the raiment of Huitzilopochtli, or possibly that of Painal; they differed from one another, as Sahagún's artists depicted in both the *Primeros Memoriales* and in the *Florentine Codex* (Sahagún 1950–82, bk 1: 1–2; 1993, 93–94). Certainly, according to Sahagún (1950–82, bk 2: 145), this small dough figure was called Painal. Others are silent on its name, but suggest that it was an image of or related to Huitzilopochtli. In the ceremony known as *ipaina Huitzilopochtli*, this smaller image had to have been used. The other figure, as large as a man, would simply have weighed too much for a runner to carry it alone.

In Toxcatl, however, a very different image was featured. This was a larger, life-sized image of the god, built upon a framework of mesquite, probably covered with *tzoalli*. It too was decorated with colorful seeds and other touches to make it more life-like. As with the image of Painal, it too was dressed in the array of a god, undoubtedly of Huitzilopochtli. This image was placed on a platform or bier and then carried by at least four men from the Huiznahuac district to the Templo Mayor. At the Templo Mayor it was hoisted to the sanctuary of Huitzilopochtli on top of the temple. There it was probably stored until some later date when it would be ritually executed, only to be replaced by another. The testimony provided by both Cortés and Tapia suggests that what they saw was this life-sized image.

There is an additional option. It is quite possible that in the *ipaina Huitzilopochtli* running ceremony, a team of priests also carried a larger image of Huitzilopochtli as part of the retinue. The Nahuatl is equivocal as to how many images participated in the ritual. Indeed, at one point about a third of the way through, another image is added to the procession, that of Cuahuitl Icac, a brother or companion of Huitzilopochtli (Mazzetto 2019). Nonetheless, none of the extant sources mention a life-sized figure when describing the running ceremony.

What attracts our attention is that these two different representations of Huitzilopochtli were so central to their respective rituals, but became so confused in the minds of the colonial authors who described them. Quite clearly logic demands that the smaller image was used in the *ipaina Huitzilopochtli* run, while the larger took part in the Toxcatl feast. Yet Huitzilopochtli was such an important deity that his presence seems to have overwhelmed many Spanish observers.

NOTES

1. One reason why *teixiptlah* appears less frequently is that "his, her, or its" *ixiptla* (that is an object possessed by a specific person) would be "*iixiptlah*." But the two i's generally get fused in writing. Secondly, the "h" at the end signifies that the word ends with a glottal stop, a consonant in Nahuatl, which while present in English, lacks a graphic character, so by convention in Nahuatl it is nowadays written with the letter "h." For a more detailed discussion of the notion of *teixiptlah*, see Bassett (2015, 132-35). In this chapter, when the referent is known, generally I will use *ixiptlah* (its local embodiment), but when the referent is not known or speaking in general terms, *teixiptlah* (someone's local embodiment).

2. While Sahagún's description of the running ceremony begins on p. 145 of Book II of the *Florentine Codex*, he does not mention that the figure is made of amaranth dough until p. 146 (Sahagún 1950–82, bk 2: 145–46).

3. "*Auh in muchioaia, in tlacatia Vitzilobuchtli ixiptla: vmpa in itocaiocan Itepeioc,*" "And when the image of Uitzilopochtli was made when it took human form, it was there at Itepeyoc" (Sahagún

1950–82, bk 2: 175). Here the verb *tlacati* can mean "to take human form" or "to become animate" (on this topic, see also Olivier in this volume, Chapter Two).

4. On this topic, see also Chinchilla Mazariegos in this volume (Chapter One).

5. At least one dough image was sent to Europe in the sixteenth century, as in that there are records of it being given by Francesco de Medici to Albrecht V. See Keating and Markey (2011, 292).

6. A fuller description and analysis of the Panquetzaliztli celebrations can be found in Schwaller (2019).

7. In Nahuatl, there is no difference between "i" and "y." Thus, in some instances authors prefer Painal, while others use Paynal.

8. Sahagún offers different details on the nature of the image. In Book II, Chapter 34, very late in his description, he notes that the image was made of amaranth. In Book II, Appendix, "Temple of Uitzilopochtli," he insists that there were two amaranth dough images, but that the image of the "Swiftness of Huitzilopochtli" was only made of sticks (Sahagún 1950–82, bk 2: 145–46 versus 175).

9. For a detailed discussion of the category of this priest, the *tlamacazqui*, see Contel and Mikulska Dąbrowska (2011, 32–35).

10. Several scholars have demonstrated that Sahagún and other Franciscan missionaries frequently attempted to categorize the Mexica pantheon according to the Greco-Roman tradition with which they were already familiar. See Botta (2010); Olivier (2010, 2016). The suggestion that Painal was similar to Mercury helps to demonstrate that one must be judicious in using Sahagún because of intrusive material.

11. This has led to confusion about the number of figurines.

12. On this topic, see also Olivier in this volume (Chapter Two).

13. The day is conjectural, counting backwards from the known ceremony of Painal that occurred on the 20th of the month.

REFERENCES

Bassett, Molly H. 2015. *The Fate of Earthly Things: Aztec Gods and God-Bodies*. Austin: University of Texas Press.

Boone, Elizabeth H. 1989. *Incarnations of the Aztec Supernatural: The Image of Huitzilopochtli in Mexico and Europe*. Philadelphia: American Philosophical Society.

Botta, Sergio. 2010. "The Franciscan Invention of Mexican Polytheism: The Case of the Water Gods." *Studi e Materiali di Storia delle Religioni* 76, no. 2: 411–32.

Caso, Alfonso. 1967. *Los calendarios prehispánicos*. Mexico City: Universidad Nacional Autónoma de México-Instituto de Investigaciones Históricas.

Contel, José, and Katarzyna Mikulska Dąbrowska. 2011. "'Mas nosotros que somos dioses nunca morimos.' Ensayo sobre *Tlamacazqui*: ¿Dios, sacerdote o qué otro demonio?." In *De dioses y hombres: Creencias y rituales mesoamericanos y sus supervivencias*, edited by Katarzyna Mikulska Dąbrowska and José Contel, 23–65. Warsaw: University of Warsaw.

Cortés, Hernán. 1963. *Cartas y documentos*. Mexico City: Porrúa.

Díaz del Castillo, Bernal. 1977. *La historia verdadera de la conquista de la Nueva España*. 2 vols. Mexico City: Porrúa.

Durán, Diego. 1971. *Book of the Gods and Rites and the Ancient Calendar*. Translated and edited by Fernando Horcasitas and Doris Heyden. Norman: University of Oklahoma Press.

Fuentes, Patricia de. 1963. *The Conquistadores: First-Person Accounts of the Conquest of Mexico.* New York: Orion.

Hvidtfeldt, Arild. 1958. *Teotl and *Ixiptlatli: Some Central Conceptions in Ancient Mexican Religion.* Copenhagen: Muksgaard.

Kartunnen, Frances. 1992. *An Analytical Dictionary of Nahuatl.* Norman: University of Oklahoma Press.

Keating, Jessica, and Lia Markey. 2011. "'Indians' Objects in Medici and Austrian-Habsburg Inventories." *Journal of the History of Collections* 23: 283–300.

Martínez, José Luis, ed. 1990–92. *Documentos cortesianos.* 4 vols. Mexico City: Fondo de Cultura Económica.

Mazzetto, Elena. 2014. "Las *ayauhcalli* en el ciclo de las veintenas del año solar. Funciones y ubicación de las casas de niebla y sus relaciones con la liturgia del maíz." *Estudios de Cultura Náhuatl* 48: 135–75.

———. 2017. "¿Miel o sangre? Nuevas problemáticas acerca de la elaboración de las efigies de *tzoalli* de las divinidades nahuas." *Estudios de Cultura Náhuatl* 53: 73–118.

———. 2019. "Mitos y recorridos divinos en la veintena de Panquetzaliztli." *Trace* 75: 46–85.

Morán, Elizabeth. 2016. *Sacred Consumption: Food and Ritual in Aztec Art and Culture.* Austin: University of Texas Press.

Olivier, Guilhem. 2003. *Mockeries and Metamorphoses of an Aztec God: Tezcatlipoca, "Lord of the Smoking Mirror."* Translated by Michel Besson. Niwot: University of Colorado Press.

———. 2010. "El panteón mexica a la luz del politeísmo grecolatino: el ejemplo de la obra de fray Bernardino de Sahagún." *Studi e Materiali di Storia delle Religioni* 76, no. 2: 389–410.

———. 2016. "The Mexica Pantheon in Light of Graeco-Roman Polytheism: Uses, Abuses, and Proposals." In *Altera Roma. Art and Empire from Mérida to Mexico,* edited by John M. D. Pohl and Claire L. Lyons, 189–214. Los Angeles: University of California Press, Cotsen Institute of Archaeology Press.

Reyes Equiguas, Salvador. 2005. "El *huauhtli* en la cultura náhuatl." MA thesis, Universidad Nacional Autónoma de México.

Sahagún, Bernardino de. 1950–82. *Florentine Codex: General History of the Things of New Spain, Fray Bernardino de Sahagún.* Translated with notes and illustrations by Arthur J. O. Anderson and Charles E. Dibble. 13 vols. Santa Fe: The School of American Research, University of Utah Press.

———. 1979. *Códice Florentino. El manuscrito 218–220 de la colección palatina de la Biblioteca Medicea Laurenziana.* 3 vols. Florence, Mexico City: Giunti Barbéra, Archivo General de la Nación.

———. 1993. *Primeros Memoriales: Facsimile Edition.* Norman: University of Oklahoma Press.

———. 1997. *Primeros Memoriales.* Edited and translated by Thelma Sullivan. Completed and revised, with additions, by Henry B. Nicholson, Arthur J. O. Anderson, Charles E. Dibble, Eloise Quiñones Keber, and Wayne Ruwet. Norman: University of Oklahoma Press.

Schwaller, John F. 2019. *The Fifteenth Month: Aztec History in the Rituals of Panquetzaliztli.* Norman: University of Oklahoma Press.

Torquemada, Juan de. 1975–83. *Monarquía Indiana.* Edited by Miguel León-Portilla. 7 vols. Mexico City: Universidad Nacional Autónoma de México-Instituto de Investigaciones Históricas.

CHAPTER EIGHT

Myths, Rites, and the Agricultural Cycle

The *Huixtotin* Priests and the *Veintenas*

SYLVIE PEPERSTRAETE

In the descriptions and images of *veintena* festivals that have come down to the present, although Huixtotin priests are involved in rites addressed to deities associated with water, such as the Salt Goddess Huixtocihuatl or the Rain God Tlaloc and his helpers the Tlaloque, they also participate in rites that imply ties to maize goddesses such as Chicomecoatl and Xilonen. However, the latter had their own priests, respectively known as the Chichicomecoa and the "women who belonged to Xilonen," which raises the question: what were the roles and the symbolism of the Huixtotin priests in rites dedicated to these goddesses? This query, a starting point and guiding thread throughout the present discussion, leads to a reconsideration of the Mexica priestly organization and how the *veintena* festivals took place in light of the indigenous thought system and its categories. Through this line of inquiry, it will also be possible to demonstrate the interest in as well as the need for a global study of the *veintena* cycle and the continuities between the different fiestas.[1]

This chapter focusing on the figure of Huixtotin priests in *veintena* rites is part of a broader research project undertaken on the priestly organization among the Mexicas (e.g. Peperstraete 2014, 2015, 2016). After an introduction to the state of current knowledge on Mexica priests, discussion zeroes in on the Huixtotin. In the first place, the word and its connotations are analyzed, studying its etymology and its occurrence in the context of speech. Then the insignia worn by Huixtotin priests is assessed, as is the role of these ritual specialists in the *veintena* fiestas in which they participated. Finally, the study concludes by offering a reflection on what it adds to our current understanding of this priestly organization among the Mexicas, and how this organization and *veintena* rites reflected the dynamism of indigenous thought.

PRIESTS AND PRIESTLY ORGANIZATION AMONG THE MEXICA

The subject of the priestly organization among the Mexica has received little scholarly attention to date, with the notable exception being an article by Miguel Acosta Saignes and a book by Miguel Pastrana Flores, which nonetheless solely deals with the *calpulli* priests (Acosta Saignes 1946; Pastrana Flores 2008). This is a consequence of the lack of interest on the part of colonial-period authors in pre-Hispanic priests. Sadly, they established virtually no distinctions among priests. They always employed the same general words, such as "ministers of idols," whereas in Nahuatl there were several dozen of different words to refer to priests (*teohuatzin, tlenamacac, cuacuilli,* etc.; only the detailed descriptions of rites in Nahuatl, such as those of Sahagún's informants, provided specific terms) (Sahagún 1950–82, especially bk 2).

Furthermore, colonial-period European authors described indigenous priests in such a way that their categories of thought were implicit and had little to do with the indigenous world, as was the custom among these chroniclers who were obviously unaware of modern anthropological methods. Consequently, *fray* Bernardino de Sahagún, not knowing of the overlap between political and religious power in pre-Hispanic Mexico, dedicated an entire volume of his *General History of the Things of New Spain* to Mexica kings and lords without addressing the question of their priestly function (Sahagún 1950–82, bk 8). As for the priests that colonial authors identified as such, they described them in light of their knowledge on the Western world, despite the divergences that at times were considerable. Thus, *fray* Diego Durán (1995, 1: 210) compared the denominations of Mexica priests to those of the sixteenth-century Spanish Catholic clergy, despite the lack of correspondence between the categories in these two universes. What is more, the author observed, in another chapter of his work (Durán 1995, 2: 36, 40), that in ancient Mexico, the numerous servants of the gods only acted as such for a limited period of time, usually a year. In this way, the sort of "planning for the priestly vocation" laid out by Sahagún (1950–82, bk 3: 67), besides being overly simplistic, is inadequate, because with few exceptions, ritual specialists rarely devoted their entire lives to the service of the gods. Indeed, some ranks were more important than others, but the Mexica had a broad spectrum of ritual specialists, with highly diverse rules and purposes, and they were organized in a much more complex way than what is presented by colonial authors. The Nahuatl vocabulary for designating priests, particularly in descriptions of rites, attests to their ample variety. The terms can, for example, refer to their function (as is the case of the *tonalpouhque* who were specialists in the *tonalpohualli*, the 260-day ritual calendar), or their rank (the *tlamacaztoton* were literally "small *tlamacazque*" or "small priests"), or the deity that they served (the *chichicomecoa* were the priests of Chicomecoatl), or their age (*ihuehue*—"their elders"), or their appearance (*papahuaque*—the "hairy ones"), or to the duration of their participation in rites (*mocexiuhzauhque*—"those who fasted for a year"), and so forth. The fact that the words used to refer to a single priest may vary from one passage to another in colonial indigenous discourses (e.g. Sahagún 1950–82, bk 2: 50, 75, 81–82, 196–97; bk 3: 67; see also Peperstraete 2016, 9–10) is perhaps the most interesting feature. Depending on the circumstances, these variations can be more or less precise and reveal different aspects. Above all, these designations were not mutually exclusive, as demonstrated by the existence of long lists resembling litanies when it was necessary to evoke various characteristics simultaneously. Therefore, in Teotl Eco, the arrival of Tezcatlipoca was awaited by a figure known as the *cuacuilli*, the *huehue*, the god's *teohuatzin* (Sahagún 1950–82, bk 2: 119) to simultaneously evoke the high rank, age, and relationship to Tezcatlipoca of this ritual specialist. This highly flexible and ingenious system was adapted to the dynamism of the Mexica pantheon and to the networks of symbolic associations characteristic of Nahua thought.

The iconography of the priests was equally diversified. In codices, priests are habitually shown with their bodies smeared with black pigment, but they can also possess numerous other attributes as a function, for instance, of their rank or their role in the ritual. Accordingly, in images of the *veintena* festivals in the *Primeros Memoriales* (Sahagún 1993, fol. 250r–253r) each priest is depicted with his own insignia. In this case, a comparison of the iconographic data with the information from texts may make it possible to identify some of these figures with precision. For example, in the *Primeros Memoriales* the images and Nahuatl text on the ritual specialists in the fiestas of Atlcahualo (or Cuahuitlehua) and Panquetzaliztli (Sahagún 1993, fol. 250r, 252v; 1997, 55–56, 64–65; see also Espinosa Pineda 2010, 71–73, 102–06) reveal that the *tlenamacac*, a high-ranking priest, has long hair and carries a gourd with tobacco, as well as a *xiquipilli* copal bag; the *tlenamacac* is literally he who "makes fire offerings," hence his close relationship with the act of burning copal (Figure 8.1). In addition, iconographic variations appear as a function of the fiestas and the gods that the priests served. For instance, in Atlcahualo (or Cuahuitlehua), the *tlenamacaque* (plural of *tlenamacac*) wear a blue *xicolli* vest, a color that refers to the Tlaloque (Sahagún 1993, fol. 250r; see also Peperstraete 2015, 5–9).

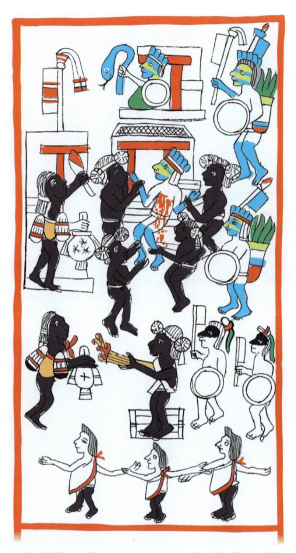

Figure 8.1. Panquetzaliztli. Detail of *Primeros Memoriales*, fol. 252v. Source: Drawing courtesy of Nicolas Latsanopoulos.

HUIXTOTL **AND** *HUIXTOTIN*

Before studying Huixtotin priests, it is essential to analyze the word *huixtotl* (plural *huixtotin*) and its multiple connotations. Assessing its appearance in the context of speech as well as its etymology can shed greater light on its meaning. The word *huixtotl* occurs *a priori* in quite different contexts: in the name of the Salt Goddess,

Huixtocihuatl, in the name of the Olmeca-Huixtotin, a group whose land was identified with the east coast (Sahagún 1950–82, bk 10: 187–88) and in the name that refers to one of the heavens depicted in the first folio of the *Codex Vaticanus A* or *Ríos* (*Códice Vaticano A* 1996, fol. 1v), *ilhuicatl huixtotlan* (Figure 8.2). In the latter image, the figure represented in the heaven has a sort of paper fan on the back of its neck, the *tlaquechpaniotl*, referring to water; this is highly suggestive, because the common denominator in Huixtocihuatl, the Olmeca-Huixtotin, and *ilhuicatl huixtotlan* is precisely the sea.

In fact, the root *huix-* means, according to Eduard Seler (1909, 112–13), saltwater or the sea, because it appears constantly in movement. That said, there are other related Nahuatl words, such as *huihuixca*, which means "to tremble, shiver," or *huihuixoa* which means "to shake, sway, rock, awake," or *huihuixalhuia* which means "to shake, sway, rock back and forth, swing something at some-one."[2] In this way, if *huixtotlan* refers to one of the heavens, it is because, as the informants of Sahagún (1950–82, bk 11: 247) explain "The people of old, the people here of New Spain, thought and took as truth that the heavens were just like a house; it stood resting in every direction, and it extended reaching to the water. It was as if the water walls were joined to it" (*in ie vecauhtlaca, in njcan nueva españa tlaca, momatia, ioan iuhquj neltocaia, ca in ilhujcatl, çan iuhqujnma calli, noviiampa tlacçaticac: auh itech acitoc in atl, iuhqujnma acaltechtli itech mot-latzoa: auh ic qujtocaiotique*). And hence they called it *ilhuicaatl,* in other words "celestial water," "because it stretched extending to the heavens" (*iehica acitimanj in ilhujcatl*).

Thus, the word Huixtotl refers to the sea. In this context, we understand why Huixtocihuatl, who is literally "Huixtotl woman," is the goddess of salt or salt-water. As seen in the *Primeros Memoriales* (Sahagún 1997, 106), the insignia of Huixtocihuatl (*Vixtociuatl, inechichiuh*) were her yellow face paint (*yxaval cuztic*), paper headdress with quetzal feather crest (*y yamacal quetzalmiavayo*), gold ear ornaments (*yteucuitlanacuch*), *huipil* (tunic) with water designs (*yvipil atlacuiloli*), skirt with water motifs (*yn icue atlacuiloli*), her bells (*ytzitzil*), sandals (*ycac*), shield with white water lily (*Nymphaea odorata*) (*ychimal atlacueçonayo*), and the *oztopilli* stick (*y yoztopil imac icac*) in her hand.

Figure 8.2. The *ilhuicatl huixtotlan*. Detail of *Codex Vaticanus A* or *Ríos*, fol. 1v. Source: Drawing courtesy of Nicolas Latsanopoulos.

The preceding attests to the close relationship of this goddess with water. Furthermore, the *Florentine Codex* states that she is *inveltiuh in tlaloque*, "the elder sister of the *tlaloque*" (Sahagún 1950–82, bk 2: 86). In fact, she might share certain accoutrements with them. Thus, for example, the *Codex Vaticanus A* or *Ríos* (*Códice Vaticano A* 1996, fol. 45v) and the *Codex Telleriano-Remensis* (1995, fol. 1r) represent Huixtocihuatl as an emblem of the celebration of Tecuilhuitontli in which the goddess's personification was sacrificed (Figure 8.3). She wears paper ornaments splattered with rubber and a pleated paper fan, the *tlaquechpaniotl*, just as many other water deities (e.g. Chalchiuhtlicue and Tlaloc: *Códice Borbónico* 1991, pl. 5, 7, 23, etc.). Her skirt is bedecked with motifs resembling those on the *xicolli* vest found in Templo Mayor Offering 102, which was associated with rain deities (Barrera Rivera et al. 2001, 74). Moreover, Huixtocihuatl is particularly close to the Water Goddess Chalchiuhtlicue, who, like her, is an "elder sister of the *tlaloque*" according to the *Florentine Codex* (Sahagún 1950–82, bk 1: 21). In fact, the attributes of Huixtocihuatl might be confused with those of Chalchiuhtlicue and, according to the data from the *Primeros Memoriales* (Sahagún 1997, 104, 106), there is a similarity in garb, particularly in the costume of the two goddesses—both

Figure 8.3. Huixtocihuatl as the emblem of the Tecuilhuitontli *veintena*. Detail of *Codex Vaticanus A* or *Ríos*, fol. 45v. Source: Drawing courtesy of Nicolas Latsanopoulos.

are painted with lines indicating water or blue waves (Franconi 2014, 9–11; Seler 1909, 112). All of this reinforces the aquatic symbolism.

However, we can also see in these images and in the description from the *Primeros Memoriales* that Huixtocihuatl has yellow face paint, which indicates that Huixtocihuatl also has a kinship with deities of food and fertility. In fact, the *Florentine Codex* specifies that during the rites of Tecuilhuitontli, the face paint of the personification of Huixtocihuatl was made of yellow from *tecozahuitl*, a yellow compared with that of the corn flower (Sahagún 1950–82, bk 2: 86). Élodie Dupey García has noted that two groups of female deities had face paint made with *tecozahuitl*: personifications of food—salt, growing maize—and mother-goddesses, which incarnate fertility (Dupey García 2016, 24; 2018). We shall return to this connection, which, reinforced by iconography and deity attributes, links water, foodstuffs, and fertility.

Through the sea and its associations with fertility, Huixtotl referred to origins and primordial waters, which in turn also evoked Tollan, Tlalocan, and their extraordinary and boundless wealth. As a result, Huixtocihuatl, the female Huixtotl, belonged to the people known as the Olmeca-Huixtotin, whose domains were the tropical, moist, fertile lands of the Gulf of Mexico. That said, these Olmeca-Huixtotin had a longstanding reputation with ancient roots: they were associated with the beginning of history. Michel Graulich has underscored that, at times, they were confused with giants (Graulich 2005, 277)—whose king had been Tlaloc, according to Ixtlilxóchitl (1975–77, 2: 273). Sullivan (in Sahagún 1997, 106, n. 70) added that even in 1566, the cacique of Xaltocan, Pablo Nazareo (1970, 29), mentioned the *Vixtocanorum* (Huixtocans) among the peoples who had reigned in pre-Toltec times.

It is precisely for the wealth and prestige derived from their antiquity that the land of the Olmeca-Huixtotin was associated with Tollan. Thus, Sahagún's informants (Sahagún 1950–82, bk 10: 187–88) describe the Olmeca-Huixtotin as the children of Quetzalcoatl and Toltecs, for the riches of their territory, whose features were blurred with the attributes of the mythical Tollan (Sahagún 1950–82, bk 10: 165–70). Moreover, they dwelled in a region of abundance equivalent to the mythical home of Tlaloc, known as Tlalocan; Sahagún's informants say of the Olmeca Vixtoti Mixteca (Olmeca-Huixtotin Mixteca) (Sahagún 1950–82, bk 10: 187–88): "They were rich; their home, their land, was really a land of riches, a land of flowers, a land of wealth, a land of abundance ... The old people gave it the name of Tlalocan, which is to say, 'place of wealth'" (*Injque y, mocujltonoa in jnchan, in jntlalpan, vel tonacatlalpan, xuchitlalpan, necujltonoloian ... qujtocaiotitivi in vevetque Tlalocan quitoznequi necujltonoloia*). The Franciscan friar echoes this idea and develops it in the adaptation of the Spanish text (Sahagún 1969, 3: 206): "surely a most fertile land, for which the ancient [people] called it Tlalocan, which means land of riches and earthly paradise" (*tierra cierto fertilísima, por lo cual*

la llamaron los antiguos Tlalocan, que quiere decir, tierra de riquezas y paraíso terrenal).
It was, thus, a place so rich and fertile, so paradisiacal for the friar that he gathered
these words, as Alfredo López Austin highlighted, which were worthy of the name
of Tlalocan (López Austin 1997, 214–15). In fact, the description is quite similar
to that of Sahagún's informants:

> And in Tlalocan all prospered greatly; all enjoyed much wealth. Never did one suffer. Never
> was there lack of ears of green maize, [nor] squash, squash blossoms, heads of amaranth,
> green *chilis*, tomatoes, green beans, [nor] the *Tagetes* flower ... And so, they said that in
> Tlalocan all is ever green, always in growth, always spring; it is always spring time (*auh in*
> *tlalocan cenca netlamachtilo, cenca necuiltonolo, aic mihjiovia, aic polivi in elotl, in aiotetl, yn*
> *aioxochquilitl, in oauhtzontli, in chilchotl, i xitomatl, yn exotl, in cempoalxochitl ... iuh qujtoa in*
> *tlalocan, muchipa tlacelia, muchipa tlatzmolini, muchipa xopantla tlaxopanmamanj).* (Sahagún
> 1950–82, bk 3: 45; see also Anderson 1988, 151–55)

This takes us, once again, to the connection with water, vegetation, foodstuffs,
and fertility, and it is precisely all of this in turn that the Huixtotin priests evoked
in rites.

WHO WERE THE *HUIXTOTIN* PRIESTS?

In an earlier article, I emphasized the fact that two gods, Quetzalcoatl and Tlaloc,
were particularly linked to the priesthood (Peperstraete 2014, 9–11). The former
is often painted black, holding the *xiquipilli* copal bag and priestly implements of
autosacrifice (e.g. *Códice Borbónico* 1991, pl. 22), while at the conclusion of the Tollan
myth, he appears as the archetype of priests. Sahagún's informants say of him:

> And this Quetzalcoatl also did penances. He bled the calf of his leg to stain thorns with
> blood. And he bathed at midnight. And he bathed there where his bathing place was, at
> a place named Xippacoyan ... And the priests took their manner of conduct from the life
> of Quetzalcoatl. (*auh yoan in iehoatl in Quetzalcoatl no tlamaceoaia qujçoaia, in itlanitz ynjc*
> *quezviaia in vitztli, yoan maltiaia iooalnepantla: auh in vmpa onmaltia, in inealtiaia catca, ito-*
> *caiocan xippacoian ... inemiliz in quetzalcoatl in qujmonemiliztiaia in tlamacazque).* (Sahagún
> 1950–82, bk 3: 14)

It is probably in reference to this mythical model that in Mexico-Tenochtitlan,
the two high priests were given the title of *quetzalcoatl.* Just like this god, the *quet-*
zalcoatl priests lived a reclusive life and rarely left their shrines (Sahagún 1950–82,
bk 6: 210).

However, priests also resembled Tlaloc, whose epithet Tlamacazqui, literally
"he who gives" or "the provider," is also one of the most frequent appellations for
priests. As the god of rain as well as the earth (Contel 2006; Klein 1980; Sullivan
1974), and by extension, of vegetation and fertility, Tlaloc was responsible for all

sustenance. From Tlalocan he sent everything needed for life; he offered favors to human beings, hence his name Tlamacazqui (López Austin 1997, 209). "Being called Tlaloc Tlamacazqui," wrote Sahagún (1969, 1: 45), "means that he is [the] god who dwells in the earthly paradise, and he gives men the food necessary for bodily life." That being so, priests often wear his insignia in rites, to the extent that at times they can be confused with him. Just as José Contel and Katarzyna Mikulska Dąbrowska proposed, this ambiguity was probably intentional (Contel and Mikulska Dąbrowska 2011, 31–39). The word *tlamacazqui* (pl. *tlamacazque*) underscores the proximity between priests and the divine world they accessed, thus making them mediators between the two universes, much like Tlaloc. However, just as Tlaloc Tlamacazqui, the provider deity, held back all food resources and ensured the survival of human beings, *tlamacazque* priests were responsible for the gods' needs in a relationship of reciprocity. The parallel between rain gods and priests is closer with the *tlenamacaque* priests because, just as Tlaloc is the origin of clouds and fertilizes the earth, the *tlenamacaque*, "givers of fire," waft sacrificial victims with incense[3] and "smite" them by slitting them open with their flint knife, the stone generating sparks of fire and life itself (Graulich 2005, 230–31). The Rain God offers water to humankind for agriculture and they, in turn, give him another type of water: sacrificial blood, known as *chalchiuh-atl*, "precious water" (Botta 2004, 113–14).

It comes as no surprise that the Huixtotin priests bear a strong resemblance to Tlaloc and, as we shall see, even more to the Tlaloque. According to written sources, they participated in certain *veintena* festivals, where they wore Tlaloque accoutrements (the pleated *tlaquechpaniotl* and other paper ornaments splattered with rubber). They had the typical face paint (*texotli* blue on the forehead and a wave motif), as well as the emblem of the Olmeca-Huixtotin, an insignia in the form of an eagle claw. This claw was made of quetzal head feathers and eagle down arranged on a wood structure that was tied to the head (Sahagún 1950–82, bk 2: 88). A similar claw adorned the head of one of the figures on the stone sculpture known as Teocalli of Sacred Warfare (Caso 1927, 21–23) (Figure 8.4a). Significantly, this personage has Tlaloc's face. The same insignia is represented in the headdress of Yohualtecuhtli in the central part of the *Codex Borgia* (*Códice Borgia* 1993, pl. 35; Guilhem Olivier 2016, personal communication) (Figure 8.4b), which relates this claw to the night and, by extension, to death; this is also the case of the figure on the Teocalli, who has a fleshless jaw and wears paper rosettes characteristic of figures linked to death (Caso 1927, 18–19; Klein 1984, 36–38). The inverted eagle claw can perhaps be tied to descending birds seen in other images in the *Codex Borgia*, especially in plate 18 where an eagle descends holding a flint knife in its beak. Be that as it may, Huixtotin priests are also linked to death, for in *veintena* festivals they intervene in sacrifices.

Figure 8.4. (a) Figure wearing the eagle claw on the Teocalli of Sacred Warfare. Source: Drawing courtesy of Nicolas Latsanopoulos; (b) Yohualtecuhtli. Detail of *Codex Borgia*, pl. 35. Source: Drawings courtesy of Nicolas Latsanopoulos.

In the sources consulted, four *veintena* rites involved *huixtotin* priests. The first is that of Etzalcualiztli, a *veintena* dedicated to Chalchiuhtlicue, Tlaloc, and the Tlaloque. It is probably in the guise of the Huixtotin that the priests performed the *veintena* sacrifices and punished negligent priests. In fact, at the start of the day of the sacrifice of the Tlaloque impersonators, these priests wore paper insignia (*tlaquechpaniotl*, and so forth), they blackened their bodies, and as detailed by Sahagún's informants, "*yoan neixquatexoujlo, mjxquatexoujaia, yoan michioaia, moujxtoichioaia*" (Sahagún 1950–82, bk 2: 82), which Dibble and Anderson translate as, "their foreheads were stained blue—they were colored blue—and their bodies were stained. They were painted after the manner of Uixtociuatl." However, a more literal translation, "they painted their forehead blue, they put blue on their forehead, they adorned themselves, they adorned themselves like the Uixtotin" (the author's translation) seems more appropriate. In fact, Seler (1927, 125) translates the same passage "they painted their face as water in movement" (*bemalt das Gesicht in der Art des bewegten Wassers*), and in Alexis Wimmer's dictionary, the word *huixtohihchihua* is translated as "to paint the face as the Olmecs, to paint the face with waves" (*se peindre, se parer le visage à la manière des Olmèques, se peindre le visage de vagues*) (Wimmer 2006). Thus, this is a description of the face paint of the Huixtotin instead of that of Huixtocihuatl, who had a yellow face, as noted earlier. Moreover, this face paint with the wave motif and blue on the forehead also appears in Durán's (1995, 1: pl. 34) book, on the face of a priest wearing garb with the water motif and performing a ceremony at the inauguration of the aqueduct built by Ahuitzotl. In all likelihood, it depicts a Huixtotl priest. As for the blue pigment (*texotli*) used, Dupey García (2010a, 438–43) notes that it was regarded as a complement, or even as a substitute, for rubber or *olli* in Nahuatl. All of these features confirm the symbolic context is that of moisture and fertility. We should bear in mind that this painting also evokes the Tlaloque, evident in the description of the insignia of the deceased destined for Tlalocan: "These, when they died, they did not burn, but only buried. They applied liquid rubber to their faces; and with fish amaranth [paste] they covered their cheeks; and they colored their foreheads blue. And they gave them [each] a paper lock of hair at the back of the head" (*in iehoan jn, yn iquac miqui, amo tlatla, can qujntocaia, quimixolviaia, yoan michioauhtli, incamapan conpachooa, yoan quimjxquatexoviaia, yoan quimahamacuexpaltiaia*) (Sahagún 1950–82, bk 3: 45).

Given that the *veintena* of Etzalcualiztli was primarily dedicated to Tlaloc and the Tlaloque, the insignia of the Huixtotin, entities with aquatic connotations similar to the Tlaloque, were completely appropriate. The priest who led the celebrants were the Tlalocan Tlenamacac, one of the two high priests, dressed as Tlaloc for the occasion; his face was smeared with rubber, while he wore a quetzal and heron feather headdress, an *ayauhxicolli* (mist jacket), and a Tlaloc mask, and his hair was long and matted. He performed rites related to rain and fertility: he struck four jade stones placed on a reed mat with a curved blue staff, going back and forth, and around in circles, then he scattered dried sweet-scented marigold flowers (*Tagetes lucida*), called *yauhtli* in Nahuatl, and shook the *ayauhchicahuaztli* (Sahagún 1950–82, bk 2: 82–83).[4] At midnight the captives were sacrificed—to serve as the "fundament" of the divine impersonators—and then the sacrifice of the personifications of the Tlaloque. The *tlamacazque* took offerings, along with the hearts of the victims to Pantitlan, where the *tlenamacac* cast the hearts into the water. At dawn, the priests washed the blue paint from their foreheads at a place called *nealtiaian tlamacazque*, "the priests' bathing place." They also punished those who had not observed the fast for Tlaloc by casting them into the water (Sahagún 1950–82, bk 2: 83–85). Unfortunately, no image related to this *veintena* shows the Huixtotin priests in action.[5]

Huixtotin priests appear in rites for the Tecuilhuitontli *veintena*. In the *Florentine Codex*, a woman who impersonated Huixtocihuatl was sacrificed at the temple of Tlaloc during this *veintena* (Sahagún 1950–82, bk 2: 88–89). Davíd Carrasco (1999, 201) interpreted the attribution of this name to the priests as a metamorphosis of the place within the ritual. It was regarded as part of the archetypical domains of the Olmeca-Huixtotin, this rich and mythical place of origin on the coast. In turn, Graulich (2005, 123), for whom the paradise of Tamoanchan and the end of Tollan were evoked in Tecuilhuitontli, believes that the festival recreates a place of origin, specifically among the Olmeca-Huixtotin and the ancient denizens of Tlalocan. That said, as Contel observed (2016, §10), Tlalocan, "where and when Tlaloc is," is not only a place, but also a concept that encompasses the group of spatial and temporal domains under the influence of Tlaloc. This god assumes control of places, things, and animate beings; therefore the priests under discussion are converted into Huixtotin in the framework of this ritual context linked to Tlalocan and to places of origin associated with riches in myths. At dawn, according to the *Florentine Codex* (Sahagún 1950–82, bk 2: 88), the priests were bedecked as Huixtotin—they wore their face paint, their insignia in the form of the eagle claw, a *tlaquechpaniotl*, and another creased paper ornament that was placed at the neck, the *amacuexpalli*—and they took some captives and Huixtocihuatl to the Tlaloc pyramid. They began to kill the prisoners. Then, they put the rostrum of a sawfish on the neck of Huixtocihuatl and the sacrificer sliced open her chest and ripped out her heart. As Graulich (1999, 376–77) has emphasized, the sawfish, *acipactli*, possibly refers to *cipactli*, the creature with saurian features forming the earth and the sky in origin myths (e.g. "Historia de los mexicanos por sus pinturas" 1965, 25–26; Thévet 1905, 28–29).[6]

Unfortunately, the images of the rites in this *veintena* are extremely simplified and they do not allow us to observe the typical Huixtotin attributes worn by the priests depicted. Consequently, in the *Florentine Codex* (Sahagún 1979, fol. 49r), although the text says that they are Huixtotin, the priests do not wear any specific insignia. And in the *Primeros Memoriales* (Sahagún 1993, fol. 251r; see also Espinosa Pineda 2010, 85–87), the priest is blackened and carries a tobacco gourd and a *xiquipilli* (copal bag)—which clearly indicate that he is a *tlenamacac*, a high-ranking priest—but he lacks the accoutrements of the Huixtotin, and even the sacrificial implement in the image is not the correct tool, for he brandishes a flint knife and not a sawfish rostrum.

Huixtotin priests are also featured in two other *veintenas*, where they participated in rites involving maize deities. In Huey Tecuilhuitl, the ritual led to the death of the impersonator of the Young Maize Goddess, Xilonen. Women "who belonged to Xilonen," *cihuatlamacazque* who wore the same insignia as the goddess—yellow and red face paint, yellow body paint, red feathers on the arms and legs, and garlands of Mexican marigold (*Tagetes erecta*), known as *cempoalxochitl*—surrounded the personification as they sang to her. Warriors danced with maize stalks before Xilonen, while the *tlamacazque* awaited the procession as they played wind instruments and tossed sweet-scented marigold flowers (*yauhtli*) before the goddess (Sahagún 1950–82, bk 2: 98). The sacrificial priest was a *tlenamacac* who wore an eagle claw and paper *tlaquechpaniotl* on his back. This identified him as one of the Huixtotin. When Xilonen reached the place where she was to die, the priest shook an *ayauhchicahuaztli* in front of her. She was taken to the temple of Cinteotl, where her throat was slit as she was carried on a priest's back (Sahagún 1950–82, bk 2: 99; see also Mazzetto, forthcoming). After this, her heart was extracted and deposited in a blue vessel. Lords of rain and foodstuffs, the Tlaloque could in effect deprive humankind of their favors and, in particular, take the "hearts" of the foodstuffs and lock them up, as recounted in the *Florentine Codex*:

verily, now, the gods, the Tlamacazque ... have hidden for themselves [that which is as] the precious green stone, the bracelet, the precious turquoise; they have taken with them their older sister Chicome coatl, the sustenance, and the red woman, the chili (*a can elle axcan ca omotoptenque, ca omopetlacaltenque in teteu in tlamacazque ... a ca ocommotlatilique in chalchivitl in maqujztli, in teuxivitl: a ca oconmoviqujlitiaque in jnveltioatzin yn chicome covatl in tonacaiutl: auh in tlatlauhquj civatl in chiltzintli*).

The consequences are, alas, woeful:

And here, verily, now already the sustenance lieth suffering, the older sister of the gods lieth outstretched. The sustenance already lieth covered with dust, already it lieth enclosed in a spider web, already it endureth fatigue, already it suffereth ... And the nourishment: there is no more of it; it is gone, it hath disappeared. The gods, the Tlamacazque, carried it away, introduced it there into Tlalocan (*Auh iz nelle axcan ca ie tlajhijovitoc in tonacaiutl, ca ie ma vilantoc in teteu inveltiuh: in tonacaiutl ca ie teuhpachiuhtoc, ca ie toca tzaoalqujmjliuhtoc ca ie tlaihiiovia, ca ie tlaciavi ... Auh ie iehoatl in iolcaiutl, aoc tle oia, opoliuh: oqujtqujque, oqujcalaqujque in teteu in tlamacazque in vmpa tlallocan*). (Sahagún 1950–82, bk 6: 35–36)[7]

In Huey Tecuilhuitl, the Huixtotl sacrificer, like one of the Tlaloque, intervened in order to bring about the opposite effect: he oversaw the fertilization of Xilonen, whose heart, carefully deposited in a blue vessel that evoked water and vegetation, had to ensure the abundant growth of maize. The wind instruments, *yauhtli* flowers, and the *ayauhchicahuaztli* used in the rite were supplementary allusions to rain, and by extension, to the Tlaloque.[8]

Once again, the images available are highly simplified and they do not show the insignia of the Huixtotin, insignia that, nevertheless, are described in the texts. Thus, in the *Primeros Memoriales*, the priest is smeared in black paint and wears paper rosettes on his head (Sahagún 1993, fol. 251r; see also Espinosa Pineda 2010, 87–88). He holds a sacrificial knife in his left hand and a *xiquipilli* in the right. Therefore, he is a *tlenamacac*, which is confirmed in the text. However, he does not wear the ornaments characteristic of the Huixtotl priest.

Finally, the last *veintena* to be discussed, Ochpaniztli, led to a celebration in honor of earth, water, and maize deities, the three elements linked to fertility and agricultural growth. One of the sacrificial victims was a female slave who personified the goddess of ripe maize, Chicomecoatl. She was beheaded in her sanctuary on a litter of seeds, bedecked with corncobs and chilies (Durán 1995, 2: 146). The priest who sacrificed Chicomecoatl was probably a *tlenamacac*, perhaps in the attire of a Huixtotl. Nonetheless, in the *Codex Borbonicus* we see two Huixtotin priests in the Ochpaniztli rites to Chicomecoatl. This codex has three plates with images of this *veintena* (*Códice Borbónico* 1991, pl. 29–31); in the first half of the first image, three figures stand facing five others (Figure 8.5). Among the first three, the main figure is the impersonator of Chicomecoatl, who wears the goddess's typical headdress. The two figures above Chicomecoatl are priests (with black body paint and a

Figure 8.5. *Huixtotin* priests in the *veintena* of Ochpaniztli. Detail of *Codex Borbonicus*, pl. 29. Source: photograph courtesy of Bibliothèque de l'Assemblée nationale, Paris.

xicolli vest) wearing rubber-spattered paper, characteristic of rain gods. Four of the five figures facing Chicomecoatl play musical instruments: a shell, an *ayauhchica-huaztli*, and trumpet shells (from above to below). As Graulich (1999, 98–99) has pointed out, the latter two wear the eagle claw on their heads that identify them as Huixtotin priests. As for the individual directly in front of Chicomecoatl, the richness of his attire identifies him as the main priest. He has a *xiquipilli*, which leaves little room for doubt that he is a *tlenamacac*. The blue serpent staff (*coatopilli*), which he extends toward Chicomecoatl or toward one of the four blue balls in front of her, represents the fertilizing thunderclap (Graulich 1999, 99), while other priests play instruments to imitate the sound of wind and falling rain. The footprints indicate that the priest with the *coatopilli* walks back and forth or in circles before the goddess (Graulich 1999, 99). This ceremony recalls that performed by the Tlalocan Tlenamacac at the Templo Mayor during the Etzalcualiztli fiesta. Doris Heyden has already observed the water goddesses and the goddesses of sustenance share a number of similar or identical features in iconography, which indicates their close and complementary character (Heyden 1983, 141–42). Furthermore, they play a shared role: the fertilization of the earth, which remains sterile without the water that makes the planted seed sprout. The cooperation between these conceptual spheres is explicit, as shown in Sahagún (1969, 1: 51) when he writes of Chalchiuhtlicue: "Lords and kings held this goddess in great veneration along with two others, who were the goddess of sustenance that they called Chicomecoatl and the goddess of salt that they called Uixtocihuatl, because they used to say that these three goddesses maintained the commoners to be able to live and multiply." *(Los señores y reyes veneraban mucho a esta diosa, con otras dos, que eran la diosa de los mantenimientos que llamaban Chicomecóatl, y la diosa de la sal, que llamaban Uixtocihuatl, por que decían que estas tres diosas mantenían a la gente popular para que pudiese vivir y multiplicar).* This connection, which is overtly expressed in the iconography, is also revealed in rites. Given the permeability between aquatic and plant spheres, we can understand why priests with aquatic connotations could officiate the sacrifice of a maize goddess.

MEXICA PRIESTLY ORGANIZATION AND THE DYNAMISM OF INDIGENOUS THOUGHT

Through the systematic study of Huixtotin priests in the framework of *veintena* festivals, it is possible to gain greater insight into their character. With regard to water and Huixtocihuatl, as well as origins and Tlalocan more broadly, blue face paint with wave motifs and rubber-splattered paper are insignia closely associated with the Tlaloque, with whom they were at times apparently blurred in rites. Like the Tlaloque, in their role as providers, they make rain, but they also fertilize the earth and permit the growth of vegetation for abundant food. Thus, the Huixtotin priests do not intervene solely in rites involving rain deities, but also in those related to earth and maize deities. They have close ties to the sacrifice of deity impersonators related to these elements and they play a role in rites in which the hearts of victims—of which the Tlaloque are the lords who can take and make use of them—are deposited in blue or green vessels, colors that evoke the agricultural riches and fertility that are petitioned.[9] The Huixtotin priests also have close symbolic ties to nighttime and death, as the inverted eagle claw in their headdress, perhaps a symbol of the setting sun, seems to connote. Like the Tlaloque, they are ambiguous beings, in contact with the divine world and with Tlalocan, which probably explains the role they play in the sacrifice/fertilization of sacrificial victims.

Furthermore, the particular way that the symbolic universe of the Huixtotin priests was integrated into rites has led to a reassessment of Mexica priestly organization and how it was deployed in *veintena* festivals in light of the indigenous thought system, its categories, and its inherent dynamism. Remarkably fluid, this system of thought was not based on generalized and rigid concepts, but rather it adapted to the context, bringing out the most pertinent aspects in any given situation. Guided by a network of associations of ideas and analogies, it interwove these facets to allow for reshaping in each case depending on the specific needs and qualities of the ritual.

Elena Mazzetto has already demonstrated that the places of veneration used in *veintena* rites could fluctuate to reflect the permeability of deities' spheres of action and be adapted to the specific context of a given festival (Mazzetto 2014). Thus, in Ochpaniztli, although each deity celebrated had its own places for veneration, the *veintena* rites, which associated the domains of Toci-Teteo Innan, Chicomecoatl, and Atlantonan, dynamically blended temples and personifications of the goddesses (Mazzetto 2014, 196–228). Similarly, the religious responsibilities of the Mexica were also adapted to this dynamic system of thought. Huixtotin priests are found symbolically connected to the aquatic world and involved in the sacrifice of the maize goddesses Chicomecoatl and Xilonen (Mazzetto 2014, 194–95, 228). The study of the participation of ritual specialists in *veintena* festivals enables us to conclude that the same logic operated for other priests, who did not exclusively participate in rites dedicated only to the particular deity they served. For instance, during Ochpaniztli the priests of the Corn Goddess Chicomecoatl, the *chichicomecoa*, participate in rites involving a deity associated with the earth, Toci or Teteo Innan (Sahagún 1950–82, bk 2: 111); thus, in plate 30 of the *Codex Borbonicus*, a procession is guided by a priest attired as Chicomecoatl and armed with a *coatopilli* (serpent staff), which he raises to Teteo Innan (Figure 8.6).

Moreover, religious responsibilities reflect what López Austin (1983, 76) defined as the capacity for "fusion and fission" of Mexica gods, in other words: "the cases in which a group of gods is also conceived as a singular, unitary divinity; and the opposite cases, of division, in those in which a deity is divided into distinct numens, sharing their attributes." *(los casos en los que un conjunto de dioses se concibe también como una divinidad singular, unitaria; y los casos opuestos, de división, en los que una deidad se separa en distintos númenes, repartiendo sus atributos).* Just like the gods whom they serve, priests can, depending on the context, put on insignia that pertain to different gods; thus, in the *Codex Borbonicus*, the figures

Figure 8.6. Rites of the *veintena* of Ochpaniztli. *Codex Borbonicus*, pl. 30. Source: Photograph courtesy of Bibliothèque de l'Assemblée nationale, Paris.

that flank the personification of Chicomecoatl simultaneously seem to be maize and rain priests (*Códice Borbónico* 1991, pl. 30) (Figure 8.6). Their accoutrements strongly resemble those of Chicomecoatl and, like the goddess, they hold ears of maize in their hands. However, the Tlaloc mask at the base of their blocky *amacalli* headgear and the fan-like *tlaquechpaniotl* also identify them as Tlaloque. They are rendered in four different hues, as certain gods that can be separated into different numens, identical in all details with the exception of their color (*cf.* Dupey García 2010b). This represents an example of both fusion and fission, not of the gods, but of those who serve them, namely their priests.

This phenomenon implies that, just like the gods that they serve, the priests, whose insignia shifted in relation to the specific context in which they served, are at times difficult to identify. Thus, in the case of the figures flanking the personification of Chicomecoatl in the *Codex Borbonicus*, Couch (1985, 72) emphasizes that although they wear the paraphernalia characteristic of Chicomecoatl and Tlaloc, they are in overall appearance closer to Chicomecoatl, whereas Klein (1980, 194) and Anders, Jansen and Reyes García (1991, 211–12) identify them as Tlaloc priests based on the mask in their headdresses, and Broda (1987, 237), given their division into four colors, considers them to be Tlaloque of the four directions. Therefore, the iconography of priests must be studied as meticulously as that of deities and, in this regard, I reference the proposal of Mikulska Dąbrowska (2008, 80–84) to distinguish in each image between the distinctive features (which are diagnostic of a god—or here, of a priest), the discretionary (which vary depending on the context), and the aesthetic ones.

My aim here has been to contribute to reconsidering the Mexica priestly organization and particularly to de-constructing overly rigid associations that are often established between a priest and a temple or a deity. I also demonstrate the need for a global study of the *veintena* festival cycle, for the indispensable analysis of variations as a function of contexts can only be undertaken through a systematic study of the different rites. Without doubt, future research extended to consider the role of each ritual specialist in the framework of *veintena* fiestas will permit a more comprehensive and precise view of these rites as well as their participants.

NOTES

1. Numerous studies have focused on specific *veintenas*—for example, on Ochpaniztli, see Brown (1984), DiCesare (2009), and Grave (2004)—or a group of *veintenas*—for example, on the *veintenas* of the rain gods, see Broda (1971)—but very few authors have analyzed these fiestas globally as part of an integral whole. The key point in the present chapter is the study by Graulich (1999), in addition to the short pioneering article by Kirchhoff (1971), the work of Couch (1985) and Mazzetto (2014), the latter dealing with images of the *veintenas* in the *Codex Borbonicus* and to the places of veneration and ceremonial routes in *veintena* rites, respectively.

2. See Molina's dictionary: *viuixca*: "to tremble"; *viuixoa*: "to shake or move a tree, or rock the baby's cradle, or to shake someone awake, or to strike with shame"; *viuixalhuia*: "shake, sway or rock something back and forth" (Molina 1970, part II, fol. 158r); and Wimmer's dictionary: *huihuixca*: "tremble, get chills"; *huihuixoa*: "shake, move around, rock [a baby], awaken"; *huihuixalhuia*: "shake, move around, stir something in someone" (Wimmer 2006).

3. In Nahua symbolic thought smoke was equated with clouds and Tlaloc, the maker of clouds, was also described as *copalloe*, "lord of copal" (Sahagún 1950–82, bk 6: 35, 244).

4. The *ayauhchicahuaztli*, "mist rattle staff," was an instrument that made a noise to summon clouds and rain through an imitating sound. The rattle staff also served to open holes in the earth, where seeds were placed (Soustelle 1940, 37; see also Couvreur 2011).

5. For a comparison of the representations of this *veintena* in different manuscripts, see Nicholson 2002, 85–91.

6. Dozens of sawfish rostrums were found in the Templo Mayor offerings (Robles Cortés et al. 2018).

7. On the "hearts" of foods, their relationship with Tlalocan and the goddesses that embody them, see also López Austin (1997, 219–20) and Carrasco (2002, 205–08).

8. On the use of the *ayauhchicahuaztli* and *yauhtli* flowers in rites devoted to rain, earth, and agricultural fertility deities, see also Dupey García, 2020.

9. There might be a relationship between rites involving hearts deposited in stone vessels and those placed in a *tepetlacalli*, a container whose walls, sometimes decorated with agricultural symbols, could be used as receptacles of divine images or offerings (López Luján and López Austin 2010, 2011). On the *tepetlacalli* discovered in the Templo Mayor of Mexico-Tenochtitlan, see López Austin and López Luján (2009, 321–31), and on the relationship between these receptacles and rain in Zapotec culture, see Urcid (2011).

REFERENCES

Acosta Saignes, Miguel. 1946. "Los *teopixque*. Organización sacerdotal entre los mexicas." *Revista Mexicana de Estudios Históricos* 8: 147–206.

Anders, Ferdinand, Maarten Jansen, and Luis Reyes García. 1991. *El libro del Ciuacoatl: Homenaje para el año del Fuego Nuevo: Libro explicativo del llamado Códice Borbónico*. Graz, Madrid, Mexico City: ADEVA, Sociedad Estatal Quinto Centenario, Fondo de Cultura Económica.

Anderson, Arthur J. O. 1988. "Sahagún's Informants on the Nature of Tlalocan." In *The Work of Bernardino de Sahagún: Pioneer Ethnographer of Sixteenth-Century Aztec Mexico*, edited by José Jorge Klor de Alva, Henry B. Nicholson, and Eloise Quiñones Keber, 151–60. New York: Institute of Mesoamerican Studies, The University of Albany, State University of New York.

Barrera Rivera, José Álvaro, María de Lourdes Gallardo Parodi, and Aurora Montúfar López. 2001. "La ofrenda 102 del Templo Mayor." *Arqueología Mexicana* 48: 70–77.

Botta, Sergio. 2004. "Los dioses preciosos. Un acercamiento histórico-religioso a las divinidades aztecas de la lluvia." *Estudios de Cultura Náhuatl* 35: 89–120.

Broda, Johanna (de Casas). 1971. "Las fiestas aztecas de los dioses de la lluvia: una reconstrucción según las fuentes del siglo XVI." *Revista Española de Antropología Americana* 6: 245–327.

———. 1987. "The Provenience of the Offerings: Tribute and Cosmovision." In *The Aztec Templo Mayor*, edited by Elizabeth H. Boone, 211–56. Washington, DC: Dumbarton Oaks.

Brown, Betty Ann. 1984. "Ochpaniztli in Historical Perspective." In *Sacrifice in Mesoamerica*, edited by Elizabeth H. Boone, 195–209. Washington, DC: Dumbarton Oaks.

Carrasco, Davíd. 1999. *City of Sacrifice: the Aztec Empire and the Role of Violence in Civilization*. Boston: Beacon Press.

———. 2002. "The Sacrifice of Women in the *Florentine Codex*. The Hearts of Plants and Players in War Games." In *Representing Aztec Ritual: Performance, Text, and Image in the Work of Sahagún*, edited by Eloise Quiñones Keber, 197–225. Boulder: University Press of Colorado.

Caso, Alfonso. 1927. *El Teocalli de la Guerra Sagrada: descripción y estudio del monolito encontrado en los cimientos del Palacio Nacional*. Mexico City: Secretaría de Educación Pública.

Codex Telleriano Remensis: Ritual, Divination, and History in a Pictorial Aztec Manuscript. 1995. Edited by Eloise Quiñones Keber. Austin: University of Texas Press.

Códice Borbónico. 1991. Edited by Ferdinand Anders, Maarten Jansen, and Luis Reyes García. Graz, Madrid, Mexico City: ADEVA, Sociedad Estatal Quinto Centenario, Fondo de Cultura Económica.

Códice Borgia. 1993. Edited by Ferdinand Anders, Maarten Jansen, and Luis Reyes García. Graz, Madrid, Mexico City: ADEVA, Sociedad Estatal Quinto Centenario, Fondo de Cultura Económica.

Códice Vaticano A 3738. 1996. Edited by Ferdinand Anders and Maarten Jansen. Graz, Mexico City: ADEVA, Fondo de Cultura Económica.

Contel, José. 2006. "Tlalloc, le dieu aztèque de la terre et de l'eau." *Annuaire de l'École Pratique des Hautes Études, Section des Sciences Religieuses* 113: 57–60.

———. 2016. "Tlalloc-Tlallocan: el *altepetl* arquetípico." *Americae.* Accessed April 4, 2017. http://www.mae.parisnanterre.fr/americae-dossiers/americae-dossier-altepetl/tlalloc-tlallocan-el-altepetl-arquetipico/.

Contel, José, and Katarzyna Mikulska Dąbrowska. 2011. "'Mas nosotros que somos dioses nunca morimos.' Ensayo sobre *Tlamacazqui:* ¿Dios, sacerdote o qué otro demonio?" In *De dioses y hombres: Creencias y rituales mesoamericanos y sus supervivencias,* edited by Katarzyna Mikulska Dąbrowska and José Contel, 23–65. Warsaw: University of Warsaw.

Couch, Christopher N. C. 1985. *The Festival Cycle of the Aztec Codex Borbonicus.* Oxford: British Archaeological Reports.

Couvreur, Aurélie. 2011. "Entre sceptres divins et instruments de musique cérémoniels: le symbolisme des bâtons de sonnailles aztèques." In *La quête du Serpent à Plumes. Arts et religions de l'Amérique précolombienne. Hommage à Michel Graulich,* edited by Nathalie Ragot, Sylvie Peperstraete, and Guilhem Olivier, 235–50. Turnhout: Brepols Publishers, Bibliothèque de l'École Pratique des Hautes Études-Sciences Religieuses.

Di Cesare, Catherine. 2009. *Sweeping the Way. Divine Transformation in the Aztec Festival of Ochpaniztli.* Boulder: University Press of Colorado.

Dupey García, Élodie. 2010a. "Les couleurs dans les pratiques et les représentations des Nahuas du Mexique central (XIVe–XVIe siècles)." PhD diss., École Pratique des Hautes Études.

———. 2010b. "Les métamorphoses chromatiques des dieux mésoaméricains: un nouvel éclairage par l'analyse de leur identité et de leurs fonctions." *Studi e Materiali di Storia delle Religioni* 76, no. 2: 351–71.

———. 2016. "El cuerpo del color. Materialidad y significado del adorno corporal en la cultura náhuatl prehispánica." In *El color de los dioses: Policromía en la Antigüedad clásica y Mesoamérica,* edited by Evelyn Useda Miranda, María Helena Rangel Guerrero, and Mariana Casanova Zamudi, 20–33. Mexico City: Instituto Nacional de Bellas Artes, Museo del Palacio de Bellas Artes.

———. 2018. "The Yellow Women: Naked Skin, Everyday Cosmetics, and Ritual Body Painting in Aztec Society." In *Painting the Skin. Pigments on Bodies and Codices in Pre-Columbian Mesoamerica,* edited by Élodie Dupey García and María Luisa Vázquez de Ágredos Pascual, 88–101. Tucson: The University of Arizona Press.

———. 2020. "Lo que el viento se lleva. Ofrendas odoríferas y sonoras en la ritualidad náhuatl prehispánica." In *De olfato. Aproximaciones a los olores en la historia de México,* edited by Élodie Dupey García and Guadalupe Pinzón Ríos, 83–131. Mexico City: Fondo de Cultura Económica, Universidad Nacional Autónoma de México, Centro de Estudios Mexicanos y Centroamericanos.

Durán, Diego. 1995. *Historia de las Indias de Nueva España e islas de Tierra Firme.* Edited by José Rubén Romero and Rosa Camelo. 2 vols. Mexico City: Consejo Nacional para la Cultura y las Artes.

Espinosa Pineda, Gabriel. 2010. "Las viñetas de las 18 fiestas del año en los *Primeros memoriales.*" In *Tepeapulco: Región en perspectivas,* edited by Manuel Alberto Morales Damián, 69–116. Pachuca, Mexico City: Universidad Autónoma del Estado de Hidalgo, Plaza y Valdés.

Franconi, Antoine. 2014. "Huixtocihuatl et le sel dans le *Codex de Florence*." *Les Dossiers du GEMESO* 3. Accessed April 4, 2017. http://www.gemeso.com/nahuatl/dossiers/.

Graulich, Michel. 1999. *Ritos aztecas. Las fiestas de las veintenas.* Mexico City: Instituto Nacional Indigenista.

———. 2005. *Le sacrifice humain chez les Aztèques.* Paris: Fayard.

Grave Tirado, Luis Alfonso. 2004. "Barriendo en lo ya barrido. Un nuevo repaso a Ochpaniztli." *Estudios de Cultura Náhuatl* 35: 157–77.

Heyden, Doris. 1983. "Las diosas del agua y la vegetación." *Anales de Antropología* 20, no. 2: 129–45.

"Historia de los mexicanos por sus pinturas." 1965. In *Teogonía e historia de los mexicanos*, edited by Ángel M. Garibay, 23–66. Mexico City: Porrúa.

Ixtlilxóchitl, Fernando de Alva. 1975–1977. *Obras históricas.* Edited by Edmundo O'Gorman. 2 vols. Mexico City: Universidad Nacional Autónoma de México-Instituto de Investigaciones Históricas.

Kirchhoff, Paul. 1971. "Las 18 fiestas anuales en Mesoamérica: 6 fiestas sencillas y 6 fiestas dobles." In *Verhandlungen des XXXVIII Internationalen Amerikanisten-Kongresses, Stuttgart-München, 12 bis. 18 August 1968.* Vol. 3, 207–21. Munich: Klaus Renner Verlag.

Klein, Cecelia F. 1980. "Who Was Tlaloc?" *Journal of Latin American Lore* 6, no. 2: 155–204.

———. 1984. "¿Dioses de la lluvia o sacerdotes ofrendadores del fuego? Un estudio socio-político de algunas representaciones mexicas del dios Tláloc." *Estudios de Cultura Náhuatl* 17: 33–50.

López Austin, Alfredo. 1983. "Nota sobre la fusión y fisión de los dioses en el panteón mexica." *Anales de antropología* 20, no. 2: 75–87.

———. 1997. *Tamoanchan, Tlalocan: Places of Mist.* Boulder: University Press of Colorado.

López Austin, Alfredo, and Leonardo López Luján. 2009. *Monte Sagrado. Templo Mayor.* Mexico City: Universidad Nacional Autónoma de México, Instituto Nacional de Antropología e Historia.

López Luján, Leonardo, and Alfredo López Austin. 2010. "El Cuartillo de Santo Tomás Ajusco y los cultos agrícolas." *Arqueología Mexicana* 18, no. 106: 18–23.

———. 2011. "Cartas." *Arqueología Mexicana* 18, no. 107: 6.

Mazzetto, Elena. 2014. *Lieux de culte et parcours cérémoniels dans les fêtes des vingtaines à Mexico-Tenoch-titlan.* Oxford: British Archaeological Reports.

———. Forthcoming. "Cuando la tierra ríe. Apuntes sobre el humor ritual entre los nahuas prehispánicos." *Revista Española de Antropología Americana.*

Mikulska Dąbrowska, Katarzyna. 2008. *El lenguaje enmascarado. Un acercamiento a las representaciones gráficas de deidades nahuas.* Mexico City: Universidad Nacional Autónoma de México, Sociedad Polaca de Estudios Latinoamericanos, Warsaw University.

Molina, Alonso de. 1970. *Vocabulario en Lengua Castellana y Mexicana y Mexicana y Castellana.* Edited by Miguel León-Portilla. Mexico City: Porrúa.

Nazareo, Pablo. 1970. "Dritte Brief des Don Pablo de Nazareo an Philipp II." In *Briefe der indianischen Nobilität aus Neuspanien an Karl V und Philipp II um die Mitte des 16. Jahrhunderts*, edited by Günter Zimmermann, 23–31. Munich: Klaus Renner Verlag.

Nicholson, Henry B. 2002. "Representing the Veintena Ceremonies in the *Primeros Memoriales*." In *Representing Aztec Ritual: Performance, Text, and Image in the Work of Sahagún*, edited by Eloise Quiñones Keber, 63–106. Boulder: University Press of Colorado.

Pastrana Flores, Miguel. 2008. *Entre los hombres y los dioses. Acercamiento al sacerdocio de calpulli entre los antiguos nahuas.* Mexico City: Universidad Nacional Autónoma de México-Instituto de Investigaciones Históricas.

Peperstraete, Sylvie. 2014. "La fonction sacerdotale au Mexique préhispanique." *Annuaire de l'École Pratique des Hautes Études, Section des Sciences Religieuses* 121: 1–11.

————. 2015. "La fonction sacerdotale au Mexique préhispanique (II)." *Annuaire de l'École Pratique des Hautes Études, Section des Sciences Religieuses* 122: 1–10.

————. 2016. "La fonction sacerdotale au Mexique préhispanique (III)." *Annuaire de l'École Pratique des Hautes Études, Section des Sciences Religieuses* 123: 9–15.

Robles Cortés, Érika Lucero, Adriana Sanromán Peyron, María Barajas Rocha, Karla Valeria Hernández Ascencio, Nataly Bolaño Martínez, and Oscar Uriel Mendoza Vargas. 2018. "Un pez marino tierra adentro. Los peces sierra del Templo Mayor de Tenochtitlan." *Arqueología Mexicana* 25, no. 151: 20–27.

Sahagún, Bernardino de. 1950–82. *Florentine Codex: General History of the Things of New Spain, Fray Bernardino de Sahagún.* Translated with notes and illustrations by Arthur J. O. Anderson and Charles E. Dibble. 13 vols. Santa Fe: The School of American Research, University of Utah Press.

————. 1969. *Historia general de las cosas de Nueva España.* Edited by Ángel M. Garibay. 4 vols. Mexico City: Porrúa.

————. 1979. *Códice Florentino. El manuscrito 218–220 de la Colección Palatina de la Biblioteca Medicea Laurenziana.* 3 vols. Florence, Mexico City: Giunti Barbéra, Archivo General de la Nación.

————. 1993. *Primeros Memoriales: Facsimile Edition.* Norman: University of Oklahoma Press.

————. 1997. *Primeros Memoriales.* Edited and translated by Thelma Sullivan. Completed and revised, with additions, by Henry B. Nicholson, Arthur J. O. Anderson, Charles E. Dibble, Eloise Quiñones Keber, and Wayne Ruwet. Norman: University of Oklahoma Press.

Seler, Eduard. 1909. "Costumes et attributs des divinités du Mexique selon le P. Sahagún." *Journal de la Société des Américanistes de Paris,* nouvelle série, 6: 101–46.

————. 1927. *Einige Kapitel aus dem Geschichtswerk des Fray Bernardino de Sahagún, aus dem aztekischen übersetzt von Eduard Seler.* Edited by Caecilie Seler-Sachs, Walter Lehmann, and Walter Krickeberg. Stuttgart: Strecker und Schröder.

Soustelle, Jacques. 1940. *La pensée cosmologique des anciens Mexicains (représentations du monde et de l'espace).* Paris: Hermann.

Sullivan, Thelma D. 1974. "Tlaloc: A New Etymological Interpretation of the God's Name and What It Reveals of his Essence and Nature." In *Atti del XL Congresso Internazionale degli Americanisti, Roma-Genova, 3–10 Settembre 1972.* Vol. 2, edited by Ernesta Cerulli, 213–19. Genova: Tilgher.

Thévet, André. 1905. "Histoyre du Mechique, manuscrit français inédit du xvie siècle." Edited by Edouard de Jonghe. *Journal de la Société des Américanistes* 2: 1–41.

Urcid, Javier. 2011. "Sobre la antigüedad de cofres para augurar y propiciar la lluvia." *Arqueología Mexicana* 19, no. 110: 16–21.

Wimmer, Alexis. 2006. *Dictionnaire de la langue nahuatl classique.* Accessed April 4, 2017. http://sites.estvideo.net/malinal/.

PART III

Pre-Columbian Categories, Colonial Interpretations

CHAPTER NINE

Dance and Sacrificial Rituals in the *Veintena* Ceremonies

MIRJANA DANILOVIĆ

From the late eighteenth century onwards, scholars have shown significant interest in the study of human sacrifice in ancient Mexico.[1] The studies of the ritual killing of humans, before Europeans came to the Valley of Mexico, have focused mainly on its appearance in the myths of origin, the correlation between human victims and animals, sacrificial techniques and the process of identification between the victims and their sacrificers (e.g. Boone 1984; González Torres 1985; Graulich 2005; López Luján and Olivier 2010).

According to colonial narratives, a dance was included in almost every performance of human sacrifice during the eighteen *veintena* ceremonies of the Mexica. Most modern studies of these native religious practices and of the belief systems which they reflect did not consider the role of dance in sacrificial rituals, but focused principally on other aspects of the Mexica festivals, or on the different features of the practice of dance (Graulich 1999; Martí 1961; Martí and Prokosch 1964; Mazzetto 2014; Sten 1990; Turrent 2006). While some scholars have recently examined the relationship between dance and sacrifice, they have tended to limit their studies to the dances of certain *veintenas*.[2]

This chapter provides a brief overview of all the dances that took place during the sacrificial rituals of the *veintena* festivals among the Mexica during the Postclassic period.[3] When possible, I describe the elements of each dance (when it was performed, the movements), the participants (dancers), and the use of the dancers' body parts as paraphernalia. Likewise, this work explores the overlap between dancing and other ritual acts, which raises questions about the nature of these acts.

Ultimately, this chapter aims to show the close integration of dance and sacrifice among the Mexica in ancient Mexico.

My research draws largely from the descriptions of Spanish missionaries, the chronicles written by the authors born in the New World, as well as the indigenous pictorial manuscripts, known as codices. Most of the data comes from the remarkable *Florentine Codex*, a twelve-volume manuscript, written in Nahuatl and Spanish, that deals with numerous aspects of the Mexica culture, which is the result of a systematic study by the Franciscan friar Bernardino de Sahagún.

This chapter begins with a description of the two main categories of victims destined to be sacrificed and the conditions they had to fulfill in order to be taken to the sacrificial stone. As early colonial sources agree that dancing was present from the beginning until the end of the sacrificial ceremonies, the rest of this chapter follows the stages of the practice of human sacrifice, examining the dances that took place before, during and after the ritual killing, which involved the victims and the sacrificers. Finally, it explores moments of potential overlap between dance and other ritual acts, and concludes by commenting on the crucial importance of dance and sacrifice in the personal and political lives of the Mexica.

SLAVES AND PRISONERS OF WAR: THE VICTIMS WILL DANCE

In central Mexico, before the Spanish conquest, the sacrificial victims were classified into two main categories: the slaves (*tlatlacotin*),[4] who were bathed (*tlaaltiltin*) or purified in order to represent deities (*teotl ixiptla*);[5] and the prisoners (*mamaltin*), who had been caught on the battlefield. Both slaves and captive warriors were required to dance, at different times, before and during the rituals.

According to Sahagún's informants, purchased slaves "should dance well" (*inic uel mitotiaia*). In the *Florentine Codex*, they provide an account of the public sale of slaves, highlighting that the slave dealers were looking for someone "who sang well, who made his dance accompany [the beat of] the two-toned drum" (*in cenca uel cuica: in quiuicaltia, inetotiliz teponaztli*). The text also indicates that slaves who had the ability to dance were more highly esteemed: "If he was not highly skilled as a dancer, his price was thirty large capes. But if he danced well, if he was clean of body, his price was forty large capes" (*Jn amo cenca mimati ic mitotia in ipatiuh cenquimilli onmatlactli. Auh in qualli ic mitotia in chipaoac inacaio in ipatiuh onquimilli in quachtli*) (Sahagún 1950–82, bk 9: 46).

Prisoners of war were also required to dance. During the migration of the Mexica from Aztlan in search of the promised land, their god Huitzilopochtli ordered them to make the captives dance during the festivals. Cristóbal del Castillo (2001, 100–01) includes these instructions in his writings:

Third thing: captives will be painted in white; they will be adorned with light feathers. You will make them eat a lot in order to gain weight. And whenever a month of twenty days ends, you will kill them. Over the course of the festival they will dance. The night before their death, they will stay awake the whole night; they will eat, dance and get drunk (*Auh inic etlamantli in aquique mamaltin yezque quintizaozazque quimihuipotonizque quimpatizque tomahuac mecatl in quinxillaxilpizque, quimaztapiloltizque, cenca quintlaqualtizque quintomahuazque cecempohualilhuitica in quimmictizque inic ilhuichihualozque mitotitinemizque. Auh in iquac imoztlayoc miquizque cenyohual tozozque tlaquazque mitotizque tlahuanazque*).[6]

The Mexica chronicler Fernando de Alvarado Tezozómoc (1997, 163–68) specifies that captive warriors danced and sang as they used to do in their homeland. Indeed, before they were transported from their territories by the enemy, they would begin to dance and raise their voices, expressing pain and shame. In addition, the prisoners of war began to dance upon arrival in Mexico-Tenochtitlan. As early chroniclers recorded, war prisoners entered the city dancing. For instance, Diego Durán (1994, 186) explains that after defeating Coaixtlauaca, "the Aztecs arrived in Tenochtitlan with slaves, people captured in the war. They were all bound and entered the city dancing and singing loudly."

Slaves and captives danced throughout the year. Written sources document both categories of victims dancing over the course of the *veintena* festivals calendar, usually accompanied by other victims or, in the case of the captives, by their captors. On occasion, they danced as living images of a specific deity and, on others, they accompanied embodiments of the honored gods, who danced with a group of people who protected and guided them.

The future victims moved in different dance formations. The two most frequent dances were the serpent (or winding) dance and the circle dance. During the *veintena* festivals of Toxcatl, Panquetzaliztli, and Xocotl Huetzi, dancers imitated the snake's rhythmic movements (Sahagún 1974, 41, 44–45; 1950–82, bk 2: 76, 108, 131; 2000, 248). The circle dance was performed in the sacrificial context of Huey Tecuilhuitl (Sahagún 2000, 218), Tlacaxipehualiztli (Sahagún 1950–82, bk 2: 53), Toxcatl (Durán 1995, 2: 54), Xocotl Huetzi (Sahagún 2000, 152), and Izcalli (Sahagún 1950–82, bk 2: 152; 2000, 265). In addition, during the festival of Panquetzaliztli (Sahagún 2000, 248), a dance was characterized by leaps, and there is evidence of a hand-to-hand dance in Tecuilhuitontli and Xocotl Huetzi (Sahagún 2000, 211, 225).

Often, however, the historical sources do not specify the dancers' movements. For instance, in the case of the dances of the *ixiptla* of Tlaloc, the Rain God, in Etzalcualiztli and of the living image of Ilamatecuhtli in Tititl, the dance features are not described. The *Primeros Memoriales* only states that "during one night they made the Tlaloc dance" (*auh ce youal in quitotiaya Tlaloc*) (Sahagún 1974, 34), while the *Florentine Codex* indicates that the woman danced to the rhythm of the drums: "And before she died, she danced. The old men beat the drums for her"

(*Auh in aiamo mjquj mjtotiaia, qujtlatzotzonjliaia in vevetque*) (Sahagún 1950–82, bk 2: 156). What is consistent in the historical sources, though, is the mention of dance before, during, and after the ritual killing.

PREPARATORY RITUALS AND DANCING BEFORE THE SACRIFICE

Sacrificial victims, both slaves and prisoners of war, danced on days prior to the ritual killing. The former danced as or with deities, while the latter danced alone or with their captors. The accounts concerning sacrifice tend to begin with the preparation of the slaves to take on the appearance of the deity that was to be honored and thus became an *ixiptla*, or of the captives who acted as an *ixiptla's* "deathbed".[7]

A slave who was selected to be a "deity image" after having presented his or her dance skills in the market, "became" a deity by dancing unceasingly, as well as through numerous other preparatory rites such as all-night vigils, fasting, cleansing or ritual baths, autosacrifice, body painting and changing of attire. Clothed in insignia and regalia of the deities, these slaves were transformed into a visual presence of the worshiped god or goddess,[8] who was brought into existence through dancing. The future victim was thus transformed by his participation in ritual dances.

In pre-Columbian times, the *ixiptla* danced in the annual festivals of Etzalcualiztli, Tecuilhuitontli, Huey Tecuilhuitl, and Ochpaniztli. During the ceremony of Etzalcualiztli, the living images or *ixiptla* of Tlaloc and Chalchiuhtlicue, the Water Goddess, danced. According to the Franciscan friar Motolinía (1971, 63–64), two slaves dressed in the garments and distinctive attributes of the god and the goddess, danced all day until midnight, when they were sacrificed. Similar information was given to Sahagún by his indigenous informants. The *Primeros Memoriales* describes: "During one night they made Tlaloc [his impersonator] dance. At the break of the dawn Tlaloc died" (*Auh ce youal in quitotiaya Tlaloc. Auh inicuac ye tlatlachipaua, icuac miquia in Tlaloc*) (Náhuatl: Sahagún 1974, 34–35; author's translation).

In the festival of Tecuilhuitontli, the Salt Goddess Huixtocihuatl was venerated with dance movements. The slave embodying the goddess, accompanied by other women, danced and sang for ten days in the temple of Tlaloc. Historical records in Nahuatl offer a picture of this dance:

> When she danced, she kept swinging the shield around in a circle; with it she crouched around. And her reed staff was hung with papers; it had papers. And they were spattered with liquid rubber; they had rubber. In three places [the staff] had cup-like flowers; it had

various cup-like flowers (*Jn iquac mjtotiaia, qujmamalacachoa ynjchimal, ic momamana: Yoan yoztopil tlaamaiotilli, haamaio, yoan tlaulhujlli, vllo: excan in tecomaio, tetecomaio*). (Sahagún 1950–82, bk 2: 92)

Thanks to the evidence provided by Sahagún's informants, we know that while Huixtocihuatl danced, so did the prisoners of war who would be sacrificed to become her deathbed (Sahagún 2000, 1: 211). As reported by the *Florentine Codex*: "Likewise the captives danced all the night—those who were to be first to die, who would be as her fundament, who they would make her fundament" (*No iuh ceiooal in mjtotia mamalti, in iacatiazque mjquizque, in iuhquj ypepechoan iezque, in qujnmopepechtizque*) (Sahagún 1950–82, bk 2: 93).

In the same document we find that, during the festival of Huey Tecuilhuitl, a living image of Xilonen, the Tender Maize Goddess, danced with offering priestesses (*cihuatlacamazque*): "likewise the women dance, those who belonged to Xilonen ... They went encircling [the likeness of] Xilonen. They went singing for her after the manner of women" (*no mjtotia in cioa, yn tech pouja in xilonen ... cololujtiuj, qujtepeujtiuj in Xilonen: qujcioapācujcatitiuj*) (Sahagún 1950–82, bk 2: 104). Finally, during the festival of Ochpaniztli, dedicated to the three goddesses Atlatonan ("Our Mother of Water"), Chicomecoatl ("Seven Snake") and Toci ("Our Grandmother"), an *ixiptla* dance also took place. In Duran's account of the rituals, once Atlatonan had been sacrificed, a 12-year-old image of Chicomecoatl danced with a tiara of red paper upon her hair, ears of maize in her hands and a necklace of corn (Durán 1995, 2: 143).

As noted above, victims from conquered groups also danced during the rigorous preparatory rituals that occurred the day before the sacrifice. Over the course of the 365-day calendar, the "captives' dance" was presented three times: the brave war captives danced with their captors before the main ceremony of the festivals of Atlcahualo or Cuahuitlehua, Tlacaxipehualiztli, and Xocotl Huetzi. In addition, before being sacrificed in the religious ceremonies, these foreign warriors were often painted and adorned in the same way as those who had captured them on the battlefield. The accounts given by Bernardino de Sahagún's informants state that in the first days of Atlcahualo: "... the captors, those who had captured men, who had captives, who had taken men, also anointed themselves with ochre; they covered themselves with feather down; they covered their arms, their legs with white turkey feathers" (*Auh in tlamanj, in temanji, in male, in teacinj, no motlauhoça, mopotonja, motzomaia ynjma, yn icxi iztac totoliujtica*) (Sahagún 1950–82, bk 2: 45–46).

During the following *veintena*, Tlacaxipehualiztli, celebrated in honor of Xipe Totec ("Our Lord the Flayed one"), "[t]hose who had captives, when, on the morrow, their captives were to die, then began to dance the captives' dance, when the sun had passed noon" (*Jn maleque, in ie iuh muztla miqujzque inmalhoan, iquac peoa, in momalitotia, in ie onmotzcaloa tonatiuh*) (Sahagún 1950–82, bk 2: 47). In Xocotl Huetzi, the captives were ritually prepared along with their captors before being taken for sacrifice:[9] their bodies were painted with ochre and covered with feathers (Sahagún 1950–82, bk 2: 113). After these preparatory rituals, a day before being thrown into the fire, the captives danced together with their enemies: "Thus did they go dancing. They went dancing with the captives; they went winding back and forth. Thus, they proceeded by twos. The captives, they who were to be cast into the fire, also went dancing" (*Ic mjtotitivi, momalitotitivi, momamātivi: ic vmpatitivi in mamalti in motlepantlaçazque, no mjtotivi*) (Sahagún 1950–82, bk 2: 113).

DANCING TOWARDS THE SACRIFICIAL STONE: THE DAY OF THE SACRIFICE

Studies of the 365-day calendar show that on numerous occasions the future victims, both captives and slaves, danced immediately before their sacrifice. In the case of the captives, the ceremony called *tlahuahuanaliztli* or "striping,"[10] stands out as one of the most remarkable (Figure 9.1). This ritual was performed during Tlacaxipehualiztli and is also known, although inaccurately, as the "gladiator sacrifice." In fact, warfare, human sacrifice and dance come together in this unequal fight between the brave captured enemies using mock weapons and the most courageous, fully armed Mexica warriors.

Figure 9.1. *Tlahuahuanaliztli* during the festival of Tlacaxipehualiztli. Detail of *Codex Tovar* or *Codex Ramírez*, fol. 27. Source: Drawing courtesy of Elbis Domínguez.

This ritual fight was enacted by means of dance (Sahagún 2000, 1: 181). More precisely, the contenders began to dance as soon as they appeared. The *Florentine Codex* states that "they came dancing; they each went turning about" (*mitotitiujtze, momamantiuj*) (Sahagún 1950–82, bk 2: 51). Additionally, while the captive was dancing and fighting, the person who provided the victim "stopped where he had been standing before; he stood dancing; from where he was he stood looking at his captive" (*vncan oalmoquetza yn icaia, mihtotiticac, ixqujchcapa otlachixticac, yn jmal conitzicac*) (Sahagún 1950–82, bk 2: 52–53). Finally, the *tlahuahuanque* ("stripers, scrapers of skin") sought to mark the skin of the prisoner, tied to a horizontal circular stone (*temalacatl*), with stripes before the sacrifice. Once the victim was wounded or striped by his opponents, he was sacrificed.

In the case of the slaves embodying deities, they sang, danced and expressed their emotions while climbing towards the sacrificial stone. During Izcalli, "those [adorned as] Ixcoçauhqui, the impersonators of Xiuhtecutli" (*Ixcoçauhque, in jxiptlaoan Xiuhtecutli*) (Sahagún 1950–82, bk 2: 162) arrived at the place where they were to die after several days of preparing for their death. The text in Nahuatl clarifies that "thereupon they danced, they sang; they made an effort. It was said that [they sang until] their voices cracked; it was said that they were hoarse" (*njmā ie ic mjtotia, mocujca ellaquaoa: omach intozquj tzatzaian, omach ihiçaoacaque*) (Sahagún 1950–82, bk 2: 163). Similarly, on the last day of Toxcatl, the *ixiptla* of Ixteucale Tlacahuepan Teicautzin guided the serpent dance on his way to the sacrificial stone, donning several gold rattles around his ankle that produced a sound (Sahagún 1950–82, bk 2: 76). Interestingly, this young man, wearing adornments of the deity, had the opportunity to choose the moment of his death: "When he was to wish it, when he wished it, thereupon he delivered himself into the hands of those where he was to die" (*in quēman connequiz, yn oqujnec, njman ie ic onmotemaca, yn vncan mjquiz*) (Sahagún 1950–82, bk 2: 76).

As in Izcalli, the dancing of slaves or *ixiptla* before the sacrifice was often linked to the expression of emotions. For instance, historical data reveals that, in Quecholli, the slaves wept while dancing, expressing sadness and anxiety about what was going to happen: "When they ascended, they went singing lustily. Some went dancing. Some indeed wept. And the escorts went holding them by the hand" (*In jquac tleco, cenca cujcativi, cequjntin mjtotivi, in cequjntin vel choca: auh in teanque qujmaantivi*) (Sahagún 1950–82, bk 2: 140). Likewise, an *ixiptla* of Ilamatecuhtli expressed her sorrow in Tititl by shedding tears: "And before she died, she danced. The old men beat the drums for her; the singers sang for her; they intoned her song. And as she danced she could weep for herself, and she sighed; she felt anguish" (*Auh in aiamo mjquj mjtotiaia, qujtlatzotzonjliaia in vevetque, in cujcanjme, qujcujcatia, quevilia in jcujc. Auh in jquac mjtotiaia, vel mochoqujliaia, yoan elcicivia, mociappoa*) (Sahagún 1950–82, bk 2: 156).

By contrast, during Tecuilhuitontli, Huey Tecuilhuitl and Ochpaniztli, women victims had to show contentment or joy in spite of their imminent death. Writing about the sacrifice of a living image of Xilonen in Huey Tecuilhuitl, Juan de Torquemada notes that she was joined in dance by offering priestesses. They danced and sang with her, showing admiration for her death and encouraging her to die with spirit (Torquemada 1975–83, 3: 390). Durán (1995, 2: 267) completes this description by stating that if it was noticed that she did not dance with a feeling of pleasure, she was made to drink until she became content. The same encouragement and support was given to the *ixiptla* of Huixtocihuatl in Tecuilhuitontli. Sahagún (2000, 211) indicates that for ten days she danced with other women, the salt makers, who attempted to cheer her up, while his informants state that "for ten days they sang [and danced] for her in the manner of women" (*auh matlaqujlhujtl, in qujcioapancujcatiaia ixqujchtin*) (Sahagún 1950–82, bk 2: 92–93). However, they differ in the narration of events in that the women were not described as joyful. Instead, "they went singing; they cried out loudly; they sang in a very high treble" (*yoan cujcatiuj, cenca tzatzi, cenca tlapitzaoa*) (Sahagún 1950–82, bk 2: 93).

Thus, during the eighteen *veintena* festivals, the individuals who were to be sacrificed often danced their way to death, but dancing also took place during the act of immolation, as will be explored in the following section.

DANCING AT THE TIME OF THE SACRIFICE: THE DANCE OF THE SACRIFICER

Ritual killings during the *veintenas* took different forms, including extraction of the heart, beheading and immolation. Often, bystanders danced while the sacrifice occurred. However, the only indications of a dance carried out by the sacrificer at the moment of the ritual killing refer to immolations. Indeed, the colonial writings of the Spanish friars indicate that, during the immolation, sacrificers often danced.

As can be seen from the route of the festival of Teotleco, the victims were thrown into the fire alive: "And at this time then there began the casting [of victims] into the fire there on the large altar" (*Auh in jquac in, njmanicpeoa in tetlepantlaxo, vncan in teccalco*) (Sahagún 1950–82, bk 2: 129). As they were being sacrificed, a specific kind of dance was performed around the bonfire. The references in the *Florentine Codex* show that the men who pushed them were dancing dressed as *techalotl* ("squirrel")[11] and *tzinacan* ("bat"): "And when they were being cast into the fire, [one arrayed as a] squirrel went dancing there … When they cast one into the fire, [the dancer] whistled repeatedly through his fingers. And one [in the likeness of a] bat was there. He went dancing" (*Auh in vncan tetlepātlaxo, vncan mjtotininemj techalotl … In jquac ce contlaça tleco, mapipitzoa: Yoan ce tzinacan vncan nenca, mjtotitinemj*) (Sahagún 1950–82, bk 2: 129).

A similar dance occurred during the festival of Xocotl Huetzi. In honor of the Fire God, Xiuhtecuhtli, the warriors would carry their captives on their shoulders and, while dancing around the fire, would throw them into the burning mass of firewood (Torquemada 1975–83, 3: 394–95). Documentary sources agree that after the death of the victims, the dance did not come to an end.

DANCING AFTER THE DEATH OF THE VICTIM

A Celebratory Dance. The sacrifice was commonly followed by a dance performed by the participants of the sacrificial ritual. Torquemada (1975–83, 3: 404), writing at the beginning of the seventeenth century, describes how, after a massive slaughter of captives, the feast of Quecholli ended with much dancing and singing. The chronicler also describes how, during the festival of Panquetzaliztli, "they were killing first the war captives and after them the fat slaves" (*mataban los cautivos en guerra primero y tras ellos los esclavos cebones*). He adds that this was celebrated "with much music, dance and joy" (*con mucha música ... con muchos bailes y regocijos*) (Torquemada 1975–83, 3: 406).

Similarly, to commemorate the sacrifice of the female victim in Huey Tozoztli, all the women danced and became inebriated throughout the day ("Costumbres ..." 1945, 41). Durán (1995, 2: 54) provides an account of the rituals carried out after the death of the impersonator of Tezcatlipoca in Toxcatl. The Dominican friar states that all the participants in the main event celebrated by dancing and singing accompanied by drums. The description of the *tlahuahuanaliztli* or "striping" indicates that, once the dance began, it did not cease. As stated previously, the enemy combatants and the Mexica warriors danced from the moment the ritual began. They presented themselves dancing; they fought moving their bodies rhythmically and, after the sacrificial death, all the people present rejoiced and began to dance around the sacrificial stone (Sahagún 1950–82, bk 2: 54).

It should be noted that the early chronicles mention the presence of the Mexica ruler Moctezuma in the celebratory dance of Izcalli. Every four years, the *huey tlatoani* honored the ritual deaths by leading "the dance of the lords" (*netecuitotoli*). Sahagún's informants described the dance as follows:

And when they had come descending, then they went encircling [the courtyard]. Only four times did they go encircling. And when they had danced, then there was dispersing on the part of each one; there was dispersing of each person. Thereupon there was entering the palace; there was going into the palace. And of this it was said: "There is lordly dancing; the lords dance the lordly dance." It was the privilege only of the rulers that they should dance the lordly dance (*Auh in otemoco: njmā ie ic tlaiaoaloa, çā nappa in tlaiaoaloa: auh in ommj-totique mec nexixitinjlo, texixitinjlo, njmā ie ic calacoa in tecpan tlatecpanoloz. Auh in iehoatl y, moteneoa: netecujtotilo, motecujtotia in tetecutin, çan inneixcavil catca in tlatoque, in motecujto-tiaia*). (Sahagún 1950–82, bk 2: 164)

Figure 9.2. Dance with severed heads. Detail of *Codex Borgia*, pl. 32. Source: Drawing courtesy of Elbis Domínguez.

Dance with the Severed Head. In addition to the celebratory dances that took place after the sacrifice, occasionally dances were performed with the victim's body parts. This post-mortem treatment of their bodies allowed them to continue to dance in spite of the fact that they were no longer alive. The two dances that probably upset the European missionaries and conquistadors most are the dance with the severed head and the dance with the flayed skin of the victim.

According to documentary sources, the dance with the severed heads (Figure 9.2)[12] was an integral component of two festivals in the Mexica calendar: Tlacaxipehualiztli and Tititl. After the sacrifice of victims to the gods Xipe Totec and Ilamatecuhtli, respectively, the festivals' central rites were brought to an end with this singular dance. Once the act of striping (*tlahuahuanaliztli*) of war prisoners was over, the participants "all severally took with them the head of a captive, of a striped one; with them they danced. It was said: 'They dance with the severed heads'" (*muchintin cecentetl intlan ca ana, yn jntzontecon mamalti, in oaoanti, ic mjottiuj: mjtoa, motzontecomaitotia*) (Sahagún 1950–82, bk 2: 54).

The Nahuatl text of the *Florentine Codex* is more precise when recounting the dance with the head of the victim in Tititl. After they sacrificed her [the female *ixiptla* Ilamatecuhtli] by opening her breast, "they severed her head. And her head they gave to him who went leading [the vicar, the other *ixiptla* of Ilamatecuhtli]. He took it with him; in his right hand, he went grasping it; he went dancing; with the severed head he went making dance gestures" (*njmā ic qujoalquechcotona: auh in jtzontecō, qujoalmaca in teiacantiuh, itlan conana imaiauhcampa in qujtzitzqujtiuh, mjtotitiuh ic ontlaiiauhtiuh in tzōtecomatl*) (Sahagún 1950–82, bk 2: 156). The man who received her head danced backwards, guiding other impersonators of deities who danced in line circling the temple.

Dancing with the Victims' Flayed Skin. In certain rituals, the sacrificed *ixiptla* were flayed.[13] After the victims were sacrificed and the flaying process was completed, their skin was used for dances, combats, and processions. The flayed skin of the sacrificial victim was worn by individuals—mainly warriors and priests—called *xixipeme* ("Flayed Ones") o *tototecti* ("Our Lords"), after the name of the god with the flayed skin, Xipe Totec. The Spanish chronicles of the sixteenth and seventeenth centuries document the skin-wearing dance in Tlacaxipehualiztli (Acosta 2003, 342; Cervantes de Salazar 1985, 36; "Costumbres ..." 1945, 40; Durán 1995, 2: 248; Sahagún 1974, 23–26), Tecuilhuitontli ("Costumbres ..." 1945, 44), Ochpaniztli ("Costumbres ..." 1945, 48; Durán 1995, 2: 146, 150, 152; Motolinía 1971, 63; Torquemada 1975–83, 3: 231), and Izcalli (Torquemada 1975–83, 3: 410–11).

Francisco Cervantes de Salazar, the author of the *Crónica de la Nueva España*, explains that the fresh skin flayed during Tlacaxipehualiztli was worn by the warriors who had just triumphed by the *temalacatl* stone (Figure 9.3).[14] We read: "removing the skin of the tiger [that he had on during the fight], he put on the skin of the dead and danced in front of the devil called Tlacateutezcatepotl" (Cervantes de Salazar 1985, 36). According to the *Primeros Memoriales*, the dance lasted for twenty days; in the words of Sahagún's informants: "for twenty days they danced with it" (*cempoualilhuitl ipan mitotinenca*) (Sahagún 1974, 23).

Figure 9.3. Tlacaxipehualiztli. Detail of *Florentine Codex* (Ms. Med. Palat. 219), 1: bk 2: fol. 20v. Source: Drawing courtesy of Elbis Domínguez.

Regarding the sacrificial rituals of Tecuilhuitontli, the text "Costumbres, Fiestas, Enterramientos y Diversas Formas de Proceder de los Indios de Nueva España" (1945, 44) notes that the priests killed the *ixiptla* of Xochipilli ("Flower Prince") and removed his skin. After the victim had his skin stripped away, a priest performed a dance covering his own body with the flayed skin.

Within the context of Ochpaniztli, the living images of Atlatonan, Chicomecoatl, and Toci were sacrificed and flayed. The morning after Atlatonan's sacrifice, a priest solemnly danced in a procession, carrying her skin (Torquemada 1975–83, 3: 231). Once the skin of Chicomecoatl was stripped off, a priest guided a dance dressed in the flayed skin and the adornments of the sacrificed goddess (Durán 1995, 2: 146). Finally, the skin removed from the body of Toci was used in subsequent combat and dance. As described by Durán, a dancer, covered with Toci's skin, fought vigorously, with the help of the midwives and the Huastecs, against the noble lords and the dignitaries (Durán 1995, 2: 151–52). Another source describes two dancers, one donning a mask made with the skin of Toci's thigh and the other dancing with her skin turned inside out ("Costumbres ..." 1945, 48).

According to Torquemada (1975–83, 3: 410–11), during the festival of Izcalli more than eight thousand people came to Cuauhtitlan, a city located near Tenochtitlan, to witness the sacrifice of two women on top of a temple. Afterwards the skin of the sacrificial women was removed intact and used for a dance.

OVERLAP BETWEEN DANCE AND OTHER SACRIFICIAL ACTS

In a ceremonial sequence, dance, song, music, procession, feasts, and offerings were inseparably interwoven. Often it is not possible to tell the difference between dance, battle, sacrifice, and procession. In fact, certain ritual acts seem to encompass more than one at the same time. Therefore, it is not surprising that the combat between warriors and captives in the *tlahuahuanaliztli* was performed through dance. In a similar vein, several colonial sources show that the lives of victims were offered while dancing, thus making it difficult to distinguish between this dance and the sacrifice itself. As stated previously, there were two festivals, Xocotl Huetzi and Teotleco, in which prisoners were thrown alive into the fire while the sacrificers danced.

Frequently, a dance and a procession cannot be differentiated. For instance, during Izcalli, when the time of the sacrifice came, the impersonators of Xiuhtecutli danced in procession (Sahagún 1950–82, bk 2: 162; 2000, 264). Similarly, the *Primeros Memoriales* indicates that after the victims were sacrificed in Xocotl Huetzi, a procession and a serpent dance took place around the *xocotl* tree (Sahagún 1974, 41, 44–45). Following the sacrifice in Tlacaxipehualiztli, the participants proceeded in an orderly manner around the sacrificial stone. We read: "And when this was done, when they had finished with the striped ones, then they danced, they went in procession about the round sacrificial stone" (*Auh in ie iuhquj, yn ontlanque oaoanti, njman ic mjtotia, qujiaoaloa in temalacatl*) (Sahagún 1950–82, bk 2: 54).

In addition, the movements described in the sources are sometimes identical, but the documents do not mention dance. Such is the case of Teotleco, when the priests moved hand-to-hand in a procession around the fire (Sahagún 2000, 238). In Tlacaxipehualiztli and Tititl, the sacrifice of the *ixiptla* ended with a dance with the heads of the victims; in the case of Quecholli, it ended in a procession with the participants holding the head of the victim in one hand (Durán 1995, 2: 85). In this case, it is difficult to ascertain whether the ceremonial use of victims' severed heads differs fundamentally, or whether it can also be considered a dance.

Likewise, colonial manuscripts sometimes fail to agree on whether a specific ritual included a dance or not. For example, the Nahuatl and Spanish texts of the *Florentine Codex* differ in their description of a ritual act in Panquetzaliztli. While the Nahuatl description mentions only trotting, running and hurrying (Sahagún 1950–82, bk 2: 143), the Spanish text states that the future victims danced, jumped and ran (Sahagún 2000, 248). The information about the beginning of the *tla-huahuanaliztli* varies as well. According to the friar, captives moved in a procession waving their sword and shield (Sahagún 2000, 182), whereas according to his informants, they emerged dancing (Sahagún 1950–82, bk 2: 51; see also Durán 1995, 2: 225). Therefore, the difficulty of delineating and determining the nature of specific ritual acts did not only fall to modern scholars. Rather, while collecting and recording information from elders and interpreters, Spanish chroniclers some-times expressed their doubt about the nature of the ritual acts described. Another example of this kind of uncertainty is provided by Sahagún, who points out that a "hand-waving dance" performed in silence during Ochpaniztli did not include typical dance movements like swaying; rather, the dancers walked and waved their hands (Sahagún 2000, 233).

Finally, in spite of the fact that war dances use weapons and fighting move-ments in many parts of the world, and that dancing processions have adopted different forms for centuries, it is important to acknowledge the possibility that the Mexica had different concepts of body movements, making our categories unpro-ductive. My data shows that dance and sacrifice are inextricably interwoven, which simultaneously raises various questions. What was the nature of the relationship between ritual killing and dancing among the Mexica before the arrival of the Europeans? At what point(s) do they converge? How can boundaries between them be determined? How do we define the nature of the different ritual acts that often overlap? Can these ritual acts be more than one thing at the same time? In other words, can they be considered different categories? Are sacrifice and dance separate categories or not?

These questions suggest that the limits of our categories may need to be expanded in order to further understand the nature of dance among the Mexica. Specifically, concepts such as "dance," "sacrifice," "ritual fight," and "procession," along with other terms we use in order to analyze the *veintena* festivals, should be re-examined.[15] Rather than forcing our categories to describe the native's point of view, it is important to keep in mind that we are facing distinct knowledge systems.[16] In this sense, the relationship between different, but at times indistinguishable, ritual practices should be a matter of great concern and constant reflection.

CONCLUSIONS

In pre-Columbian times, dance was a widespread practice in the ritual and sacrificial offerings of the Mexica. From the process of selecting or capturing victims until the ritual use of their dismembered bodies, the act of dancing appears prominently in the sources. Furthermore, in the context of the *veintena* festivals, it seems impossible to separate the dance from the sacrificial rituals.

Two valuable testimonies offer special insight as to the crucial importance of dance throughout the sacrificial rituals. In his reconstruction of the military expansion of the Mexica, Durán includes an unfortunate episode for Mexico-Tenochtitlan. The Chalca killed three brothers of the ruler of Tenochtitlan, when "the day of the feast of Xocotl was due" (Durán 1994, 142). They also took Ezhuahuacatl, "a first cousin of King Motecuhzoma." He refused the proposal of the Chalca to become their leader and asked the enemies "that they bring a tree trunk about twenty *brazas* high and that they place a platform on top," in order to recreate the specific ceremonies of Xocotl Huetzi. Durán's (1994, 143) informants recalled his last dance in detail:

> A drum was brought out and all began to dance around the pole. After dancing, Ezhua-huacatl said farewell to the Aztecs, crying out, "Brothers, the time has come! Die like brave men!" Having said these words, he began to climb the pole. When he arrived at the wooden platform at the summit, he began to dance and sing. When he finished singing, he shouted in a loud voice, "O Chalcas, know that with my death I shall have bought your lives and, in the future, you will serve my children and grandchildren! My royal blood will be paid for with yours!" And on this last cry he cast himself off the platform and was shattered to bits.

Ezhuahuacatl's actions sheds light on the importance of dance and its association with bravery, particularly in the face of death.

Some years later, when the conquerors arrived to the New World, dance movements were once again associated with brave conduct. Cervantes de Salazar (1985, 547–49) states that thirty or forty natives, captured by the soldiers under Hernán Cortés' command, understanding that they were to die, removed their clothes and danced for half an hour before dying. Undoubtedly, for the indigenous people of pre-Hispanic Mexico, a good death meant to die dancing.

Table 9.1. Dance in the sacrificial rituals of the *veintena* festivals.

Name of the festival	Time of dance	Participants	Dance movements	Overlap with other ritual acts
Atlcahualo	?	Captives and captors	?	
Tlacaxipehualiztli	One day before the sacrifice	Captives and captors	?	
Tlacaxipehualiztli	The day of the sacrifice, before the sacrifice was completed	Captives	?	Procession?
Tlacaxipehualiztli	The day of the sacrifice, before the sacrifice was carried out	All the participants, except the captives	?	Procession, combat
Tlacaxipehualiztli	The day of the sacrifice, before the sacrifice was carried out	Captives and Mexica warriors (*tlahuahuanaliztli*)	?	Combat
Tlacaxipehualiztli	The day of the sacrifice, before the sacrifice was carried out	Captor	?	
Tlacaxipehualiztli	Once the sacrifice was carried out	All participants	Circle dance	Procession
Tlacaxipehualiztli	Once the sacrifice was carried out	Captors, other living images of deities and sacrificers	"Dance of the severed head"	
Tlacaxipehualiztli	Once the sacrifice was carried out	?	Dancing with the victim's flayed skin	
Huey Tozoztli	Once the sacrifice was carried out	Women	?	
Toxcatl	The day of the sacrifice, before the sacrifice was carried out	*Ixiptla* of Ixteucale Tlacahuepan Teicautzin	Serpent (or winding) dance	
Etzalcualiztli	The night before the sacrifice	*Ixiptla* of Tlaloc	?	

Continued

Table 9.1. Continued

Name of the festival	Time of dance	Participants	Dance movements	Overlap with other ritual acts
Etzalcualiztli	The night before the sacrifice	*Ixiptla* of Tlaloc and Chalchiuhtlicue	?	
Tecuilhuitontli	Ten days before the sacrifice	*Ixiptla* of Huixtocihuatl with the women salt-makers	Hand-to-hand and circle dance	
Tecuilhuitontli	The night before the sacrifice	Captives and *ixiptla* of Huixtocihuatl with the women salt-makers	?	
Tecuilhuitontli	?	Those who wanted to participate	?	
Tecuilhuitontli	Once the sacrifice was carried out	Priest	Dancing with the victim's flayed skin	
Huey Tecuilhuitl	The day and the night before the sacrifice	Priestesses	?	
Huey Tecuilhuitl	The day of the sacrifice, before the sacrifice was carried out	*Ixiptla* of Xilonen	?	
Huey Tecuilhuitl	The day of the sacrifice, before the sacrifice was carried out	*Ixiptla* of Xilonen with the priestesses	?	
Huey Tecuilhuitl	The day of the sacrifice, before the sacrifice was carried out	The masters of the youths	Hand-to-hand and serpent (or winding) dance	
Huey Tecuilhuitl	The day of the sacrifice, before the sacrifice was carried out	Priest	Turning around	

Table 9.1. Continued

Name of the festival	Time of dance	Participants	Dance movements	Overlap with other ritual acts
Xocotl Huetzi	One day before the sacrifice	Captives and captors	Serpent (or winding) dance	
Xocotl Huetzi	During the sacrificial rituals	Captives and captors	Circle dance	Sacrifice
Xocotl Huetzi	During the sacrificial rituals	Future victim	?	Sacrifice
Xocotl Huetzi	Once the sacrifice was carried out	?	Hand-to-hand, serpent (or winding) dance and circle dance	Procession?
Ochpaniztli	One day before the sacrifice of Chicomecoatl	*Ixiptla* of Chicomecoatl	?	
Ochpaniztli	Once the sacrifice of Chicomecoatl was carried out	The one who wore the skin of Chicomecoatl	Dancing with the victim's flayed skin	
Ochpaniztli	For seven days before the sacrifice of Toci	*Ixiptla* of Toci	?	
Ochpaniztli	For seven days before the sacrifice of Toci	Young boys and girls	Hand-to-hand	
Ochpaniztli	Once the sacrifice of Toci was carried out	The one who wore the skin of Toci	Dancing with the victim's flayed skin	
Ochpaniztli	Once the sacrifice of Toci was carried out	The women physicians	?	
Ochpaniztli	Once the sacrifice of Toci was carried out	Warriors	"The hand-waving dance"	Walking

Continued

Table 9.1. Continued

Name of the festival	Time of dance	Participants	Dance movements	Overlap with other ritual acts
Teotl Eco	During the sacrificial rituals	One young man dressed as a squirrel and another one as a bat	Circle dance	Sacrifice
Quecholli	The day of the sacrifice, before the sacrifice was carried out	Female victims	?	
Panquetzaliztli	Nine days before the sacrifice	The bathed victims	Hand-to-hand	
Panquetzaliztli	Five days before the sacrifice	The bathed victims, the owners of slaves and other participants.	Hand-to-hand and serpent (or winding) dance	
Panquetzaliztli	Five days before the sacrifice	The bathed victims	Jumping, running	Jumping, running
Panquetzaliztli	One day before the sacrifice	The bathed victims	?	
Panquetzaliztli	Once the sacrifice was carried out	?		
Tititl	The day of the sacrifice, before the sacrifice was carried out	*Ixiptla* of Ilamatecuhtli		
Tititl	Once the sacrifice was carried out	The second living image of Ilamatecuhtli	"Dance of the severed head" and stepping back	
Tititl	Once the sacrifice was carried out	The second living image of Ilamatecuhtli and other living images of deities	Circle dance	

Table 9.1. Continued

Name of the festival	Time of dance	Participants	Dance movements	Overlap with other ritual acts
Izcalli	The day of the sacrifice, before the sacrifice was carried out	Future victims, captives and *ixiptla* of Ixcozauhqui		Procession
Izcalli	Once the sacrifice was carried out	Rulers and dignitaries ("The dance of the Lords")	Hand-to-hand	
Izcalli	Once the sacrifice was carried out	Rulers and dignitaries ("The dance of the Lords")	Circle dance	
Izcalli	Once the sacrifice was carried out	Priests	Dancing with the victims' flayed skin	

NOTES

1. This chapter, copy-edited by Susana Kolb Cadwell, is derived from my PhD research entitled: "El concepto de danza entre los mexicas en la época posclásica," Universidad Nacional Autónoma de México, 2016.
2. For instance, Danilović (2009) carried out a study of female dances in Tecuilhuitontli, Huey Tecuilhuitl, Ochpaniztli, and Tititl; Claude-François Baudez (2011) examined the dance performed during *tlahuahuanaliztli*, the central ceremony of Tlacaxipehualiztli; and Paul A. Scolieri (2013, 70–89) describes some of the dances in Atlcahualo, Tlacaxipehualiztli, Tecuilhuitontli, Huey Tecuilhuitl, Ochpaniztli, Quecholli, and Tititl.
3. The dances performed during the sacrificial rituals over the course of the 365-day calendar are listed in Table 9.1 at the end of the chapter.
4. As Alfredo López Austin and Leonardo López Luján (2011, 214) have shown, the *tlatlacoliztli* was a Mexica institution that has been compared to slavery. One became a *tlacotli* by not paying debts or by being penalized for committing a serious crime. A *tlacotli* was forced to work for his creditor with no pay except his daily food. However, he did not lose his family or the ability to own property, including a *tlacotli* of his own.
5. The Nahuatl word *ixiptla* (or *teotl ixiptla*) was used to refer to an image, a likeness, a representative, an impersonator of deities. The deity likeness could be a person, a stone image, a seed-dough figure, and an object, to name but a few.

6. My translation into English of Navarrete's translation of the Nahuatl (Castillo 2001).

7. The captives were killed in order to become a sort of support or foundation upon which the *ixiptla*'s body was sacrificed.

8. See Hvidtfeldt (1958) and Dehouve (2016) regarding ceremonial insignia and adornments that served to visualize and embody deities.

9. A bond between prisoners of war and their captors was established immediately. Upon capturing a future victim, the warrior would name him his son. The *Florentine Codex* explains: "For when he took [the captive], he said: 'He is as my beloved son.' And the captive had said: 'He is my beloved father'" (*Ca yn iquac caci, qujtoa, ca iuhquj nopiltiz: Auh in malli, qujtoa ca notatzin*) (Sahagún 1950–82, bk 2: 54). Therefore, the captor could not participate in the ritual consumption of the captive's corpse. For more information on the alliance formed between prisoners of war and their captors, see, for example, Baudez (2010, 431–51) and Olivier (2015, 645–53).

10. For more information on the *tlahuahuanaliztli* ritual see, for example, Broda (1970, 197–274), Graulich (1999, 282–305), and González González (2011, 355–71).

11. Agnieszka Brylak (2015) examines the domain of this figure in her study of the Nahua pre-Hispanic god called Techalotl. As she points out, he resembles the Macuiltonaleque, gods associated with the number five, on the iconographic level, which links him to the field of dances, songs, performances, mockery, and excesses. In addition, Brylak refers to the sexual connotations of the squirrel and its connection to sexuality and transgression.

12. Pictographic descriptions of rituals with severed heads can also be seen in the codices *Vaticanus B* (*Códice Vaticano B* 1993, pl. 24), *Cospi* (*Códice Cospi* 1994, pl. 1–3, 5–8), *Fejérváry-Mayer* (*Códice Fejérváry-Mayer* 1994, pl. 41), and *Laud* (*Códice Laud* 1961, pl. 20, 24).

13. One example can be found during the festival of Ochpaniztli, in which the skin of the impersonators of Atlatonan, Chicomecoatl, and Toci was peeled off. As reported by Sahagún's informants, the skin of Toci was removed from her body as follows: "And when they had taken her to where she was to die, they seized her. They stretched her out on the back of one [of them]. Then they quickly cut off her head. And when they had cut off her head, they also flayed her. And when they had flayed her, then a man [a priest] quickly put on her skin. He was called Teccizquacuilli" (*Auh in oconaxitique vncā mjqujz: njmā ic qujoalana, çan tecujtlapan in cōteca, njmā ic qujoalquecheotontivetzi: auh in ocōquechcotonque, njmā no iciuhca qujxipeuhtivetzi, qujxipeuhtiquiça. Auh in oqujxipeuhque: njmā ic cōmaqujtivetzi ce tlacatl in jeoaio: itoca Tecizcuajli*) (Sahagún 1950–82, bk 2: 120). On the flaying of sacrificial victims, see also Mazzetto in this volume (Chapter 6).

14. See also the *Florentine Codex* (Sahagún 1979, bk 2: fol. 10r, 10v, 26r) and the codices *Borbonicus* (*Códice Borbónico* 1991, pl. 24), *Vaticanus B* (*Códice Vaticano B* 1993, pl. 42), *Fejérváry-Mayer* (*Códice Fejérváry-Mayer*, pl. 43), *Tudela* (1980, pl. 12r), and *Tovar* or *Ramírez* (Tovar 1979, pl. 147).

15. Until recently, most research assumed an equivalence between the pre-Columbian term, the Colonial concept, and the modern idea of dance for the Nahuatl-speaking groups of Central Mexico. There was no critical consideration of the use of the term. In my PhD thesis (Danilović 2016), I examine the concept itself and re-examine the terminology we apply and its consequences for our understanding of Mexica dance.

16. Another indicator of different concepts of body movements among the Mexica is their language. My linguistic analysis of vocabularies and texts in Nahuatl provides a list of ten verbs which include a meaning of "dance": *i'tōtia, mācēhua, cuicoanoa, āna, cōānecuiloa, nāhua, mātlāza, cōcōloa, tlayahua* and *chocholoa* (Danilović 2016, 116–68).

REFERENCES

Acosta, José de. 2003. *Historia natural y moral de las Indias*. Madrid: Dastin.

Alvarado Tezozómoc, Fernando. 1997. *Crónica mexicana*. Madrid: Dastin.

Baudez, Claude-François. 2010. "Sacrificio de 'sí', sacrificio del 'otro'." In *El sacrificio humano en la tradición religiosa mesoamericana*, edited by Leonardo López Lujan and Guilhem Olivier, 431–51. Mexico City: Instituto Nacional de Antropología e Historia, Universidad Nacional Autónoma de México.

_____2011. "La danse de l'éraflure (*tlauauanaliztli*) ou la réconciliation des antagonismes." In *La Quête du serpent à plumes. Arts et religions de l'Amérique précolombienne*, edited by Sylvie Peperstraete, Nathalie Ragot, and Guilhem Olivier, 137–45. Turnhout: Brepols Publishers, Bibliothèque de l'École Pratique des Hautes Études-Sciences religieuses.

Boone, Elizabeth H., ed. 1984. *Ritual Human Sacrifice in Mesoamerica*. Washington D.C.: Dumbarton Oaks.

Broda, Johanna (de Casas). 1970. "Tlacaxipehualiztli: A Reconstruction of an Aztec Calendar Festival from 16th Century Sources." *Revista Española de Antropología Americana* 5: 197–274.

Brylak, Agnieszka. 2015. "Truhanería y sexualidad: *techalotl* entre los nahuas prehispánicos," *Itinerarios* 21: 57–78.

Castillo, Cristóbal del. 2001. *Historia de la venida de los mexicanos y otros pueblos e historia de la conquista*. Edited by Federico Navarrete Linares. Mexico City: Consejo Nacional para la Cultura y las Artes.

Cervantes de Salazar, Francisco. 1985. *Crónica de la Nueva España*. Mexico City: Porrúa.

Códice Borbónico. 1991. Edited by Ferdinand Anders, Maarten Jansen, and Luis Reyes García. Graz, Madrid, Mexico City: ADEVA, Sociedad Estatal Quinto Centenario, Fondo de Cultura Económica.

Códice Cospi. 1994. Edited by Ferdinand Anders, Maarten Jansen, and Luis Reyes García. Graz, Mexico City: ADEVA, Fondo de Cultura Económica.

Códice Fejérváry-Mayer. 1994. Edited by Ferdinand Anders, Maarten Jansen, and Luis Reyes García. Graz, Mexico City: ADEVA, Fondo de Cultura Económica.

Códice Laud. 1961. Edited by Carlos Martínez. Mexico City: Instituto Nacional de Antropología e Historia.

Códice Tudela. 1980. Edited by José Tudela de la Orden. Madrid: Ediciones Cultura Hispánica del Instituto de Cooperación Iberoamericano.

Códice Vaticano B 3773. 1993. Edited by Ferdinand Anders, Maarten Jansen, and Luis Reyes García. Graz, Madrid, Mexico City: ADEVA, Sociedad Estatal Quinto Centenario, Fondo de Cultura Económica.

"Costumbres, fiestas, enterramientos y diversas formas de proceder de los Indios de Nueva España." 1945. Edited by Federico Gómez de Orozco. *Tlalocan* 2, no. 1: 37–63.

Danilović, Mirjana. 2009. "El valor simbólico de las danzas femeninas en el caso de las fiestas de *tecuilhuitontli*, *huey tecuilhuitl*, *ochpaniztli* y *tititl*." MA diss., Universidad Nacional Autónoma de México.

———. 2016. "El concepto de danza entre los mexicas." PhD diss., Universidad Nacional Autónoma de México.

Dehouve, Danièle. 2016. "El papel de la vestimenta en los rituales mexicas de 'personificación'." http://journals.openedition.org/nuevomundo/69305

Durán, Diego. 1994. *The History of the Indies of New Spain.* Translated and edited by Doris Heyden. Norman: University of Oklahoma Press.

———. 1995. *Historia de las Indias de Nueva España e islas de Tierra Firme.* Edited by José Rubén Romero and Rosa Camelo. 2 vols. Mexico City: Consejo Nacional para la Cultura y las Artes.

González González, Carlos. 2011. *Xipe Tótec. Guerra y regeneración del maíz en la religión mexica.* Mexico City: Instituto Nacional de Antropología e Historia, Fondo de Cultura Económica.

González Torres, Yolotl. 1985. *El sacrificio humano entre los mexicas.* Mexico City: Fondo de Cultura Económica.

Graulich, Michel. 1999. *Ritos aztecas. Las fiestas de las veintenas.* Mexico City: Instituto Nacional Indigenista.

———. 2005. *Le sacrifice humain chez les Aztèques.* Paris: Fayard.

Hvidtfeldt, Arild. 1958. *Teotl and *Ixiptlatli. Some Central Conceptions in Ancient Mexican Religion.* Copenhagen: Munksgaard.

López Austin, Alfredo, and Leonardo López Luján. 2011. *Mexico's Indigenous Past.* Translated by Bernard R. Ortiz de Montellano. Norman: University Press of Oklahoma.

López Luján, Leonardo, and Guilhem Olivier, eds. 2010. *El sacrificio humano en la tradición religiosa mesoamericana.* Mexico City: Instituto Nacional de Antropología e Historia, Universidad Nacional Autónoma de México.

Martí, Samuel. 1961. *Canto, danza y música precortesianos.* Mexico City: Fondo de Cultura Económica.

Martí, Samuel, and Gertrude Prokosch Kurath. 1964. *Dances of Anahuac. The Choreography and Music of Precortesian Dances.* Chicago: Aldine.

Mazzetto, Elena. 2014. *Lieux de culte et parcours cérémoniels dans les fêtes des vingtaines à Mexico Tenochtitlan.* Oxford: British Archaeological Reports.

Motolinía, or Benavente, Toribio de. 1971. *Memoriales o Libro de las cosas de la Nueva España y de los naturales de ella.* Edited by Edmundo O'Gorman. Mexico City: Universidad Nacional Autónoma de México-Instituto de Investigaciones Históricas.

Olivier, Guilhem. 2015. *Cacería, sacrificio y poder en Mesoamérica. Tras las huellas de Mixcóatl, "Serpiente de Nube."* Mexico City: Fondo de Cultura Económica, Universidad Nacional Autónoma de México, Centro de Estudios Mexicanos y Centroamericanos.

Sahagún, Bernardino de. 1950–82. *Florentine Codex: General History of the Things of New Spain, Fray Bernardino de Sahagún.* Translated with notes and illustrations by Arthur J. O. Anderson and Charles E. Dibble. 13 vols. Santa Fe: The School of American Research, University of Utah Press.

———. 1974. *"Primeros Memoriales" de Fray Bernardino de Sahagún.* Edited and translated by Wigberto Jiménez Moreno. Mexico City: Instituto Nacional de Antropología e Historia, Secretaría de Educación Pública.

———. 1979. *Códice Florentino. El manuscrito 218–220 de la Colección Palatina de la Biblioteca Medicea Laurenziana.* 3 vols. Florence, Mexico City: Giunti Barbéra, Archivo General de la Nación.

———. 1997. *Primeros Memoriales.* Edited and translated by Thelma Sullivan. Completed and revised, with additions, by Henry B. Nicholson, Arthur J. O. Anderson, Charles E. Dibble, Eloise Quiñones Keber, and Wayne Ruwet. Norman: University of Oklahoma Press.

———. 2000. *Historia General de las Cosas de Nueva España.* Edited by Alfredo López Austin and Josefina García Quintana. 3 vols. Mexico City: Consejo Nacional para la Cultura y las Artes.

Scolieri, Paul. 2013. *Dancing the New World: Aztecs, Spaniards, and the Choreography of Conquest.* Austin: University of Texas Press.

Sten, María. 1990. *Ponte a bailar, tú que reinas: Antropología de la danza prehispánica.* Mexico City: J. Mortiz.

Torquemada, Juan de. 1975–83. *Monarquía indiana.* Edited by Miguel León-Portilla. 7 vols. Mexico City: Universidad Nacional Autónoma de México-Instituto de Investigaciones Históricas.

Tovar, Juan de. 1979. *Códice Ramírez, manuscrito del siglo XVI intitulado: Relación del origen de los indios que habitan esta Nueva España, según sus historias.* Mexico City: Innovación.

Turrent, Lourdes. 2006. *La conquista musical de México.* Mexico City: Fondo de Cultura Económica.

CHAPTER TEN

Ritual and Religious Practices Described in the *Florentine Codex*

Ritual Unit as a Structural Concept

ANDREA B. RODRÍGUEZ FIGUEROA, MARIO CORTINA BORJA,
AND LEOPOLDO VALIÑAS COALLA

INTRODUCTION

This chapter is part of the research project "The translation of Sahagún's work from a linguistic perspective," which aims to reconstruct the festival landscape in the Basin of Mexico in the fifteenth and sixteenth centuries. To achieve this, we analyzed all the information related to the *sêsempôwallapôwalli*[1] or the account of each one of the *veintenas* described in two of Sahagún's manuscripts that were written between 1559 and 1580 in Castilian and Classical Nahuatl, although there are sections written only in one of these languages and also some very few parts written in Latin (see Bartl et al. 1989, 76).

These two documents are: (1) the one known as *Códice Matritense de Real Palacio*, which is one of two sets of documents kept in the Real Biblioteca del Palacio Real de Madrid, Spain, and entitled by Sahagún *Universal History of the Things of New Spain* (*historia vnjuersal, de las cosas dela nueua españa*). A section of this collection is known as *Primeros Memoriales* and is written mainly in Classical Nahuatl. (2) The *Florentine Codex* (Sahagún 1979), the original of which is in the Biblioteca Medicea Laurenziana in Florence.

Our main objective is to *demonstrate the pertinence of a nuclear analytical term*, here called a ritual unit, as part of the structure of any festival, based on the analyses shown in Rodríguez Figueroa (2014). This proposal is based on our analytical work, first, of the contents of each of the textual headings of chapters 20 to 37 of

Book II of the *Florentine Codex* (Sahagún 1979, bk 2: fol. 15r–96r), and, second, on the reading of what is described in the chapters that address the first four *veintenas*: *kʷawitl êwa* or *âtl kâwalo, tlâkašipêwalistli, tôssôstôntli* and *wêyi tôssôstli* (Sahagún 1979, bk 2: fol. 15r–29v).

Since Sahagún's texts are written in Classical Nahuatl and in Castilian,[2] in order to respect them as historical evidence, we decided to present the written sections in Castilian and in Classical Nahuatl in paleography. Since rather than working with documents we were working with languages, we decided to normalize the texts in Classical Nahuatl which were written using the alphabetic strategies of fifteenth-century Castilian (Parodi 1995). Thus, we decided to *rewrite* the Classical Nahuatl texts following linguistic principles based on their assumed phonological and morphological reality (see Rodríguez Figueroa 2014). At the same time, we made the decision to translate the Classical Nahuatl text into English because: (1) for the purposes of this research most of the existing translations were not clear enough to understand them contextually,[3] and (2) naturally, each translation has different intentions and ours is to reconstruct the festival landscape.

We used: (1) Molina's *Vocabulario* that has two sections: the Castilian to Classical Nahuatl (or Mexican, as it was named in the sixteenth century) one, and the Classical Nahuatl to Castilian one (Molina 2004); (2) Sahagún's *Escolios*, a manuscript also known as *Memoriales en tres columnas*, included in the *Matritenses de la Real Academia*, the set of documents collected and lodged in the Real Academia de Historia, Spain. These *Escolios* are a set of lexicography notes added to the Classical Nahuatl texts that define some words. We decided not to translate proper names, since they have no meaning.

To better distinguish the citations to Molina's *Vocabulario*, its two sections will be denoted with roman numerals. For example, Molina (2004, part II: fol. 125v) indicates that the definition is in the Classical Nahuatl to Castilian section in folio 125v.

Only some Castilian sections were translated into Spanish in the first place because some words and expressions have changed their meanings over the last four centuries; following this they were translated into English. As the first step, we used the *Diccionario de Autoridades* (Real Academia Española 1969) because it utilizes a number of Castilian texts to support its definitions. We quote this dictionary by referencing the volume number of the facsimile version.

As humans, we all give meaning to what we *read* of the world (i.e. to interpret what we perceive), and the written word is no exception. Some passages of the existing translations may be unclear or "not so well understood," for example when we are trying to identify the relationship among festivals, rites, and *veintenas*. This uncertainty is present in our translation proposal because we were not always clear about what the text was about. This initial misunderstanding led us to the following questions: Are the names (assuming that they are names) that appear in Sahagún's texts the festivals' names or the *veintenas*' names? Was there a single festival or more than one in each veintena? Was there a major festival in each *veintena*? If so, how could it be identified?

These questions led us to propose a structured hierarchy to characterize the *veintena* festivals.

CONVENTIONS

Finally, to simplify the reading of the text we decided to use the following conventions: the Classical Nahuatl words will appear in italics (except the proper names); the Classical Nahuatl morphemes, between {}; the meanings, between single quotation marks '; and the citations, between double quotation marks ".

RITUAL UNIT AS A FESTIVAL STRUCTURAL CONCEPT

To describe and analyze each one of the practices that were carried out in each *veintena* we propose the concept of ritual unity. Further, we propose a hierarchy of the highest levels of the structure of the religious practices. This will function as an axis for a set of practices that integrate the festival. The ritual unit must be materialized in a festival to achieve its function. We define ritual unity as the rite or set of nuclear rites that are needed to fulfill a festival. This means that every festival must have at least one ritual unity.

So far, in the descriptions of the first four *veintenas*, we have identified four ritual units (three of them are named in the headings of each of the 18 *veintenas* described in Book 2 of the *Florentine Codex* or within their descriptions): TLAMAWISTÎLÎLISTLI, NEŠTLÂWALISTLI, TLAMANALISTLI y NENEHTOLTÎLISTLI (from now on the names of the ritual units will appear in small caps). The last one is not mentioned in the headings but is indeed described within the tlâkašipêwal-istli *veintena*. But what allows us to identify such terms as ritual units?

STRUCTURE OF THE HEADINGS OF THE DESCRIPTIONS OF THE *VEINTENAS*

To answer this question, we firstly look at the headings of each one of the chapters 20 to 37 of Book 2 of the *Florentine Codex* (Sahagún 1979, bk 2: fol. 15r–96r). Evidently each one of the headings is structured according to a scheme which can be represented in terms of four fields:

1. Chapter number.
2. Thematic reference, which includes the word *ilwitl* 'day/festival' plus a derived noun, whose morphological ending is basically {-listli} (whose function is to nominalize a verb focusing the event).
3. Temporal reference.
4. The name of the *veintena*.

Table 10.1 shows the headings of the 18 *veintenas* in the Castilian version, the Classical Nahuatl version, the normalized Classical Nahuatl version, and, our suggested English translation.

We first focus on three headings (those of chapters 20, 28 and 35) in which the word *ilwitl* 'festival' is accompanied by one of the following three nouns in Classical Nahuatl: NEŠTLÂWALISTLI, TLAMAWISTÎLÎLISTLI, and TLAMANALISTLI (in the following examples these words are highlighted in bold type). In the Castilian version, however, there appears the word *fiesta*, festival, which is accompanied only by two words: *sacrificios*, sacrifices, and *cerimonias*, ceremonies.

In each of the following cases the normalized Classical Nahuatl version appears in the first line; in the second, our translation, and in the third, the Castilian version.

Heading of the twentieth chapter

1. In ik 20 capitulo.
Twentieth chapter.
Capitulo veynte

2. Itechpa tlahtoa in **ilwitl** iwân in **neštlâwalistli**
It talks about the **festival** and the **NEŠTLÂWALISTLI**
de la **fiesta** y **sacrificios**

3. in kichîwayah in ipan wel ik semilwitl mêtstli
that were made on the first day of the month
que hazian en las kalendas del primero mes,

4. in kitôkâyôtiâyah in kihtoâyah âtl kâwalo ahnoso kʷawitl êwa.
called *âtl kâwalo* or *kʷawitl êwa*.
que se llamaua, atl caoalo, o quaujtleoa

Heading of the twenty-eighth chapter

1. In ik sempôwalli onchikʷêyi capitulo.
Twenty-eighth chapter.
Capitulo decimo .28,

Table 10.1. Headings of the *veintenas* in the *Florentine Codex*

Castilian	Classical Nahuatl	Classical Nahuatl Normalized	English Translation
	fol. 15r		
Capitulo veynte de la fiesta y sacrificios que hazian en las kalendas del primero mes, que se llamaua, atl caoalo, o quauitleoa.	Inic. 20. capitulo, yrechpa tlatoa yn ilhuitl, yoan in nextlaoaliztli: in quichioaia, yn ipan vel ic cemilhuitl metztli: in quitocaiotiaia, in quitoaia atl caoalo, anoço quauitleoa.	In ik 20 capitulo. Itechpa tlahtoa in ilwitl iwân in neštlâwalistli in kichîwayah in ipan wel ik semilwitl mêtstli in kitôkâyôtiâyah in kihtoâyah âtl kâwalo ahnoso kʷawitl êwa.	Twentieth chapter. It talks about the festival and the *neštlâwalistli* that were made on the first day of the month called *âtl kâwalo* or *kʷawitl êwa*.
	fol. 17v		
Capitulo tercero 21, de las cerimonjas, y sacrificios, que hazian en el segundo mes: que se llamaua tlacaxipeoaliztli.	Inic ᶜᵉᵐᵖᵒᵃˡⁱᵒⁿᶜᵉ eycapitulo, yrechpa tlatoa intlamauiztililiztli, yoan in nextlaoaliztli, in qujchioaia, yn ipan vel ic vntetl metztli, in mjtoaia, tlacaxipeoaliztli.	In ik sempôwalli onsê capitulo. Itechpa tlahtoa in tlamawistîlistli iwân in neštlâwalistli in kichîwâyah in ipan wel ik ôntetl mêtstli in mihtoaya tlâkašipêwalistli.	Twenty-first chapter. It talks about the *tlamawistîlistli* and the *neštlâwalistli* that were made on the first day of the month called *tlâkašipêwalistli*.
	fol. 24r		
Capitulo quarto 22, de la fiesta y sacrificios: que hazian en el postrero dia, del segundo mes, que se dezia tlacaxipeoaliztli.	Inic vmei ᶜᵉᵐᵖᵒᵃˡⁱᵒᵐᵘᵐᵉ capitulo: vncā̄ moteneoa yn ilhuitl, yoan in nextlaoaliztli in quichioaia in ipan ic vme metztli: in mitoaia, in moteneoaia, tlacaxipeoaliztli.	In ik sempôwalli omôme capitulo. Onkân moténêwa in ilwitl iwân in neštlâwalistli in kichîwayah in ipan ik ôme mêtstli in mihtoâya in moténêwaya tlâkašipêwalistli.	Twenty-second chapter. The festival and the *neštlâwalistli*, that were made on the second month called *tlâkašipêwalistli*, are described here.
	fol. 27r		
Capitulo quinto 23, de la fiesta, y cerimonias, que haziā en las kalendas del quarto mes que se llamaua vey toçoztli.	Inic cempoualli ᵛᵐᵉⁱ capitulo, yrechpa tlatoa in ilhujtl: yoan in tlamauistililiztli, in qujchioaia, yn jpan ic cemilhujtl yc nauj metztli: in mitoaia vey toçoztli.	In ik sempôwalli omêyi capitulo. Itechpa tlahtoa in ilwitl iwân in tlamawistîlistli in kichîwayah in ipan ik semilwitl ik nâwi mêtstli in mihtoâya wêyi tôssostli.	Twenty-third chapter. It talks about the festival and tla *tlamawistîlistli* that were made on the first day of the fourth month called *wêyi tôssostli*.

Continued

Table 10.1. Continued

Castilian	*Classical Nahuatl*	*Classical Nahuatl Normalized*	*English Translation*
	fol. 30r		
Capitulo ~~sesto~~ 24, de la fiesta, que se hazian en las kalendas del qujnto mes, que se llamaua Toxcatl.	Inic chiquacen capitulo, ytechpa tlatoa, yn ilhujtil; yoã in nextlaoalli, in muchioaia, yn ipan ic cemjlhujtl, ic macujlli metztli: in mitoaia, Toxcatl.	In ik chikʷasen capitulo. Itechpa tlahtoa in ilwitl iwân in neštlâwalli in mochîwaya in ipan ik semilwitl ik mâkʷilli mêtstli in mihtoâya toškatl.	Sixth chapter. It talks about the festival and the *neštlâwalli* that were made on the first day of the fifth month called *toškatl.*
	fol. 37v		
Capitulo ~~septimo~~ 25, de la fiesta y sacrificios, que se hazian, en las kalendas del sexto mes: que se llamaua etzalqualiztli.	Inic cempoualli vmmacuilli capitulo, itechpa tlatoa yn ilhujtl, yoan ynjn tlamanaliz in quichioaia, yn ipan ic cemilhujtl, ynic chiquacen metztli, in moteneoaia Etzalqualiztli.	In ik sempôwalli ommâkʷilli capitulo. Itechpa tlahtoa in ilwitl iwân in intlamanalis in kichîwayah in ipan ik semilwitl in ik chikʷasen mêtstli in motênêwaya etsalkʷâlistli.	Twenty-fifth chapter. It talks about the festival and their *tlamanalistli* that they made on the first day of the sixth month called *etsalkʷâlistli.*
	fol. 46r		
Capitulo ~~septimo~~ .26. de la fiesta y cerimonjas, que se hazian, en las kalendas del septimo mes, que se nombraua Tecujlhujtontli.	Inic cẽpovalli onchiquacê capitulo, vncan moteneoa yn ilhuitl, yoan in tlamauiztililiztli, in muchioaia, yn ipan vel ic cemilhujtl, ic chicome metztli, in mjtoaia: Tecujlhujtontli.	In ik sempôwalli onchikʷase capitulo. Onkân motênêwa in ilwitl iwân in tlamawistîlilistli in mochîwaya in ipan wel ik semilwitl ik chikʷôme mêtstli in mihtoâya têkʷilwitôntli.	Twenty-sixth chapter. The festival and the *tlamawistîlilistli* that were made on the first day of the seventh month called *têkʷilwitôntli* are described here.
	fol. 49v		
Capitulo ~~nono~~ .27. de la fiesta y sacrificios, que se hazian en las kalendas, del octauo mes, que se dezia, vei tecujlhujtl.	Inic cempoalli on chicunæ~~uj~~ capitulo, ytechpa tlatoa in ilhujtl yoan in nextlaoaliztli, in quichioaia, yn ipan ic cemilhujtl ynic chicuey metztli; in mitoaia Vei tecujlhujtl.	In ik sempôwalli onchikʷnâwi capitu_o. Itechpa tlahtoa in ilwitl iwân in neštlâwalistli in kichîwayah in ipan ik semilwitl in ik chikʷêyi mêtstli in mihtoâya wêyi têkʷilwitl.	Twenty-ninth chapter. It talks about the festival and the *neštlâwalistli* that were made on the first day of the eighth month called *wêyi têkʷilwitl.*

Castilian	Classical Nahuatl	Classical Nahuatl Normalized	English Translation
	fol. 58v		
Capitulo decimo .28, dela fiesta, y sacrificios: que se hazian, en las kalendas, del nono mes, que se llamaua, tlasuchimaco.	Inic cepualli onchicuei capitulo, itechpa tlatoa in ilhuitl, yoan in tlamanaliztli: in quichioaia inipan ic cemilhuitl, ic chicunauhtetl metztli, in moteneoaia tlasuchimaco.	In ik sempõwalli onchik^wēyi capitulo. Itechpa tlahtoa in ilwitl iwān tlamanalistli in kichîwayah in ipan ik semilwitl ik chik^wnâwtetl mêtstli in motênêwaya tlašôchimako.	Twenty-eighth chapter. It talks about the festival and the *tlamanalistli* that were made on the first day of the ninth month named *tlašôchimako*.
	fol. 61r		
Capitulo .29. dela fiesta, y sacrificios: que se hazian, en las kalendas, del dezimo mes: que se llamaua Xocotl vetzi.	Inic cempoalli on chicunauj capitulo, vncan moteneoa in ilhujtl, yoan in nextlaoaliztli: in qujchioaia, inipan ic cemilhujtl, ic matlactetl metztli: in mitoaia Xocotl vetzi.	In ik sempõwalli onchik^wnâwi capitulo. Onkân motênêwa in ilwitl iwān in neštlâwalistli in kichîwayah in ipan ik semilwitl ik mahtlaktetl mêtstli in mihtoâya šokotl wetsi.	Twenty-ninth chapter. The festival and the *neštlâwalistli* that were made on the first day of the tenth month called *šokotl wetsi* are described here.
	fol. 66r		
Capitulo doze .30., dela fiesta, y ceriminjas, que se hazian en las kalendas del onzeno mes: que se llamaua Ochpanizdi.	Inic cempoalli on matlactli omume capitulo: vncā moteneoa in ilhujtl, yoā in tlamaviztililizdi; in muchioaia in jpā ic cemjlhujtl, ic matlactetl oce metzdi; in mjtoaia, in moteneoaia: Ochpanizdi.	In ik sempõwalli onmahtlaktli omêyi capitulo. Onkân motênêwa in ilwitl iwān in tlamawistfílistli in mochîwaya in ipan ik semilwitl ik mahtlaktetl onsê mêtstli in mihtoâya in motênêwaya ochpanistli.	Thirtieth chapter. The festival and the *tlamawistfílistli* that were made on the first day of the eleventh month called *ochpanistli* are described here.
	fol. 73r		
Capitulo trezze .31., dela fiesta, y sacrificios: que se hazian, en las kalēdas, del dozeno mes: que se llamaua teutleco.	Inic cempoalli on matlactli omei capitulo: itechpa tlatoa in ilhujtl, yoan in nextlaoaliztli; in muchioaia, in jpā vel ic cemjlhujtl, injc matlactetl omume metztli; in motocaiotiaia, Teutleco.	In ik sempõwalli onmahtlaktli omêyi capitulo. Itechpa tlahtoa in ilwitl iwān in neštlâwalistli in mochîwaya in ipan wel ik semilwitl in ik mahtlaktetl omôme mêtstli in motôkâyôtiâya teôtl ehko.	Thirty-third chapter. It talks about the festival and the *neštlâwalistli* that were made just on the first day of the twelfth month named *teôtl ehko*.

Continued

Table 10.1. Continued

Castilian	Classical Nahuatl	Classical Nahuatl Normalized	English Translation
fol. 75v			
Capitulo. 32. de la fiesta, y sacrificios, que se hazian enlas kalendas, del trezeno mes: que se dezia Tepeilhujtl.	Inic cempoalli on matlactli ōmomex. capitulo: vncan moteneoa in jlhujtl, yoan in nextlaoalli, in muchioaia in jpāic cemjlhujtl, ic matlactetl omei metztli in moteneoaia, in mjtoaia Tepilhujtl.	In ik sempōwalli onmahtlaktli omōme capitulo. Onkān motēnēwa in ilwitl iwān in neštlāwalli in mochīwaya in ipan ik semilwitl ik mahtlaktetl omēyi mētstli in motēnēwaya in mihtoāya tepēilwitl.	Thirty-second chapter. The festival and the neštlāwalli that were made on the first day of the thirteenth month called tepēilwitl are described here.
fol. 77v			
Capitulo. 34. 33 de la fiesta, y sacrificios, que se hazian enlas kalendas, del catorzeno mes: que se llamaua Quecholli.	Inic cempoallio matlactli omei capitulo: vncan moteneoa in ilhujtl, yoā in nextlaoalli, injc tlacotia: in qujchioaia, in jpā ic cemjlhujtl, ic matlactetl onnavi metztli, in moteneoaia. Quecholli.	In ik sempōwalli onmahtlaktli omēyi capitulo. Onkān motēnēwa in ilwitl iwān in neštlāwalli in ik tlakotiyah in kichīwayah in ipan ik semilwitl ik mahtlaktetl onnāwi mētstli in motēnēwaya kechōlli.	Thirty-third chapter. The festival and the neštlāwalli with which [tlakotiyah][a] that were made on the first day of the fourteenth month called kechōlli are described here.
fol. 82v			
Capitulo.346. de la fiesta, y sacrificios, que se hazian enlas kalendas, del quizeno mes, que se dezia panquetzaliztli.	Inic caxtolli oce 34 capitulo: itechpa tlatoa in ilhujtl, yoan in nextlaoaliztli, in muchioaia injpan ic cemjlhujtl, ic caxtoltetl metztli, in mjtoaia: Panquetzaliztli.	In ik 34 capitulo. Itechpa tlahtoa in ilwitl iwān in neštlāwalistli in mochīwaya in ipan ik semilwitl ik kaštoltetl mētstli in mihtoāya panketsalistli.	Thirty-fourth chapter. It talks about the festival and the neštlāwalistli that were made on the first day of the fifteenth month called panketsalistli.
fol. 90r			
Capitulo.35.37. de la fiesta, y cerimonjas, que se hazian en las kalendas del. 16. mes, que se llamaua Atemuztli.	Inic cempoalli on caxtolli omume capitulo: itechpa tlatoa in jlhujtl, yoan in tlamaviztililiztli, in qujchioaia in jpan ic cemjlhujtl ic caxtoltetl occe metztli in moteneoa Atemoztli.	In ik sempōwalli kaštolli capitulo. Itechpa tlahtoa in ilwitl iwān in tlamawistililistli in kichīwayah in ipan ik semilwitl ik kaštoltetl oksē mēstli in motēnēwa ātemostli.	Thirty-fifth chapter. It talks about the festival and the tlamawistililistli that were made on the first day of the sixteenth month named ātemostli.

Castilian	Classical Nahuatl	Classical Nahuatl Normalized	English Translation
Capitulo.36.38. de la fiesta, y sacrificios, que se hazian en las kalendas del decimo septimo mes que se llamaua Tititl.	fol. 93r Inic ᶜᵉᵐᵖᵒᵃˡˡⁱ ᵒⁿ caxtolli ōmēi: capitulo vncan moteneoa in ilhujtl. yoā in nextlaoalli in muchioaia in jpan vel ic cemjlhujtl ic caxtoltetl omume metztli in mjtoaia Tititl.	In ik sempôwalli onkaštolli capitulo. Onkán moténêwa in ilwitl iwán in neštláwalli in mochîwaya in ipan wel ik semilwitl ik kaštoltetl omôme mêtstli in mihtoâya tititl.	Thirty-fifth chapter. The festival and the *neštláwalli* that were made just on the first day of the seventeenth month called *tititl* are described here.
Capitulo.37.39. de la fiesta, y cerimonjas, que se hazian, en las kalendas del. 18. mes, que se llamaua Izcalli.	fol. 15v Inic cempoalli on caxtolli omume. capt. ytechpa tlatoa, yn ilhuitl, yoan intlamauiztililiztli, in motequjpanoaia, in jpan vel ic cemilhujtl, ic caxtoltetl omey metztli, in mjtoaia in moteneoaia Yzcalli.	In ik sempôwalli onkaštolli omôme capitulo. Irechpa tlahtoa in ilwitl iwán in tlamawistlilistli in motekipanoaya in ipan wel ik semilwitl ik kaštoltetl omêyi mêtstli in mihtoâya in moténêwaya iskalli.	Thirty-seventh chapter. It talks about the festival and the *tlamawistlilistli* that were made just on the first day of the eighteenth month named *iskalli*.

ᵃ We don't know what *injc tlacotia* mean. Anderson and Dibble translated it as "with which they gave service" (Sahagún 1950–82, bk 2: 134), relating it with *tlåkobti* "to work as a slave" or "to become a slave." We do not agree with their translation and interpretation because *injc tlacotia* in this context violates two conversational maxims, the one of quantity and the one of relation (*cf.* Grice 1975), and our generated conversational implicatures do not satisfy us.

Continued

2. Itechpa tlahtoa in **ilwitl** iwân **tlamanalistli**
It talks about the **festival** and the TLAMANALISTLI
de la fiesta, y sacrificios:

3. in kichîwayah in ipan ik semilwitl ik chik^wnâwtetl mêtstli
that were made on the first day of the ninth month
que se hazian, en las kalendas, del nono mes,

4. in motênêwaya tlašôchimako.
named *tlašôchimako*.
que se llamaua, tlasuchimaco.

Heading of the thirty-fifth chapter.

1. In ik sempôwalli kaštolli capitulo.
Thirty-fifth chapter.
Capitulo.35.3̶7̶.

2. In Itechpa tlahtoa in **ilwitl** iwân in **tlamawistîlîlistli**
It talks about the **festival** and the TLAMAWISTÎLÎLISTLI
de la fiesta, y cerimonjas,

3. in kichîwayah in ipan ik semilwitl ik kaštoltetl oksê mêstli
that were made on the first day of the sixteenth month
que se hazian en las kalendas del. 16. mes,

4. in motênêwa âtemostli.
named *âtemostli*.
que se llamaua Atemuztli.

As mentioned, in the second field (thematic references), the word *ilwitl* (which corresponds to *fiesta* in the Castilian version) always appears in the lines written in Classical Nahuatl accompanied with a noun ended in {-listli}. *Ilwitl* appears in seventeen headings and always, in all cases, with 'festival,' *fiesta*, as a Castilian equivalent; *neštlâwalistli* or *neštlâwalli*, in 11 cases (seven, the first and four, the second) and always as 'sacrifices,' *sacrificios*, as the lexical equivalent; *tlamawistîlîlistli*, appears in six cases and always as 'ceremonies,' *cerimonias*, as a Castilian lexical equivalent, and *tlamanalistli*, in two cases and always as 'sacrifices.'

However, what do the words in the first and second columns in Table 10.2 mean? Why are there four terms in Classical Nahuatl and only three in Castilian? Why does *ilwitl* appear accompanied by any of the other three words? Are these

Table 10.2. Correlation between the Classical Nahuatl and Castilian terms in the headings of the descriptions of the *veintenas* in Book II of the *Florentine Codex*

Classical Nahuatl *Florentine Codex*	Castilian *Florentine Codex*	Veintena/month *Florentine Codex*
ilwitl	fiesta	âtl kâwalo/kʷawitl êwa
		tôssôstôntli
		wêyi tôssôstli
		toškatl
		etsalkʷâlistli
		têkʷilwitôntli
		têkʷilwitl
		tlašôchimako
		šokotl wetsi
		ochpanistli
		teôtl ehko
		tepêilwitl
		kecholli
		panketsalistli
		âtemostli
		tititl
		iskalli
neštlâwalistli or neštlâwalli	sacrificios	âtl kâwalo/kʷawitl êwa
		tlâkašipêwalistli
		tôssôstôntli
		toškatl (neštlâwalli)
		wêyi têkʷilwitl
		šokotl wetsi
		teôtl ehko
		tepêilwitl (neštlâwalli)
		kecholli (neštlâwalli)
		panketsalistli
		tititl (neštlâwalli)
tlamawistîlîlistli	ceremonias	tlâkašipêwalistli
		wêyi tôssôstli
		têkʷilwitôntli
		ochpanistli
		âtemostli
		iskalli
tlamanalistli	sacrificios	etsalkʷâlistli
		tlašôchimako

sacrifices and ceremonies the festivals? What is described in every *veintena*? One or several festivals, or one or more ceremonies or one or more sacrifices? To answer these questions, we need to define the Castilian words involved: *fiesta* (or 'festival'), 'ceremony' and 'sacrifice,' as well as the Nahuatl words: *ilwitl, tlamawistililistli, neštlâwalistli* or *neštlâwalli*, and *tlamanalistli*.

FIESTA, CERIMONIA, AND SACRIFICIO

We begin by considering that whatever was understood by "celebration", "ceremony" and "sacrifice" in the sixteenth century does not correspond to our current understanding of these terms. To know what meaning they may have had in those times, we used the *Diccionario de Autoridades* (Real Academia Española 1969) that was published at the beginning of the eighteenth century, assuming that it would be a valid means of approximating an appropriate meaning (as a result of its relative temporal proximity).

According to the *Diccionario de Autoridades*, which is written in the Castilian language, *fiesta* has seven meanings, two of which are: "*el día que la Iglesia celebra con mayor solemnidad que otros, mandando se oyga Missa y se gaste en obras santas, y prohibiendo el trabajo servil*" (the day the Church celebrates with greater solemnity than others, commanding that Mass be heard and spent in holy works, and prohibiting servile work) and "*por extensión se llama la solemnidad con que la Iglésia celebra el Martyrio o tránsito de algún Santo*" (by extension is called the solemnity that the church celebrates the Martyrdom or date of death of a particular Saint). (Real Academia Española 1969, 3: 1732, 747). In contemporary English, the two definitions given by the *Diccionario de Autoridades* (both made from a Roman Catholic perspective) explain "festival" as a day when religious authorities celebrate a deity with a major public ceremony; such days are dedicated to pious work and menial work is prohibited. Thus, for the *Diccionario de Autoridades* the *fiesta* 'festival' is exclusively a religious celebration.

This is confirmed by the fact that Sahagún's descriptive model faithfully followed the scheme of the *Chronographia y reportorio de los tiempos* (sixteenth-century almanacs, i.e. books on astronomy and astrology related to everyday life, *cf.* De Chaves 1584; Tappan Valázquez 2012),[4] in which the day on which a festival was celebrated within the context of each of the months of the year and their days was marked. The first eighteen chapters of Book 2 of the *Florentine Codex* (Sahagún 1979, bk 2: fol. 3r–12r) and the pages 126v to 129r of the *Codices Matritenses de Real Palacio* followed this model (Figure 10.1).

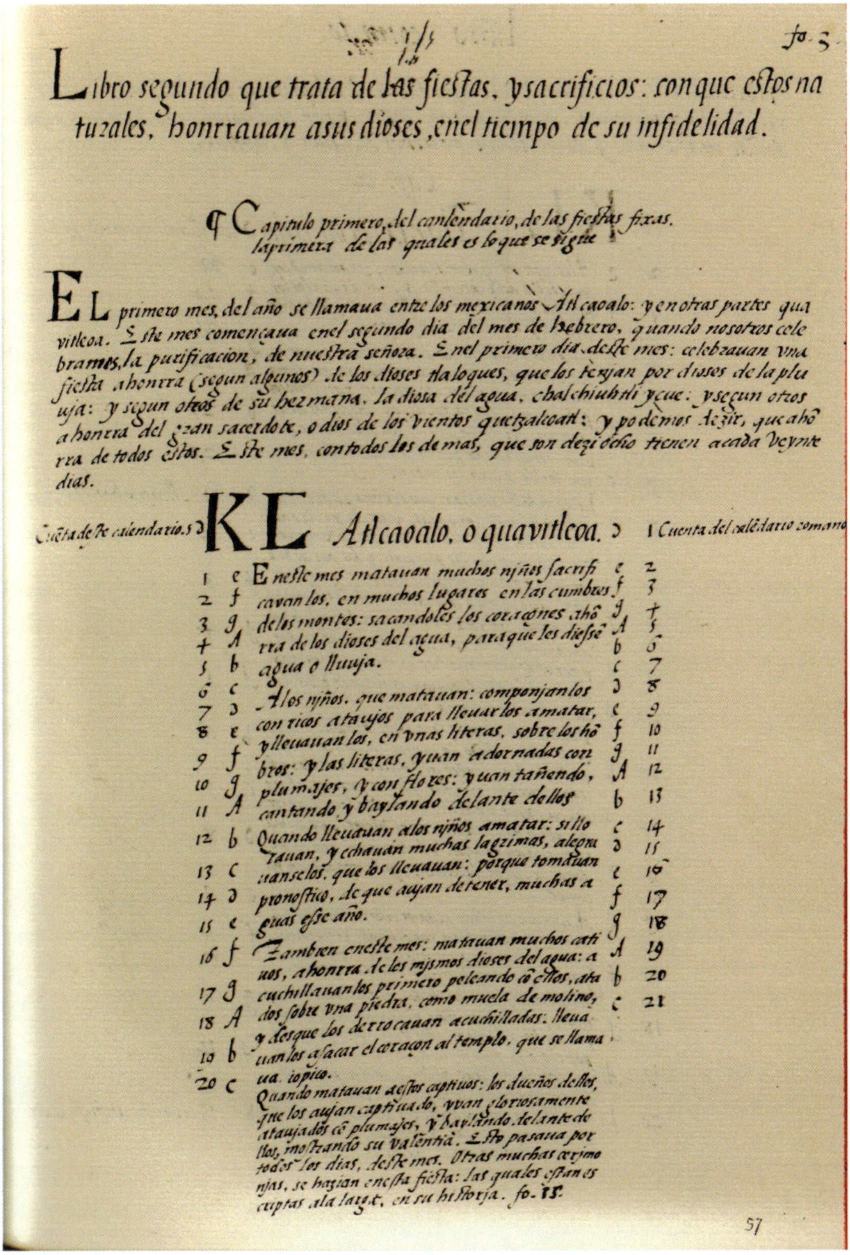

Libro segundo que trata de las fiestas, y sacrificios: conque estos na tuзales, honrrauan asus dioses, enel tiempo de su infidelidad.

¶ Capitulo primero, del calendario, de las fiestas fixas. la primera de las quales es lo que se sigue

EL primero mes, del año se llamaua entre los mexicanos Atlcaoalo: y en otras partes qua uitleoa. Este mes començaua enel segundo dia del mes de hebrero, quando nosotros cele bramos, la purificacion, de nuestra señora. Enel primero dia deste mes: celebrauan vna fiesta ahonrra (segun algunos) de los dioses tlaloques, que los tenian por dioses de la plu uia: y segun otros de su hezmana. la diosa del agua, chalchiuhtli yeue: y segun otros a honrra del gran sacerdote, o dios de los vientos quetzalcoatl: y podemos dezir, que aho rra de todos estos. Este mes, con todos los demas, que son dezi ocho tienen acada veynte dias.

Cuẽta de se calendario.s KL Atlcaoalo, o quauitleoa. Cuenta del calẽdario romano

1 c E neste mes matauan muchos niños sacrifi c 2
2 f cauan los, en muchos lugares enlas cumbres f 3
3 g delos montes: sacandoles los coraçones, ahõ g 4
4 A rra de los dioses del agua, paraque les diese A 5
5 b agua o lluuia. b 6
6 c - A los niños, que matauan: componianlos c 7
7 d con ricos atauios para lleuarlos amatar, d 8
8 e y lleuauan los, en vnas literas, sobre los hõ e 9
9 f bres: y las literas, yuan adornadas con f 10
10 g plumajes, y con flores: yuan tañendo, g 11
11 A cantando y baylando delante dellos A 12
                                              b 13
12 b Quando lleuauan alos niños amatar: si llo c 14
13 c rauan, y echauan muchas lagrimas, alegra d 15
      uanse los, que los lleuauan: porque tomauan e 16
14 d pronostico, de que ayan de tener, muchas a f 17
15 e guas ese año. g 18
16 f Tambien eneste mes: matauan muchos cati A 19
      uos, ahonrra de los mismos dioses del agua: a b 20
17 g cuchillauanlos primero peleando cõ ellos, ata c 21
18 A dos sobre vna piedra, como muela de molino,
      y desque los derrocauan acuchillados: lleua
19 b uanlos a sacar el coraçon al templo, que se llama
20 c ua. iopico.
      Quando matauan aestos captiuos: los dueños dellos,
      que los auian captiuado, yuan gloriosamente
      atauiados cõ plumajes, y baylando delante de
      llos, mostrando su valentia. Esto paraua por
      todos los dias, deste mes. Otras muchas cerimo
      nias, se hazian enesta fiesta: las quales estan es
      cuptas ala larga, en su historia. fo. 15.

57

Figure 10.1. Festivals in the *Florentine Codex*. Ms. Med. Palat. 218, bk. 2: fol. 3r.
Source: Photograph courtesy of Biblioteca Medicea Laurenziana, Florence.

Cerimonia or *ceremonia* 'ceremony' is for the *Diccionario de Autoridades* equivalent to "*Acción, o acto exterior arreglado por ley, estatúto, o costumbre, para dar culto a las cosas divinas, y reverencia, o honor a las profanas*" (action, or external act organized by law, statute, or custom, to worship divine things, and to reverence or honor the profane) (Real Academia Española 1969, 2: 1729, 282). In contrast, *sacrificio*, 'sacrifice,' is "*cualquier cosa hecha u ofrecida en reconocimiento de una deidad*" (anything done or offered in acknowledgment of a deity) (Real Academia Española 1969, 6: 1739, 13). Thus, at least in the eighteenth century (and we assume also in the sixteenth), the word ceremony was equivalent to 'to honor' and the word sacrifice, to 'to offer.' This should coincide with the meanings of the Classical Nahuatl verbs used in the Sahagun's text:

- If ceremony is 'to honor,' *tlamawistilia*, its equivalent, should be 'to honor.'
- If sacrifice is 'to offer,' *moštlâwa* and *tlamana* should be 'to offer.'

Importantly, sacrifice does not necessarily imply blood acts but is generally defined by the offering of anything in acknowledgment of someone.

In other words, festival, ceremony, and sacrifice are different events. Festival is a *celebration* and ceremony and sacrifice are *acts*. But are festival and *ilwitl* fully equivalent social practices? Taking into account that the structure of Sahagún's work is European, it is necessary to precisely define the festival *concept* in order to objectively analyze such relationship.

FESTIVAL AND RITUAL

In this chapter, the concept of festival, intimately related to, though differing from, that of ritual, is understood as a system of social practices characterized by communal participation which is developed under institutional rules and is divided into solemn and non-solemn moments. Festival, as a system, is hierarchically shaped by a *ritual structure* (whose function is nodal) and by events (which are not nodal).

Ritual structure is divided into nuclear rituals (those that properly define the festival, fundamentally celebrated on the festival day) and non-nuclear rituals (which may or may not be simultaneous with nuclear rituals); and events (non-ritual practices). Starting from the bottom nodes in Figure 10.2, we see that nuclear rituals specifically define the nodal festival in the strictest sense but by themselves are not the festival (they are nuclear rituals). The nuclear and non-nuclear rituals make up the ritual structure of the festival in a broader sense, but neither of them is the festival (they are the ritual structure of the festival). The ritual structure together with the various events make up the festival in the broadest sense, noting that in every festival there must be a ritual unit, which is the festival's *raison d'être*.

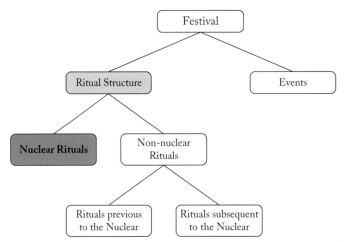

Figure 10.2. Festival structure. Source: Diagram by Andrea B. Rodríguez Figueroa and Leopoldo Valiñas Coalla.

Every festival is characterized by having the following overarching structure: (1) calendar temporality, (2) ritual structure, (3) argument structure, (4) spatial structure, and (5) temporal structure (internal and external). Since the ritual structure defines the festival, it is necessary to define ritual first.

Ritual is a social practice including these features: (1) it is institutional, (2) it is repetitive, (3) it is performative, (4) it has an argument structure, (5) it has internal temporal structure, (6) it has spatial structure and (7) it has symbolic plot. Within a festival all rituals are articulated with all the other rituals that are celebrated in that festival, and together they constitute its ritual structure. The ritual structure is characterized by being dominated by only one nuclear ritual and, additionally, included non nuclear rituals (see Rodríguez Figueroa 2014).

In the particular case of the Nahua of the Basin of Mexico, the nuclear moment of the festival was celebrated in a single day. This is because, unlike the concept of ritual, festival does have a lexical equivalent in Nahuatl: *ilwitl*, which also means 'day.' The identity between 'day' and 'festival' suggests a temporal co-occurrence, which is further supported by the phrase 'to celebrate a festival,' *kisa ilwitl*, which is constructed with the verb *kisa* 'to get out, to end,' literally meaning 'the festivals leaves' or 'the festival ends.' This leaves us with the question of the semantic nature of the terms that appear with *ilwitl* in the headings: *tlamanalistli, neštlâwalistli,* and *tlamawistililistli*.

The three words just presented end with {-listli}; linguistically, this element indicates the verbal nominalization that refers to the action designated by the verb, which can be glossed as 'act of.' In the Mexican and Castilian section of his

Vocabulario, Molina translates, on the one hand, *tlamanalistli* as "*el acto de ofrecer don o ofrenda*" (the act of offering a gift or offering) (Molina 2004, part II: fol. 125v), while in the Castilian and Mexican section as "*sacrificio o ofrenda*" (sacrifice or offering) (Molina 2004, part I: fol. 106v). If we take into account the morphological value of the {-listli} suffix, then we must understand *tlamanalistli* as the act of sacrificing or offering.

In the Mexican and Castilian section, however, Molina translates *neštlâwalli* (because he did not register the nominal *neštlâwalistli*) as "*sacrificio de sangre, que ofrecian alos ydolos, sajandose o horadando alguna parte del cuerpo*" (blood sacrifice, which they offered to the idols, cutting or piercing some part of the body) (Molina 2004, part I: fol. 71v), and in the Castilian and Mexican section, as "*sacrificio o ofrenda*" (sacrifice or offering) (Molina 2004, part I: fol. 106v). Knowing the relationship between the nouns that end with {-li} and those with {-listli}, a possible translation of *neštlâwalistli* would be 'the act of self-sacrificing' or 'the act of offering.'

Something similar occurs in the Castilian and Mexican section of Molina's *Vocabulario*, where the word *tlamawistililli* (because the nominal *tlamawistililistli* was not recorded) is translated as "*dignificado y honrado de otros*" (dignified and honored by others) (Molina 2004, part I: fol. 126r). In Sahagún's *Códices Matritenses de la Real Academia*, the word *tlamawistilia* (the verb) is translated as "*reverenciar o honrar*" (to reverence or to honor) (*Matritenses de la Real Academia*, fol. 89r). Thus, we believe that *tlamawistililistli* should be translated as 'the act of honoring.'

We can translate {-listli} as 'ritual' if and only if the word that carries this suffix in the textual context in which it appears meets the seven features defining ritual. For example, *tlamanalistli* would literally be 'the act of laying something out' or 'the act of offering,' but its ritual nature is achieved only if it fulfills the seven features already listed. In other words, 'the act of offering' may be a ritual only if its performance were characterized by the above-mentioned seven features. However, there is another condition besides the semantic content: the verbal stem that gives origin to the noun ended in {-listli} should have as one of its arguments or syntactic subject a human, and its function is as an agent-argument with respect to action (that is to say, he must have volition). The words {mana} 'to lay something out,' {ištlâwa} 'to pay,' and {tlamawistilia} 'to honor' satisfy the semantic conditions just mentioned. Each of these verbal stems requires a human agent, someone who performs the action intentionally.

THE FESTIVALS IN THE FIRST FOUR *VEINTENAS*

We have seen in Book II of the *Florentine Codex* that the heading of each chapter describes a festival and a rite (which we have proposed to be a ritual unit: TLAMANALISTLI, NEŠTLÂWALISTLI y TLAMAWISTÎLÎLISTLI). However, neither *ilwitl* nor any of these three terms had a plural form in Classical Nahuatl. This means that it is possible that, in each *veintena*, several festivals and rites were celebrated. After analyzing the first four *veintenas*, we hypothesize that in each chapter, several festivals are described and that the heading gives account of only one ritual unit corresponding to the nuclear rite of one of the festivals. Below, we present the festivals that we have identified through an intertextual reading of the descriptions of those first four *veintenas*, as well as the rites that we identified as the nuclear ones.

Âtl kâwalo or *kʷawitl êwa*. In this *veintena* we identified three festivals: (1) the one dedicated to the Tlâlôk, whose nuclear ritual was the *neštlâwalistli* or the self-payment ritual; (2) the Kʷawitl êwa, whose nuclear ritual was the *tlakʷawit-lêwaltîlistli* or the rite of the presentation; and (3) that dedicated to Chikʷnâwe-hekatl, whose nuclear ritual was the *tlamiktîlistli* or the sacrificial death ritual (see Rodríguez Figueroa 2010).

Tlâkašipêwalistli. In this *veintena* we identified five festivals: (1) the one dedicated to the Tlâlôk, whose nuclear ritual was the *neštlâwalistli* or the self-payment ritual; (2) the Tlâkašipêwalistli, dedicated to Witsilôpôchtli, whose nuclear ritual was the *tlâkašipêwalistli* or the human flaying rite; (3) the Tlawawanalistli, dedicated to Šipêw Totêkʷ, whose nuclear ritual was the *tlawawânalistli* or the scratching ritual; (4) the Tekikîštîlistli, and (5) the Âyakachpišôlo. We could not accurately identify the nuclear ritual of these last two festivals. We only know that the *nehtotîlistli* or dance was one of the rites; apparently, the first one was dedicated to the *tlatoâni*, and the second to Totêkʷ Yowallawân.

Tôsôstôntli. In this *veintena* we identified two festivals: (1) the one dedicated to the Tlâlôk, whose nuclear ritual was the *neštlâwalistli* or the self-payment ritual, and (2) the Êwatlâtîlistli, dedicated to Šipêw and Totêkʷ, whose nuclear ritual was the *êwatlâtîlistli* or the ritual of concealing the skin [of the flayed victims]. We also identified three practices that, due to a lack of information, we have not been able to determine if they were festivals or rites: *šôchimanalistli, kôwâiškalmanalistli* and *tsatsapaltamalmanalistli*.

Wêyi tôssôstli. We were able to identify two festivals in this *veintena*: (1) the one dedicated to the Tlâlôk, whose nuclear ritual was the *neštlâwalistli* or the self-payment ritual, and (2) the one dedicated to Chikʷôme Kôwâtl, whose nuclear ritual was the *tlamiktîlistli* or the sacrificial death ritual.

The nuclear rituals of the festivals described above do not correspond with the terms that appear in the headings: TLAMANALISTLI, NEŠTLÂWALISTLI and TLAMAWISTÎLÎLISTLI. So, what does the nuclear ritual of each festival have that allows us to relate it to one of the three terms in the heading that accompanies *ilwitl?* Let us reconsider the first four *veintenas*.

In the first *veintena* there was a festival dedicated to the Tlâlôk in which a *neštlâwalistli* was performed. This clearly corresponds to the word in the heading

(NEŠTLÂWALISTLI). In the second *veintena* the term NEŠTLÂWALISTLI mentioned in the heading also appears, and since a festival dedicated to the Tlâlôk was also celebrated, its nuclear ritual corresponded to the announced ritual unit. And in this same *veintena*, both the Tlâkašipêwalistli festival and the Tlawawanalistli one, with their respective nuclear rituals, were to honor Witsilôpôchtli and Šipêw Totêkᵂ, respectively. This honor related to the TLAMAWISTÎLÎLISTLI, a term used in the heading of this *veintena*. In the third veintena, the festival Êwâtlâtîlistli, whose nuclear ritual had the same name, *êwâtlâtîlistli*, the ritual of hiding the skin, is described. This ritual is clearly not a way to offer or to celebrate a NEŠTLÂWALISTLI (as indicated in the heading), but in the description of this festival, it is explicitly stated that, with the ritual of concealing the skin [of the flayed victims], the people that realized it made a vow or, in the Nahuatl language, celebrated the NENEH-TOLTÎLISTLI (Sahagun 1979, bk 2: fol. 24v, 25r):

Classical Nahuatl:	Aw sekîntin ik monehtoltiah in êwâtlâtiskeh
English translation:	In this way, some people made vows or celebrated *nenehtoltîlistli* by concealing the skin or performing the *êwâtlâtîlistli*.
Castilian:	Algunos enfermos de sarna, o de los ojos, hazian promesa de yr a ayudar asconder estos pellejos.

If the *êwâtlâtîlistli* ritual corresponds to the ritual unit NENEHTOLTÎLISTLI (which does not appear in the headings), which one relates to the ritual unit NEŠTLÂWALISTLI, that does appear in the heading of this *veintena*? It corresponds to the nuclear ritual of the festival dedicated to the Tlâlôk.

In the fourth *veintena*, only the festival dedicated to Chikᵂôme Kôwâtl is described, whose nuclear rite was the *tlamiktîlistli* (or the sacrificial death ritual) with which that divinity was honored. This honor corresponded to the TLAMAW-ISTÎLÎLISTLI, a term used in the heading of the *veintena*.

As we have seen, the four ritual units do not always appear explicitly. In analyzing the descriptions of the festivals, we found that each ritual unit meets certain conditions, of which two stand out: its basic function and the directionality of the actions (that is to say, who is the agent and who is the patient, and the hierarchical relationship between them). This helped us to identify the ritual units of the remainder of the festivals, whenever there was sufficient information.

RITUAL UNIT

As we have pointed out, the ritual unit is one of the highest levels of religious practices; it works as an axis for a set of practices that constitutes a whole and that is manifested in the nuclear rituals or ritual structure of each festival (see Figure 10.3).

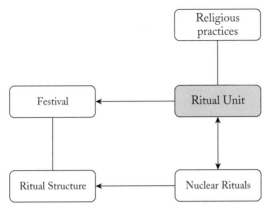

Figure 10.3. The Ritual Unit and its relations with the festival. Source: Diagram by Andrea B. Rodríguez Figueroa and Leopoldo Valiñas Coalla.

We now describe each of the ritual units and their specification in terms of their function and their directionality:

1. TLAMAWISTÎLÎLISTLI. It was performed with the purpose of honoring a *teôtl* or someone of importance (such as the *tlahtoâni*). The relationship between the participants was unidirectional: either from a *tlâkatl* 'person' to the *teôtl* 'god' or from a *kʷitlapilli ahtlapalli* 'the people' to the *tlahtoâni*.

2. TLAMANALISTLI. It was performed with the purpose of making an offering to a *teôtl*. In this case a unidirectional relationship was also manifested: from a *tlâkatl* to a *teôtl*.

3. NEŠTLÂWALISTLI. It was performed with the purpose of giving a gift in reciprocity to offer thanks or make a request. In this case it was a bidirectional relationship in which both *teôtl* and *tlâkatl* participate in reciprocal exchange of gifts by paying themselves.

4. NENEHTOLTÎLISTLI. It was performed with the purpose of making a vow or promise to a *teôtl*. In this case it established a bidirectional relationship because the *tlâkatl* made an oath to a *teôtl* for having committed a fault or even granting him the ability to perform effectively and adequately some particular task.

The main proposal of this chapter is that a festival was not only to honor a particular *teôtl*, but to make a payment, to make offerings, or to promise or to make a vow through specific rites. For example, a divinity could be honored by sacrificing somebody or something in their honor (TLAMAWISTÎLÎLISTLI), but in other instances one could make a promise to a *teôtl* (NENEHTOLTÎLISTLI) by bleeding oneself, or another person or an animal.

The four ritual units detected can be divided into two major categories:

- The ritual units that manifest a one-way relationship: the TLAMANALISTLI and the TLAMAWISTILÎLISTLI.
- The ritual units that manifest a two-way relationship: the NEŠTLÂWALISTLI and the NENEHTOLTÎLISTLI.

With the above characterization, we were able to identify the ritual units of each of the festivities associated with the first four *veintenas*. These are shown in Table 10.3. In the rows highlighted in black, the names of the *veintenas* are registered; in the first column are the festivals identified in each of the *veintenas*; in the second, the rite we consider, based on the description given, to be the nuclear one, and in the third, the ritual unit that corresponds to the festival. The terms that

Table 10.3. The ritual units in each of the festivals of the first four *veintenas*

Festival	Nuclear ritual	Ritual Unit
âtl kâwalo or *kʷawitl êwa*		
Festival dedicated to Tlâlôk	*neštlâwalistli* or the self-payment ritual	NEŠTLÂWALISTLI
Kʷawitl êwa	*tlakʷawitlêwaltilistli* or the presentation ritual	TLAMAWISTÎLÎLISTLI
Festival dedicated to Chikʷnâwehekatl	*tlamiktilistli* or the sacrificial death ritual	TLAMAWISTÎLÎLISTLI
tlâkašipêwalistli		
Festival dedicated to Tlâlôk	*neštlâwalistli* or the self-payment ritual	NEŠTLÂWALISTLI
Tlâkašipêwalistli	*tlâkašipêwalistli* or the human flaying ritual	TLAMAWISTÎLÎLISTLI
Tlawawânalistli	*tlawawânalistli* or the scratching ritual	TLAMAWISTÎLÎLISTLI
Tekikîštîlistli	(without information)	
Âyakachpišôlo	(without information)	
tôssôstôntli		
Festival dedicated to Tlâlôk	*neštlâwalistli* or the self-payment ritual	NEŠTLÂWALISTLI
Êwatlâtîlistli	*êwatlâtîlistli* or the ritual of concealing the skin [of the flayed victims]	NENEHTOLTÎLISTLI
wêyi tôssôstli		
Festival dedicated to Tlâlôk	*neštlâwalistli* or the self-payment ritual	NEŠTLÂWALISTLI
Festival dedicated to Chikʷôme Kôwâtl	*tlamiktilistli* or the sacrificial death ritual	TLAMAWISTÎLÎLISTLI

name a ritual unit and that appear in the heading of the chapter accompanying the word *ilwitl* appear in boldface. As mentioned, the only ritual unit that does not appear in any heading is NENEHTOLTÎLISTLI, which is reconstructed from what is said in the description of the festival Êwatlâtîlistli.

CONCLUSIONS

This chapter offers a linguistic approach, as opposed to a historical one, to narrow down and clarify possible interpretations, and to avoid any weak or poorly argued ones of the texts written in Classical Nahuatl and Castilian.

This chapter also presents an anthropological approach to the historical sources, in this case, Sahagún's work. This approach lets us see the festival as a structured and hierarchical social practice with a nuclear ritual unit.

The interaction between both approaches helps us to propose both a translation (that is to say, a set of semantic equivalences) and an interpretation (that is to say, a reconstruction of cultural facts) of the events described.

As the analysis included both Classical Nahuatl and Castilian and two approaches, it allowed us to identify the ritual units of the festivals of the *veintenas*: TLAMAWISTÎLÎLISTLI, TLAMANALISTLI, NEŠTLÂWALISTLI, and NENEHTOLTÎLISTLI. These ritual units are the essence of the festivals. Each festival has its own ritual unit. This means that the festival was not only to honor particular divinities; we have found four reasons which define the purpose of a festival: to honor a divinity or an authority, to offer something to a divinity, to give a reciprocal gift in thanks or for a request, and to make a vow or promise to a divinity or group of divinities for them to make something. As far as we know, this approach has not been explicitly outlined.

This also means that each festival (*ilwitl*), understood as a system, has its own ritual and festival structure. If a festival is to be described, in addition to the ethnographic aspect, such work will require further analysis to account for the ritual structure and the ritual unity that characterize the festival.

NOTES

1. We use the symbols of the International Phonetic Alphabet to represent both vowels and consonants in Nahua words. There are, however, seven exceptions as follow. Due to graphical complexity, we represent the <ts>, <ch>, <tl> and <y> with their actual values in Spanish. We use š instead of <x> in order to avoid ambiguities arising from their values [s], [š], [x], and [ks]. Regarding the saltillo, we represent it with <h> since this symbol does not exist in Times New Roman font. Finally, to indicate a long vowel we use a circumflex, for example â.

2. We propose, based on phonological, morphological, syntactic, and semantic evidence, that the language used in the sixteenth and seventeenth centuries, and in the first half of the eighteenth century, is Castilian, not Spanish.

3. There are translations made by many specialists: for example, Arthur Anderson and Charles Dibble (Sahagún 1950–82), Ángel M. Garibay (1952), Wigberto Jiménez Moreno (Sahagún 1974), Miguel León-Portilla (1992), Alfredo López Austin (1967), and Thelma Sullivan (Sahagún 1997).

4. Especially the chapter dedicated to the annual calendar that points out every day and all the festivals dedicated to the saints.

REFERENCES

Bartl, Renate, Barbara Göbel, and Hanns J. Prem. 1989. "Los calendarios aztecas de Sahagún." *Estudios de Cultura Náhuatl* 19: 13–82.

Códice Matritenses del Real Palacio. Manuscript of *fray* Bernardino de Sahagún, collected and deposited in the Royal Library of the Royal Palace of Madrid, Spain. The Mexican Digital Library named it as Códices matritenses de la Real Biblioteca (Madrid*), II-3280*.

Códice Matritenses de la Real Academia. Manuscript of *fray* Bernardino de Sahagún, collected and deposited in the Library of the Royal Academy of History, Spain.

De Chaves, Hieronimo. 1584. *Chronographia o reportorio de tiempos, el mas copioso y precisso, que hasta ahora ha salido a luz*. Sevilla. https://archive.org/details/ARes21320.

Garibay, Ángel María. 1952. "Versiones discutibles del texto náhuatl de Sahagún." *Tlalocan* 2: 187–90.

Grice, H.P. 1975. "Logic and Conversation." In *Syntax and Semantics 3: Speech Acts*, edited by Peter Cole and Jerry L. Morgan, 41–58. New York: Academic Press.

León-Portilla, Miguel. 1992. *Ritos, sacerdotes y atavíos de los dioses*. Mexico City: Universidad Nacional Autónoma de México.

López Austin, Alfredo. 1967. *Juegos rituales aztecas. Versión, introducción y notas de Alfredo López Austin*. Mexico City: Universidad Nacional Autónoma de México.

Molina, Alonso de. 2004. *Vocabulario en lengua castellana y mexicana y mexicana y castellana*. Mexico City: Porrúa.

Parodi, Claudia. 1995. *Orígenes del español americano*. Mexico City: Centro de Lingüística Hispánica, Universidad Nacional Autónoma de México.

Real Academia Española. 1969. *Diccionario de Autoridades*. Facsimilar Edition. 3 vols. Madrid: Editorial Gredos, S.A.

Rodríguez Figueroa, Andrea B. 2010. "Paisaje e imaginario colectivo del altiplano central mesoamericano: el paisaje ritual en *Atl cahualo* o *Cuahuilt ehua* según las fuentes sahaguntinas." MA thesis, Universidad Nacional Autónoma de México.

———. 2014. "El paisaje festivo en el *cecempohuallapohualli* de la cuenca de México del siglo XVI, según las fuentes sahaguntinas." PhD diss., Universidad Nacional Autónoma de México.

Sahagún, Bernardino de. 1950–82. *Florentine Codex: General History of the Things of New Spain, Fray Bernardino de Sahagún*. Translated with notes and illustrations by Arthur J. O. Anderson and Charles E. Dibble. 13 vols. Santa Fe: The School of American Research, University of Utah Press.

————. 1974. *"Primeros Memoriales" de Fray Bernardino de Sahagún*. Edited and translated by Wigberto Jiménez Moreno. Mexico City: Instituto Nacional de Antropología e Historia, Secretaría de Educación Pública.

————. 1979 [1569]. *Códice Florentino. El manuscrito 218–220 de la colección palatina de la Biblioteca Medicea Laurenziana*. 3 vols. Florence, Mexico City: Giunti Barbéra, Archivo General de la Nación.

————. 1997. *Primeros Memoriales*. Edited and translated by Thelma D. Sullivan. Completed and revised, with additions, by Henry B. Nicholson, Arthur J. O. Anderson, Charles E. Dibble, Eloise Quiñones Keber, and Wayne Ruwet. Norman: University of Oklahoma Press.

Tappan Velázquez, Martha. 2012. "La representación del tiempo en un género de escritura del siglo XVI: los repertorios de los tiempos." *Revista Fuentes Humanísticas* 45: 33–49.

CHAPTER ELEVEN

An Augustinian Political Theology in New Spain

Towards a Franciscan Interpretation of the *Veintenas*

SERGIO BOTTA

In recent years, since works such as those of Jaime Marroquín Arredondo (2014), Victoria Ríos Castaño (2014), and David Solodkow (2014), the debate concerning the very nature of the Novohispanic ethnographic discourse has come back to the focused center of historiographical attention. These new reflections have also reinvigorated the theoretical discussion about the hermeneutical quality of the testimonies on indigenous cultures produced by the missionary orders. In the first place, this theoretical and methodological turn led to a reflection on the heuristic value of missionary interpretations based on the notion of colonial ethnographic discourse proposed by Solodkow, which he considered as a Foucauldian *dispositif* acting in colonial contexts and exercising a symbolic and material influence over the cultures of the New World (Solodkow 2014, 15–53). In the second place, Ríos Castaño, in a work dedicated to Bernardino de Sahagún, proposed the notion of cultural translation to describe the missionary re-conceptualization of the Nahua world and contrasted the historiographic image (Garibay 1953–54; Jiménez Moreno 1938; León-Portilla 1999, 2002) of the friar as a "pioneering anthropologist, ethnographer, and ethnologist" (Ríos Castaño 2014, 16). Despite the significant contribution that these critical perspectives provided for contextualizing the missionary "spiritual conquest" of New Spain (Ricard 1933)—and also to assess the influence of the European thought in the representation of the indigenous religious systems—this view runs the risk of overestimating the effectiveness of the instruments that the chroniclers used in an "interreligious" confrontation. That is to say, although these ethnographic projects created a violent and dramatic "colonial semiosis" (Mignolo 1995), they have not always been able to manufacture discourses capable of definitively assimilating the indigenous religions.

In an effort to show the ambivalent nature of these Novohispanic missionary works, the aim of this chapter is to examine the construction of a Franciscan representation of religious otherness (Botta 2010, 2013), focusing on the image of the *veintenas* and of this peculiar form of indigenous organization of time (Graulich 1987). For this purpose, I will address the use and development by Franciscan chroniclers of one of the most authorized conceptual models of the Christian tradition—Augustine of Hippo's *De civitate Dei* (*The City of God*) (Brown 1967), written in Latin in the early fifth century—which played a leading role in the deconstruction of ancient paganism and in the invention of an idolatrous representation of indigenous gods in the course of Novohispanic history (Botta 2017).

Through a critical Augustinian understanding of the ancient tripartite theology, the Franciscans succeeded in developing an intricate discursive production. According to the hermeneutical instruments contained in *The City of God*, the friars proposed an analogical hypothesis according to which the cycle of eighteen *veintenas* would provide a place for the expression of a "political" or "civil" theology. For example, as will be evident later, the Augustinian interpretation played an important role in the work of Sahagún. In order to justify the investigation of indigenous idolatry, the friar explicitly quoted *The City of God* in the Prologue to Book III of his *Historia general* dedicated to "the Origin of the Gods":

> The divine Augustine did not consider it superfluous or vain to deal with the fictitious theology [*theologia fabulosa*] of the gentiles in the sixth Book of The City of God, because, as he says, the empty fictions and falsehoods which the gentiles held regarding their false gods being known, [true believers] could easily make them understand that those were not gods nor could they provide anything that would be beneficial to a rational being. For this reason, the fictions and falsehoods these natives held regarding their gods are placed in this third Book, because the vanities they believed regarding their lying gods being understood, they may come more easily, through Gospel doctrine, to know the true God and to know that those they held as gods were not gods but lying devils and deceivers (*No tuvo por cosa superflua ni vana el divino Augustino tratar de la teología fabulosa de los gentiles en el sexto libro de La ciudad de Dios, porque, como él dice, conocidas las fábulas y ficciones vanas que los gentiles tenían cerca de sus dioses fingidos, pudiesen fácilmente darles a entender que aquéllos no eran dioses ni podían dar cosa ninguna que fuese provechosa a la criatura racional. A este propósito en este Tercer Libro se ponen las fábulas y ficciones que estos naturales tenían cerca de sus dioses, porque entendidas las vanidades que ellos tenían por fe cerca de sus mentirosos dioses, vengan más fácilmente por la doctrina evangélica a conocer al verdadero Dios, y que aquellos que ellos tenían por dioses no eran dioses, sino diablos mentirosos y engañadores*). (Sahagún 1950–82, *Introduction and Indices*, 59; 1988, 201–02)

In this section of his encyclopedic project, the Franciscan devoted himself to a brief account of some pre-Hispanic myths related to indigenous gods (López Austin 2000) and, of course, to the deconstruction of a "mythical" and "fabulous" theology, founded on the cult of these *dioses fingidos* ("false gods"). The *fábulas* ("fictions") and *ficciones* ("falsehoods") that the Gentiles told about their gods showed that—as had already happened in the time of ancient paganism—the Nahua believed in irrational gods—that is to say in *diablos mentirosos* ("lying devils") and *engañadores* ("deceivers")—and in *vanidades* ("vanities"), which they had by faith. Therefore, in Sahaguntine reflection, pre-Hispanic myths—according to one of the most important Augustinian topics concerning the knowledge of the poets—manifested a lack of rationality that blocked the indigenous peoples from the path to salvation.

This brief text on Nahua myths is the only explicit quotation from the Augustinian discourse on tripartite theology in Sahagún's work (Browne 2000). Nevertheless, there are elements that suggest the presence of a more systematic usage of the scheme provided by Augustine. As Mariana C. Zinni has recently noted, Sahagún's work does not present a unified thought, a finished system, but is dispersed, disordered, scattered in different places according to the needs of the moment (Zinni 2012, 164). Additionally, it is important to consider that the content of Augustine's quotation was not simply directed against the myths themselves, but rather reveals a project of deconstruction of the entire indigenous religion. In fact, the Augustinian interpretation authorized the incorporation of Nahua mythology in a broader framework and, consequently, it was employed as an instrument for the analogical construction of an indigenous *cultus deorum*. That is to say, indigenous myths represented the narrative part of a complex system of worship directed towards the gods, which was capable—as in ancient Roman polytheism—of organizing the whole reality.

Before analyzing the Franciscan discourse on the *veintenas*, it will be useful to focus briefly on the Christian definition of Roman polytheism contained in *The City of God*. This review may also contribute to a study concerning the very nature of Mesoamerican polytheism, since it allows an analysis of the recurrent theological pillars and the philosophical statements that the Franciscans, whether implicitly or explicitly, proposed during the first century of Novohispanic history. Augustine's work offered to the Franciscans the instruments to present a comprehensive interpretation of indigenous religion through a comparison with the ancient gods (Laird 2016; Lupher 2003; MacCormack 1995; Olivier 2002, 2010, 2016). In fact, the Father of the Church had promoted the deconstruction of the tripartite theology by means of which the Roman scholar and writer Marcus Terentius Varro, in his lost *Antiquitates rerum humanarum et divinarum libri XLI* written in the first century BC, tried to "defend" a form of philosophical reflection about the gods. Although he was profoundly skeptical about the "truth" of Roman polytheism, Varro still recognized the importance of ancient theology to public life. In the first place, Varro recognized in the religious thought of the Ancients a sort of "mythical" or "fabulous" theology (which we have already observed in the Sahaguntine prologue of the Book III) used by the poets in theaters to produce allegorical meditations by means of the images of the gods. Second, Varro described a "physical" or "natural" theology produced by the philosophers through a reflection on the rational nature of the gods themselves; this form of theology represented, from Varro's skeptical point of view, the only true form of knowledge produced by a polytheistic religion. Finally, in the third place, Varro discussed a "political" or "civil" theology produced by the priests, which was vital to rule the people and control the cities. It encompassed any public form of worship of the gods, all of the rites and sacrifices that each person had to offer them.

Although this form of theology was established on beliefs that appeared erroneous to Varro himself, the Romans could not give up the public usage of these religious instruments for the functioning of the ancient city, which Augustine therefore opposed to the "City of God." It is worth emphasizing that the Augustinian interpretation of the three forms of Varronian theology was definitely negative. On the one side, Varro tried to defend at least some philosophical features of the "physical" theology while, on the other hand, preserving the positive function of a "political" theology, which played a central role in the welfare of the city. On the other side, Augustine completely dismantled Roman paganism, criticizing all three forms of theology and showing that all the ancient gods were, in fact, the product of a same type of idolatrous error: that is, the confusion between created beings and the creator himself.

As noted before, through the deconstruction of Varro's theology, Augustine provided a descriptive model (Brading 1988) that permitted the first step towards the "invention" of a Mesoamerican polytheism. In essence, it was both an instrument to reveal the falsity of indigenous beliefs and a comparative configuration endowed with great authority. It was not only used to dismantle the indigenous religious system, which had already been interpreted as idolatrous, but it also served to manipulate indigenous beliefs and practices, so they could be understood through the lens of an ancient polytheism. Paradoxically, the representation of indigenous religion was the result of a process of assimilation, since it was based on reproducing the Christian image of Roman polytheism. In fact, in the third chapter of Book VI of *De civitate Dei*, Augustine portrayed Roman polytheism in accordance with a model that Varro exposed in his forty-one books devoted to Roman antiquities, which were divided into divine and human subjects. The sixteen books devoted to the divine subject described men (i.e. the priests), places of worship, times of the rites, divine worship, and, finally, the gods, divided into three types: the certain, the uncertain, and the select gods.[1] Undoubtedly, the Augustinian description—and demolition— of Varronian ancient theologies was one of the most successful theological models in Christian history. Consequently, its *auctoritas* legitimized the rhetorical strategies of the Franciscan discourses and the cultural translation of indigenous religious diversity.

However, it is questionable as to what extent these discourses were effective in producing a positive perception of indigenous religion. That is to say, it would be worth questioning whether in the Franciscan context something similar to the process described by Carmen Bernard and Serge Gruzinski with respect to the work of Bartolomé de Las Casas occurred (Bernand and Gruzinski 1988). In fact, the interpretive model of the Dominican emerges in the New World as a hermeneutical product authorized by the scholastic theology. Despite its *auctoritas*, the Lascasian pattern would have soon shown its limitations, its inability to exercise a definitive colonial influence because of the non-adaptability of indigenous beliefs and rites to the Christian and Western notions of religion.

Focusing again on Franciscan works, it should be noted how Augustinian arguments appear in their chronicles only starting with the Sahaguntine period of their missionary work, which means after the failure of the prophetic and eschatological perspective of the first friars (Cipolloni 1994, 172–73). The initial phase of the Franciscan discourse on indigenous religion—which started with the arrival of the Twelve and closed as a result of the crisis of the 1550s—had primarily developed within an optimistic perception of their missionary labor, which finds its most important expression in the ethnographic works produced in the context of the Colegio of Tlatelolco (Kobayashi 1974). With regard to this ethnographic stage, little information on the *veintenas* can be obtained from the work of *fray* Andrés de Olmos. Although Gerónimo de Mendieta, Juan de Torquemada, and the *oidor* Alonso de Zorita often mentioned fragments of his lost *Tratado de antigüedades mexicanas*, it is not possible to arrive at a detailed interpretation of Olmos' view on indigenous religion (Baudot 1976). However, important traces of an interest in indigenous calendrical systems can be found in the work of *fray* Toribio de Benavente Motolinía (Botta 2008). In the fifth chapter of the *Historia de los indios de la Nueva España*, the friar devotes himself to a careful synthesis of the different indigenous calendrical systems (Motolinía 2014, 39–43), while in the corresponding chapter of the *Memoriales* (Motolinía 1996, 159–84), Motolinía provides a more detailed exposition of the solar calendar and the *tonalpohualli*. The issue concerning the indigenous computation of time was part of a wider effort made by Motolinía to defend at least part of these systems, limiting the symbolic and practical accusations and repression only to those explicit manifestations of worship of the gods that were connected to time (Cipolloni 1994, 319–20).

In Motolinía's optimistic view, historical memory and the computation of time could be separated from religious phenomena. On one hand, it was evident in his account of pre-Hispanic history that Motolinía considered idolatry as a remote historical event, which was definitively relegated to the past. To the contrary, Sahagún would have considered idolatry as a "contemporary" issue, since it continued to show its devilish face and its penetrating presence in the Novohispanic context. As already noted, in a well-known passage of his *Epistola proemial*,

Motolinía exposed the strong relationship between the computation of time and the indigenous construction of memory, which was articulated in five different literary genres. While the first spoke of the years and time, the second spoke of the days and festivals they celebrated annually. The others spoke of dreams and augurs, of baptism and the names they gave to children, and of the rites, ceremonies, and omens they had in marriages. Of these contents, Motolinía affirmed that only the first genre could be accepted because, despite their barbarism and ignorance, indigenous cultures carefully devoted themselves to an ordered and trustworthy way of counting days, weeks, months, years, etc.[2] Therefore, he needed to dismantle the logical unity constituted by the calendar, the festivals, the ceremonies, and the so-called sacraments, separating calendrical aspects, which could be considered as rational, and establishing an artificial distinction between profane and religious phenomena. The latter were, of course, the product of the action of the devil, the universal actor who permitted the Franciscans to impose their prescriptive eye on religious difference (Cervantes 2005).

This attempt to "secularize" the indigenous calendar also allowed an apparently harmless comparison with the calendrical systems of "different nations" (the Greeks, the Egyptians, the Romans, the Jews, etc.). From this perspective, Motolinía mentioned the traditional form of dividing time in ten parts (year, month, week, day, quadrant, hour, point, moment, ounce, and atom), which became the norm during the Middle Ages through the work of Isidore of Seville and Bede the Venerable, among others. However, in New Spain, this medieval ecclesiastical model was transformed into a generalized instrument that served to recognize an alleged "pure" calendrical function. As an example of this comparative effort, in his *Memoriales*, Motolinía applied the Latin notion of the month (*mes*) as an analogical instrument to compare and describe the *veintenas*, as they were just variations of a natural and universal way of measuring time (Motolinía 1996, 161).[3]

Nevertheless, Motolinía's interpretation of indigenous organization of time shows its ambiguous nature, since the separation between these two temporalities—the religious and the profane—reveals its artificial character. After describing the functioning of indigenous calendars, Motolinía analyzes in detail the content of some of the *veintenas*. Although in the *Historia* the friar dedicated his attention only to Panquetzaliztli (Motolinía 2014, 44–46), Xocotl Huetzi (Motolinía 2014, 47–48), Atemoztli (Motolinía 2014, 49–50), Huey Tozoztli (Motolinía 2014, 51), and Tititl (Motolinía 2014, 52–53), ten *veintenas* are analyzed in detail in the *Memoriales*: Panquetzaliztli, Tlacaxipehualiztli, Ochpaniztli, Etzalcualiztli, Xocotl Huetzi, Izcalli, Atemoztli, Tozoztli, Huey Tozoztli, and Tititl (Motolinía 1996, 185–87, 189, 193–95). In these descriptions of the *veintenas*, an interpretive framework focusing on demonic action took control of the discourse, and Motolinía's lexicon became judgmental and severe. As a matter of fact, the pages that Motolinía devoted to the description of the *veintenas* are full of *ídolos, sacrificios, homicidios, matanzas, destrucciones, crueldades,* etc. ("idols," "sacrifices," "homicides," "killings," "destructions," "cruelties," etc.).

In this context, it is not only important to reflect on the ethnographic quality of these accounts on the *veintenas,* but it could be useful to observe the purpose of this interpretive model. From a hermeneutical point of view, the division between two modes of measuring time is ineffective, since the separation between a profane and religious quality of time is contradicted by Motolinía's descriptions, which indicate how in these indigenous ceremonies most of the ritual actions are connected to a religious agenda. Therefore, Motolinía's attempt to invent a profane time represents one of the indications of the hermeneutic disaster of the prophetic-eschatological model of the first Franciscans, which failed the challenge to defend and preserve some features of the indigenous cultures, separating them from their idolatrous aspects.

Subsequently, the work of Sahagún embodied the shift towards a pessimistic missionary phase, and it represented the reaction to the failure of the first ethnographic projects. By the time Sahagún began his work, the conditions in New Spain under which the Franciscans operated had totally changed. As already noted, the crisis materialized in the 1550s when, for example, the plans to form an indigenous clergy—even though Franciscans were not unified in terms of supporting this idea—were abandoned, as the seculars were progressively gaining space in New Spain. The increasing presence of the secular clergy and the stronger control imposed by the Viceroy to the indigenous peoples limited the power of the Franciscans. At that time, the indigenous nobles had, at least in name, adopted Christianity and the secular clergy pressed for the natives to be subjected to the common diocesan ecclesiastic life. To counter this attempt to reduce the power of the Franciscans, Sahagún proposed a counter-image of indigenous religion as a dangerous reality that had not yet been defeated and eradicated. Consequently, the innovative apostolic and inquisitorial missionary model proposed by this new generation of Franciscans also represented the determination to preserve their privileges and to continue exerting their hegemony in the transformation of the indigenous society.

Clear evidence of this change can be seen in Sahagún's pessimism and is visible in the harsh texts against idolatry contained in the appendix of Book I of his impressive encyclopedia. Sahaguntine work began around 1558 in Tepeapulco, where he expanded and deepened the ethnographic projects of the 1530s that seemed unable to definitively extirpate indigenous idolatry. Sahagún was openly critical of the optimism of his confreres and, at the same time, severely disapproved of the Novohispanic institutions that did not recognize the fundamental role played by the Franciscans as the only mediators able to preserve social and political harmony in New Spain. The friars had always believed that only by involving indigenous people in the process of conversion to Christianity could long-term consequences be produced. For this reason, Sahagún undertook his celebrated two-decade long project of researching and writing that was shared with his indigenous informants and produced his famous encyclopedia in twelve books. This work constitutes the most important Novohispanic representation of indigenous history and culture. However, it should be noted that this phase was also innovative and groundbreaking with respect to the use of Christian sources and models (Cipolloni 1994, 178).

It is noticeable that the rhetorical usage of authoritative sources by Motolinía was no longer effective. The sole *auctoritas* of these literary models was no longer sufficient to legitimize Franciscan purposes and should have been converted into a real hermeneutical methodology. As the failure of Motolinía's interpretation had already shown, the indigenous *cosas divinas* were so "peculiar" that the only possible foundation of missionary work was the production of a renewed and meticulous ethnography, now based on a refined apostolic and inquisitorial methodology. In this perspective, the Sahaguntine view of the *veintenas* is different from that of Motolinía, for Sahagún refused to designate a profane indigenous calendrical system and abandoned the defense of the indigenous representation of time, memory and history. In his interpretative model, idolatry was still alive. Consequently, his inquisitorial methodology should have operated on a synchronic level. Yet, to the contrary, Motolinía had interpreted indigenous organization of time on a diachronic level and had sought for those positive aspects of the indigenous culture and past to imagine an optimistic future for New Spain. Because of these different colonial conditions, the distinctive genre of the first Franciscan missionary phase was the *Historia*, while, on the contrary, the Sahaguntine privileged genre was the encyclopedia.

In this transformed literary context, the Sahaguntine operation required new hermeneutical instruments. Among them, Augustinian interpretations were used not only because of their *auctoritas*, but as they offered the opportunity of describing all the indigenous religious phenomena as idolatrous. In the prologue to Book III, Sahagún justified his missionary project by presenting a systematic plan of attack against idolatry (Solodkow 2014, 350). According to Browne (2000, 195), this "is virtually the only place where Sahagún makes an explicit reference to an author and used a model for his own work." Augustine, though, played a decisive role in the work of the friar. First, despite the fact that it was already used by *fray* Andrés de Olmos in his *Tratado de hechicerías y sortilegios* (1979), Sahagún took up the well-known image of the physician and the metaphor of the "spiritual healing" of the *indios* from the first book of Augustine's *De doctrina Christiana*.[4] Consequently, it is necessary to look at the Augustinian quality of the organization of the first five Sahaguntine books to reveal the presence of a precise structural model (Browne 2000, 205–06).

While Book III is devoted to an analysis of the myths that concern the actions of the main gods, Book I and II also seem to fulfill an Augustinian function (Bustamante 2018, 154–62). It should be noted, for example, how Sahagún's arguments in the appendix to Book I reutilized the theological framework used by Augustine to dismantle the Varronian physical and natural theology and to provide a rationalization for the images of pagan gods (Browne 2000, 199). This could be observed, for example, in Sahaguntine usage of the well-known formula *Omnes dii gentium demonia* ("All the gods of the Gentiles are demons"). As noted before, according to Augustine, the ancient philosophers used this form of theology to expose what the Romans knew about their gods, about their gender and quality, about their origin, etc. On this subject, Nicolau d'Owler stressed that the Sahaguntine *Exclamaciones del autor* ("Exclamation of the Author")—a text that closes the appendix to Book I and gives a general sence of the struggle against the indigenous gods—exposed a "heartfelt prayer of Augustinian flavor" (Nicolau d'Olwer 1952, 67). However, it is evident, as Ríos Castaño (2014, 132–36) noted, that the distribution of the divine subject matter follows, albeit in a reverse order, the Varronian classification model. Actually, if we look in detail at the structure of the Sahaguntine work, it will be observed that Book I would correspond to the XIV, XV and XVI of the *Antiquitates*. Book II has its parallel in the books that Varro dedicated to the divine cult (VIII, XI, XII and XIII). The appendix to Book II, dedicated to the priests and to the sacred buildings of Mexico-Tenochtitlan, would correspond to the books II to VII of the *Antiquitates*. Finally, Books IV and V by Sahagún would correspond to the fourth and third by Varro (Ríos Castaño 2014, 133–34).

The Sahaguntine usage of the Varronian scheme was essential to establish an implicit comparison between a Roman and an alleged indigenous polytheism. Nevertheless, it is worth observing the hermeneutical efficacy of the Augustinian view and its capability to mobilize a coherent Christian interpretation of the indigenous divine subject matter. Therefore, diverging from Motolinía's view, Sahagún could not interpret the *veintenas* outside of a religious framework, since they represented an indissoluble expression of the indigenous *cultus deorum*. In fact, in the well-known appendix of Book IV of his work, Sahagún tried to defend his interpretation of the indigenous calendar against the interpretation proposed by a previous Franciscan, who was probably Motolinía himself. As a result, in the brief prologue to that book, Sahagún described the entire indigenous calendar system as an unnatural and demonic menace to free will (Sahagún 1988, 231–32).

Moreover, additional evidence that Sahagún considered the *veintenas* as merely an aspect of a complex divine worship is the fact that, in the *Primeros memoriales* (Sahagún 1997), the first of four chapters was dedicated both to rites and gods together. The questionnaires that Sahagún used in Tepeapulco—which "might have proceeded from general queries, such as 'who were their deities' and 'how many festivities did you hold in their honor?', to specific ones" (Ríos Castaño 2014, 175)—revealed a unitary interpretation of these two features of the religious field. That is, the union between indigenous gods and festivals was the product of a theological perspective that considered the Christian relationship with God as natural: ritual action could not be interpreted as a complex social phenomenon, but rather as an expression of worship, which is naturally influenced by the "verticality" of Christian theology.

However, it was during the encyclopedic writing of the *Florentine Codex*—that is, when the hermeneutical needs of Sahagún became urgent—that the Augustinian scheme became explicit so that the divine subject matter, on the one hand, could be organized according to the Varronian scheme and, on the other hand, could be theoretically dismantled through the Augustinian interpretation of tripartite theology. Regarding Book I of the *Florentine Codex*—implicitly devoted to describing an indigenous physical and natural theology—it should be noted that, although the analogical project had not yet become systematic, the circulation of the Augustinian arguments produced important hermeneutical effects. For example, almost every confrontation between indigenous and ancient gods was actually proposed by the friar himself. As noted by Olivier (2002, 2010), during the first stage of his ethnographic work, Sahagún offered only a few comparisons in some brief notations to the *Códice Matritense del Real Palacio* and, afterwards, he fashioned more systematic efforts in his later *Historia general*. It is worth noting that the indigenous informants did not provide any comparisons in the Nahuatl texts of the *Primeros memoriales* and the *Florentine Codex*. Rather, the greater part of the comparative Sahaguntine attempts revealed their Augustinian nature. In fact, every comparison of an indigenous god with a Roman one was based on the hermeneutical possibility given by the list of twenty select gods contained in chapter II of Book VII of *De civitate Dei*.[5] At the same time, the classification contained in the Sahaguntine Book I reveals a tripartite Augustinian order, which categorized indigenous divine subject matter into three groups of gods, goddesses and minor gods.

Therefore, it is critical to analyze the organization of Book II of the *Florentine Codex*, which "deals with holidays and sacrifices with which these natives honored their gods in times of infidelity" *(que trata de las fiestas y sacrificios con que estos naturales honraban a sus dioses en el tiempo de su infidelidad)* (Sahagún 1988, 77–80). In this context, the Sahaguntine hermeneutical strategies are evocative. For example, the description of the ceremonies of the *veintenas* that were held in the city of Mexico-Tenochtitlan offers an image of a complex cycle of festivals articulated around the worship of different gods. In this context, Sahagún tried to impose a descriptive "rule" that connects a single god to every *veintena*. Despite an evident reduction of ritual complexity, from our point of view it is important to reflect on this imperfect attempt to invent a sort of Augustinian political and civil theology.

The artificial nature of this project can be observed, for example, in the chapters I to XIX of Book II of the *Historia general*, since these brief descriptions in Spanish did not derive from any text in Nahuatl (López Austin 1974, 125). Here, Sahagún was trying to comprehend and diminish the indigenous ritual complexity, which in contrast exhibited a dispersed and multifaceted presence of the gods in the diverse festivals. Paradoxically, the opposite situation can be perceived in the following chapters of Book II, where Sahagún provided longer and meticulous descriptions of the eighteen *veintenas*—mainly using data that derived from his indigenous informants. For example, it is worth noting the apparent lack of correlation between the brief and long descriptions of the *veintenas*, by observing the text of chapter II introducing the feast of Tlacaxipehualiztli:

> The second month they named Tlacaxipehualiztli. On the first day of this month they celebrated a feast in honor of the god called Totec—and, as another name, called Xipe—when they slew and flayed many slaves and captives (*Al segundo mes llamaban tlacaxipehualiztli. En el primero día deste mes hacían fiesta a honra del dios llamado Tótec, y por otro nombre se llamaba Xipe, donde mataban muchos esclavos y captivos*). (Sahagún 1950–82, bk 2: 3; 1988, 82)

While Sahagún affirms here that they celebrated the feast only in honor of Xipe Totec, in the extensive description of the *veintena* ritual actions dedicated to Huitzilopochtli also appeared (Sahagún 1950–82, bk 2: 47–56);[6] the same focus on a single deity can be observed more than a few times in Book II. For example, in the brief description of the fourth *veintena* contained in chapter IV, the feast is associated only with Cinteotl (Sahagún 1988, 83), while in chapter XXIII Chicomecoatl is also involved (Sahagún 1950–82, bk 2: 61–65). Despite the artificial attempt to connect a god to every specific feast, it is even more important to observe the ineffective reduction of the *veintenas'* ritual complexity to a form of veneration of an individual deity. Conversely, the larger descriptions in Nahuatl of the *veintenas*—impossible to fit within an effective Augustinian scheme—emerged as an open space for expression for the indigenous informants and resisted any attempts of Christian assimilation (López Austin 1974, 126).

There is no doubt that in his Book II, Sahagún aimed to obtain detailed information in order to promote the extirpation of idolatry. Although the inability to apply his interpretive model to the plain descriptions of the *veintenas* unintentionally leaves room for an indigenous point of view, it is in the Sahaguntine prologues and appendices that the strongest expression of his hermeneutical project must be sought. In this perspective, prologues could be seen "as a way to cover the newly opened hermeneutic space between authors, readers, signs, and things, however, belies the notion that he felt had achieved complete success in his endeavor" (Browne 2000, 142). That is to say, with Zinni (2012, 182), that Sahagún's prologues represented the main space of the doctrinal labor, but also a space for a permanent re-interpretation of his own point of view.

In addition, it is worth noting that the peculiar nature of the prologue to Book II (Ríos Castaño 2014, 173) is not accidental. In this text, one would expect to find—as in the cases of Books I and III—a systematic theological reflection on the "falsehood" of the indigenous political and civil theology, which Sahagún would eventually expand upon in the rest of the book. On the contrary, the prologue surprisingly provided one of the most interesting self-reflective moments within the entire Sahaguntine work. As Solodkow noted, the friar begins the prologue to Book II by making clear that he is aware of the authorizing strategies when communicating Western knowledge and he also recognizes the lack of *auctoritas* of the ethnographic sources that serve to validate the comprehension of indigenous festivals. This sort of confession is extremely remarkable because it shows that Sahagún was aware of the fact that his description could no longer be based on the Holy Scriptures or the Church Fathers like Augustine or Thomas Aquinas. Nevertheless, it could not be entirely based on the "theologically unreliable" indigenous informants of Tepeapulco (Solodkov 2014, 353).[7] For that reason, it is significant that Sahagún, in the middle of the hermeneutical failure of his descriptive project on the *veintenas*, clearly exposes the fragility of his "ethnographic authority" (Clifford 1983). As Jesús Bustamante has shown, Sahagún's style is scientifically refined, to the point that the author seems almost absent throughout the whole text (Bustamante 2003, 221–36). However, Sahagun's subjectivity appears in this prologue for the first time, revealing its paradoxical character. As Zinni (2012, 181) has pointed out, if the prologues usually function as a textual frontier, as a threshold that make us perceive the contact between the exteriority of the description and the interiority of the author, that of Book II shows Sahagún's weakness in proposing an effective evangelizing method and the withdrawal into a skeptical and self-reflexive condition.

To conclude—although any argument *in absentia* could not represent a certain proof—it is possible to find the traces of this failure in the works of another Franciscan, *fray* Juan de Torquemada, who used the same Augustinian model to describe indigenous gods. Despite the fact that Torquemada took this scheme to its transcendent hermeneutical consequences, he only used it with respect to the description of the gods, that is, with respect to a detailed representation of physical and natural theology (Frost 1975–83, 7: 69–85).[8] In his *Monarquía indiana*, the friar proposed a systematic use of the Augustinian scheme, for example, when, comparing indigenous and ancient gods, he claimed that in the *Indias Occidentales* gods were divided into "three parts or genders," as was the case among the "ancient nations of the Gentiles." That is to say that Torquemada took up the enumeration and description of the Roman gods—provided by Varro, criticized by Augustine, and reproduced by Sahagún—with the aim of assimilating all of the indigenous gods, since he supposed a complete merging of those two worlds (Bernand and Gruzinski 1988). Surprisingly, and despite the systematic use of Augustinian arguments concerning indigenous gods, Torquemada dedicated Book X of the *Monarquía Indiana* to the analysis of the *veintenas* without making a single reference to these hermeneutical instruments. In his systematic description of indigenous ceremonies, there are no traces of arguments or quotations from *De civitate Dei.* On the contrary, in his interpretation of the *veintenas,* we can perceive a surprising return to a systematic demonic interpretation. Along these lines, the reappearance of judgmental language—used to severely describe the idolatrous action of the devil—reveals the limits of the Augustinian model and its inability to produce definitive control over indigenous religion. This failure of control is a result of the inexhaustible ritual complexity of the indigenous religious system, whose non-adaptability to Christian thought clearly reflected the hermeneutical failure of the Franciscans in New Spain.

NOTES

1. "*Quadraginta et unum libros scripsit Antiquitatum; hos in res humanas divinasque divisit, rebus humanis viginti quinque, divinis sedecim tribuit, istam secutus in ea partitione rationem, ut rerum humanarum libros senos quattuor partibus daret. Intendit enim qui agant, ubi agant, quando agant, quid agant. In sex itaque primis de hominibus scripsit, in secundis sex de locis, sex tertios de temporibus, sex quartos eosdemque postremos de rebus absolvit. Quater autem seni viginti et quattuor fiunt. Sed unum singularem, qui communiter prius de omnibus loqueretur, in capite posuit. In divinis identidem rebus eadem ab illo divisionis forma servata est, quantum attinet ad ea, quae diis exhibenda sunt. Exhibentur enim ab hominibus in locis et temporibus sacra. Haec quattuor, quae dixi, libris complexus est ternis: nam tres priores de hominibus scripsit, sequentes de locis, tertios de temporibus, quartos de sacris, etiam hic, qui exhibeant, ubi exhibeant, quando exhibeant, quid exhibeant, subtilissima distinctione commendans. Sed quia oportebat dicere et maxime id exspectabatur, quibus exhibeant, de ipsis quoque diis tres conscripsit extremos, ut quinquies terni quindecim fierent. Sunt autem omnes, ut diximus, sedecim, quia et istorum exordio unum singularem, qui prius de omnibus loqueretur, apposuit. Quo absoluto consequenter ex illa quinquepertita distributione tres praecedentes, qui ad homines pertinent, ita subdivisit, ut primus sit de pontificibus, secundus de auguribus, tertius de quindecimviris sacrorum; secundos tres ad loca pertinentes ita, ut in uno eorum de sacellis, altero de sacris aedibus diceret, tertio de locis religiosis; tres porro, qui istos sequuntur et ad tempora pertinent, id est ad dies festos, ita, ut unum eorum faceret de feriis, alterum de ludis circensibus, de scaenicis tertium; quartorum trium ad sacra pertinentium uni dedit consecrationes, alteri sacra privata, ultimo publica. Hanc velut pompam obsequiorum in tribus, qui restant, dii ipsi sequuntur extremi, quibus iste universus cultus impensus est: in primo dii certi, in secundo incerti, in tertio cunctorum novissimo dii praecipui atque selecti*" (Augustinus Hipponensis 1955, bk. 6, ch. 3).

2. "*Había entre estos naturales cinco libros, como dije, de figuras y caracteres: el primero habla de los años y tiempos; el segundo, de los días y fiestas que tenían todo el año; el tercero, de los sueños, embaimientos y vanidades y agüeros en que crían; el cuarto era del bautismo y nombres que daban a los niños; el quinto, de los ritos y ceremonias y agüeros que tenían en los matrimonios. De todo éstos, del uno, que es el primero, se puede dar crédito porque habla en la verdad, que, aunque bárbaros y sin letras, mucha orden tenían en contar los tiempos, días, semanas, meses y años y fiestas*" (Motolinía 2014, 5).

3. "*Mensis a mensura do el mes se dice de medir o contar, porquel año se cuenta por meses y se diuide y reparte en doze meses. Los indios de Anavac tenían año de trezientos y sesenta y çinco días; tenían mes de a veynte días, e tenían diez y ocho meses y çinco días en vn año, como dicho es. El día postrero del mes, solemne y muy festival entrellos, e nombraban a los meses por la orden siguiente: al primer mes dezían tlacaxipehualiztli; al segundo tozcoztli ...*" (Motolinía 1996, 161).

4. "*Sicut autem curatio via est ad sanitatem, sic ista curatio peccatores sanandos reficiendosque suscepit. Et quemadmodum medici cum alligant vulnera, non incomposite sed apte id faciunt, ut vinculi utilitatem quaedam pulchritudo etiam consequatur, sic medicina Sapientiae per hominis susceptionem nostris est accomodata vulneribus, de quibusdam contrariis curans et de quibusdam similibus*" (Augustinus Hipponensis 1962, bk 1: 14.13).

5. "*Hos certe deos selectos Varro unius libri contextione commendat: Ianum, Iovem, Saturnum, Genium, Mercurium, Apollinem, Martem, Vulcanum, Neptunum, Solem, Orcum, Liberum patrem, Tellurem, Cererem, Iunonem, Lunam, Dianam, Minervam, Venerem, Vestam; in quibus omnibus ferme viginti duodecim mares, octo sunt feminae*" (Augustinus Hipponensis 1955, bk 7, ch. 2).

6. On the celebration of Huitzilopochtli in this festival, see also Rodríguez Figueroa et al. (Chapter 10) in this volume.

7. "*Todos los escriptores trabaxan de autorizar sus escripturas lo mejor que pueden, unos con testigos fidedignos, otros con otros escriptores que ante dellos han escripto, los testimonios de los cuales son habidos por ciertos; otros con testimonios de la Sagrada Escriptura. A mí me han faltado todos estos fundamentos para autorizar lo que en estos doce libros tengo escripto, y no hallo otro fundamento para autorizarlo sino poner aquí la relación de la diligencia que hice para saber la verdad de todo lo que en estos libros he escripto*" (Sahagún 1988, 77).

8. "*De los antiguos sabemos (según San Agustín, en los libros de la Ciudad de Dios), cómo dividieron sus dioses en tres partes o géneros, el primero de los cuales nombraron selectos, que quiere decir apartados o escogidos; el segundo género era de los medio dioses, y el tercero, de los dioses rústicos o agrestes*" (Torquemada 1975–83, bk 6: 58).

REFERENCES

Augustinus Hipponensis. 1955. *De civitate Dei libri I-X* (CPL 313, CHL 202), edited by Bernhard Dombart and Alfons Kalb. Turnholti: Brepols.

Augustinus Hipponensis. 1962. *De doctrina christiana. De vera religione* (CCSL 32), edited by Klaus-Detlef Daur and Josef Martin. Turnholti: Brepols.

Baudot, Georges. 1976. *Utopie et histoire au Mexique. Les premiers chroniqueurs de la civilisation mexicaine (1520–1569).* Toulouse: E. Privat.

Bernand, Carmen, and Serge Gruzinski. 1988. *De l'idolâtrie. Une archéologie des sciences religieuses.* Paris: Seuil.

Botta, Sergio. 2008. "El politeísmo como sistema de traducción. La obra misionera de Toribio de Benavente Motolinía frente a la alteridad religiosa de la Nueva España." *Guaraguao. Revista de Cultura Latinoamericana* 28, no. 12: 9–26.

———. 2010. "The Franciscan Invention of Mexican Polytheism: the Case of the Water Gods." *Studi e Materiali di Storia delle Religioni* 76, no. 2: 411–32.

———. 2013. "Towards a Missionary Theory of Polytheism: The Franciscans in the Face of the Indigenous Religions of New Spain." In *Manufacturing Otherness. Missions and Indigenous Cultures in Latin America*, edited by Sergio Botta, 11–36. Newcastle Upon Tyne: Cambridge Scholars Publishing.

———. 2017. "Representar a los dioses indígenas a través de San Agustín. Huellas del *De civitate Dei* en las obras de fray Bernardino de Sahagún y fray Juan de Torquemada." In *Mudables representaciones: el indio en la Nueva España a través de crónicas, impresos y manuscritos*, edited by Clementina Battcock and Berenice Bravo Rubio, 49–78. Mexico City: Instituto Nacional de Antropología e Historia.

Brading, David. 1988. *Mito y profecía en la historia de México*. Mexico City: Vuelta.

Brown, Peter. 1967. *Augustine of Hippo. A Biography*. Berkeley: University of California Press.

Browne, Walden. 2000. *Sahagún and the Transition to Modernity*. Norman: University of Oklahoma Press.

Bustamante, Jesús. 2003. "Problemas con las fuentes escritas y su interpretación: de cuestionarios, franciscanos e 'indios' en México, siglo XVI." *Revista de Dialectología y Tradiciones Populares* LVIII, no. 1: 221–36.

———. 2018. "Fuentes y modelos usados por Sahagún en su obra etnográfica. Dioses, rituales y teología fabulosa de los antiguos mexicanos." In *Lo múltiple y lo singular. Diversidad de perspectivas en las crónicas de la Nueva España*, edited by Luis Barjau and Clementina Battcock, 153–70. Mexico City: Secretaría de Cultura, Instituto Nacional de Antropología e Historia.

Cervantes, Fernando. 2005. *The Devil in the New World: The Impact of Diabolism in New Spain*. New Haven: Yale University Press.

Cipolloni, Marco. 1994. *Tra memoria apostolica e racconto profetico: il compromesso etnografico francescano e le cosas della Nuova Spagna (1524–1621)*. Roma: Bulzoni.

Clifford, James. 1983. "On Ethnographic Authority." *Representations* 2: 118–46.

Frost, Elsa Cecilia. 1975–83. "El plan y la estructura de la obra." In Juan de Torquemada, *Monarquía indiana*. Vol. 7, edited by Miguel León-Portilla, 69–85. Mexico City: Universidad Nacional Autónoma de México-Instituto de Investigaciones Históricas.

Garibay, Ángel María. 1953–54. *Historia de la literatura náhuatl*. 2 vols. Mexico City: Porrúa.

Graulich, Michel. 1987. *Mythes et rituels du Mexique ancien préhispanique*. Brussels: Académie Royale de Belgique.

Jiménez Moreno, Wigberto. 1938. "Fray Bernardino de Sahagún y su obra." In Bernardino de Sahagún, *Historia general de las cosas de Nueva España*, XIII-LXXXIV, edited by Joaquín Ramírez Cabañas. Mexico City: Editorial de Pedro Robredo.

Kobayashi, José María. 1974. *La educación como conquista (empresa franciscana en México)*. Mexico City: El Colegio de México.

Laird, Andrew. 2016. "Aztec and Roman Gods in Sixteenth-Century Mexico: Strategic Uses of Classical Learning in Sahagún's Historia *General*." In *Altera Roma: Art and Empire from Mérida to México*, edited by John M. D. Pohl and Claire L. Lyons, 167–87. Los Angeles: The Cotsen Institute of Archaeology Press.

León-Portilla, Miguel. 1999. *Bernardino de Sahagún. Pionero de la antropología*. Mexico City: Universidad Nacional Autónoma de México.

———. 2002. *Cantos y crónicas del México antiguo*. Madrid: Dastin.

López Austin, Alfredo. 1974. "The Research Method of Fray Bernardino de Sahagún: The Questionnaires." In *Sixteenth-Century Mexico. The Work of Sahagún*, edited by Munro Edmonson, 111–50. Albuquerque: University of New Mexico Press.

———. 2000. "Fray Bernardino de Sahagún frente a los mitos indígenas." *Ciencias* 60–61: 6–14.

Lupher, David A. 2003. *Romans in a New World: Classical Models in Sixteenth-Century Spanish America*. Ann Arbor: University of Michigan Press.

MacCormack, Sabine. 1995. "Limits of Understanding: Perceptions of Greco-Roman and Amerindian Paganism in Early Modern Europe." In *America in European Consciousness 1493–1750*, edited by Karen Ordhal Kupperman, 79–129. Chapel Hill: University of North Carolina Press.

Marroquín Arredondo, Jaime. 2014. *Diálogos con Quetzalcóatl: humanismo, etnografía y ciencia (1492–1577)*. Madrid, Frankfurt am Main: Iberoamericana, Vervuert.

Mignolo, Walter. 1995. *The Darker Side of the Renaissance. Literacy, Territoriality, and Colonization*. Ann Arbor: University of Michigan Press.

Motolinía, or Benavente, Toribio de. 1996. *Memoriales (Libro de oro, MS JGI 31)*. Edited by Nancy J. Dyer. Mexico City: Colegio de México.

———. 2014. *Historia de los indios de la Nueva España*. Edited by Mercedes Serna Arnaiz, and Bernat Castany Prado. Madrid: Real Academia Española.

Nicolau d'Olwer, Luis. 1952. *Fray Bernardino de Sahagún (1499–1590)*. Mexico City: Instituto Panamericano de Geografía e Historia.

Olivier, Guilhem. 2002. "El panteón en la *Historia general de las cosas de Nueva España* de fray Bernardino de Sahagún." In *Bernardino de Sahagún. Quinientos años de presencia*, edited by Miguel León-Portilla, 61–80. Mexico City: Universidad Nacional Autónoma de México.

———. 2010. "El panteón mexica a la luz del politeísmo grecolatino: el ejemplo de la obra de Fray Bernardino de Sahagún." *Studi e Materiali di Storia delle Religioni*, 76, no. 2: 389–410.

———. 2016. "The Mexica Pantheon in Light of Graeco-Roman Polytheism: Uses, Abuses, and Proposals." In *Altera Roma: Art and Empire from Mérida to México*, edited by John M. D. Pohl and Claire L. Lyons, 189–214. Los Angeles: The Cotsen Institute of Archaeology Press.

Olmos, Andrés de. 1979. *Tratado de hechicerías y sortilegios*. Edited by Georges Baudot. Mexico City: Mission Archéologique et Éthnologique Française.

Ricard, Robert. 1933. *La conquête spirituelle du Mexique. Essai sur l'apostolat et les méthodes missionaires des ordres mendiants en Nouvelle-Espagne de 1523–24 à 1572*. Paris: Institut d'Éthnologie.

Ríos Castaño, Victoria. 2014. *Translation as Conquest. Sahagún and the Universal History of the Things of New Spain*. Madrid, Frankfurt am Main: Iberoamericana, Vervuert.

Sahagún, Bernardino de. 1950–82. *Florentine Codex: General History of the Things of New Spain, Fray Bernardino de Sahagún*. Translated with notes and illustrations by Arthur J. O. Anderson and Charles E. Dibble. 13 vols. Santa Fe: The School of American Research, University of Utah Press.

———. 1988. *Historia general de las cosas de Nueva España*. Edited by Alfredo López Austin and Josefina García Quintana. 2 vols. Madrid: Alianza editorial.

———. 1997. *Primeros Memoriales*. Edited and translated by Thelma Sullivan. Completed and revised, with additions, by Henry B. Nicholson, Arthur J. O. Anderson, Charles E. Dibble, Eloise Quiñones Keber, and Wayne Ruwet. Norman: University of Oklahoma Press.

Solodkow, David M. 2014. *Etnógrafos coloniales: alteridad y escritura en la Conquista de América (siglo XVI)*. Madrid, Frankfurt am Main: Iberoamericana, Vervuert.

Zinni, Mariana C. 2012. "Umbrales hermenéuticos: los 'prólogos' y 'advertencias' de fray Bernardino de Sahagún." *Estudios de Cultura Náhuatl* 43: 161–83.

CHAPTER TWELVE

Bright Plumages, Teary Children, and Blessed Rains

Possible Reminiscences of Atlcahualo during the Indigenous Ceremonial Pomp of Saint Francis in Post-Conquest Mexico City

ROSSEND ROVIRA-MORGADO

PROLOGUE

In March 1564, a heterogeneous and buoyant group of Mexico City *maceguales* began to gain the attention of the judicial bureaus of the Real Audiencia de la Nueva España. The intent of those Nahua middle-ranked commoners was to threaten a lawsuit against Tenochtitlan Indian *cabildo*[1] main officers and nobles in response to deep-rooted grievances (AGN, Civil, vol. 644, exp. 1, 196 fols).[2] Encouraged by both their Spanish procurator Agustín Pinto and the Dominican friar Diego de Toral, these plebeian journeymen, who clamored for justice, presented nineteen overwhelming charges (AGN, Civil, vol. 644, exp. 1, fol. 2r–3r, 18r; *Anales de Juan Bautista* 2001, 139–41). Among the most intriguing accusations that the local native council deputies faced, the sixth and the seventh involved complaints concerning the profound questioning about the strengthening of the Christianization program—or *poliçia christiana*—in the four urban districts of Santa María La Redonda, San Juan, San Pablo, and San Sebastián. Specifically, these complaints were about the persistence of certain Pre-Columbian funerary and festive behaviors, as well as the regular usage of ancient ritual clothing and feather headdresses, displayed by Tenochca dignitaries during various Christian celebrations orchestrated in the city (AGN, Civil, vol. 644, exp. 1, fol. 2r). The Saint Francis of Assisi yearly festivity on 4 October—having once been one of the most ostentatious, bustling, and admired celebrations performed by Indian elites at the very end of the wet season—started to sound to the Real Audiencia magistrates' ears like a highly suspicious religious event requiring investigation, that could have been masking long-held, gentile ritual memories for four decades.

Notwithstanding, it ought to be remembered that incipient Nahua Christianity in Post-Conquest Central Mexico developed in a negotiated atmosphere described by Charles Dibble (1974) and Louise M. Burkhart (1989, 28 and ff.) as a sort of indigenized Catholicism. Regarding pristine Christian life at Tenochtitlan, pioneering Franciscan friars competed against Dominican, Augustinian, and later Jesuit and Carmelite ministers for control of indigenous parishioners, together with their activism against the recurring interference of the diocesan clergy regarding the ecclesiastical rights granted to them (Alcántara Rojas 2008; Álvarez Icaza Longoria 2010; Castañeda de la Paz 2013, 251–57; Gibson 1986, 384; Moreno de los Arcos 1992, 10–12; Mundy 2015, 178–80; Pérez Puente 2010; Ramírez 2008, 16; 2014, 1026–68; 2015; Rovira-Morgado 2016a, 483–90; 2017, 46–47, 52–53, 84–85, 138–43; Truitt 2003, 2009, 2018). Additionally, harsh and punitive judgments of Tenochca evangelization were also commonplace for the Spanish *cabildo* and the Real Audiencia personnel in Mexico City (Rovira-Morgado 2016b; 2017, 136–46).

In this way, the conflicting and poorly organized early Colonial religious arena may have contextualized the integration of many symbolic and communicative features of the ancient *xiuhpohualli* festive cycle into the new pre-Tridentine Christian Nahua liturgy. As is well known, it was sponsored by the mendicant orders—namely, the Franciscan family—and their Indian aristocratic neophytes. Consequently, the focus of this chapter is on elucidating how various semiological aspects of the *veintena* of Atlcahualo—or "Cessation of Waters," also known by the supplementary epithets of Cuahuitlehua ("Raising of Poles") and Xilomanaliztli ("Offering of Tender Maize Ears") (*Codex Magliabechiano* c. 1550, fol. 29r–29v; *Codex Tudela* c. 1540, fol. 11r; Sahagún 2003, 1: 112)—could have been reinterpreted and fragmented within this embryonic indigenous Christianity in Mexico City. Regular orders' literature, native sources, urban landscape imaginaries, archival records, and compilations of legal regulations are all analyzed in order to shed light on such cultural and sociological issues as revealed by the 1564 lawsuit.

ATLCAHUALO AND OTHER TLALOC-WORSHIPPED *VEINTENAS* AT ANCIENT TENOCHTITLAN

From early Colonial documentary evidence, little can be conclusively understood about the ceremonial activities held in several *veintenas* related to Tlaloc cults in

Late Postclassic Mexico-Tenochtitlan's major *calpolli* neighborhoods or their *cal-polteteo* patron deities (Figure 12.1). Revered personnel and divine impersonators (*ixiptlahuan*), solemn performances, ritual timing, sacred urban topographies, and hierophanic lacustrine sceneries are mentioned in sixteenth-century reports, but often in a scattered, obscure way that obfuscates awareness about their persistence in early Post-Conquest times (Broda 1971, 1991, 2001, 2016, 2019; Mazzetto 2014a). Furthermore, it must be considered that ancient rain-petitioning festivals in the capital—in the manner of Atlcahualo, but also Tepeilhuitl, Atemoztli or Etzal-cualiztli—involved a great number of occupational specialists and participants, who

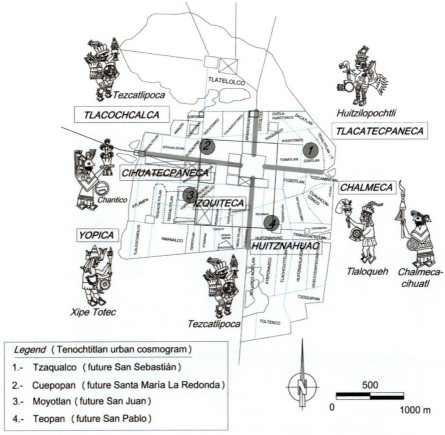

Figure 12.1. Map of Late Postclassic Mexico-Tenochtitlan neighboring plots, with the quadripartite urban arrangement and seven main *calpolli* with some of their *calpolteteo*.
Source: Design by Rossend Rovira-Morgado, after *Primeros Memoriales*; *Codex Chavero de Ixhuatepec* c. 1650; *Títulos del pueblo de Santa Isabel Tola* 1714; Caso 1956; González Aparicio 1973; Van Zantwijk 1963, 1966, 1985; Calnek 2003; González González 2011; Mazzetto 2014a; Rovira-Morgado 2014.

resided, worshipped, and labored in both urban corporate groups and peripheral subject areas. Therefore, institutionalized ceremonial celebration of seasonal storms involved the entire Tenochca society *locus enuntiationis*. Tlaloc and his avatars and assistants might be considered devices of "ritual technology" as part of a collective response to annual environmental hardships, as conceptualized analogously by William H. Walker (2001, 87 and ff.) and Holley Moyes et al. (2009, 197–201).

Consonant with Franciscan friar Bernardino de Sahagún's work, among other important indigenous accounts, it is commonly believed that the *xiuhpohualli* calendar in Late Pre-Columbian Aztec society started with the *veintena* of Atlcahualo. Following Sahagún's detailed assessment of the sequence of this celebration, sixteenth-century Atlcahualo began in February to glorify the *tlaloqueh*, or mountain and rain deities (*Florentine Codex* 1950–82, bk 2: 42–45; *Primeros Memoriales* 1997, fol. 250r; Sahagún 2003, 1: 112–13, 144–46, 257). The yearly inaugural event paralleled the erection of wooden poles in many places and the gathering of *tlacateteuhme* children and *xixioti* lepers in Atempan.[3] Atempan hosted an *ayauhcalli* holy house assumed to be located in Tenochtitlan's southeastern edges and aquatic ditches, which was proximate to either the Xolloco area or in the ward called Temazcaltitlan (Mazzetto 2014b, 163; Mazzetto and Rovira-Morgado 2014, 103–04). Immediately after the first overnight stay in Atempan, *tlacateteuhme* infants that were to be sacrificed were elaborately decorated with precious stones, feathers, and paper. A ritual procession was carried out afterwards in order to move these special messengers by canoe to seven hills around the Basin of Mexico and the watery cave of Pantitlan. Amidst these propitiatory places, the mountain islands of Tepetzinco and Tepepolco, Pantitlan whirlpool, as well as the Cocotl promontory in the Chalco region, were apparently paramount. Concurrent activities were also typical of other similar *veintenas*, like Tepeilhuitl, when small mountains and lightning-shaped figures were used as a sympathetic means of strengthening water gods' benevolence (Sahagún 2003, 1: 201–02).

To summarize: rituals involving lake travel and sacrificial offerings to Tlaloc all combined wooden pole raising, ecstatic dancing-chanting, feathers and textile intensive ritual consumption, as well as ceremonial weeping by children. In fact, children's crying, sadness, sorrow, compassionate body language, and emotional dramatization would all have been important. They all served to bind ritual human tears to celestial waters through the mediation provided by the Lord of Tlalocan and his little avatars Opochtli, Atlahua, Amimitl, Yiauhquemeh, Tomiauhtecuhtli, Totoltecatl, and Chachalmeca (Arnold 1991, 219–32; Aveni 1991, 58 and ff.; Botta 2009, 182; Díaz Barriga 2012, 24–28; Escalante Gonzalbo 2004, 247–49; Graña 2009, 162–63; Read 2005, 55 and ff.). It should be noted that pre-Columbian Nahua breastfed infants and very young children were supposed to allegorize ontological categories connected to a kind of pre-human, pre-cultural existence (Ardren 2011, 134; Echeverría García 2015, 144, 147–49). This leads to the consideration that children were viewed as beings privileged with the ability to foster benign communication with supernatural entities in exchange for rainfall, crops, nourishment, social reproduction, and the healthy safeguarding of civilization, or *toltecayotl*.

In addition to erecting large poles or the emulation of infants moaning through ritual singing, three other elements might have also been important to ancient *veintenas* in which Tlaloc was worshiped in the capital, especially, during the Atlcahualo festive cycle. Those were Pre-Columbian temporality; embroiled religious theatres in southeastern Tenochtitlan or outer areas; and, finally, politically expressive feather attires, such as the *aztatzontli* headdress. As noted above, a general consensus existed in Post-Conquest narrative sources about Atlcahualo opening in mid-February, a moment close to the midpoint of the dry season. It must be taken into account that Atlcahualo's proposed etymology—"Cessation of Waters"—seems to contradict the reported sixteenth-century descriptions of aquatic glorification. This issue enabled Michel Graulich (1992, 34; 1999, 44 and ff.) to argue that Atlcahualo would have originally fallen—according to a calendar reform initiated in Epiclassic Mesoamerica—during the entire month of September, just at the very end of the annual rainy period. Solar year movements through the centuries in Epiclassic and Postclassic Central Mexico therefore explained the Atlcahualo ritual cycle, which, in 1519, "had slipped into February-March, so that the immolation of children typical of this month coincided with those linked to the tropical year" (Graulich 1992, 34). Although it is a topic not lacking in controversy, Tenochca ritual remembrance in the sixteenth-century *veintena* framework could consequently have classified Atlcahualo as an time period related semiotically to the final wet season.

The southeastern districts of Tenochtitlan were a primary focus of the Atlcahualo rituals, an area of the city that, from Post-Conquest times onward, housed the urban quarter, *barrio grande*, or *parcialidad* of San Pablo de México. As depicted in Figure 12.1, ancient *calpolli* residential corporations in the Teopan urban area flourished according to Colonial-period sources. Indian chronicler Hernando de Alvarado Tezozomoc described how San Pablo marketplaces and neighborhoods were the places where Huitznahuac Ayauhcaltitlan had once been situated; this was one of the foundational *calpolli* in the city (Tezozomoc 1998, 26–27, 74–75; 2001, 304; see also Rovira-Morgado 2010, 43–46; 2012, 38, 46). Subsidiary documentary materials and data are available in the *Codex Chavero de Ixhuatepec* (c. 1650) and the *Títulos del pueblo de Santa Isabel Tola* (1714). As explained by Ana Rita Valero de García (2004, 220 and ff.), both sources illuminate the ancient *calpolli* of Chalman as another relevant social cluster in what became San Pablo, where it was called *Chalmeca* or *Chalmecapan*. It ought to be remembered that Chalman was traditionally patronized by certain Nahua telluric and aquatic extra-human essences, such as Cihuacoatl/Chalmecacihuatl, Mixcoatl, and the aforementioned avatars of Tlaloc, or *tlaloqueh* (Klein 1984, 39–47; Olivier 2015, 156, Fig. II.10). Furthermore, and in line with Rudolph van Zantwijk (1963, 92, 102; 1966, 182; 1994, 105), it is more than likely that Chalmeca were directly implied in several passages concerning Mexico-Tenochtitlan ethnogenesis, and, as such, symbolized early ritual leadership and legitimate sovereignty. Most meaningful, they retained an ancestral origin in the aforesaid Chalco province (Torquemada 1975, 3: 357). It should be highlighted here that Cuauhtlequetzqui/Cuauhcoatl and Axollohua, two priests who were Malinalxoch's or the Chalman lady's followers, led the discovery of the Toltzallan Acatzallan spring at the aforementioned Temazcaltitlan and the later, well-known "eagle-on-cactus" manifestation. In fact, it was said that Axollohua met Tlaloc during such paramount events (Torquemada 1975, 3: 397–98).

So, of the two Pre-Columbian *calpolli* documented in Colonial San Pablo, the Chalmeca seemingly fit with ancient Atlcahualo in terms of rituality, sacred aquatic landscape, and chronometrical and spatial preeminence. Given the fact that Pre-Hispanic Atempan and the noble office of *atempanecatl* were also reported among Temazcaltitlan and its high-ranked residents (Chimalpahin 1997, 1: 208–09; 2: 114–15; Tezozomoc 2001, 98; see also Mazzetto and Rovira-Morgado 2014, 95), it is possible that Atempan, child sacrifices, *calpolli* Chalman, and Atlcahualo festivals might have been partly related to the southern margin of Tenochtitlan's main core island, which bordered with the Lagoon of Mexico (Dehouve 2013, 61, Fig. 1). According to the Conquest-era *Map of Nüremberg* (c. 1524), this city zone was identified with suburban domestic units and estates just behind *huey tlahtoani* Motecuhzoma II Xocoyotzin's palatine compound, as well as the *totocalco* orchards, aviaries, and craft workshops. The early Colonial *Map of Uppsala* (c. 1537–50) also describes this area as intimately connected to the aquatic canal of Xolloco, which drained directly to the swamps around Tepetzinco, Tepepolco, and Pantitlan (Figure 12.2).

As recorded by Sahagún (2003, 1: 113, 145–46), large amounts of feather crafts were ritually consumed in the Atlcahualo festivity during performances and processions. Local waterfowl hunting in the lakes and the transportation of plumages to urban workshops must therefore have been important seasonal activities. When looking at narrative or pictographic descriptions of Atlcahualo, as well as Tepeilhuitl and Atemoztli, contained in Early Colonial Franciscan-inspired compositions and native codices, feather artifacts are particularly noteworthy (*Codex Borbonicus* c. 1563, pl. 23, 29, 32, 36; *Codex Magliabechiano* c. 1550, fol. 29r–29v; *Codex Telleriano-Remensis* c. 1563, fol. 5v, 9v; *Codex Tudela* c. 1540, fol. 11r; *Codex Vaticanus 3738* c. 1566, fol. 42v; *Primeros Memoriales* 1997, fol. 77r, 260r–260v). These records repeatedly emphasized the *aztatzontli* headdress as a distinctive insignia of Tlaloc, his assistants and impersonators, as well as the pulque gods, during the fertility festivals to petition the rains (Olko 2014, 59, 125, 406; Seler 1902–23; Vauzelle 2017, 81 and ff.) (Figure 12.3).

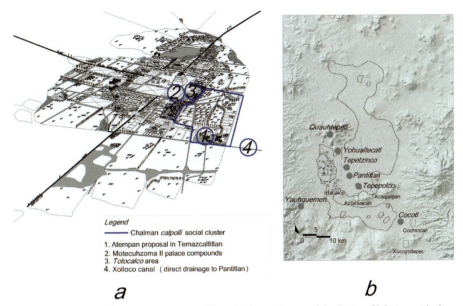

a

b

Figure 12.2. Idealized axonometric view of Tenochtitlan and map of the Basin of Mexico with the places and some locations discussed. Source: Design by Rossend Rovira-Morgado.

Figure 12.3. Tlaloc's *aztatzontli* headdresses depicted in relation to the *veintena* of Atlcahualo/Cuahuitl ehua/Xilomaniliztli. Detail of *Codex Tudela* c. 1540, fol. 11r. Source: Drawing by Rossend Rovira-Morgado.

It is well known that the primary resource for the *aztatzontli* decorative implements was the magnificent white plumage of the *aztatl*, which is translated by the Franciscan friar Alonso de Molina (1970, part II, fol. 10r) as *garça*, or heron (*Casmerodius albus*). Netting of herons must have been a routine enterprise in the most central-eastern, deep-water area of Lake Texcoco. These seasonal ponds were located near previously mentioned Tepetzinco, Pantitlan, Tepepolco, the coastal hamlets in the Santa Catalina peninsula, and the Chalcan fields (*Map of Uppsala* c. 1537–50; Espinosa Pineda 1996, 126; González Aparicio 1973; Hodge 2008, 324; Parsons 2006, 243–44; Rojas 1985, 126; Villanueva García and Manrique-Eternod 2007, 42). Although the collection of heron feathers could have been one of the most important economic tasks in this area, it is also likely that the transfer of captive specimens to Tenochtitlan might have been important as well, since the ancient capital housed specialized wards, aviaries and dependent workshops (*Map of Nüremberg* c. 1524; see also Blanco Padilla et al. 2009, 34–35; López Luján et al. 2012, 26–29; Nicholson 1955, 4). As mentioned, one of these aviaries and craft centers, Motecuhzoma II's palatine *totocalco*, was located adjacent to the Chalman *calpolli* neighboring corporate landholdings. As late as the 1550s and 1570s, nearby indigenous vicinities were still reported as places inhabited by specialized collectors of lake food and water birds (Benson Latin American Collection, University of Texas, Genaro García Collection, Ms. 30, fol. 1v) and of "merchants, dealers and officers of all the occupations and fishermen" (*mercaderes, tratantes y oficiales de todos los oficios y pescadores*) (*Descripción del Arzobispado de México* 1897, 278). Consistent with these persuasive lines of evidence, prior Aztec residents who had dwelled in this urban area are the best candidates to have been daily palatial avian caretakers and featherwork artisans. They were mentioned by the first Spanish eyewitnesses, Hernán Cortés (2000, 146) and Bernal Díaz del Castillo (1999, 255), as well as in Bernardino de Sahagún's later encyclopedic compilations (Sahagún 2003, 2: 668).

SAINT FRANCIS AS NEW DEMIURGE IN THE EARLY CHRISTIAN INDIAN COSMIC DRAMA IN MEXICO CITY

Considering that Tlaloc adoration and specialized featherwork *amantecayotl* was critical to ancient Tenochtitlan society, an analysis of Atlcahualo should reveal an intrinsic linkage with Chalman *calpolli* membership and its traditional expertise in fishing, hunting, captive bird breeding, and precious plumage crafting. Documentary evidence serves to corroborate that the Late Postclassic Chalmeca social cluster adjoined Motecuhzoma II Xocoyotzin's royal palace (*huey tecpan*), courtyards, and apartment compounds, an urban zone identifiable with the later most northern *tlaxilacalli* wards of San Pablo de México. According to Edward E. Cal-nek (1976, 296) and Luis Reyes García et al. (1996, 56), those *tlaxilacaltin*—the Colonial-Nahuatl plural form for *tlaxilacalli*—were wards, or residential subdi-visions, of the *calpolli* and the four great urban quarters in the city. As reviewed previously by scholars like Alfonso Caso (1956, 22–23), Luis González Apari-cio (1973), Ana Rita Valero de García (1991, 185–88), Francisco Morales (1994, 367–68), Edward E. Calnek (2003, 167, 185–86, 190), Rossend Rovira-Morgado (2014, 164–78; 2017, 51), Barbara E. Mundy (2015, 144–46), and others, this area included at least six Post-Conquest indigenous *tlaxilacaltin*: Tozcamincan, Cozot-lan, (Cuauh)Contzinco-Atlixco, Tozanitlan, Ometochtitlan, and the previously mentioned Temazcaltitlan. Even though the Christian evangelization agenda advanced—albeit slowly—in Mexico City during the first decades that followed the Conquest, several Chalmeca traditions endured in such northern wards of San Pablo. This assertion allows us to make some assumptions regarding accusations of heathendom aired in the 1564 lawsuit.

Indeed, the names of the barrios are consistent with local Pre-Columbian identity and professional skills. Thus, Tozanitlan and Cozotlan were etymologi-cally connected to the *toznene* parrot birds, the precious white-yellow coloration of their feathers, and the yellow waters (Mundy 2015, 146; Olaguíbel 1898, 39), while Contzinco turned into Santa Cruz, conceivably reminiscent of Tlaloc avatar cults (Broda 1997, 130). Ometochtitlan may be linked with one of the ancient pulque gods. Tozcamincan was likewise believed to have housed renowned feath-erworkers, in as much as artisans and sellers of plume cloaks were located there (Reyes García et al. 1996, 186; Rojas Rabiela 1999). In fact, the early Post-Con-quest Tenochca government not only derived political support from those neigh-borhoods, but they further stimulated the production of feather work, organized centralized storage, and featured feather work in both clandestine displays and public processions. These feathered objects served as symbolic capital and a cul-tural symbol of the new Indian Christian republic. Actually, it was reported in 1539 that Temazcaltitlan had furtively housed the *tlaquimilolli* sacred bundle of Huitzilopochtil (González Obregón 1902, 124). Because of this, from 1525 onward, Andrés de Tapia Motelchiuhtzin, recently appointed as *quauhtlahtoani*, or interim ruler, of the Tenochca people, resolved to move the political seat to his palace in adjoining Tozanitlan, afterwards known as *Casa de Tapia* (Calnek 1974, 2003; Rovira-Morgado 2013, 2015; Evans 2005). Friar Juan de Zumarraga (1870, 142), who was the first prelate and bishop of Mexico, affirmed that this Tenochca chief, "who for the Christians was named Tapia ... owned rich plumages, with which he rejoiced" (*que por nombre de cristianos se dice fulano de Tapia ... tenía unos plumajes muy ricos, con que se regocijaba*). One observation recorded in 1576 was even more explicit in asserting that later governors Diego Huanitzin (c.1539–41) and Diego de San Francisco Tehuetzquititzin (c.1541–54) also dwelled in *Casa de Tapia*. According to this source, "the community gatherings were usually held [there] … and, as a communal place, [the governors]… housed in there their feather crafts and ancient paintings" (*solían hacerse fiestas en ellas de la comunidad …y como era casa de común … tenían en ellas su plumería y pinturas antiguas*) (AGN, Tierras, vol. 37, exp. 2, fol. 99v).

Moreover, Post-Conquest patronage featherwork seemed to have received certain endorsement by Seraphic ministers who administered San José de los Naturales' doctrinal circumscriptions, matrix chapel, and workshops, where the stunning and technically complex *Misa de San Gregorio* [Mass of San Gregorio] was also manufactured by 1539 (Bartolomé 2008, 164; Estrada de Gerlero et al. 1990; Mundy 2015, 104, 119; Osowski 2010, 29). While its official sponsorship is attributed to Governor Huanitzin, the identities of *amantecah* who were involved remain obscure (Muñoz 2006, 134, n. 29). Nevertheless, the later *Anales de Juan Bautista* records on daily crafting activities of the mid-sixteenth-century San José identified Martín Mixcohuatl and Juan Ycnotzin, residents from San Pablo, as the great masters in painting and precious artistic plumage assemblies for the Franciscans (*Anales de Juan Bautista* 2001, 143, 181, 199, 251, 255, 265, 275). In fact, Martín Mixcohuatl's second name mirrored one of the most striking Chalmeca deities, pointing to a plausible association with the northern San Pablo *tlaxilacaltin*. Apparently, therefore, a new group of Seraphic native parishioners were tying featherwork technical knowledge, traditional occupational corporatism, residential adscription, long-lived ritualistic practices, and collective identity to the *doctrina christiana* arrangements in San José (Truitt 2009, 2010, 2018).

Early on, Franciscan monks attempted to find balance between empowering and legitimizing such Nahua re-actualized practices and habits into their *ars praedicandi*. Friar Toribio de Benavente "Motolinía" (2017, 95) noted that one Saint Francis apology passage occurred in Tlaxcala, where a theatrical performance was performed for praising the saint's benevolence when he decided to preach to birds. Doctrinarian warnings had such an effect that fowls succumbed to God, and so a fierce beast, presumably Tepeyollotl, another terrestrial facet of Tlaloc (Olivier 1998, 104, 113), immediately fled the mountain. Reaching this point, it must be recalled that Seraphic friars promptly equated precious flying animals, shining plumages, and sacred arboreal dwellings with the new celestial messengers and redeemers for the Nahuas. As researched by Berenice Alcántara Rojas (2008, 165; 2015, 150) with her analyses on the *Psalmodia Christiana* (c.1558–83) and the *Cantares Mexicanos* (c.1582), birds with bright feathers, sweet singing, and special flowery trees possessed "mantic" qualities that enabled Indian neophytes to communicate ritually with the Christian entities. As a matter of fact, one of the best examples was the early indigenous festival of Saint Francis, when the *pilcuicatl* or *piltoncuicatl* ("song of the [little] children," in Nahuatl) was chanted.[4]

This ritual singing was compiled in the late sixteenth-century *Cantares Mexicanos*, although it is presumed to have been composed around the 1530s in the Franciscan convent in Mexico City, during Sebastián Ramírez de Fuenleal's Segunda Audiencia presidency and under friar Peter of Ghent's direct sponsorship (Bierhorst 1985, 286–97; *Cantares Mexicanos* 2011, 2: 668–709, 1207, n. 532, 541, 542, 1208, n. 557; Garibay 1987, 2: 116, 331). Imaginaries in the *pilcuicatl* evoked the native wet season and misty landscapes, populated with hallowed waters, houses, trees, and birds. And the most important thing, it was presumably inhabited by a kind of infantile, Levitical priesthood as well:

> Let us Huexotzinca start up a song, strike up a song. And aya! We little children will make creation of flowers. Let many be pleasured in the Picture House ... Who made the sky and the earth? Our father God, he is the one ... Let us little children all be taken in. Then the pleasured child, the baby smiler, once again will weep ... We're the Huexotzinca, we're the little children ... Let's make troupial-and-turquoise-swan plumes twirl ... They're twirling as parrot colors, these, your beautiful songs, your beautiful watery flowers ... (*Ya man toncuicatlatocan tihuexotinzca ma toncuicapepehuacan aya xochitl totlayocol in toconyachihuzque in tipipiltzinti ma onahahuilon amoxcali ... y acon y ye quichiuh ilhuˀ. yn tlaˀpc. aya anqui ya yehuatl totatzin Dios ... Ma calacoa in tipipiltzitzinti ye no cuel chocaz in topilahuiltil yxhuetzcatocato ... Tihuexotzinca netle tipipiltzintzinti ... yman Tiquetzalçaquaxiuhquechol-huihuico ...*). (Bierhorst 1985, 287–93)

As can be seen, metaphorical children, who are the main characters in this canticle, are portrayed as *huexotzincah*, or dwellers of the *huexotl*, the sacred willow that are linked to God's beings (*Cantares Mexicanos* 2011, 669). It can be assumed that this *huexotl* resembled a sort of tabernacle or temple of unrevealed mysteries, safeguarded by those who were training and being initiated in faith (Orozco y Berra 1880, 3: 70; Torquemada 1975, 2: 114). These *huexotzincah* chant and weep painfully, but their tears and sorrows can be consoled by Saint Francis's relief, which drives them up to the Heavenly Father like *zaquan*, *tlauhquechol*, *xiuhquechol*, or *tzinitzcan* birds (*Cantares Mexicanos* 2011, 677–79, 681, 685).[5] Nahuatl rhetorical strategies also emerge here with the formula *ilhuicatl yyollo* ("his Heart of the Heaven") for God and his saints, which echoes the ancient expression *tepetl yyollo*, or "his Heart of the Mountain" (*Cantares Mexicanos* 2011, 670, 1206, n. 528), the aforementioned personality of Tlaloc. Furthermore, these *huexotzincah* children are imagined to carry ceremonial paper, called *toconteocuitlaamatlayehuaca*, for dispelling sadness (*Cantares Mexicanos* 2011, 679, 1207, n. 536). They are also compelled to believe that a being called 1 Rabbit (*ce to*[ch]*tzi*[n]) crumbled into the water, on the same date that Tlaloc-Tlaltecuhtli determined to initiate human life on earth and establish calendrical cycles (*Cantares Mexicanos* 2011, 690–91, 1207, n. 543; see also Boone 2016; Broda 1987, 240 and ff.). *Pilcuicatl* songs, once composed in Mexico City, were distributed in the manner of oral prototypes in

Highland New Spain's local headquarters of the Seraphic order, or *guardianías*, for annually celebrating Saint Francis on October 4th. So, friar Jerónimo de Mendieta (2012, 329) could only express admiration to remember in the 1590s how Nahua children and their families, chanting and dancing with the Franciscan habit during this festivity, had elevated "… the shouting that seemed to come from a great herd of little goats and lambs …" (*las gritas, que no parece sino una gran manada de cabritos o corderos*). Unfortunately, native inspirational sources used by Seraphic friars in their *pilcuicatl* Christian chant to Saint Francis in Mexico City are unknown. Even Ángel María Garibay (1987, 2: 116) observed that Peter of Ghent "could have sought aid in contexts from old [Nahua] mythology." On the basis of the importance of hidden messages contained in the *pilcuicatl* concerning Tlaloc essences, childlike weeping, and ceremonial aquatic environments, several details suggest a reasonable connection with those Pre-Columbian reverberating sacred *teocuicatl* of the *Codices Matritenses* that were related to Tlaloc himself, Amimitl, Atlahua, or Cihuacoatl—namely, the Chalmeca ancient rain and fertility gods—and their ritual intoning in *veintenas* like Atlcahualo (Léon-Portilla 2002, 97–99, 103–06, 111–12).

However, *pilcuicatl* collective chanting was just one of many celebrations held by the Tenochca during early Post-Conquest Saint Francis festivals. While documentary evidence is scant, complementary activities are observed in 1564, with precious featherworking at San José displayed by Martín Mixcohuatl from San Pablo, *volador* pole raising, Nahua performers attired with *tlauhquechol* feathers, as well as communal preaching under a *huexotl*, conducted by friar Bernardino de Sahagún (*Anales de Juan Bautista* 2001, 265, 267). Three years later, on 4 October 1567, it was said that a great crowd executed a superb *pipilcuicatl*. In September, friar Peter of Ghent had commanded church Indian personnel who held religious offices (*teopantlaca*) to rehearse the chant and to feed choir men for a month in order to support the performance a few weeks later. For this occasion, four prestigious dancers were summoned, of whom Tomás de Aquino Huixtopolcatl was possibly one of the most important (*Anales de Juan Bautista* 2001, 165). Huixtopolcatl had a long career in Tenochtitlan public affairs, since he had already held many positions in the local *cabildo* for San Pablo alcaldeship and regidorship (AGN, Civil, vol. 644, exp. 1, fol. 147r, 148r, 164r, 170v). Carrying bulky insignias and ritual clothing, chorus dancers' most visible feature was the *aztatzontli* accessory, cultural patrimony associated with the hamlet of Aztahuacan, a rural center subjected to San Pablo. In summary, there are too many documentary indications that should not be ignored about certain San Pablo Indian persons' engagement in the ritual design of Saint Francis celebrations in Early Colonial Mexico City. The circumstances that would have made that involvement possible are examined in the next section.

A FRAGILE, AUTO-SUSTAINING CHRISTIANITY:
SERAPHIC LED URBAN EVANGELIZATION QUESTIONED

Several groups of Franciscans in New Spain tended to be, at least until the 1550s provincialates of friars Francisco de Bustamante and Francisco de Toral, very sympathetic to hybrid spiritual behavior as long as it did not threaten the functioning of their own evangelizing project or lead to the neglect of basic Christian dogmas and proper *poliçia* (Botta 2011, 45, 49, 53–54). It is not overlooked in current scholarship that certain sixteenth-century Seraphic erudite authors were very familiar with ancient Roman law sources and political philosophy concerning *ius naturale* and *ius gentium*. Alongside some early customary law agreements (Puga 1563, fol. 53r–56v, 54r), natural and human laws both constituted cornerstones for later Medieval and Early Modern Western European territorial expansion into non-Christian kingdoms. This was exemplified by the Crown of Castile and its viceregal dominions in the Americas (Sahagún 2003, 2: 633; see also Borah 1996, 18–19, 40–41; Luque Talaván 2008, 45–46; McClure 2016, 32; Owensby 2008, 257). In this light, the more the Nahuas could cooperate with friars in dismantling idolatry, the better they were able to mount a successful collective enterprise of cultural survival and identity reformulation. As stated by Friar Alonso de Molina in his 1552 *Ordenanças* (Sell 2002, 88) or by the 1569 *Franciscan Codex* (1889, 62–64), Indigenous lords, council officers, rich artisans, and merchants were sought to be observers supervising the process.

If Martín Mixcohuatl, Juan Ycnotzin, Tomás de Aquino Huixtopolcatl, and other civil and ecclesiastic deputies living in San Pablo designed the ritual ceremonies as Saint Francis in Post-Conquest Mexico City, it was through their legal condition of *yndios reservados*, or native vassals unburdened from economic obligations (Zavala 1985, 2: 57). The newly installed archbishop Alonso de Montúfar was scandalized by this situation, noting that, in parallel to elected officers and the traditional nobility, a growing number of non-tributary individuals of Indian descent in New Spain and their co-residential kinship groups owed their privileged status to religious service in local monasteries and doctrinal chapels (ENE 1940, 7: 296–97). Indeed, a 1555–64 administrative computation of Tenochtitlan corporate neighborhoods' yearly draft rotary labors, or *coatequitl*, provides some clues about specialized tasks, internal social hierarchy, and such fiscal release in northern San Pablo. The *tlaxilacalli* of Cozotlan was fully exempted from public works and Tozcamincan seems to have been partially excused. Tozanitlan, Ometochtitlan, and Temazcaltitlan showed comparable tax ratios, but Contzinco bore the heaviest labor tributary weight (AGN, Civil, vol. 644, exp. 1, fol. 145r–173v). Rather than reflecting patterns of low-ranked stratification in the latter ward, this patterning disguised indigenous elite forms of socioeconomic dependency, as we will see. In light of these data, Cozotlan clearly appears to have enjoyed the highest level of institutional protection in the area, due to its connections with almsgiving and public institutions promoted by the Franciscans, as this *tlaxilacalli* was also adjacent to the Seraphic Clarist nuns' early sanctorum located at the Santísima Trinidad prior 1579 (*Map of Uppsala* c. 1537–50; Montoya 1984, 34).

In this regard, it is not surprising that one of the very first Seraphic Tenochca allies was Martín Coçotecatl, likely an inhabitant of San Pablo Cozotlan. He held religious stewardships in the early 1550s, holding later regidorship offices in 1554, and again in 1561 and 1564 (AGN, Civil, vol. 644, exp. 1, fol. 165v, 172r; León-Portilla 2001, 252). Supposedly, this indigenous noble, or *pilli*, might have been in charge of coordinating the scheduling of neighborhood *amantecah* for San José feather workshops. Momentary estrangements with the Franciscans might explain, nonetheless, accusations of wrongdoing by him during the *juicio de residencia* made by the Xochimilca noble Esteban de Guzmán in 1554–1557 (Rovira-Morgado 2017, 93–94).

As expected, increasing tributary immunity over certain Indian elite social strata and occupational collectives, as well as the apparent continuity of "gentile religion," did not go unnoticed by Spanish central authorities. In 1556, Mexico City Spanish *cabildo* officers did not hide their reluctance toward Tenochca's *poliçia christiana* (O'Gorman 1970, 313). Furthermore, the 66th chapter of the First Mexican Provincial Council's constitutions (1555) regulated native religious chanting and dancing, which recalled the 33rd decree of the former 1546 Royal Ordinances (O'Gorman 1940). Another campaign, centered on public burning of ancient codices, was issued on 17 March 1560 (*Codex Aubin* 1576, fol. 52r). In 1561, the *oidor* Francisco Ceinos (1958, 36) impugned local native temporal and spiritual governorship. In the same year, a royal *cedula* was issued on 19 February, when Philip II acted to regulate New Spain convents and Indian chapels in view of "the excess and superfluity [that there was] in that country …, with the difference of musical instruments and singers" (*el exceso y superfluidad en esa tierra … con la diferencia de instrumentos de música y cantores*) (*Cedulario Indiano*, 2: 48). For his part, the canon Francisco Cervantes de Salazar (2017, 59) expressed his concerns about the use of feathers and animal skins in urban indigenous dances, as well as the possibility that ancient *teocuicatl* could be disguised in Christian chanted praises. His distrust for such native aristocratic attitudes was analogous to those experienced by some censorious Dominican friars, like the deceased Domingo de Betanzos (Sempat 1998, 532–33), Diego Durán (1880, 2: 169), and likely the aforementioned Diego de Toral.

In fact, when in mid-1563 Jerónimo de Valderrama, Philip II's *visitador general* to the Mexican viceregal court, disembarked in New Spain, multi-ethnic relations were disharmonious, to say the least. It must be noted that his tributary and sociopolitical structural transformations in January 1564 marked the start of the litigation described earlier, led by a group of *maceguales* and *yndios ofiçiales* who were the injured parties (Connell 2011, 22; Rovira-Morgado 2017, 151–53; Ruiz Medrano 2010, 48). As previously noted, from March 1564 onward, offenses taken into account at the Real Audiencia included a combination of private, civil, and criminal matters, which were susceptible to having violated general ordinances and public morals for years. Focusing solely on the sixth and seventh judicial charges, commoner plaintiffs denounced the apparent continuity of subversive Pre-Columbian traditions in Christian festivals. Five witnesses provided by these complainants and their procurator Agustín Pinto testified that calendrical Aztec-era rituals of generosity and competitive feasting still sprang up at baptisms, weddings, and funerals among Tenochca residents, who lavished Indian *cabildo* bureaucrats and noble headmen with gifts and services like in ancient times (AGN, Civil, vol. 644, exp. 1, fol. 2r, 4v, 6r, 10r, 11v). One of the observers who testified declared that many such celebrations used to start "the previous day, just before the dawn comes" (*el otro día antes que amanezca*) (AGN, Civil, vol. 644, exp. 1, fol. 4v). When required to clarify whether feather headdress and panoply usage in Christian celebrations, such as Saint Francis's, reflected the custom "of dressing in the ancient ancestral ways when worshipping idols and sacrificing people" (*era costumbre de ponerse y vestirse aquellos viejos antepasados cuando iban a idolatrar y hacer sacrificio de alguna persona*), they put forward that those things were "very public and prominent" (*muy público y notorio*) everywhere in Mexico City (AGN, Civil, vol. 644, exp. 1, fol. 2r, 4v, 6r–6v, 10r, 11v).

As anticipated, council officers' and traditional aristocrats' voices did not remain silent. The administrative response was commissioned by the Spaniard Juan Caro, a procurator related consanguineously to a Franciscan friar who was his namesake and well connected to the pro-Seraphic *oidor* Alonso de Zorita as well (Mendieta 2012, 404; Ruiz Medrano 2010, 48, 55). His judicial disclaimers relied on of iusnaturalistic and iuspositivistic techniques. Ceremonial banquets for Tenochca dignitaries that adopted the social protocol of Christian events were simply qualified by him as "nothing new but permitted both in this country and in the kingdoms of Castile, where the highest-ranking are invited" (*cosa no nueva sino permitida así en estas partes y en los Reinos de Castilla, donde se convidan las personas más principales*) (AGN, Civil, vol. 644, exp. 1, fol. 16r). Moreover, ritual dancing and the exhibition of feathered insignia did not presume a return to "heathendom," because they were rigidly displayed to

> only rejoice in their celebrations with songs that glorify God and the Christian religion and all the Saints, excoriating the Demon and their ancient ceremonies with the endorsement of religious priests and the others who administer the doctrinaire Catholic faith and sacraments among all the natives of New Spain (*solamente regocijarse en sus fiestas con canciones que alaban a Dios y a la religión cristiana y a todos los santos vituperando al demonio y sus cerimonias antiguas con aprobación de religiosos sacerdotes y de los demás que administran la doctrina*

fe católica y sacramentos entre todos los naturales de la Nueva España). (AGN, Civil, vol. 644, exp. 1, fol. 16v)

As pointed out by Barry D. Sell and Susan Kellogg (1997, 336–37), this matter had been distorted by the friars in the Nahuatl language exegesis of the 1546 Ordinances in the mid-1550s, and Peter of Ghent had explained in 1558 how he monitored such indigenous dances (Torre 1974, 58–59). At this point, it should be mentioned that Franciscan-influenced Juan Caro led a simultaneous legal dispute in 1564. He also defended the Tenochca *principales* from the tributary *tlaxilacalli* of San Pablo Contzinco and their patrimonial estates in the adjacent, dependent vicinity of Atlixco against the Spaniards (AGN, Tierras, vol. 20, 2a parte, exp. 7, fol. 310r–322v). Native plaintiffs Martín Yzcuin, Miguel Xuarez, Pablo Ayogua, Pedro Yxtopolcatl, Martín Yaotl, Martín Caunen, Domingo Caçitl, Miguel Achacatl, and Juan Aquayaguacatl (*sic*) reported how the Spanish *cabildo* of Mexico City had removed neighboring boundaries. This reallocation meant that *ejidos*, or Spaniards' common lands, invaded their *pillalli*, or inherited noble possessions (AGN, Tierras, vol. 20, 2a parte, exp. 7, fol. 310r–313r; Rovira-Morgado 2010, 53–54). Suggestively, the *Anales de Juan Bautista* (2001, 221, 251) identified several civil and religious officers who handled the 1564 native *cabildo* of Tenochtitlan, since one Miguel Xuarez was *amatlacuillo*, or notary, while another, Martin Yaotl(aloc), was identified as a religious steward *mayordomo*. Furthermore, Pedro Yxtopolcatl (*sic*) might have been Tomás de Aquino Huixtopolcatl's relative. With all this, it is not surprising that Contzinco-Atlixco traditional privileges were threatened during social debates about the process of Christianization and Westernization of Tenochca society. As noted by Ethelia Ruiz Medrano and Perla Valle (1998, 231–32), as well as Susan Kellogg (2005, 39–40), mid-sixteenth-century indigenous litigation routinely included legal defense through both pictographic manuscripts with visual images, and oral testimony. Therefore, in line with Pablo Escalante Gonzalbo (2012, 101–10) as well, the neighboring parcels present in the *Beinecke Map* (c. 1565) might have portrayed Atlixco households inhabited by the traditional tenant renters (*mayequeh*); that is, by servile groups subject to payments in kind or labor supplied to Nahua noble patrons' domestic and public requirements. If Contzinco-Atlixco *principales* and bureaucrats used this pictographic source in the 1564 complaint to safeguard the hidden patrimonial workforce for periodical *coatequitl*, and so to further carry on with their tax exempt, full-time Christian lifestyle in light of Franciscan agreements, Juan Caro's arguments sounded convincing when he alleged that corporate possessions:

> ... of San Pablo located in the suburb (*tlaxilacalli*) of Atlixco Conçingo ... are and have been theirs, and they have always cultivated and sowed and collected from them the maize and the nourishment; as did my clients' parents, grandparents, and ancestors since time

immemorial to the present (... *de San Pablo del barrio de Atlixco Conçingo ... son y han sido suyas y las han siempre labrado y sembrado y cogido de ellas de maíz y sustento y lo mismo hicieron de tiempo inmemorial a esta parte los padres abuelos y antepasados de mis partes*). (AGN, Tierras, vol. 20, 2a parte, exp. 7, fol. 313r, 321r–321v)

FINAL REMARKS

The 1564 lawsuits were eventually resolved or dropped. However, their legal consequences lingered in terms of diminishing institutional reputability and spiritual self-management of the indigenous community. Despite friar Peter of Ghent's and other religious leaders' attempts to protect *amantecah* and scribes in San José de los Naturales, their devoted Indian neighborhoods and ecclesiastical civil officers, as well as Christian experimentations with the Christian faith undertaken at the end of the annual wet rainy season in honor of Saint Francis, sociocultural changes were underway that could not be ignored (Olarte 1892, 33). Both diocesan Second and Third Mexican Provincial Councils, celebrated in 1565 and 1585, respectively, saw the greatest drop in Seraphic missionary expectations (Lira González et al. 2013; Pérez Puente 2010), meaning that new evangelization strategies were required. Consistent with this, indigenous accounts from the 1580s, including devotional manuscripts, and growing printing activities under Seraphic directorship, attested by the *Anales de Juan Bautista*, the *Psalmodia Christiana* and the *Cantares Mexicanos*, may be partially viewed as a final attempt to preserve a rich religious realm about to dissipate. In other words, a desperate recorded remembrance of the pristine Christian *toltecayotl* that was once woven by both Franciscans and Tenochca people for the sake of *veintena* ritual oblivion and monthly glorification of Catholic saints and apostles. Not surprisingly, by circa 1585, "syncretic" *pilcuicatl* was recalled as an old-fashioned, outdated chant "that used to be sung there in Mexico at the feast of Saint Francisco" (Bierhorst 1985, 287). Surely that was one of the many reasons why friar Jéronimo de Mendieta tirelessly claimed to the Third Mexican Provincial Council members "that no distinction be made between Indians and Spaniards with regard to being named as Christians, since ... Indians were Christians for more than sixty years" (*que no se haga distinción entre indios y españoles con nombre de cristianos, pues ... los indios también lo son de más de sesenta años ...*) (Luque Alcaide 1992, 321).

ACKNOWLEDGMENTS

I would like to express my sincere thanks for the supportive feedback provided by Dr. Berenice Alcántara Rojas (IIH-UNAM) and by the scholars of the *Seminario Internacional Conquista, etnohistoria y arte de las Américas* (ICANH-UASLP-Le

Mans Université main directorship). Both Dr. Élodie Dupey García and Dr. Elena Mazzetto additionally afforded me priceless support and feedback. I am also indebted to the anonymous evaluator for their comments and suggestions. Finally, I extend my deep gratitude to Dr. Jon C. Lohse (Moore Archaeological Consulting; Regional Division for Coastal Environments, Inc., University of Texas at San Antonio) for his assistance in both reviewing the preliminary draft and further correcting it in English.

NOTES

1. As is well known, two autonomous community councils—or *cabildos*—were progressively institutionalized in Tenochtitlan and Tlatelolco after the Conquest. Both Indian municipalities lived side by side with the Spaniards in Mexico City, who were also represented by their own *cabildo* beginning in 1524.

2. Luis Chávez Orozco (1947, 13–170) published a substantial part of this complaint with a deficient paleography and analysis, not to mention the absence of page numbers. We have used the AGN archival source in order to avoid additional edition errors and misunderstandings of the data.

3. According to the English version of the *Primeros Memoriales* (1997, fol. 250r), *tlacateteuhme* literally meant "human sacrificial papers" and referred to children chosen for sacrifice in the festivals dedicated to the aquatic deities. Furthermore, friar Bernardino de Sahagún (2003, 1: 257) argued that *xixioti* were leprous slaves.

4. *Pilcuicatl* and *piltoncuicatl* are synonyms used in the *Cantares Mexicanos* corpus. A chant likely accompanied by dance—called *pipilcuicatl*—is reported in *Anales de Juan Bautista* (2001, 165) for 1567. Arthur J. O. Anderson (1990, 26; 1993, XXII-XXIII), Gary Tomlinson (2007, 59–60), and Berenice Alcántara Rojas (2008, 126, n. 210, 131) have noted the connections between them and established their interchangeable character.

5. Sahagún provides information about these precious birds. The *zaquan* is pictured with a "tawny plumage" (Sahagún 2003, 2: 893); the *tlauhquechol* is portrayed as "a duck … that is the prince of white herons" (Sahagún 2003, 2: 892–93); the *xiuhquechol* possesses "green feathers like grass" (Sahagún 2003, 2: 893); and the *tzinitzcan* is "the colored plumage that quetzal birds have on their throats or necks" (Sahagún 2003, 2: 892). In Late Postclassic Mexico-Tenochtitlan, most of them were housed in the aforementioned ancient royal aviaries, or *totocalco* (Sahagún 2003, 2: 668).

REFERENCES

Alcántara Rojas, Berenice. 2008. "Cantos para bailar un cristianismo reinventado: La nahuatlización del discurso de evangelización en la *Psalmodia Christiana* de Fray Bernardino de Sahagún." PhD diss., Universidad Nacional Autónoma de México.

———. 2015. "Of Feathers and Songs: Birds and Rich Plumage in Nahua *Cantares*." In *Image Take Flight: Feather Art in Mexico and Europe, 1400–1700*, edited by Alessandra Russo et al., 145–55. Trento: Hirmer.

Álvarez Icaza Longoria, María Teresa. 2010. "La secularización de doctrinas de indios en la ciudad de México." In *Los indios y las ciudades de Nueva España*, edited by Felipe Castro Gutiérrez, 303–25. Mexico City: Universidad Nacional Autónoma de México.

Anales de Juan Bautista. 2001. In *¿Cómo te confundes? ¿Acaso no somos conquistados? Anales de Juan Bautista*, edited by Luis Reyes García. Mexico City: Centro de Investigaciones y Estudios Superiores en Antropología Social, Biblioteca Lorenzo Boturini de la Insigne, Nacional Basílica de Guadalupe.

Anderson, Arthur J. O. 1990. "La Salmodia de Sahagún." *Estudios de Cultura Náhuatl* 20: 17–38.

———. 1993. *Bernardino de Sahagún's Psalmodia Christiana (Christian Psalmody)*. Salt Lake City: University of Utah Press.

Ardren, Traci. 2011. "The Divine Power of Childhood in Ancient Mesoamerica." In *(Re)Thinking the Little Ancestor: New Perspectives on the Archaeology of Infancy and Childhood*, edited by Mike Lally and Alison Moore, 133–38. Oxford: Archaeopress, British Archaeological Reports.

Arnold, Philip P. 1991. "Eating Landscape: Human Sacrifice and Sustenance in Aztec Mexico." In *Aztec Ceremonial Landscapes*, edited by Davíd Carrasco, 219–32. Boulder: University Press of Colorado.

Aveni, Anthony F. 1991. "Mapping the Ritual Landscape: Debt Payment to Tlaloc During the Month of *Atlcahualo*." In *Aztec Ceremonial Landscapes*, edited by Davíd Carrasco, 58–73. Boulder: University Press of Colorado.

Bartolomé, Fernando R. 2008. "Un conjunto de arte plumario mexicano en Manurga (Álava)." *Sancho el Sabio. Revista de Cultura e Investigación Vasca* 28: 157–69.

Bierhorst, John. 1985. *Cantares Mexicanos: Songs of the Aztecs*. Palo Alto: Stanford University Press.

Blanco Padilla, Alicia, et al. 2009. "El zoológico de Moctezuma: ¿Mito o realidad?" *Revista de la Asociación Mexicana de Médicos Veterinarios Zootecnistas en Pequeñas Especies* 20, no. 2: 28–39.

Boone, Elizabeth Hill. 2016. *Ciclos de tiempo y significado en los libros mexicanos del destino*. Mexico City: Fondo de Cultura Económica.

Borah, Woodrow. 1996 [1985]. *El Juzgado General de Indios en la Nueva España*. Mexico City: Fondo de Cultura Económica.

Botta, Sergio. 2009. "De la tierra al territorio: Límites interpretativos del naturismo y aspectos políticos del culto a Tláloc." *Estudios de Cultura Náhuatl* 40: 175–99.

———. 2011. "Una negación teológico-política en la Nueva España: reflexiones sobre la obra franciscana (siglo XVI)." In *La cruz de maíz. Política, religión, identidad en México: entre la crisis colonial y la crisis de la modernidad*, edited by María Isabel Campos and Massimo de Giuseppe, 39–61. Mexico City: Escuela Nacional de Antropología e Historia.

Broda, Johanna (de Casas). 1971. "Las fiestas aztecas de los dioses de la lluvia." In *Revista Española de Antropología Americana* 6: 245–328.

———. 1987. "The Provenience of the Offerings: Tribute and *Cosmovisión*." In *The Aztec Templo Mayor*, edited by Elizabeth Hill Boone, 211–56. Washington, DC: Dumbarton Oaks.

———. 1991. "The Sacred Landscape of Aztec Calendar Festivals: Myth, Nature, and Society." In *Aztec Ceremonial Landscapes*, edited by Davíd Carrasco, 74–120. Boulder: University Press of Colorado.

———, ed. 1997. *Graniceros: Cosmovisión y meteorología indígenas de Mesoamérica*. Mexico City: El Colegio Mexiquense, Universidad Nacional Autónoma de México.

———. 2001. "Ritos mexicas en los cerros de la Cuenca: Los sacrificios de niños." In *La montaña en el paisaje ritual*, edited by Johanna Broda et al., 173–98. Mexico City: Escuela Nacional de Antropología e Historia.

————. 2016. "Processions and Aztec State Rituals in the Landscape of the Valley of Mexico." In *Processions in the Ancient Americas*, edited by Susan Toby Evans, 179–211. Harrisburg: Pennsylvania State University.

————. 2019. "La fiesta de Atlcahualo y el paisaje ritual de la Cuenca de México." *Trace* 75: 9–45.

Burkhart, Louise M. 1989. *The Slippery Earth: Nahua-Christian Moral Dialogue in Sixteenth Century Mexico.* Tucson: University of Arizona Press.

Calnek, Edward E. 1974. "Conjunto urbano y modelo residencial en Tenochtitlan." In *Ensayos sobre el desarrollo urbano en México*, edited by Woodrow Borah et al., 11–65. Mexico City: Secretaría de Educación Pública.

————. 1976. "The Internal Structure of Tenochtitlan." In *The Valley of Mexico. Studies in Pre-Hispanic Ecology and Society*, edited by Eric R. Wolf, 287–302. Albuquerque: University of New Mexico Press.

————. 2003. "Tenochtitlan-Tlatelolco: The Natural History of a City." In *Urbanism in Mesoamerica.* Vol. I, edited by William T. Sanders et al., 149–202. Mexico City: Instituto Nacional de Antropología e Historia, Pennsylvania University Press.

Cantares Mexicanos. 2011. Edited by Miguel León-Portilla et al. 2 vols. Mexico City: Universidad Nacional Autónoma de México.

Caso, Alfonso. 1956. "Los barrios antiguos de Tenochtitlán y Tlatelolco." *Memorias de la Academia Mexicana de la Historia* 15, no. 1: 7–63.

Castañeda de la Paz, María. 2013. *Conflictos y alianzas en tiempos de cambio: Azcapotzalco, Tlacopan, Tenochtitlan y Tlatelolco.* Mexico City: Universidad Nacional Autónoma de México.

Cedulario Indiano (CI). 1945. Edited by Alfonso García Gallo. 4 vols. Madrid: Ediciones de Cultura Hispánica.

Ceinos, Francisco. 1958. "Parecer del doctor Ceynos oidor de su Majestad. México, 20 de agosto de 1561." In *Documentos para la Historia de México colonial.* Vol. V, *Sobre el modo de tributar los indios de Nueva España a Su Majestad (1561–1564)*, edited by Frances V. Scholes and Eleanor B. Adams, 35–40. Mexico City: Porrúa.

Cervantes de Salazar, Francisco. 2017. *Crónica de la Nueva España.* Barcelona: Linkgua.

Chávez Orozco, Luis. 1947. *Códice Osuna: Reproducción facsimilar de la obra del mismo título, editada en Madrid, 1878. Acompañada de 158 páginas inéditas encontradas en el Archivo General de la Nación.* Mexico City: Instituto Indigenista Interamericano.

Chimalpahin, Domingo Francisco de San Antón Muñón. 1997. *Codex Chimalpahin*, edited by Arthur O. J. Anderson and Susan Schroeder. Norman: University of Oklahoma Press.

Connell, William F. 2011. *After Moctezuma. Indigenous Politics and Self-Government in Mexico City, 1523–1730.* Norman: University of Oklahoma Press.

Cortés, Hernán. 2000. *Cartas de relación.* Madrid: Dastin.

Dehouve, Danièle. 2013. "Las funciones rituales de los altos personajes mexicas." *Estudios de Cultura Náhuatl* 45: 37–68.

Descripción del Arzobispado de México. 1897. Edited by VV.AA. Mexico City: Imprenta de J. J. Terrazas e Hijas.

Díaz Barriga, Alejandro. 2012. "La representación social de la infancia mexica a principios del siglo XVI." In *Nuevas miradas a la historia de la infancia en América Latina. Entre prácticas y representaciones*, edited by Susana Sosenski and Elena Jackson Albarrán, 23–62. Mexico City: Universidad Nacional Autónoma de México.

Díaz del Castillo, Bernal. 1999. *Historia verdadera de la conquista de la Nueva España.* Madrid: Castalia.

Dibble, Charles. 1974. "The Nahuatlization of Christianity." In *Sixteenth-Century Mexico: The Work of Sahagún*, edited by Munro S. Edmonson, 225–33. Albuquerque: University of New Mexico Press.

Durán, Diego. 1880. *Historia de las Indias de Nueva España e islas de Tierra Firme*. Mexico City: Imprenta de Ignacio Escalante.

Echeverría García, Jaime. 2015. "Los excesos del mono: salvajismo, transgresión y deshumanización en el pensamiento nahua del siglo XVI." *Journal de la Société des Américanistes* 101, no. 1–2: 137–72.

Epistolario de la Nueva España, 1505–1818 (ENE). 1940. Edited by Francisco del Paso y Troncoso. 16 vols. Mexico City: Porrúa.

Escalante Gonzalbo, Pablo. 2004. "La casa, el cuerpo y las emociones." In *Historia de la vida cotidiana en México*. Vol. I, *Mesoamérica y los ámbitos indígenas de la Nueva España*, edited by Pablo Escalante Gonzalbo, 231–60. Mexico City: El Colegio de México, Fondo de Cultura Económica.

———. 2012. "On the Margins of Mexico City: What the Beinecke Map Shows." In *Painting a Map of Sixteenth-Century Mexico City: Land, Writing, and Native Rule*, edited by Mary E. Miller and Barbara E. Mundy, 101–10. New Haven: Yale University, Beinecke Rare Book and Manuscript Library.

Espinosa Pineda, Gabriel. 1996. *El embrujo del lago: El sistema lacustre de la Cuenca de México en la cosmovisión mexica*. Mexico City: Universidad Nacional Autónoma de México.

Estrada de Gerlero, Elena Isabel, et al. 1990. "The Mass of St. Gregory." In *Mexico: Splendors of Thirty Centuries*, edited by VV. AA, 258–60. New York: Metropolitan Museum of Arts.

Evans, Susan Toby. 2005. "The Aztec Palace under the Spanish Rule: Disk Motifs in the *Mapa de México de 1550* (Uppsala Map or *Mapa de Santa Cruz*)." In *The Postclassic to Spanish-Era Transition in Mesoamerica. Archaeological Perspectives*, edited by Susan Kepecs and Rani T. Alexander, 14–33. Albuquerque: University of New Mexico Press.

Florentine Codex. 1950–82. In *Florentine Codex: General History of the Things of New Spain, Fray Bernardino de Sahagún*. Translated with notes and illustrations by Arthur J. O. Anderson and Charles E. Dibble. 13 vols. Santa Fe: The School of American Research, University of Utah Press.

Franciscan Codex. 1889. In *Nueva Colección de Documentos para la Historia de México*. Vol. II, edited by Joaquín García Icazbalceta. Mexico City: Imprenta de Francisco Díaz de León.

Garibay, Ángel M. 1987. *Historia de la literatura Nahuatl*. Vol. II. Mexico City: Porrúa.

Gibson, Charles. 1986. *Los aztecas bajo el dominio español, 1519–1810*. Mexico City: Siglo XXI.

González Aparicio, Luis. 1973. *Plano reconstructivo de la región de Tenochtitlan*. Mexico City: Instituto Nacional de Antropología e Historia.

González González, Carlos Javier. 2011. *Xipe Tótec: Guerra y regeneración del maíz en la religión mexica*. Mexico City: Fondo de Cultura Económica.

González Obregón, Luis, ed. 1902. *Procesos de indios idólatras y hechiceros*. Mexico City: Archivo General de la Nación.

Graña Behrens, Daniel. 2009. "El llorar entre los nahuas y otras culturas prehispánicas." *Estudios de Cultura Náhuatl* 40: 155–74.

Graulich, Michel. 1992. "Aztec Festivals of the Rain Gods." *Indiana* 12: 21–54.

———. 1999. *Ritos aztecas: Las fiestas de las veintenas*. Mexico City: Instituto Nacional Indigenista.

Hodge, Mary G., ed. 2008. *Place of Jade: Society and Economy in Ancient Chalco*. Mexico City: Instituto Nacional de Antropología e Historia, University of Pittsburgh.

Kellogg, Susan. 2005. *Law and the Transformation of Aztec Culture, 1500–1700*. Norman: University of Oklahoma Press.

Klein, Cecilia F. 1984. "¿Dioses de la lluvia o sacerdotes ofrendadores del fuego? Un estudio socio-político de algunas representaciones del dios Tláloc." *Estudios de Cultura Náhuatl* 17: 33–50.

León-Portilla, Miguel. 2001. "La autonomía indígena. Carta al Príncipe Felipe de los principales de México en 1554." *Estudios de Cultura Náhuatl* 32: 235–56.

———. 2002. *Cantos y crónicas del México antiguo*. Madrid: Dastin.

Lira González, Andrés, et al. 2013. *Derecho, política y sociedad en Nueva España a la luz del Tercer Concilio Provincial Mexicano (1585)*. Zamora: El Colegio de Michoacán, El Colegio de México.

López Luján, Leonardo, et al. 2012. "Un portal al inframundo: Ofrendas de animales al pie del Templo Mayor de Tenochtitlan." *Estudios de Cultura Náhuatl* 44: 9–40.

Luque Alcaide, Elisa. 1992. "El memorial inédito de Jerónimo de Mendieta al III Concilio Provincial de México. Estudio preliminar y transcripción." *Anuario de Historia de la Iglesia* 1: 305–23.

Luque Talaván, Miguel. 2008. "Perdurar en tiempos de cambio: las otras noblezas hispánicas (Canaria, Nazarita e Indiana) y su adaptación al ordenamiento socio-jurídico castellano durante la Edad Moderna." In *Poder local, poder global en América Latina*, edited by Gabriela Dalla Corte et al., 35–52. Barcelona: Publicacions i Edicions de la Universitat de Barcelona.

Mazzetto, Elena. 2014a. *Lieux de culte et parcours cérémoniels dans les fêtes des vingtaines à Mexico Tenochtitlan*. Oxford: British Archaeological Reports.

———. 2014b. "Las *ayauhcalli* en el ciclo de las veintenas del año solar. Funciones y ubicación de las casas de niebla y sus relaciones con la liturgia del maíz." *Estudios de Cultura Náhuatl* 48: 135–75.

Mazzetto, Elena, and Rossend Rovira-Morgado. 2014. "Sobre la orilla del agua: En torno a la dignidad de *atenpanecatl* y de ciertos espacios de culto a la diosa Toci en México-Tenochtitlan." *Cuicuilco* 21, no. 59: 93–120.

McClure, Julia. 2016. *The Franciscan Invention of the New World*. Cham: Palgrave Macmillan, Springer.

Mendieta, Jéronimo de. 2012. *Historia eclesiástica indiana*. Barcelona: Linkgua.

Molina, Alonso de. 1970. *Vocabulario en Lengua Castellana y Mexicana y Mexicana y Castellana*. Edited by Miguel León-Portilla. Mexico City: Porrúa.

Montoya, María Cristina. 1984. *La Iglesia de la Santísima Trinidad*. Mexico City: Universidad Nacional Autónoma de México.

Morales, Francisco. 1994. "Santoral franciscano en los barrios indios de la ciudad de México." *Estudios de Cultura Náhuatl* 24: 351–85.

Moreno de los Arcos, Roberto. 1992. "Los territorios parroquiales de la ciudad arzobispal, 1325–1980." *Cuadernos de Arquitectura Virreinal* 12: 4–18.

Motolinía, or Toribio de Benavente. 2017. *Historia de los indios de la Nueva España*. Barcelona: Linkgua.

Moyes, Halley, et al. 2009. "The Ancient Maya Drought Cult: Late Classic Cave Use in Belize." *Latin American Antiquity* 20, no. 1: 175–206.

Mundy, Barbara E. 2015. *The Death of Aztec Tenochtitlan, the Life of Mexico City*. Austin: University of Texas Press.

Muñoz, Santiago. 2006. "El 'Arte Plumario' y sus múltiples dimensiones de significación. La Misa de San Gregorio, Virreinato de la Nueva España, 1539." *Historia Crítica* 31: 121–49.

Nicholson, Henry B. 1955. "Moctezuma's Zoo." *Pacific Discovery* 8, no. 4: 3–11.

O'Gorman, Edmundo. 1940. "Una ordenanza para el gobierno de los indios, 1546." *Boletín del Archivo General de la Nación* 11, no. 2: 8–25.

———. 1970. *Guía de las actas de cabildo de la ciudad de México, siglo XVI*. Mexico City: Fondo de Cultura Económica.

Olaguíbel, Manuel. 1898. *La Ciudad de México y el Distrito Federal. Toponimia Azteca.* Toluca de Lerdo: Lambert Hermanos.

Olarte, Diego de. 1892. "Respuesta que dió la Orden de San Francisco sobre los tributos de los indios, al Memorial que se dió de parte del Visitador, el Licenciado Valderrama." In *Códice Mendieta.* Vol. I, edited by Joaquín García Icazbalceta, 31–34. Mexico City: Imprenta de Francisco Díaz de León.

Olivier, Guilhem. 1998. "Tepeyóllotl, 'Corazón de la Montaña' y 'Señor del Eco', el dios jaguar de los antiguos mexicanos." *Estudios de Cultura Náhuatl* 28: 99–141.

———. 2015. *Cacería, sacrificio y poder en Mesoamérica: Tras las huellas de Mixcóatl, "Serpiente de Nube."* Mexico City: Fondo de Cultura Económica, Universidad Nacional Autónoma de México, Centro de Estudios Mexicanos y Centroamericanos.

Olko, Justyna. 2014. *Insignia of Rank in the Nahua World. From the Fifteenth to the Seventeenth Century.* Boulder: University of Colorado Press.

Orozco y Berra, Manuel. 1880. *Historia antigua y de la Conquista de México.* 4 vols. Mexico City: Porrúa.

Osowski, Edward W. 2010. *Indigenous Miracles: Nahua Authority in Colonial Mexico.* Tucson: University of Arizona Press.

Owensby, Brian P. 2008. *Empire of Law and Indian Justice in Colonial Mexico.* Palo Alto: Stanford University Press.

Parsons, Jeffrey R. 2006. "The Aquatic Component of Aztec Subsistence: Hunters, Fishers, and Collectors in an Urbanized Society." In *Arqueología e historia del Centro de México: Homenaje a Eduardo Matos Moctezuma,* edited by Leonardo López Luján et al., 241–56. Mexico City: Instituto Nacional de Antropología e Historia.

Pérez Puente, Leticia. 2010. *El concierto imposible: Los concilios provinciales en la disputa por las parroquias indígenas (México, 1555–1647).* Mexico City: Universidad Nacional Autónoma de México.

Primeros Memoriales. 1997. Edited and translated by Thelma Sullivan. Completed and revised, with additions, by Henry B. Nicholson, Arthur J. O. Anderson, Charles E. Dibble, Eloise Quiñones Keber, and Wayne Ruwet. Norman: University of Oklahoma Press.

Puga, Vasco de. 1563 [2012]. *Provisiones, cedulas, instrucciones de Su Magestad, ordenanças de difuntos y audiencia para la nueva expedición de los negocios y administracion de justiçia y governacion de esta Nueva España, y para el buen tratamiento y conservacion y los yndios desde el año 1525 hasta este presente de 63.* Bloomington: Indiana University.

Ramírez, Jessica. 2008. "Clérigos curas o religiosos doctrineros. La renuncia de los carmelitas descalzos a la parroquia de San Sebastián, 1606." *Secuencia* 71: 15–32.

———. 2014. "Las nuevas órdenes religiosas en las tramas semántico-espaciales de la ciudad de México, siglo XVI." *Historia Mexicana* LXIII, no. 3: 1015–75.

———. 2015. *La Provincia de San Alberto de los Carmelitas Descalzos en la Nueva España. Del activismo misional al apostolado urbano, 1585–1614.* Mexico City: Instituto Nacional de Antropología e Historia.

Read, Kay A. 2005. "Productive Tears: Weeping Speech, Water, and the Underworld in the Mexica Tradition." In *Holy Tears: Weeping in the Religious Imagination,* edited by Kimberley C. Patton and John S. Hawley, 52–66. Princeton, Oxford: Princeton University Press.

Reyes García, Luis, et al. 1996. *Documentos nauas de la ciudad de México del siglo XVI.* Mexico City: Centro de Investigaciones y Estudios Superiores en Antropología Social, Archivo General de la Nación.

Rojas Rabiela, Teresa. 1985. *La cosecha del agua: pesca, caza de aves y recolección de otros productos biológicos acuáticos de la cuenca de México*. Mexico City: Secretaría de Educación Pública, Centro de Investigaciones y Estudios Superiores en Antropología Social.

Rojas Rabiela, Teresa, et al., ed. 1999. *Vidas y bienes olvidados. Testamentos indígenas novohispanos del siglo XVII*. Vol. II. Mexico City: Centro de Investigaciones y Estudios Superiores en Antropología Social, Consejo Nacional para la Cultura y las Artes, Archivo General de la Nación.

Rovira-Morgado, Rossend. 2010. "Huitznáhuac: Ritual político y administración segmentaria en el centro de la parcialidad de Teopan (México-Tenochtitlan)." *Estudios de Cultura Náhuatl* 41: 41–64.

——. 2012. "San Pablo Teopan: pervivencia y metamorfosis virreinal de una parcialidad indígena de la ciudad de México." In *De márgenes, barrios y suburbios en la ciudad de México, siglos XVI-XXI*, edited by Márcela Dávalos, 31–51. Mexico City: Instituto Nacional de Antropología e Historia.

——. 2013. "De valeroso *quauhpilli* a denostado *quauhtlahtoani* entre los tenochcas: Radiografía histórica de don Andrés de Tapia Motelchiuhtzin." *Estudios de Cultura Náhuatl* 45: 157–95.

——. 2014. "Las cuatro parcialidades de México-Tenochtitlan: Espacialidad prehispánica, construcción virreinal y prácticas judiciales en la Real Audiencia de la Nueva España (siglo XVI)." PhD diss., Universidad Autónoma de Madrid.

——. 2015. "La *Casa de Tapia*: Imaginario público y reelaboración histórica en torno a un inmueble del cuadrante de San Pablo en México-Tenochtitlan (siglo XVI)." In *Acerca de la (des)memoria y su construcción en Mesoamérica y Andes*, edited by Clementina Battcock and Sergio Botta, 282–309. Mexico City: Quivira Ediciones.

——. 2016a. "La secularización temprana de la doctrina de indios de San Pablo en la ciudad de México: claroscuros históricos en torno a un proyecto arzobispal frustrado (c.1562–1575)." In *Entre espacios: La historia latino-americana en el contexto global. Actas del XVII Congreso Internacional de AHILA, Berlín, 9–13 de septiembre de 2014*, edited by Stephan Rinde, 482–505. Berlin: AHILA, Freie Universität.

——. 2016b. "'Se ha de suplicar que los regimientos de esta ciudad sean veinticuatrías': el cabildo de Granada como propuesta institucional interétnica en la temprana república de la ciudad de México." *Estudios de Historia Novohispana* 55: 80–98.

——. 2017. *San Francisco Padremeh: El temprano cabildo indio y las cuatro parcialidades de México-Tenochtitlan (1549–1599)*. Madrid: Consejo Superior de Investigaciones Científicas.

Ruiz Medrano, Ethelia. 2010. *Mexico's Indigenous Communities: Their Lands and Histories, 1500 to 2010*. Boulder: University of Colorado Press.

Ruiz Medrano, Ethelia, and Perla Valle. 1998. "Los colores de la justicia: códices jurídicos del siglo XVI en la Biblioteca Nacional de Francia." *Journal de la Societé des Américanistes* 84, no. 2: 228–35.

Sahagún, Bernardino de. 2003. *Historia general de las cosas de la Nueva España*. Edited by Juan Carlos Temprano. Madrid: Dastin.

Seler, Eduard. 1902–23. *Gesammelte Abhandlungen zur Amerikanischen Sprach-und Alterthumskunde*. Berlin: A. Asher.

Sell, Barry D. 2002. *Nahua Confraternities in Early Colonial Mexico: The 1552 Nahuatl Ordinances of Fray Alonso de Molina, OFM*. Berkeley: Academy of American Franciscan History.

Sell, Barry D., and Susan Kellogg. 1997. "We Want to Give Them Laws: Royal Ordinances in a Mid-Sixteenth Century Nahuatl Text." *Estudios de Cultura Náhuatl* 27: 325–67.

Sempat, Carlos. 1998. "Hacia la *Sublimis Deus*: Las discordias entre los dominicos indianos y el enfrentamiento entre el padre Testera y el padre Betanzos." *Historia Mexicana* XLVIII, no. 3: 465–536.

Tezozomoc, Hernando de Alvarado. 2001. *Crónica mexicana*. Madrid: Dastin.

————.1998. *Crónica mexicáyotl*. Mexico City: Universidad Nacional Autónoma de México.

Tomlinson, Gary. 2007. *The Singing of the New World. Indigenous Voices in the Era of European Contact*. Cambridge: Cambridge University Press.

Torquemada, Juan. 1975. *Monarquía Indiana*, Edited by VV. AA. Mexico City: Universidad Nacional Autónoma de México-Instituto de Investigaciones Históricas.

Torre, Ernesto de la. 1974. "Fray Pedro de Gante. Maestro y civilizador de América." *Estudios de Historia Novohispana* 5: 9–77.

Truitt, Jonathan G. 2003. "Franciscan Techniques of Religious Conversion and the Preservation of the Indigenous Religion in the Valley of Mexico, 1519–1650." MA diss., Minnesota State University.

————. 2009. "Nahuas and Catholicism in Mexico Tenochtitlan: Religious Faith and Practice and La Capilla de San Josef de los Naturales, 1523–1700." PhD diss., Tulane University.

————. 2010. "Adopted Pedagogies: Nahua Incorporation of European Music and Theater in Colonial Mexico City." *The Americas* 66, no. 3: 311–30.

————. 2018. *Sustaining the Divine in Mexico Tenochtitlan: Nahuas and Catholicism, 1524–1700*. Norman: University of Oklahoma Press.

Valero de García, Ana Rita. 1991. *Solares y conquistadores. Orígenes de la propiedad en la Ciudad de México*. Mexico City: Instituto Nacional de Antropología e Historia.

————. 2004. *Los códices de Ixhuatepec. Un testimonio pictográfico de dos siglos de conflicto agrario*. Mexico City: Centro de Investigaciones y Estudios Superiores en Antropología Social, Colegio de San Ignacio de Loyola/Vizcaínas.

Van Zantwijk, Rudolph. 1963. "Principios organizadores de los mexicas, una introducción al estudio del sistema interno del régimen azteca." *Estudios de Cultura Náhuatl* 4: 187–222.

————. 1966. "Los seis barrios sirvientes de Huitzilopochtli." *Estudios de Cultura Náhuatl* 6: 177–85.

————. 1985. *The Aztec Arrangement: The Social History of Pre-Spanish Mexico*. Norman: University of Oklahoma Press.

————. 1994. "Factional Divisions Within the Aztec (Colhua) Royal House." In *Factional Competition and Political Development in the New World*, edited by Elizabeth E. Brumfiel and John W. Foxs, 103–10. Cambridge: Cambridge University Press.

Vauzelle, Loïc. 2017. "Los dioses mexicas y los elementos naturales en sus atuendos: unos materiales polisémicos." *Trace* 71: 76–110.

Villanueva García, Gerardo, and Jimena Manrique-Eternod. 2007. "Fauna y flora de la cuenca de México, historia referida." In *Ciudad excavada: veinte años de arqueología de salvamento en la ciudad de México y su área metropolitana*, edited by Luis Alberto López Wario, 23–52. Mexico City: Instituto Nacional de Antropología e Historia.

Walker, William H. 2001. "Ritual Technology in an Extranatural World." In *Anthropological Perspectives on Technology*, edited by Michael Brian Schiffer, 87–106. Albuquerque: University of New Mexico Press.

Zavala, Silvio. 1985. *El servicio personal de los indios en la Nueva España. 1550–1575*. Vol. 2. Mexico City: El Colegio de México.

Zumárraga, Juan de. 1870. "Carta á su magestad del electo Obispo de México, D. Juan de Zumárraga. México, 27 de agosto de 1532." In *Colección de documentos inéditos relativos al descubrimiento, conquista y colonización de las antiguas posesiones españoles en América y Oceanía. Tomo XIII*, edited by VV.AA., 104–79. Madrid: Imprenta de José María Pérez.

Epilogue

DANIÈLE DEHOUVE

The annual solar cycle of the *veintenas*, composed of eighteen "months" of twenty days, to which five days were added, was an elaborate ritual construction. Each of the "months" was designated by one or more names, included a succession of complex rites, and mobilized a number of social groups in the sweeping ritual landscape of the Valley of Mexico. As the editors of this volume pointed out in the section of the introduction entitled "150 years of research on the *veintenas*," this cycle has been a controversial topic debated by historians of religion and anthropologists since the late nineteenth century, spawning both academic disputes and significant advances. Therefore, it is worth reassessing this history to offer a general panorama of its current status, because any researcher who approaches the subject should be aware of its extensive bibliography and the principal theoretical underpinnings.

On the other hand, the fact that 150 years of research has not been sufficient to elucidate the principles underlying the foundations of the *veintenas* shows we should not expect a simple explanation. Therefore, we cannot assume this volume will definitively resolve all the questions concerning this ritual cycle. So, what can we realistically expect from it? The very act of having brought together a diverse group of scholars and their contributions on the *veintenas* is of special interest, for it highlights what subjects are currently given priority and what questions are raised as a result of progress made in the disciplines of anthropology and ethnohistory. In other words, it should come as no surprise that certain lines of thought or inquiry arise from reading this volume. Stemming from this exercise, I have identified three of them.

The semantics of ritual acts. In the first place, the interest on the part of several contributors in ritual acts performed during the annual cycle drew my attention, particularly for their desire to understand the rituals from an *emic* perspective. We know this neologism was coined by linguist Kenneth L. Pike (1954–60), who contrasted *phonemics*, a subjective way of understanding the sounds in languages, with *phonetics*, which refers to the objective study of these sounds. Since that time, anthropologists have called their approach *emic* when they attempt to understand how diverse people thought about, categorized, and imagined the world. As Loïc Vauzelle has pointed out, this focus is congruent with that of historians who study their subject from within, in particular the branch of historical research known as the "history of representations" (Vauzelle 2018, 40–41). Given the importance of this type of study worldwide, unsurprisingly most of the contributors to this volume make an effort to shed light on the significance of the rites for their participants. Some examine flaying (Mazzetto), others the production and use of amaranth figurines (Schwaller), and the relationship between dance and sacrifice (Danilović): what does it mean to sacrifice, flay, and wear the skin of a god-impersonator, known as *ixiptla* in Nahuatl? Why make effigies with amaranth dough, ritually killing them and eating them? Why do the sacrificed victims die dancing? Why do the priests don the victims' skin or hold the decapitated heads by the hair and what is the significance of their dance? Another subject that has received little attention to date relates to conceptions and practices of the priesthood (Peperstraete): what were the different types of priests and what ritual practices were they responsible for? Others (Rodríguez, Cortiña, and Valiñas) question linguistic categories and analyze the terms used in Nahuatl to describe ritual acts.

The actors, objects, actions, and terms to name them: herein lies an entire semantics that we must parse to understand the constitution of the *veintena* ritual system. But, this is particularly difficult because these acts and objects are polysemous, in other words, their meanings differ depending on the context. Many researchers have demonstrated that a single ritual act can have numerous meanings. Some examples are Michel Graulich (2005) and Claude-François Baudez (2012) on bloodletting, Yólotl González Torres (1985) on the use of the skin of flayed individuals, Danièle Dehouve (2010) on the animals sacrificed, and Vauzelle (2018) on the materials utilized to make the gods' ornaments.

The structural principles of the rituals. One contributor, Johannes Neurath, stands out for his enumeration of the particular features of the ritual space. He applies various general principles to certain rituals of the contemporary Huichol and the Ochpaniztli *veintena*: the ritual is a transformer of ontology because its participants change their identity and become true ancestors or gods; the ritual expresses and condenses contradictory social relations; it involves ambiguous divinities and contradictory actions (such as alliance and depredation), so the key concept of ritual analysis is, in his opinion, antagonistic identification. Because Neurath looks for the general properties of ritual, his perspectives clearly stand apart from the semantic concerns discussed above.

Myths and rites. The third approach chosen by the contributors is to probe the relationship of the rites to myths: the rituals would thus be re-enactments of mythical episodes (Olivier, Dupey García). The idea is not new and many scholars who have studied the *veintenas* have helped to establish connections between myths and rites. In this regard, we should mention the re-creation of the myth of the birth of Huitzilopochtli during the festival of Panquetzaliztli, initially highlighted by Eduard Seler (Seler and Seler-Sachs 1902–23). Later, Karl Nowotny (1968) established a list of correspondences between myths and rites. Some scholars have demonstrated other ties: for instance, Johanna Broda (1971, 275) between the myth of Quetzalxoch—which relates the transference of power from the Toltecs to the Aztecs—and the sacrifice of children in Atlcahualo, and Pedro Carrasco (1979, 54) between the sacrifice of dogs to the Sun and Atemoztli.

Of course, Graulich (in his diverse works) is known for having particularly explored the relationship between myths and rites. Following in his footsteps, researchers have continued to make new connections, such as Guilhem Olivier (2003, 386–88) for whom the celebration of Toxcatl speaks of the origin of music and Élodie Dupey García (2013) who discovers the myth of the creation of flowers in the Tlacaxipehualiztli, Tozoztontli, and Ochpaniztli *veintenas*. The contributions of Olivier and Dupey García in this volume are presented as a continuation of this focus, which although classic, has not yet exhausted its interpretational possibilities.

Finally, in this volume we find two comparisons with the Maya world (Chinchilla Mazariegos, Vail) and two chapters on the evolution of the *veintenas* after the conquest (Botta, Rovira-Morgado). The extremely rich totality makes it possible to trace paths and to formulate premises. Indeed, we should not forget we have yet to discover the fundamental principles that have permitted the overall construction of the cycle of the *veintenas* as a whole and that still elude us. Below I will propose two hypotheses that came to my mind when I read this volume, which could become perspectives for future research. However, in order to consolidate these hypotheses, it will be necessary to base them on *emic* conceptions that will have to be revealed in rituals and myths.

BIRTH AND CREATION

It is interesting to observe how the birth of the gods and cyclic renovation are the common thread in a number of contributions. In the first place, the two Mayanists (Chinchilla Mazariegos, Vail) repeatedly refer to birth (that of the Maize God, for the former) and to renovation (of temples, for the latter). The benefits of comparison are evident here, because their chapters offer a new way of looking at the data for Central Mexico, as seen below.

Similarly, Olivier chooses to address the subject of the birth of the gods: in Ochpaniztli (for the birth of the Maize God), Teotl Eco (for the birth of all the gods), Quecholli and Panquetzaliztli (for the generation and birth of Huitzilopochtli). In turn, Dupey García speaks of the birth of Quetzalcoatl, a god involved in the origin of the other deities and the transition from one cosmic era to the next. Finally, various contributors have developed their reflections on ritual acts that might have been conceived of, on an *emic* level, as a birth or a ritual manipulation that enacts a birth. This is the case of the creation of amaranth effigies (Olivier, Schwaller) and of the rituals involving skin-wearing (Mazzetto, Danilović). Can the production of the effigy be conceived as the birth of the god? Can conceiving the act of dressing in a victim's skin be regarded as the god's rebirth?

Let's consider first the amaranth effigies discussed in this volume by Olivier and John Schwaller, and the subject of detailed scholarship (Bassett 2015; Mazzetto 2015, 2017; Reyes Equiguas 2005). These studies present the list of festivals when figures of amaranth dough were made (Mazzetto 2015, 410; Reyes Equiguas 2005, 109–44) as follows: the effigy of Huitzilopochtli in Toxcatl and of Tezcatlipoca and Tlacahuepan Cuexcotzin in Panquetzaliztli; of mountains and rain gods in Tepeilhuitl and Atemoztli; of Chicomecoatl in Huey Tozoztli; of *xocotl* in the shape of a bird, which perhaps represented Otontecuhtli, in Xocotl Huetzi, and of Xiuhtecuhtli in Izcalli. In addition to these effigies related to the *veintenas*, we might mention the production of the dough figurine of the goddess Tzapotlatena by the vendors of *oxitl* (an unguent made of turpentine), and that of Ome Acatl (2-Reed) during the renewal of the New Fire every fifty-two years.

Sixteenth-century sources are probably incomplete regarding the occasions when amaranth effigies were made and are not particularly detailed concerning their use in rituals. We have a fair understanding of the stages in their manufacture (studied here by Schwaller, and by Mazzetto 2017) and we know they were made to be destroyed. However, the significance of these two successive stages—their manufacture and then their destruction—is not well understood. As Olivier explains (this volume), the making of the dough figurine of Huitzilopochtli was conceived as the birth of the divinity it represented and personified. The use of the Nahuatl term *tlacati* (to be born) clearly shows the manufacture of the figurine was seen as a birth; the very god "had been born" at the end of the festival. But then, why did the ritual plan to sacrifice, dismember, and consume the effigy before the start of the following month? Olivier (this volume) points out the paradox for the celebration of Panquetzaliztli: "Instead of emphasizing the birth of the god, [the] sources insist on the ritual death of Huitzilopochtli through … a statue of the god made of amaranth dough and seeds."

I think that Chinchilla Mazariegos (this volume) offers an interpretation that can be amply applied to the sacrifices of gods in the *veintenas*. Concerning the sacrifice of the human impersonator of Tezcatlipoca in Toxcatl, he writes: "... the sacrifice at Tlacochcalco was immediately followed by the selection of a new impersonator that would embody Tezcatlipoca during the following year (Sahagún 1950–82, bk 2: 66). Arguably, this stage of the ritual amounted to a rebirth of the god ... " The death and rebirth of Tezcatlipoca, enacted in this way, would constitute a ritual act comparable to the "Maize God's death and rebirth, known from artistic representations in Classic Maya ceramics."

To more broadly apply this reasoning, first we should bear in mind what we know about the god impersonators called *ixiptla*. As demonstrated by various scholars (Bassett 2015; Dehouve 2016; Hvidtfeldt 1958; López Luján and Chávez Balderas 2010), the gods were embodied in different forms, from human impersonators—priests or sacrificial victims—to stone or wood effigies and edible amaranth figures. In the case of Toxcatl, the human impersonator of Tezcatlipoca was chosen at the end of the festival; after having played the role of the god for a year, he was wed and sacrificed. So, the ritual was cyclic and every year a new *ixiptla* took the place of the impersonator who had just been sacrificed. Chinchilla's explanation in terms of annual rebirth is, therefore, compelling.

Turning to the *ixiptla* of Huitzilopochtli in the "month" of Panquetzaliztli, at the end of the festival a young man called Yopoch, attended by a group of youths, was chosen to be dedicated for a year to the veneration of Huitzilopochtli; it would be his responsibility to carry out severe, ongoing penitence until the next Panquetzaliztli (Sahagún 1950–82, bk 3: 1–5). At that time, a dough figurine representing Huitzilopochtli was made to be bathed, sacrificed, dismembered and ceremoniously divided amongst Motecuhzoma, the district leaders, and Yopoch's assistants, who were called "the eaters of the gods" (*teoquaque*). After taking the statue of the god to the temple summit, the group of young men was freed from their obligations and those who were to take their place were designated. The cyclic ritual of Panquetzaliztli, with an annual impersonator (Yopoch, flanked by various assistants) chosen after the festival, followed the same pattern as that of Toxcatl; the difference was that, in Toxcatl, the human *ixiptla* was sacrificed in person. Expanding on Chinchilla's analysis of Toxcatl, I would suggest that the two cycles, Toxcatl and Panquetzaliztli, were seen as an annual renewal of the god.

Let us now focus on applying the hypothesis of the god's rebirth to other rituals with impersonators. The first point to be considered is the dance with the victims' flayed skin—performed during the celebrations of Tlacaxipehualiztli, Tecuilhuitontli, Ochpaniztli, and Izcalli—which Danilović analyzes in this volume. In Tlacaxipehualiztli, the fresh skin of the victims flayed during this *veintena* was worn by warriors or their representatives. In Tecuilhuitontli, priests sacrificed the *ixiptla* of Xochipilli and donned his skin. In Ochpaniztli, the impersonators of

Atlatonan, Chicomecoatl, and Toci were sacrificed and flayed; a number of priests dressed in their skin. Finally, in Izcalli, two women were flayed in the upper part of the temple of Cuauhtitlan, a town near Tenochtitlan, and their skin was worn during a dance.

Danilović is interested in the skin-wearing dance to show the overlap between dance and sacrifice. For her part, Bassett (2015, 181) reflected on the role of skin in the embodiment of the god (*teotl*): "when a ritual actor donned the flayed skin of a sacrificial victim or the attire of a *teotl*, that person underwent a major ontological transformation from human to deity embodiment." Of course, it should be added that the act of wearing skin was a highly polysemous ritual expression (González Torres 1985, 274–75, cited by Mazzetto, this volume).

Without going into such a complex analysis, here the key point seems to be that transferring a victim's skin to the body of a warrior or priest gave new life to it and could be considered a rebirth and a renewal of the god. In fact, a first *ixiptla* (the sacrificial victim) was replaced by a second one (the skin's wearer), who acted in accord with the nature of the god represented, generally in mock combats. In the case of Ochpaniztli, the skin of the first sacrificed *ixiptla* of the goddess Toci was worn by a priest, who in turn was transformed into the active *ixiptla* of Toci; then, on the second-to-last day of the festival, the skin was removed and placed onto a frame of wood at Tocititlan (Sahagún 1950–82, bk 2: 120–25), where it was to remain on display for the rest of the year until the celebration of the next festival. Thus, transferring the skin from one support to another might have been considered an act of renovation that took place in accord with an annual cycle, in the same way as the manipulation of the dough figurines described above.

Olivier (this volume) analyzes other ritual acts, such as births. In his purview, the *veintena* of Teotl Eco, whose name means "The God Arrives" or "The Gods Arrive," represents the birth of the gods or the arrival of the gods on earth. His arguments are linguistic (it was said "they descend," *temo*, a verb that also means "to be born") and mythological (because the festival was celebrated after that of Ochpaniztli, when Toci-Teteo Innan, the Mother of the Gods, was impregnated). Olivier concludes that, "This arrival of the gods can be equated to a birth." The same author, following Graulich, analyzes some of the rituals of Ochpaniztli, such as the representation of the conception and then the birth of the Maize God. He also sees in Quecholli the celebration of the generation of Huitzilopochtli and, in the next festival, Panquetzaliztli, that of his birth. Therefore, he suggests that the re-enactment of the birth of a god is expressed in three different festivals by the representation of his conception followed by his birth.

If these observations are correct, the birth of a god could be ritually represented in different ways: by sacrificing a human *ixiptla* or a dough figurine included in a cycle that encompassed the annual succession of impersonators; by flaying a human *ixiptla* followed by the transfer of the skin to successive human or wood supports, also included in an annual cycle; by the complex staging of the arrival of all the gods, or by the conception followed by the birth of some of them. I believe there were different ways of representing birth, which made it possible to repeat the same idea in different ways and on many occasions.

Maurice Godelier (2013, 420–26) has demonstrated that, given that the biological processes of conception and birth were not directly accessible for factual observation, societies had to develop interpretations and explanations that were imaginary to explain the process of making a child. Godelier distinguishes two of them in Oceania. On the one hand, among the Baruyas, descent is carried out by means of two agents: men (through sperm) and the Sun that gives the fetus human form. This representation is coherent with the patrilineal principle that structures their social relations. On the other hand, in the Trobriand Islands, where descent is matrilineal, the child is the product of an ancestor of the mother's clan who comes back to life in the body of a woman of her clan when mixing with her menstrual blood. These examples show how representations of conception and birth are cultural and social. Therefore, it is important to explore how the Mesoamerican imaginary represented these processes, because it would be an error to take it for granted. Myths and rites provide multiple versions, associated with notions of creation and renovation. A recent article by Patrick Johansson (2017) offers a timely discussion of this matter.

Considering only the few elements from the rituals of the *veintenas*, we see birth was represented in various ways.

- The model of "conception-birth" was expressed through the re-enactment of myths personified by the progenitors and their descendants. In this category, we find the union of Huitzilopochtli's parents in Quecholli, followed by the birth of their offspring in Panquetzaliztli, and the fertilization of the Earth Goddess Toci by the Mexica patron god in Ochpaniztli, from whom Cinteotl-Itztlacoliuhqui, the god of maize and frost, was born (according to Olivier's interpretation, this volume).
- The "descent-birth" model was expressed in the descent-arrival of the gods in Teotl Eco (according to Olivier's interpretation, this volume). Birth was thus seen as a descent.
- The cyclic model of renewal was expressed through the manipulation of impersonators or *ixiptla* in the form of dough figurines or through the act of wearing skin. Unlike the cases described earlier, this model was not based on a specific moment in the process of making the child, but rather in the death-rebirth cycle.
- Finally, another cyclic model was expressed in the process of making the dough figurine. In fact, shaping the figurine was conceived of as creating a living being based on its bones. We know (Schwaller, this volume; Mazzetto

2017) that dough figurines were made on wood frames and then were covered with a dough made of amaranth and agave syrup. Reyes Equiguas (2005, 112–13) demonstrated how this process reproduced the mythical sequence of the birth of Huitzilopochtli, who was born "without flesh, only with bones" ("Historia de los mexicanos por sus pinturas" 1965, 23–24). This model, which can be described as mythical, is also found in diverse narratives of the creation of humanity, according to which Quetzalcoatl modeled the first human body from one or more bones (Brotherston 1994). Therefore, it is also based on the death-rebirth cycle.

These observations show that it would be worth distinguishing with greater precision between notions of birth, rebirth, creation, and renewal. Be that as it may, one can raise the question of why rituals repeatedly represented them or referred to them. For a greater understanding, it would probably be necessary to trace homologies between the human biological cycle and other natural cycles. The most important of these natural cycles is the course of the Sun, born at dawn, reaching its zenith to then wane and die at sunset. The maize cycle also includes the birth of the ear of corn, its destruction and its rebirth in the following generation. Therefore, it should come as no surprise that the gods themselves follow a death-renewal cycle designed to reflect these natural cycles.

In the section of the *Florentine Codex* devoted to ritual speech and discourse (Sahagún 1950–82, bk 6), a series of verbs in Nahuatl expresses the emergence of a new being at the beginning of its development cycle. The list includes: childbirth, hatching of a bird, flower blossoming, sunrise, lighting of fire, lighting of a torch, and jewel drilling (for example, Sahagún 1950–82, bk 6: 17, 32). We find human birth (childbirth), animal birth (hatching of a bird), plant birth (flower blossoming), and dawn conceived as an image of these births (sunrise). It also includes the drilling of new fire, an act of prime importance in rituals of foundation and cyclic renewal (*cf.* Dehouve 2018) and its consequences: lighting of fire, lighting of a torch. Finally, drilling precious stone is included on this list for two reasons. The drilling operation carried out through rotating a cane to produce friction is the same when it comes to lighting a fire and to perforate a stone to make a jewel. This series of births is valuable for taking into account Mesoamerican representations of birth. However, of even greater interest is the context in which it was used. In fact, it served to describe the enthronement of a new sovereign (Sahagún 1950–82, bk 6: 17) and the purification of guilty individuals (Sahagún 1950–82, bk 6: 32). The notion of birth thus made it possible to represent a successful activity, as well as the cyclic purification of this activity, since to be young is to be pure.

If these hypotheses are correct, it could mean that the processes of birth and renewal were not dispersed elements in the construction of the cycle of the *veintenas*, but rather fundamental aspects providing a key to reading and ordering that should be examined systematically in the future, which would be consistent with the demonstration of Gabrielle Vail (this volume), for whom renovation and renewal were at the core of Maya *veintena* celebrations.

LAYERS OF MEANING AND MULTITEMPORALITY

The following lines were inspired principally by reading the chapter by Dupey García (this volume). They address the fact that each of the *veintenas* contains a plurality of meanings—which might seem obvious—but above all a plurality of *types* of meanings—which gives rise to reflection. To show how these meanings could belong to different categories, I will briefly review the example of the festival of Etzalcualiztli.

- The agricultural rite. Following Broda, the celebration has been regarded as a group of farming rites by various scholars. According to Broda (2004, 45–47), Etzalcualiztli occurred at the start of the rainy season. It marked the end of the irrigation cycle and the start of the rainy cycle in Tenochtitlan, as shown by the combined use of the food of *etzalli* (maize with boiled beans) from the irrigation cycle and the green *milpas* (cornfields) that began to grow in newly sowed fields. I share the idea that Etzalcualiztli had a function related to the agricultural cycle (Dehouve 2008, 29–30). Based on a comparison with the festival celebrated by the Tlapanecs of Guerrero at the end of May and early June, I proposed that this celebration marked the transition between two cycles of corn agriculture. The maize boiled and combined with beans consumed by the Tlapanecs came from the earlier harvest, whereas the planting of new maize had just taken place.
- The myth of maize stolen at Tonacatepetl. According to Alfredo López Austin and Leonardo López Luján (2004), various episodes of Etzalcualiztli enact the myth described in the *Leyenda de los Soles*, according to which the Tlaloque gods stole maize of four colors and other foodstuffs from the "Mountain of Our Sustenance," Tonacatepetl, where they were stored ("Leyenda de los Soles" 2002, 181).
- The myth of the end of the Sun of Water. We know that, for the Mexica, prior to their era known as Nahui Ollin (Sun of Movement), there were four successive eras known as the "Four Suns" (Suns of Earth, Wind, Fire, and Water) that ended in cataclysms. The goddess Chalchiuhtlicue presided over the Sun of Water, destroyed by a cataclysmic flood, a myth that the festival of Etzalcualiztli would have commemorated (Dupey García, this volume). This interpretation is particularly credible, for it does not arise solely from scholarly analysis, but is also mentioned in a sixteenth-century

document: "They made the festival to this god [Tlaloc] in memory of when the world was destroyed by water" (*Códice Vaticano A*, 1996, fol. 45r, cited by Dupey García, this volume).

I am aware that these interpretations are not unanimously accepted by researchers. The first of them (Broda) differs from that of Graulich, who, based on his theory of the time lag between the duration of the vague Mexica year and the tropical year, thinks that Etzalcualiztli took place in the dry season. As for the second interpretation (López Austin and López Luján), Graulich believes the myth of stealing maize would have been commemorated during another *veintena*, Ochpaniztli (Mazzetto 2015, 108). However, what interests me here is to point out that these interpretations allude to different temporalities: an agricultural ritual celebrated to promote corn harvests in the future, a myth of the origin of maize, and the cosmological myth of the collapse of an earlier era. Independently of the specific debates that have arisen, I am profoundly convinced that a *veintena* articulated various types of meanings of a ritual and mythical character.

What are the methodological tools that can help us understand this situation? In my opinion, these are the hermeneutical levels or layers of meaning. Hermeneutics is a branch of the theory of discourse that seeks the interpretation and analysis of underlying layers of meaning that exceed the literal and obvious signification. Its tradition, which dates back to the exegesis of sacred texts in the religions of the Bible, was introduced in semiotics by Umberto Eco (1962). This author determined five levels of interpretation on which the Exodus episode could be read: the literal level, the moral level, the allegorical level, the mystical level, and the analogical level (Angenot 2011, 268). The method can be extended to the analysis of images (*ibid.*), art expressions, and ritual. To apply it to the case of Etzalcualiztli, we will say that the rite, the origin of maize myth, and the myth of the collapse of an earlier era constitute three layers of meaning. Of course, the list of hermeneutical levels is not closed and further research can reveal others.

In this case the layers of meaning also represent different temporalities. The first is the temporality of the agricultural ritual, which traces a connection between the ceremonies of the festival and the growth of maize in the following months; the second is the myth of the origin of maize; the third layer of meaning also refers to mythical time, but this has a cosmic dimension absent in the preceding layer. It seems to me that until now scholars have not considered that the simultaneous presence of several of these temporalities within the same *veintena* might be an intrinsic characteristic of the annual ritual cycle.

This preamble brings me to the hypotheses presented by Dupey García (this volume). Some experts who preceded her sought to associate a *veintena* with a myth in an "absolute correspondence between the festival sequence and the chronology of the mythical episodes," a correspondence that Dupey García questions, following in the footsteps of Alfredo López Austin. Indeed, this scholar has stressed the dynamic relationship between myths and rituals and posited that the latter cannot be seen as mere and uninterrupted re-enactments of the former, but instead as pieces with proper functions and structures that sometimes recall the mythology for their actions, protagonists, and metaphorical meanings (López Austin 1998: 110–19; López Austin and López Luján 2004, cited by Dupey García, this volume). In turn, Dupey García's analysis of the role of Quetzalcoatl in the celebration of Huey Tecuilhuitl leads her to postulate that "a same mythical story could be evoked in diverse ritual contexts, which emphasized different aspects of a myth. Likewise, all the parts of a mythical narrative were not necessarily performed together in a particular festival; rather they may appear in different moments of the ritual sequence" (Dupey García, this volume). These observations pave the way for new paths of research on the relationship between myths and rites. In the first place, they invite us to explore the notion of myth to clarify what is understood by "myth," "mythical story," and "mythical motif." Furthermore, it has often been thought that myths refer to a temporality referred to as "mythical time." The preceding lines show that this expression is not specific enough, because myths refer to different cosmic eras that can overlap and constitute multiple layers of meaning.

In conclusion, after 150 years of research, whose principal lines of inquiry have been cited by the editors of this book, its contributors offer new analyses, above all on the meanings of a series of ritual acts. In this way, they show that we must not give up our efforts to elucidate the principles that govern the construction of the *veintena* cycle by Mesoamerican societies and to achieve this, to seek new lines of exploration that can be channeled in a true research program.

REFERENCES

Angenot, Valérie. 2011. "A Method for Ancient Egyptian Hermeneutics." In *Methodik und Didaktik in der Ägyptologie*, edited by Alexandra Verbovsek, Burkhard Backes, and Catherine Jones, 255–86. München: Wilhelm Fink Verlag.

Bassett, Molly H. 2015. *The Fate of Earthly Things: Aztec Gods and God-Bodies*. Austin: University of Texas Press.

Baudez, Claude-François. 2012. *La douleur rédemptrice. L'autosacrifice précolombien*. Paris: Riveneuve Éditions.

Broda, Johanna (de Casas). 1971. "Las fiestas aztecas de los dioses de la lluvia: una reconstrucción según las fuentes del siglo XVI." *Revista Española de Antropología Americana* 6: 245–327.

———. 2004. "Ciclos agrícolas en la cosmovisión prehispánica: el ritual mexica." In *Historia y vida ceremonial en las comunidades mesoamericanas: los ritos agrícolas*, edited by Johanna Broda and Catherine Good Eshelman, 35–60. Mexico City: Instituto Nacional de Antropología e Historia, Universidad Nacional Autónoma de México.

Brotherston, Gordon. 1994. "Huesos de muerte, huesos de vida: la compleja figura de Mictlante-cuhtli." *Cuicuilco, nueva época* 1, no. 1: 85–98.

Carrasco, Pedro. 1979. "Las fiestas de los meses mexicanos." In *Mesoamérica. Homenaje al doctor Paul Kirchhoff*, edited by Dahlgren Barbro, 52–60. Mexico City: Instituto Nacional de Antropología e Historia.

Códice Vaticano A 3738. 1996. Edited by Ferdinand Anders and Maarten Jansen. Graz, Mexico City: ADEVA, Fondo de Cultura Económica.

Dehouve, Danièle. 2008. "El venado, el maíz y el sacrificado." *Diario de campo. Cuadernos de Etnología* 4: 1–39.

———. 2010. "La polisemia del sacrificio tlapaneco." In *El sacrificio humano en la tradición religiosa mesoamericana*, edited by Leonardo López Luján and Guilhem Olivier, 499–518. Mexico City: Instituto Nacional de Antropología e Historia, Universidad Nacional Autónoma de México.

———. 2016. "El papel de la vestimenta en los rituales mexicas de 'personificación'." *Nuevo Mundo Mundos Nuevos*. https://journals.openedition.org/nuevomundo/69305?lang=en

———. 2018. "The New Fire and Corporal Penance. Comparative Perspectives Between the Tlap-anecs and the Aztecs." In *Smoke, Flames, and the Human Body in Mesoamerican Ritual Practice*, edited by Vera Tiesler and Andrew Scherer, 411–34. Washington, DC: Dumbarton Oaks.

Dupey García, Élodie. 2013. "De pieles hediondas y perfumes florales. La reactualización del mito de creación de las flores en las fiestas de las veintenas de los antiguos nahuas." *Estudios de Cultura Náhuatl* 45: 7–36.

Eco, Umberto. 1962. *Opera aperta. Forma e indeterminazione nelle poetiche contemporanee*. Milan: Bom-piani, Pórtico.

Godelier, Maurice. 2013. "L'impossible est possible. Réflexions sur les racines et les formes du croire et des croyances." In *D'une anthropologie du chamanisme vers une anthropologie du croire. Hommage à l'œuvre de Roberte Hamayon*, edited by Katia Buffetrille, Jean-Luc Lambert, Nathalie Luca, and Anne de Sales, 411–36. Paris: Centre d'Études Mongols et Sibériennes, École Pratique des Hautes Études.

González Torres, Yólotl. 1985. *El sacrificio humano entre los mexicas*. Mexico City: Fondo de Cultura Económica.

Graulich, Michel. 2005. *Le sacrifice humain chez les Aztèques*. Paris: Fayard.

"Historia de los mexicanos por sus pinturas." 1965. In *Teogonía e historia de los mexicanos*, edited by Ángel M. Garibay, 23–66. Mexico City: Porrúa.

Hvidtfeldt, Arild. 1958. *Teotl and *Ixiptlatli: Some Central Conceptions in Ancient Mexican Religion*. Copenhagen: Muksgaard.

Johansson, Patrick. 2017. "Gestación y nacimiento de Huitzilopochtli en el monte Coatépetl: consid-eraciones mítico-obstétricas." *Estudios de Cultura Náhuatl* 53: 7–54.

"Leyenda de los Soles." 2002. In *Mitos e historia de los antiguos nahuas*, edited by Rafael Tena, 169–205. Mexico City: Consejo Nacional para la Cultura y las Artes.

López Austin, Alfredo. 1998. *Los mitos del tlacuache. Caminos de la mitología mesoamericana*, 4th ed. Mexico City: Universidad Nacional Autónoma de México-Instituto de Investigaciones Antro-pológicas.

López Austin, Alfredo, and Leonardo López Luján. 2004. "El Templo Mayor de Tenochtitlan, el Tonacatépetl y el mito del robo del maíz." In *Acercarse y mirar. Homenaje a Beatriz de la Fuente*, edited by María Teresa Uriarte and Leticia Staines Cicero, 403–55. Mexico City: Universidad Nacional Autónoma de México-Instituto de Investigaciones Estéticas.

López Luján, Leonardo, and Ximena Chávez Balderas. 2010. "Al pie del Templo Mayor: excavaciones en busca de los soberanos mexicas." In *Moctezuma II. Tiempo y destino de un gobernante*, edited by Leonardo López Luján and Colin McEwan, 294–303. Mexico City: Instituto Nacional de Antropología e Historia.

Mazzetto, Elena. 2015. "El simbolismo de la *yotextli* en las fiestas del año solar mexica." *Itinerarios* 21: 147–70.

———. 2017. "¿Miel o sangre? Nuevas problemáticas acerca de la elaboración de las efigies de *tzoalli* de las divinidades nahuas." *Estudios de Cultura Náhuatl* 53: 73–118.

Nowotny, Karl A. 1968. "Die aztekischen Festkreise." *Zeitschrift für Ethnologie* 93: 84–106.

Olivier, Guilhem. 2003. *Mockeries and Metamorphoses of an Aztec God: Tezcatlipoca, "Lord of the Smoking Mirror."* Translated by Michel Besson. Niwot: University Press of Colorado.

Pike, Kenneth L. 1954–60. *Language in Relation to a Unified Theory of the Structure of Human Behavior.* Glendale: Summer Institute of Linguistics.

Reyes Equiguas, Salvador. 2005. "El *huauhtli* en la cultura náhuatl." MA thesis, Universidad Nacional Autónoma de México.

Sahagún, Bernardino de. 1950–82. *Florentine Codex: General History of the Things of New Spain, Fray Bernardino de Sahagún.* Translated with notes and illustrations by Arthur J. O. Anderson and Charles E. Dibble. 13 vols. Santa Fe: The School of American Research, University of Utah Press.

Seler, Eduard, and Caecilie Seler-Sachs. 1902–23. *Gesammelte abhandlungen zur amerikanischen sprachund alterthumskunde.* Berlin: A. Asher.

Vauzelle, Loïc. 2018. "Tlaloc et Huitzilopochtli: éléments naturels et attributs dans les parures de deux divinités aztèques aux XVe et XVIe siècles." PhD diss., PSL Research University.

Notes on Contributors

SERGIO BOTTA is Associate Professor of History of Religions at Sapienza University of Rome where he also teaches history of the Americas. Among his interests are indigenous religions, mission studies, and shamanism. He is Deputy Editor of the journal *Studi e Materiali di Storia delle Religioni*.

OSWALDO CHINCHILLA MAZARIEGOS is Associate Professor at Yale University. His books include *Art and Myth of the Ancient Maya* (2017), *Corpus of Maya Hieroglyphic Inscriptions Volume 10, Part I: Cotzumalhuapa* (2017), and *Imágenes de la Mitología Maya* (2011). He is recipient of a John Simon Guggenheim Fellowship for his research in Cotzumalguapa, Guatemala.

MARIO CORTINA BORJA studied at the Universidad Nacional Autónoma de México and the University of Bath. He is Professor of Biostatistics at University College London, and an elected member of Council at the Royal Statistical Society.

MIRJANA DANILOVIĆ holds a doctorate degree in Pre-Columbian History from the Universidad Nacional Autónoma de México. She has been the recipient of the Instituto Nacional de Antropología e Historia National Award for her PhD dissertation in 2017, and of a Summer Fellowship in Pre-Columbian Studies at Dumbarton Oaks Research Library and Collection in 2019.

DANIÈLE DEHOUVE is a French anthropologist and ethnohistorian, Emeritus Director of Studies at the CNRS (LESC-Université de Nanterre) and Emeritus Director of Studies at the EPHE, Paris. She has also taught Nahuatl at the INALCO, Paris. Her research focuses on the indigenous societies of Mexico past and present.

ÉLODIE DUPEY GARCÍA is a Research Professor at the Universidad Nacional Autónoma de México. She holds a PhD in History of Religions from the École Pratique des Hautes Études (France). She has received a fellowship in Pre-Columbian Studies from Dumbarton Oaks and a Scholar Grant from the Getty Research Institute. She is the editor of the academic journal *Estudios de Cultura Náhuatl* and of the volumes *Painting the Skin. Pigments on Bodies and Codices in Pre-Columbian Mesoamerica* (University of Arizona Press, 2018) and *De olfato. Aproximaciones a los olores en la historia de México* (FCE/UNAM/CEMCA, 2020).

ELENA MAZZETTO is Associate Professor at the Universidad Nacional Autónoma de México. She has also received a postdoctoral grant from this institution and two others from the Université Libre in Brussels. She holds a PhD in History from the Università Ca'Foscari di Venezia (Italy) and the Université Paris I Panthéon-Sorbonne (France). She is the author of *Lieux de culte et parcours cérémoniels dans les fêtes des vingtaines à Mexico-Tenochtitlan* (British Archaeological Reports, 2014).

JOHANNES NEURATH studied ethnology, philosophy, and art history at the University of Vienna and anthropology at the Universidad Nacional Autónoma de México (UNAM). He has carried out ethnographic fieldwork among Huichols, Coras, and other Mexican indigenous groups since 1992. He is Research Professor at the Museo Nacional de Antropología in Mexico City, and teaches anthropology of art, ethnographic theory, and ritual theory at the Universidad Nacional Autonóma de México.

GUILHEM OLIVIER is a Research Professor at the Universidad Nacional Autonóma de México. He has authored *Mockeries and Metamorphoses of an Aztec God: Tezcatlipoca, "Lord of the Smoking Mirror"* (University of Colorado Press, 2008) and *Cacería, sacrificio y poder en Mesoamérica: Tras las huellas de Mixcóatl* (FCE/UNAM, 2015).

SYLVIE PEPERSTRAETE is an art historian specializing in ancient Mesoamerican cultures. She is Professor at the Université Libre in Brussels and Director of Studies at the École Pratique des Hautes Études in Paris. Her research focuses on Aztec religion, which she studies from an interdisciplinary perspective.

ANDREA B. RODRÍGUEZ FIGUEROA holds a PhD in Mesoamerican Studies. She is a researcher in the School of Architecture at the Universidad Nacional Autónoma de México.

ROSSEND ROVIRA-MORGADO holds a PhD in Early Modern History from the Universidad Autónoma de Madrid. His scholarly fields are sovereignty negotiations in the Early Modern Atlantic world, the juridical interactions between the Catholic Hispanic Monarchy and American indigenous elites, and the political and religious construction of viceregal Indian communities. At present, he is an associated external researcher in the Group of Interdisciplinary Studies on Latin America at the Universidad Autónoma de Madrid (GEISAL-UAM).

JOHN F. SCHWALLER is Professor of History at the University at Albany (SUNY) and Editor of *The Americas*. He is known for his work on the secular clergy in early colonial Mexico, Nahuatl language manuscripts, the history of the Catholic Church in Latin America, the conquest of Mexico, and a study of Panquetzaliztli.

GABRIELLE VAIL is a Research Associate at UNC-Chapel Hill's Research Laboratories of Archaeology and a Research Affiliate with the non-profit InHerit: Indigenous Heritage Passed to Present. Her research focuses on the Postclassic Maya codices, and she is the author or co-author of four books, as well as the Maya Hieroglyphic Codices database (mayacodices.org).

LEOPOLDO VALIÑAS COALLA holds an MA in Linguistics. He is a researcher at the Instituto de Investigaciones Antropológicas at the Universidad Nacional Autónoma de México.

Index

Printed by
CPI books GmbH, Leck